ZAGAT®

Long Island
Restaurants
2011/12

LOCAL EDITOR
Suzi Forbes Chase with Phil Carlucci and
Donna Marino Wilkins
STAFF EDITOR
Cynthia Kilian

Published and distributed by
Zagat Survey, LLC
4 Columbus Circle
New York, NY 10019
T: 212.977.6000
E:longisland@zagat.com
www.zagat.com

ACKNOWLEDGMENTS

We thank Karen Hudes, Bernard Onken and Steven Shukow, as well as the following members of our staff: Danielle Borovoy (editorial assistant), Brian Albert, Sean Beachell, Maryanne Bertollo, Reni Chin, Larry Cohn, Nicole Diaz, Alison Flick, Jeff Freier, Matthew Hamm, Marc Henson, Natalie Lebert, Mike Liao, Polina Paley, Art Yaghci, Sharon Yates, Anna Zappia and Kyle Zolner.

The reviews in this guide are based on public opinion surveys. The ratings reflect the average scores given by the survey participants who voted on each establishment. The text is based on quotes from, or paraphrasings of, the surveyors' comments. Phone numbers, addresses and other factual data were correct to the best of our knowledge when published in this guide.

Our guides are printed using environmentally preferable inks containing 20%, by weight, renewable resources on papers sourced from well-managed forests. Deluxe editions are covered with Skivertex Recover® Double containing a minimum of 30% post-consumer waste fiber.

SUSTAINABLE FORESTRY INITIATIVE

Certified Sourcing

www.sfiprogram.org
SFI-00993

ENVIROINK™

The inks used to print the body of this publication contain a minimum of 20%, by weight, renewable resources.

Contents

Ratings & Symbols

Zagat Top Spot	Name	Symbols		Cuisine	Zagat Ratings			
					FOOD	DECOR	SERVICE	COST

Area, Address & Contact

⚡ **Tim & Nina's** ◑ *American*   ▽ 23 | 9 | 13 | $15

East Hampton | 1 Main St. (Maidendive Ln.) | 631-555-1212 | www.zagat.com

Review, surveyor comments in quotes

Locals, "celebrities" and "congenial drifters" alike "storm the hedgerows" for a taste of the "haute campground grub" at this East Hampton American; while cognoscenti crow over the "classy" yet "comforting", "cheap" cuisine, aesthetes object to "eating in a trailer" "without air-conditioning or even a fan", and suggest the "surly" staff "should be used as fish bait."

Ratings   **Food, Decor** & **Service** are rated on a 30-point scale.

0	–	9	poor to fair
10	–	15	fair to good
16	–	19	good to very good
20	–	25	very good to excellent
26	–	30	extraordinary to perfection
	▽		low response	less reliable

Cost   The estimated price of a dinner with one drink and tip. Lunch is usually 25% less. For unrated **newcomers** or **write-ins,** the price range is shown as follows:

| I | $25 and below | E | $41 to $65 |
| M | $26 to $40 | VE | $66 or above |

Symbols
⚡ highest ratings, popularity and importance
◑ serves after 11 PM
S M closed on Sunday or Monday
⊄ no credit cards accepted

About This Survey

Here are the results of our **2011/12 Long Island Restaurants Survey,** covering 901 eateries on Long Island. Like all our guides, this one is based on input from avid local consumers – 6,217 all told. Our editors have synopsized this feedback, highlighting representative comments (in quotation marks within each review). To read full surveyor comments – and share your own opinions – visit **ZAGAT.com,** where you'll also find the latest restaurant news plus special events, deals, reservations, menus, photos and lots more, all for free.

ABOUT ZAGAT: In 1979, we started asking friends to rate and review restaurants purely for fun. The term "user-generated content" had not yet been coined. That hobby grew into Zagat Survey; 32 years later, we have over 375,000 surveyors and cover everything from airlines to shopping in over 100 countries. Along the way, we evolved from being a print publisher to a digital content provider, e.g. **ZAGAT.com** and Zagat Mobile Apps (for iPad, iPhone, Android, BlackBerry, Windows Phone 7 and PalmwebOS). We also produce customized gifts and marketing tools for a wide range of corporate clients. And you can find us on Twitter (twitter.com/zagat), Facebook and just about any other social media network.

THREE SIMPLE PREMISES underlie our ratings and reviews. First, we believe that the collective opinions of large numbers of consumers are more accurate than those of any single person. (Consider that our surveyors bring some 906,000 annual meals' worth of experience to this year's survey. They also visit restaurants year-round, anonymously – and on their own dime.) Second, food quality is only part of the equation when choosing a restaurant, thus we ask surveyors to separately rate food, decor and service and report on cost. Third, since people need reliable information in a fast, easy-to-digest format, we strive to be concise and we offer our content on every platform – print, online and mobile. Our Top Ratings lists (pages 9–16) and indexes (starting on page 170) are also designed to help you quickly choose the best place for any occasion, be it business or pleasure.

THANKS: We're grateful to our editor, Suzi Forbes Chase, author of *The Hamptons, A Great Destination* as well as other travel guides and cookbooks. We also thank Phil Carlucci, a food- and golf-focused freelance writer and the creator of Golf On Long Island online, and Donna Marino Wilkins, a food, travel and lifestyle journalist. Thank you, guys. We also sincerely thank the thousands of surveyors who participated – this guide is really "theirs."

JOIN IN: To improve our guides, we solicit your comments; it's vital that we hear your opinions. Just contact us at **nina-tim@zagat.com.** We also invite you to join our surveys at **ZAGAT.com.** Do so and you'll receive a choice of rewards in exchange.

New York, NY
May 18, 2011

Nina and Tim Zagat

What's New

Long Island surveyors report eating out 2.8 times a week – just as often as two years ago – but they're paying less for the average meal: $40.42, down from $41.41 in our last Survey. That's still well above the current national average of $35.52, however, making this year's bumper crop of value-oriented newcomers well suited to surveyors, who eat 88% of their meals out for leisure rather than business.

FORK POWER: Rising up a notch to No. 1 for Food and again reigning supreme for Service is **North Fork Table & Inn,** Southold's haven for the upscale, locally sourced creations of chef-owners Gerry Hayden and Claudia Fleming. This year, the pair put their twist on the gourmet food truck craze (15% of surveyors frequent them) by christening the **Lunch Truck** – a midday take-out spot planted out back where lobster rolls, artisan hot dogs and such come at gentle prices.

SMALL IS BIG: The small-plates concept continues to thrive. Newcomers **Sugar Dining Den & Social Club** in Carle Place, **Swallow** in Huntington and **Vero** in Amityville all offer midpriced small-plates menus, and **Fork & Vine** (fka **On 3**) in Glen Head downsized to the format.

BISTRO BOOM: Bistros are popping up all over. At **Bistro 25** in Sayville, named for its $25 bottles of wine, entrees are $20 or less. **Aperitif** is a new bistro/lounge/bar in Rockville Centre, and **Metropolitan Bistro** hatched in Sea Cliff. More bistro bites are available at Greenvale's **Bar Frites,** via the **Bryant & Cooper** team, and at Greenport's former **La Cuvée,** now called **Cuvée Bistro & Bar.** Yet it's far from a casual coup – while 28% of respondents declare the formal fine-dining scene dead, a whopping 52% say it's not. And fine dining lives on at **Palm Court,** voted No. 1 for Decor.

FAREWELL: The Island lost some dining favorites this year when **Exile Bar & Grill** in Amagansett and **Camille's** in Carle Place closed, as did **Abel Conklin's** in Huntington, **Annona** in Westhampton Beach, **Soigné** in Woodmere, **Stevens Pasta Specialties** in Long Beach and **West Lake Clam & Chowder House** in Montauk.

LIVING END: The East End continues to gain ground with some notable Hamptons and North Fork arrivals. Chief among them are **Comtesse Thérèse** in Aquebogue, **Southfork Kitchen** in Bridgehampton and **The Boathouse, Grill on Pantigo, Race Lane** and **Serafina** in East Hampton. **Farmhouse** and **Portly Grape** debuted in Greenport, **South Edison** in Montauk, and **Bistro 72** and **Dark Horse** in Riverhead.

SURVEY SAYS: Long Islanders tip an average 19.3%, just over the 19.2% national average . . . 68% think restaurants should restrict how long you can linger with a laptop, book, friend, etc. during peak hours . . . 85% think restaurants should be required to post their health-inspection results.

Long Island, NY
May 18, 2011

Suzi Forbes Chase

Key Newcomers

Our editors' favorites among this year's arrivals. See a full list on page 216.

Aperitif | *French* | stylish Rockville Centre bistro, lounge and bar

Bar Frites | *French* | George and Gillis Poll's lively Greenvale bistro

Bistro 72 | *American* | farm-to-table fare in Riverhead's chic Hotel Indigo

Bistro 25 | *Eclectic* | entrees under $20 plus $25 bottles of wine in Sayville

Boathouse | *Seafood* | yachtlike setting with harbor views in East Hampton

Cedar Creek | *American* | Mill Creek Tavern owners in Glen Cove

Comtesse Thérèse | *French* | vineyard tasting room cum Aquebogue bistro

Dark Horse | *American/French* | airy brasserie hosts Riverhead scene

Domo Sushi | *Japanese* | East Setauket sushi-and-sake strip-maller

Farmhouse | *American* | cozy Greenport room and Richard Lanza's local menu

George Martin's Strip Steak | *Steak* | beef, etc. in a classy Great River setting

Grill on Pantigo | *American* | modern menu in East Hampton

Kinha Sushi | *Japanese* | alluring Garden City setting for fusion bites

LT Burger | *Burgers* | celeb chef Laurent Tourondel does Sag Harbor patties

Navy Beach | *American* | laid-back Montauk beachfront 'in' spot

Old Fields | *American/Steak* | vintage Greenlawn setting

Philippe | *Chinese* | chef Philippe Chow's Jericho offspring

Prime Catch | *Seafood* | chef Axell Urrutia in Rockville Centre

Serafina | *Italian* | East Hampton branch of Manhattan casual-chic hot spot

South Edison | *American* | Montauk debut for chef-owner Todd Mitgang

Southfork Kitchen | *Seafood* | artful takes on local fare in Bridgehampton

Sugar | *American/Asian* | Carle Place restaurant/lounge

Tate's | *American/Italian* | family-run Nesconset instant winner

Vero | *Italian* | stylish new Amityville home of chef Massimo Fedozzi

Vitae | *Continental* | classy wood-and-leather Huntington setting

---

Restaurateur Tom Schaudel (**Coolfish, A Mano**) is expecting twins. His **A Lure,** a locally focused chowder house in Southold, is due to open soon; a September debut is planned for **Jewel** in Melville's new Rubie Corporate Plaza, offering a farm-to-table menu. From the ashes of Roslyn neighbors **Mio** and **Dayboat Café** (both shuttered in a 2008 fire), a new restaurant is in the works, details to come. In Bayville, **18 Bay** is closed for an expansion. The **Olde Country Inn** in Shelter Island Heights plans to reopen by summer as **La Maison Blanche,** and the closed **Fairway** is set for a summer rebirth at Sagaponack's Poxabogue Golf Center. **A Touch of Venice** is relocating to Cutchogue. Rumor has it that the **red bar brasserie** team is scouting a Southampton location for a casual cafe and the Hillstone Group (**Houston's**) is seeking an East End anchor.

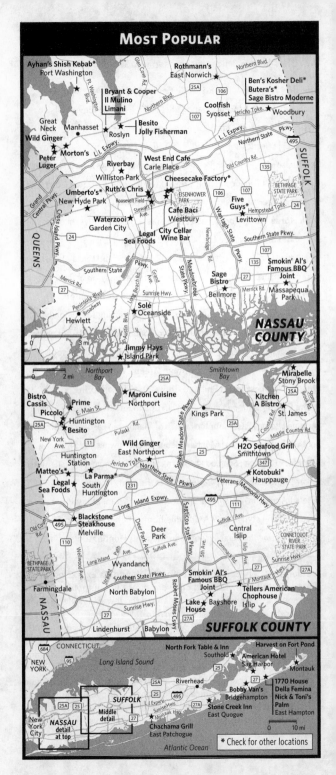

MOST POPULAR

Ayhan's Shish Kebab* Port Washington

Rothmann's East Norwich

Ben's Kosher Deli* **Butera's*** **Sage Bistro Moderne** Woodbury

Bryant & Cooper **Il Mulino** **Limani**

Coolfish Syosset

Great Neck **Wild Ginger** Manhasset

Besito **Jolly Fisherman** Roslyn

Morton's **Peter Luger**

Riverbay Williston Park

West End Cafe Carle Place

Cheesecake Factory*

Umberto's* New Hyde Park

Ruth's Chris

Five Guys* Levittown

Waterzooi Garden City

Cafe Baci Westbury

Legal Sea Foods

City Cellar Wine Bar

Sage Bistro Bellmore

Smokin' Al's Famous BBQ Joint Massapequa Park

Solé Oceanside

Hewlett

Jimmy Hays Island Park

QUEENS

NASSAU COUNTY

0 3 mi

Bistro Cassis **Piccolo**

Prime

Maroni Cuisine Northport

Mirabelle Stony Brook

Kitchen A Bistro St. James

Besito Huntington

Wild Ginger East Northport

H2O Seafood Grill Smithtown

Matteo's*

La Parma*

Kotobuki* Hauppauge

Legal Sea Foods South Huntington

Blackstone Steakhouse Melville

Deer Park

Wyandanch

Central Islip

Farmingdale

North Babylon

Smokin' Al's Famous BBQ Joint

Tellers American Chophouse Islip

Lake House Bayshore

Lindenhurst **Babylon**

NASSAU

SUFFOLK COUNTY

0 2 mi

CONNECTICUT

North Fork Table & Inn Southold

Harvest on Fort Pond

American Hotel Sag Harbor

Montauk

NEW YORK

Long Island Sound

Riverhead

Bobby Van's Bridgehampton

1770 House **Della Femina** **Nick & Toni's** **Palm** East Hampton

Stone Creek Inn East Quogue

New York City

NASSAU detail at top

SUFFOLK Middle detail

Chachama Grill East Patchogue

Atlantic Ocean

*** Check for other locations**

0 10 mi

8   Vote at ZAGAT.com

Most Popular

1. Peter Luger | *Steak*
2. Besito | *Mexican*
3. Kotobuki | *Japanese*
4. Bryant & Cooper | *Steak*
5. West End Cafe | *American*
6. North Fork Table | *American*
7. Il Mulino NY | *Italian*
8. Cheesecake Factory | *American*
9. Kitchen A Bistro | *French*
10. Smokin' Al's BBQ | *BBQ*
11. American Hotel | *Amer./French*
12. Waterzooi | *Belgian*
13. Butera's | *Italian*
14. Blackstone Steak | *Steak*
15. Prime | *American*
16. Bistro Cassis | *French*
17. Lake House | *American*
18. Tellers Chophouse | *Steak*
19. Coolfish | *Seafood*
20. Maroni | *Eclectic/Italian*
21. Morton's | *Steak*
22. Ruth's Chris | *Steak*
23. Cafe Baci | *Italian*
24. Matteo's | *Italian*
25. La Parma | *Italian*
26. Palm | *Seafood/Steak*
27. Della Femina | *American*
28. Riverbay | *Seafood*
29. Limani | *Med./Seafood*
30. Sage Bistro | *French*
31. Nick & Toni's | *Italian/Med.*
32. Ben's Kosher Deli | *Deli*
33. Rothmann's Steak | *Steak*
34. Harvest/Ft. Pond | *Italian/Med.*
35. 1770 House | *Amer.*
36. Stone Creek | *French/Med.*
37. Five Guys | *Burgers*
38. Legal Sea Foods | *Seafood*
39. Mirabelle | *French*
40. Umberto's | *Italian/Pizza*
41. Solé | *Italian*
42. H2O Seafood | *Seafood*
43. Ayhan's Shish | *Med./Turkish*
44. Chachama Grill | *American*
45. Piccolo | *American/Italian*
46. Bobby Van's | *Steak*
47. Jimmy Hays | *Steak*
48. City Cellar | *American*
49. Jolly Fisherman | *Seafood/Steak*
50. Wild Ginger | *Asian*

Many of the above restaurants are among Long Island's most expensive, but if popularity were calibrated to price, a number of other restaurants would surely join their ranks. To illustrate this, we have added two lists comprising 94 Best Buys on page 15 as well as Prix Fixe Dinner Deals on page 16.

Top Food

29 North Fork Table | *American*	Barney's | *American/French*
28 Siam Lotus | *Thai*	Plaza Cafe | *Seafood*
Mosaic | *American*	Stone Creek | *French/Med.*
Kitchen A Trattoria | *Italian*	Dario's | *Italian*
Maroni | *Eclectic/Italian*	Tellers Chophouse | *Steak*
Nagahama | *Japanese*	Limani | *Med./Seafood*
Lake House | *American*	Noah's | *American*
27 Chachama Grill | *American*	Snaps American | *American*
La Piccola Liguria | *Italian*	San Marco | *Italian*
Le Soir | *French*	Verace | *Italian*
Kitchen A Bistro | *French*	Rialto | *Italian*
Kotobuki | *Japanese*	Thai Gourmet | *Thai*
Peter Luger | *Steak*	Galleria Dominick | *Italian*
La Plage | *Eclectic*	PeraBell | *American/Eclectic*
Orient | *Chinese*	Harvest/Ft. Pond | *Italian/Med.*
Chez Noëlle | *French*	Palm | *Seafood/Steak*
Sempre Vivolo | *Italian*	Franina | *Italian*
Aji 53 | *Japanese*	Fifth Season | *American*
Dave's | *Continental/Seafood*	Solé | *Italian*
Il Mulino NY | *Italian*	25 Maureen/Daughters' | *Amer.*
Piccolo | *American/Italian*	Living Room | *American*
26 Bryant & Cooper | *Steak*	Da Ugo | *Italian*
Branzino | *Italian*	Frisky Oyster | *Eclectic*
Starr Boggs | *Amer./Seafood*	Robert's | *Italian*
Mirko's | *Eclectic*	Kumo Sushi | *Japanese*

BY CUISINE

AMERICAN (NEW)

29 North Fork Table
28 Mosaic
   Lake House
27 Chachama Grill
26 Starr Boggs

AMERICAN (TRAD.)

26 PeraBell
25 Maureen/Daughters'
   Vittorio's
   Vine Street
   American Hotel

ASIAN

25 West East Bistro
   Toku
24 Taiko
23 Dao
20 Thom Thom

BBQ/SOUTHWESTERN

24 Big Daddy's
23 Smokin' Al's BBQ
   Swingbelly's Beachside
22 RS Jones
   Turtle Crossing

CAJUN/SOUTHERN

24 Big Daddy's
23 Bayou
   LL Dent
20 Blackbirds' Grille
18 B. Smith's

CHINESE

27 Orient
24 Philippe
23 Orchid
   Pearl East
22 Fortune Wheel

Excludes places with low votes; * indicates a tie with restaurant above

Vote at ZAGAT.com

CONTINENTAL

- 27 Dave's
- 25 Barolo
- 24 Palm Court
- 23 Irish Coffee
- Frederick's

ECLECTIC

- 28 Maroni
- 27 La Plage
- 26 Mirko's
- PeraBell
- 25 Frisky Oyster

FRENCH

- 27 Le Soir
- Chez Noëlle
- 26 Barney's
- Stone Creek
- 25 Mirabelle

FRENCH (BISTRO)

- 27 Kitchen A Bistro
- 24 Voila!
- Sage Bistro
- Bistro Cassis
- 22 Bistro Toulouse

GREEK

- 23 Alexandros
- 22 Trata
- Med. Snack
- 21 Chicken Kebab
- Ethos

INDIAN

- 25 House of Dosas
- 24 Kiran Palace
- 23 Rangmahal
- Dosa Diner
- 22 Hampton Chutney

ITALIAN

- 28 Kitchen A Trattoria
- Maroni
- 27 Sempre Vivolo
- Piccolo
- 26 Verace

ITALIAN (NORTHERN)

- 27 La Piccola Liguria
- Il Mulino NY
- 26 Branzino
- Dario's
- San Marco

ITALIAN (SOUTHERN)

- 25 La Ginestra
- 24 Bravo Nader!

- 23 Mamma Lombardi's
- Matteo's
- La Parma

JAPANESE

- 28 Nagahama
- 27 Kotobuki
- Aji 53
- 25 Kumo Sushi
- Nisen Sushi

MEDITERRANEAN

- 26 Stone Creek
- Limani
- Harvest/Ft. Pond
- 24 Pier 95
- Nick & Toni's

MEXICAN

- 24 Besito
- 23 Oaxaca Mexican
- Salsa Salsa
- 22 Zim Zari
- 20 Chipotle

MIDDLE EASTERN

- 23 Kabul Afghani
- 22 Pita House
- Tel Aviv
- Azerbaijan Grill
- 21 Colbeh

PIZZA

- 25 Salvatore's
- 23 Emilio's
- Nick's
- Grimaldi's
- King Umberto

SEAFOOD

- 26 Dave's
- Starr Boggs
- Plaza Cafe
- Limani
- 25 Mill Pond House

STEAKHOUSES

- 27 Peter Luger
- 26 Bryant & Cooper
- Tellers Chophouse
- Palm
- 25 Jimmy Hays

THAI

- 28 Siam Lotus
- 26 Thai Gourmet
- 25 Sripraphai
- 24 Onzon Thai
- Thai House*

BY SPECIAL FEATURE

BREAKFAST

25 Maureen/Daughters'
24 Toast
23 Estia's Kitchen
   Rein
   Love Lane Kitchen

BRUNCH

26 Limani
25 Rothmann's Steak
24 Palm Court
   Waterzooi
   Bistro Cassis

BYO

28 Kitchen A Trattoria
27 Kitchen A Bistro
26 Thai Gourmet
24 Onzon Thai
   Kiran Palace

HOTEL DINING

29 North Fork Table
   (North Fork Table & Inn)
26 Palm
   (Huntting Inn)
25 Living Room
   (c/o The Maidstone)
   Mirabelle
   (Three Village Inn)
   Luce & Hawkins
   (Jedediah Hawkins Inn)

NEWCOMERS (RATED)

25 Aperitif
24 Philippe
23 Jack Halyards
21 Grill on Pantigo
   Stone Turtle

PEOPLE-WATCHING

27 Peter Luger
   Il Mulino NY
26 Starr Boggs
   Barney's
   Stone Creek

SINGLES SCENES

26 Bryant & Cooper
   Tellers Chophouse
   Limani
   Verace
25 Nisen Sushi

VIEWS

27 Lake House
26 Harvest/Ft. Pond
25 Amarelle
   Mill Pond House
24 Oasis Waterfront

BY LOCATION

EAST HAMPTON

26 Palm
25 Living Room
   1770 House
24 Della Femina
   Nick & Toni's

NASSAU COUNTY

28 Nagahama
27 La Piccola Liguria
   Kotobuki
   Peter Luger
   Orient

N. FORK & SHELTER IS.

29 North Fork Table
27 La Plage

26 Noah's
25 Frisky Oyster
   Luce & Hawkins

SOUTHAMPTON

26 Plaza Cafe
24 Sant Ambroeus
23 Silver's
22 La Parmigiana
   red bar

SUFFOLK COUNTY

29 North Fork Table
28 Siam Lotus
   Mosaic
   Kitchen A Trattoria
   Maroni

Top Decor

28 Palm Court	1770 House
27 Limani	Amarelle
Atlantica	Honu Kitchen
Luce & Hawkins	Living Room
Prime	**24** Lombardi's on the Bay
Tellers Chophouse	Rein
26 Toku	Nonnina
Two Steak & Sushi Den	Rare 650
Country House	Sunset Beach
East Hampton Point	American Hotel
Verace	Nisen Sushi
25 North Fork Table	Stone Creek
Trumpets	Dockers Waterside
Jamesport Manor	Four Food Studio
Barrique Kitchen & Wine Bar	Besito
Porto Vivo*	Milk & Sugar Café*
Aperitif	Aji 53
Pine Island*	Rist. Gemelli
Blackwells	Blackstone Steak
Tula Kitchen	Ram's Head

OUTDOORS

Cipollini	Maroni
Della Femina	Ram's Head
East Hampton Point	Savanna's
Fork & Vine	Starr Boggs
Harvest/Ft. Pond	Verace

ROMANCE

American Hotel	Palm Court
Barney's	Ram's Head
Country House	Robert's
Lake House	1770 House
Luce & Hawkins	Stone Creek

ROOMS

Atlantica	Porto Vivo
Four Food Studio	1770 House
Limani	Tellers Chophouse
Nisen Sushi	Toku
Palm Court	Two Steak & Sushi Den

VIEWS

Dockers Waterside	Prime
East Hampton Point	Sunset Beach
Harvest/Ft. Pond	Trumpets
Oakland's	View
Pine Island Grill	Wall's Wharf

Top Service

27 North Fork Table
Sempre Vivolo
Chachama Grill
La Piccola Liguria
Mosaic

26 Luce & Hawkins
Siam Lotus
San Marco
Lake House
Maroni
Dario's
Voila!

25 Galleria Dominick
Rialto
Chez Noëlle
Palm Court
Tellers Chophouse
Vittorio's
Verace
Tula Kitchen

Casa Rustica
Capriccio
Mario
Le Soir
Piccolo
Il Mulino NY
La Pace
Red Restaurant
Grey Horse Tavern
Kitchen A Trattoria

24 Franina
Crew Kitchen
Mirabelle
Bevanda
La Marmite
American Hotel
Limani
Barney's
Stone Creek
Morton's

Best Buys

In order of Bang for the Buck rating.

1. Five Guys
2. Chipotle
3. American Roadside
4. Maureen/Daughters'
5. Fresco Crêperie
6. Salsa Salsa
7. Bobby's Burger
8. Green Cactus
9. Baja Fresh
10. Zim Zari
11. Thomas's Eggery
12. Robinson's Tea
13. Tricia's Café
14. House of Dosas
15. Toast
16. Tasty Crepes
17. Salvatore's
18. Hampton Coffee
19. Thai Gourmet
20. Dosa Diner
21. Greenport Tea
22. Massa's
23. Hampton Chutney
24. Grimaldi's
25. Bay Burger
26. Caffe Barocco
27. La Bottega*
28. Hildebrandt's
29. Baja Grill
30. Sweet Mama's
31. Thai Table
32. Bigelow's
33. Ancient Ginger
34. Nick's
35. Pie
36. Kiran Palace
37. Oaxaca Mexican
38. Thai House
39. Lemonleaf Grill
40. International Delight

OTHER GOOD VALUES

Afghan Grill
Asian Moon
Azuma Sushi
Batata Café
Benkei Japanese
Ben's Kosher Deli
Blue Moon
BobbiQue
Bozena Polish-European
Bridgehampton Candy
Chat Noir
Chefs of New York
CPK
Crave 11025
Declan Quinn's
Dynasty
Eddie's Pizza
Emilio's
Frank-N-Burger
Galangal
Golden Pear Café
Goldmine Mexican Grill
Gonzalo's American Café
Greek Village
Harbor-Q
Jean Marie Patisserie
JT's Corner Cafe
La Panchita
Long River
Los Compadres
Madras Woodlands
Milk & Sugar Café
Minami
New Chilli & Curry
Onzon Thai House
Orient, The
Panini Café at Diane's
Perfecto Mundo
Pizza Place
Roe's Casa Dolce
Sabai Thai Bistro
Salamander's General Store
Siam Lotus
Souvlaki Palace
Spicy's Barbecue
Sripraphai
Sri Thai
Star Confectionary
Sundried Tomato Cafe
Sushi Palace
Toast & Co.
Torcellos
Tula Kitchen
Zorba the Greek

PRIX FIXE DINNER DEALS

Since hours and prices may vary, please call ahead.

$26-$30

Barney's $28	Matsulin 26
Bobby Van's 27	Mill Pond House 27
Chachama Grill 26	Plaza Cafe 29
Chez Noëlle 28	Porto Vivo 30
Coast Grill 27	Ruvo 26
Della Femina 30	Snaps American 29
Fifth Season 28	Stone Creek 30
Fresno 28	Tratt. Diane 30
Harbor Bistro 29	Uncle Bacala's 29
Jolly Fisherman 27	View 26
Jonathan's 26	Voila! 30
Le Chef 30	Wild Honey 27

$25 AND UNDER

Angelina's $25	Georgica 25
Arturo's 25	Grey Horse Tavern 19
Azerbaijan Grill 13	Grill on Pantigo 24
Babylon Carriage 25	Hemingway's 25
Bellport 22	Hudson's Mill 22
Bistro Citron 25	Il Capuccino 24
Bistro Toulouse 24	Lola's Kitchen 20
Blackbirds' Grille 24	Mama's 14
Blackwells 25	Nicholas James 23
Bliss 25	Page One 24
Bob's Place 23	Palmer's American Grille 22
Brasserie Persil 25	Patio at 54 Main 25
Brasserie 214 25	Peppercorns 22
Brio 23	Phao Thai Kitchen 25
Broadway Beanery 22	Pierre's 25
Butera's 25	Red Fish 25
Butterfields 22	Rist. Gemelli 25
Cafe Joelle 25	RS Jones 19
Cafe Max 24	San Marco 23
Chop Shop 24	Schooner 23
Cho-Sen Island 24	Sea Basin 23
Cielo 25	Shagwong 23
Crossroads Cafe 22	Thom Thom 25
Fisherman's Catch 24	Thyme 25
Garden Grill 25	Villa D'Este 24

RESTAURANT
DIRECTORY

	FOOD	DECOR	SERVICE	COST

Absolutely Mario M *Italian*   20 | 16 | 23 | $39

Farmingdale | 10 Allen Blvd. (Broad Hollow Rd.) | 631-694-7416 |
www.absolutelymario.com

The "charming" chef-owner is "always on hand making you feel like
family" at this Farmingdale "favorite" serving "good old Italian fare";
the "bustling" setting is "homey" and the staff "goes the extra mile",
so a few reviewers feel "if Mario gets his food up to the level of his
service, he'd be world-class"; P.S. there's live accordion music
on weekend nights.

Afghan Grill Kabob House *Afghan*   20 | 14 | 21 | $28

New Hyde Park | 1629 Hillside Ave. (New Hyde Park Rd.) | 516-998-4084
"Fabulous" namesake skewers are among the affordable fare at this
"family-run" Afghan, a "quaint" New Hyde Park "standout" delivering
"tasty", "plentiful" dishes that even "delight" vegetarians; sure, the
"run-down" digs could use some "personality", but the "welcoming"
servers "try very hard to please" and BYO is "a definite plus."

Z Aji 53 *Japanese*   27 | 24 | 23 | $43

Bay Shore | 53 E. Main St. (3rd Ave.) | 631-591-3107 | www.aji53.com
An "all-around hit", this "chic", "modern" Japanese brings "NYC
ambiance" to Bay Shore, with "stunning" decor, "incredible", "inventive" sushi and "charming" (if at times "almost too eager") service;
the "cool vibe" and "martinis at the bar" make "waits worthwhile",
while dishes like "to-die-for black miso cod" are so "artful" you'll
"forget about the price tag" and the "noise"; P.S. "don't even think of
going on a weekend without reservations."

Akbar *Indian*   22 | 19 | 20 | $35

Garden City | 2 South St. (Stewart Ave.) | 516-357-8300 |
www.theakbar.com

For "authentic" Indian with "just enough fire", this "upscale",
"pleasant" Garden City veteran is a "perennial favorite" thanks to
"abundant" lunch and Sunday dinner buffets presenting "well-
seasoned specialties" at "bargain" prices; true, "the tab can add up
if you order à la carte", but the "courteous" staff is a plus.

Albert's Mandarin Gourmet *Chinese*   20 | 15 | 20 | $29

Huntington | 269 New York Ave. (bet. Gerard St. & Union Pl.) |
631-673-8188

While there's "nothing new or exciting" about this "Huntington
staple", the "always reliable" Mandarin fare and "prompt" service –
helmed by "affable" owner Albert Leung – pleases "plenty" of longtime
customers, who count on it for "large get-togethers"; some critics call
for a "spruce-up" of the "frozen-in-time" decor and "clichéd cuisine",
but if you're "looking for old-school Chinese, this is your restaurant."

Alexandros *Greek/Mediterranean*   23 | 19 | 23 | $43

Mount Sinai | 1060 Rte. 25A (Pipe Stave Hollow Rd.) | 631-928-8600 |
www.alexandrosrestaurant.com

"Authentic" Greek-Med food (including "simply prepared but outstanding" fish and other "delicious" grilled specialties) entices eaters

at this "cozy", slightly upscale Mount Sinai spot where "gracious" chef-owner Sam Constantis and his "warm, welcoming" family make the whole meal "special"; though the "small" room tends to get "loud", it's "wonderful" for outdoor dining in the summer.

Allison's Amalfi Ristorante   *Italian/Mediterranean*

`21` `21` `22` `$48`

Sea Cliff | 400 Glen Cove Ave. (Glenola Ave.) | 516-656-4774 | www.allisonsamalfi.com

The winning team of "welcoming" co-owner and hostess Allison Izzo and her husband, O'Michael Zara, a "fine" chef who "accommodates special orders", adds to the "charm" of this "sophisticated" Italian-Med "tucked away" in a Sea Cliff strip mall; prices are "a trifle high", but most "enjoy" the "beautifully prepared" dishes served in a "relaxing", "rarely crowded" locale; P.S. closed Tuesdays.

Almarco   *Italian*

`20` `18` `22` `$38`

Huntington | 13 Wall St. (bet. Gerard & Main Sts.) | 631-935-1690

Many commend the "wonderful" staff at this "pleasant" Huntington Italian offering "good", "bountiful" plates and outdoor seating in back for "sunny days"; still, while the "step-above-basic" fare works for "family dining", a few naysayers knock the "plain"-Jane decor and dishes that "should be tastier" for the price.

A Mano   *Italian*

`24` `20` `22` `$47`

Mattituck | 13550 Main Rd. (bet. Love Ln. & Wickam Ave.) | 631-298-4800 | www.amanorestaurant.com

Chef/co-owner Tom Schaudel crafts "fresh local" ingredients into "tantalizing" Italian dishes – including "terrific" wood-fired pizzas – matched by an "amazing wine selection" at this "hip", "not too expensive" Mattituck osteria where a "courteous" crew "plays to a packed house every night"; though nitpickers nag about the "noise level", most either revel in the "buzzy atmosphere" or choose to eat on the patio in warm weather.

Amarelle   Ⓜ *American*

`25` `25` `23` `$52`

Wading River | 2028 N. Country Rd. (bet. N. Wading River & Sound Rds.) | 631-886-2242 | www.amarelle.net

An "innovative, clever menu" highlighting "local seasonal offerings" makes this "out-of-the-way" Wading River New American a "sublime" stop for foodies, while the "elegant" interior with a "large stone fireplace" and view of a duck pond provides a "lovely romantic atmosphere" (even if it's slightly "over-the-top for its country setting"); the service is "attentive but not obtrusive", and the "small plate option" for every entree is a "hit" too.

🅉 American Hotel, The   *American/French*

`25` `24` `24` `$67`

Sag Harbor | The American Hotel | 49 Main St. (bet. Bay & Washington Sts.) | 631-725-3535 | www.theamericanhotel.com

Ever "enchanting", this "quintessential" Sag Harbor haven brings together "sensational" American-French dishes and an "exceptional", "dizzying" wine list in a "gorgeous" 1846-vintage setting with "glittering tables" tended to by a "formal", "carefully trained" staff; you can sit by the "roaring fireplace" in winter or "on the porch" in summer and "watch the celebs go by", and while "you'll likely spend more than you originally thought", its "eternal popularity is well deserved."

American Roadside Burgers Burgers   18 | 12 | 15 | $13

Smithtown | 80 E. Main St. (bet. Landing & Lawrence Aves.) | 631-382-9500 | www.americanroadsideburgers.com

Those who "wouldn't be caught dead in a McDonald's" hail the "terrific", "juicy" hamburgers "made your way" "with just enough grease" at this Smithtown order-at-the-counter joint; sure, the "kinda cold" "motorcycle decor" isn't for everyone, and some dub the grub merely "so-so", but it's "better than the drive-thrus" – and if you eat the four-patty RoadStar "your name goes on the wall."

Ancient Ginger Chinese   21 | 17 | 22 | $26

St. James | 556 N. Country Rd. (Lake Ave.) | 631-584-8883 | www.ancientginger.com

Guests agree it's "always a pleasure" dining on the "light, fresh" and often "sumptuous" Chinese food ferried by a "gracious" staff at this "darn good" St. James option; the "cut-above" decor is "charming for a storefront", while the "bang-for-the-buck" menu keeps regulars returning "at least once a week."

Angelina's Italian   23 | 18 | 23 | $50

East Norwich | Christina's Shopping Ctr. | 1017 Oyster Bay Rd. (bet. Johnson Ct. & Northern Blvd.) | 516-922-0033 | www.angelinasofeastnorwich.com

Angelina's II Italian

Syosset | 30 Berry Hill Rd. (East St.) | 516-364-8234 | www.angelinas2.com

Fans of "down-home" Italian flock to these "upscale neighborhood" trattorias for "generous portions" of the classics, served by a "congenial" staff that's "well versed" in the "old-school" menu; the "dependable" East Norwich original with a Tuscan-style dining room serves dinner only, while the separately owned Syosset locale, set in a "comfy" converted country house, offers lunch and prix fixe specials.

NEW Aperitif French   25 | 25 | 24 | $45

Rockville Centre | 242 Sunrise Hwy. (bet. Park & Village Aves.) | 516-594-3404 | www.aperitifbistro.com

From the owners of the Sage Bistro Restaurant Group comes this "new hit" on the Rockville Centre scene – LI's No. 1 Newcomer – a "gorgeous" French bistro that pairs "enticing", slightly "eclectic" dishes (many available as part of an extensive small-plates menu) with an "excellent" 70-bottle wine list; embellished with pendant lights, red velvet and Moroccan tiles, it sets the stage for "memorable" meals, as well as late-night bites and colorful drinks from the "great bar staff."

Argyle Grill & Tavern American   22 | 21 | 21 | $37

Babylon | 90 Deer Park Ave. (bet. Grove Pl. & Main St.) | 631-321-4900 | www.theargylegrill.com

"Always packed", this "upscale pub" in Babylon attracts an avid "after-work" crowd for its "meat-and-potatoes" New American eats,

	FOOD	DECOR	SERVICE	COST

happy-hour martinis and "swinging" scene; some warn the "tight" quarters can get "too loud" and dub the dishes "not worth the wait", but most find it "comfortable" and "dependable", and dig the "specials during the week"; P.S. no reservations.

Ariana *Afghan/Vegetarian*

20	19	19	$35

Huntington | 255 Main St. (bet. New St. & New York Ave.) | 631-421-2933 | www.arianacafe.com

"Sophisticated", "delicately seasoned" dishes with an "exotic" twist (and plenty of options for "vegetarians and vegans") provide a "new" experience for many at this midpriced, "family-owned" Afghan eatery in Huntington; the service is generally "accommodating", and the "inviting" Persian-style atmosphere with "cozy pillows" is just right "for a date" or "meeting friends."

NEW Arthur Ave. ● *American*

-	-	-	M

Smithtown | 155 W. Main St. (Elliott Pl.) | 631-780-5969 | arthuraveny.com
Sports fans watch multi screens at the double-sided bar while less boisterous types head for the separate glass-enclosed dining room at this Smithtown American located beside the railroad tracks; the midpriced menu ranges from wraps to entrees such as wild-caught salmon Dijon, and live weekend entertainment varies from karaoke to bands and dancing.

Arturo's *Italian*

22	18	22	$48

Floral Park | 246-04 Jericho Tpke. (Colonial Rd.) | 516-352-7418 | www.arturorestaurant.com
A Floral Park fixture for half a century, this "oldie but goodie" caters to "special celebrations" with "terrific" Italian classics "just like grandma used to cook", some of which are "prepared tableside" for added "charm"; try to "save room" for "scrumptious" zabaglione, and let the "strolling guitarist" turn your attention from the "dated" decor.

Asian Moon *Asian*

23	22	22	$33

Garden City | 825 Franklin Ave. (bet. 9th St. & Stewart Ave.) | 516-248-6161
Massapequa Park | 4922 Merrick Rd. (bet. Southgate Circle & Whitewood Dr.) | 516-799-8800
www.asianmoononline.com
Guests are "over the moon" for this "slightly upscale" yet "reasonable" Pan-Asian pair dishing up "light, flavorful" food that's a "fresh", "eclectic" alternative to typical takeout; "pleasant" servers keep the "calm", "cool vibe" flowing through the Garden City original and its Massapequa Park offshoot, which "rocks" with a sushi menu and more fabulous "feng shui."

A Taberna *Portuguese*

23	15	19	$38

Island Park | 4135 Austin Blvd. (bet. Saratoga & Trafalgar Blvds.) | 516-432-0455
"Beautifully presented", "authentic" Portuguese fare draws a lively "local crowd" to this "casual" Island Park spot where "conviviality flows like a good red"; critics complain that they often get "squeezed in" – and "wait and wait" despite reservations – but the "zesty" eats and sangria are usually "worth it", since you get "a lot for your money."

	FOOD	DECOR	SERVICE	COST

☒ Atlantica *American/Seafood* | 20 | 27 | 19 | $55 |

Long Beach | Allegria Hotel | 80 W. Broadway (National Blvd.) | 516-992-3730 | www.allegriahotel.com

"Stunning views" of the Atlantic and "fabulous decor fit for Miami Beach" up the wow factor at this high-end Long Beach jewel in the Allegria Hotel that glimmers with beveled mirrors and jellyfish light fixtures; chef Todd Jacobs' seafood-focused New American menu is "still finding its way" among all the eye candy, and service "needs upgrading" too, so some recommend it just for "apps and drinks" (if you don't mind the "din" at the bar).

Ayhan's Fish Kebab *Seafood/Turkish* | 19 | 17 | 18 | $34 |

Port Washington | 286 Main St. (bet. Carlton Ave. & Shore Rd.) | 516-883-1515 | www.ayhansrestaurants.com

Supporters of this Turkish seafooder in Port Washington appreciate the "large portions" of "reasonably priced" fare, particularly the "simple" but "excellent" whole grilled fish; the "pretty" brick-walled space in an 1898 bank building has an "energetic" vibe and the service is "decent", though "disappointed" guests dub the meal a "mixed bag", declaring there's "nothing to do handstands over" here.

Ayhan's Mediterranean | 18 | 16 | 17 | $28 |
Cafe & Marketplace *Mediterranean/Turkish*

Port Washington | 293 Main St. (bet. Bank St. & Carlton Ave.) | 516-767-1400 | www.ayhansrestaurants.com

Ayhan's Shish Kebab *Mediterranean/Turkish*

Baldwin | 550 Sunrise Hwy. (bet. Lancaster & Rockwood Aves.) | 516-223-1414

Plainview | Plainview Ctr. | 379 S. Oyster Bay Rd. (Woodbury Rd.) | 516-827-5300

Port Washington | 283 Main St. (bet. Bank St. & Carlton Ave.) | 516-883-9309

Rockville Centre | 201 Sunrise Hwy. (N. Village Ave.) | 516-255-0005 www.ayhansrestaurants.com

"Go for the whole fish" or "tasty" kebabs at these Turkish-Med grills delivering "fast", "fairly priced" eats in a "family-friendly" setting; other items leave critics bemoaning a "mass-produced" feel, though "bargain-hunters" swear by the "well-stocked" weekend brunch buffet; P.S. the Mediterranean Cafe in Port Washington has what may be the "best view per dollar on the North Shore."

Ayhan's Trodos | ∇ 21 | 18 | 21 | $36 |
Mediterranean Restaurant *Mediterranean*

Westbury | 477 Old Country Rd. (Evelyn Ave.) | 516-222-8000 | www.trodosrestaurant.com

Ayhan Hassan's latest brings the Mediterranean to Westbury with signature grilled whole fish "seasoned to perfection", complemented by "delicious" skewers and other "traditional" fare; while a few contend the familiar menu is "no better" than what's already found at the Shish Kebab chain, others view the "personable" service and "nice digs" – furnished with a granite bar and communal table – as an "upgrade."

	FOOD	DECOR	SERVICE	COST

Azerbaijan Grill *Mideastern* — 22 | 15 | 21 | $30

Westbury | 1610 Old Country Rd. (Post Ave.) | 516-228-0001 |
www.azerbaijangrill.com

"Flavorful" kebabs sizzle inside this "unassuming" Mideastern tucked away in a Westbury strip mall, a "find" for fans of "authentic" chargrilled dishes with Persian and Turkish influences; the "zest" is in the kitchen – not in the "bare-bones" decor – so it's the "generous" plates, "welcoming" staff and "great lunch specials" that "really make the experience."

Azuma Sushi Asian Fusion *Asian/Japanese* — 23 | 14 | 22 | $29

Greenlawn | 252 Broadway (Little Plains Rd.) | 631-262-7200 |
www.azumasushiasianfusion.com

Loyalists "love the sushi, specialty salads" and extensive Asian fusion options at this "surprisingly good" Greenlawn Japanese that's definitely "better than it looks" since there's "no ambiance" to speak of; despite its shortcomings, the "wonderful hospitality" and affordable tabs keep customers "happy."

Babette's *Eclectic* — 20 | 13 | 17 | $40

East Hampton | 66 Newtown Ln. (bet. Main St. & Osborne Ln.) |
631-329-5377

"Organic, health-conscious food" from a "creative, guilt-free menu" is the specialty at this often "packed" Eclectic where, along with your grass-fed beef burger and BBQ tofu, "you might get neck strain from seeing famous people"; so while the ambiance is "one step above a diner", the service just "ok" and wallet-watchers protest that "no omelet is worth mortgaging your house for", it's still an "East Hampton classic."

Babylon Carriage House *Continental* — 21 | 23 | 21 | $42

Babylon | 21 Fire Island Ave. (Main St.) | 631-422-5161 |
www.babyloncarriagehouse.com

Regulars relish visits to this "refined" yet "friendly" Babylon Continental, set in a "romantic" 1865 carriage house with two fireplaces, a "happening" bar and a "classy stairway to the second floor" (sit upstairs "if you want a quiet meal"); while the "good", "varied" grub ("delicious" Thai calamari) and "happy-hour feeling" are a hit with most, a handful complains about "overpriced" eats and a "noisy" weekend "club" crowd that "hangs out" "looking for love the second time around"; P.S. the "Wednesday lobster bake" is a "bargain."

Baby Moon *Italian* — 18 | 13 | 18 | $35

Westhampton Beach | 238 Montauk Hwy. (bet. Rogers Ave. &
S. Country Rd.) | 631-288-6350 | www.babymoonrestaurant.com

A "go-to for locals" in Westhampton Beach, this "busy", "noisy" "red-sauce" Southern Italian offers "huge platters" of "reliable, if not memorable", "homestyle" fare, including "well-prepared" pizza, pasta and salads; still, some patrons protest it's "not worth the money" given the "uneven service" and "way too family-friendly" space that's "been around for a while, and it shows."

Backyard *Mediterranean*

▽ 23 | 23 | 21 | $49

Montauk | Solé East | 90 Second House Rd. (S. Eldert Ln.) | 631-668-2105 | www.soleeast.com

Montauk's Solé East Hotel provides the "lovely setting" for this "laid-back" Mediterranean focusing on "market-fresh" ingredients sourced from local suppliers; with an indoor fireplace and a "wonderful" outdoor poolside terrace furnished with oversized mattresses, it's a "treat" for lounging over "creative cocktails" among a "so hip, it hurts" crowd; P.S. frequent DJ sets and live music include reggae on Thursdays and Brazilian during Sunday brunch.

Baja Fresh Mexican Grill *Mexican*

18 | 12 | 15 | $14

New Hyde Park | Lake Success Shopping Ctr. | 1468 Union Tpke. (bet. Lakeville & New Hyde Park Rds.) | 516-354-2252 | www.bajafresh.com

Fans find "everything fast food usually is not" at this "always fresh" Mexican chain link in New Hyde Park, where the "fish tacos are a highlight" and the "salsa bar is a hit"; though critics find it "underspiced" with "hit-or-miss" service, most consider it "worthwhile" for a "cheap" meal "on the run."

Baja Grill *Mexican*

18 | 14 | 16 | $20

East Northport | Elwood Shopping Ctr. | 1920 Jericho Tpke. (Elwood Rd.) | 631-462-2252
Smithtown | Sleepys Shopping Plaza | 20 E. Main St. (bet. Hauppauge Rd. & Lawrence Ave.) | 631-979-2252
www.bajagrillny.com

When you're looking for an "affordable" "alternative to fast food", these East Northport and Smithtown sibs deliver "solid" Mexican fare that's big on "wraps, nachos and margaritas"; sure, they're a bit "lacking" when it comes to decor, but even if they don't "knock your socks off", they're "kid-friendly" and "handy for a quick bite."

NEW Bar Frites *French*

18 | 21 | 18 | $48

Greenvale | Wheatley Plaza | 400 Wheatley Plaza (Northern Blvd.) | 516-484-7500 | www.barfrites.com

A "lively scene" that "really hops on weekends" unfolds at this "bright, airy" French bistro in Greenvale's Wheatley Plaza run by George and Gillis Poll (Bryant & Cooper, Cipollini, Toku); admirers "love" the outdoor seating, "Parisian" atmosphere and "classic" cuisine, but a "disappointed" faction cites "deafening din", a "frantic" pace and "expensive" tabs for "unimaginative" fare, calling it the "first chink in the Poll brothers' armor."

Z Barney's M *American/French*

26 | 23 | 24 | $63

Locust Valley | 315 Buckram Rd. (Bayville Rd.) | 516-671-6300 | www.barneyslv.com

"Excellent from start to finish" say fans of this "romantic" "retreat" on a "hard-to-find" country byway in "tony Locust Valley", offering "first-rate" American-French dishes delivered by a "cordial" staff; the "chic, understated" setting "feels like a Vermont inn", especially in the "fireplace room" where a "log fire blazes and crackles" in winter, so while it can be "expensive", many consider it a "must-go"; P.S. a prix fixe is offered Sunday–Thursday and an early-bird on Friday.

Barolo ☒ *Continental/Italian*

25 | 20 | 24 | $54

Melville | 1197 Walt Whitman Rd. (Sweet Hollow Rd.) | 631-421-3750
Expect "consistently delicious" Continental-Italian fare at this "classy" "local favorite" in Melville where the "fantastic" dishes are "impeccably prepared and served" by an "eager-to-please" staff; even if the "small", "dark" room "could use a little sprucing up", it's still "highly recommended" for "special occasions."

☒ Barrique Kitchen & Wine Bar *Mediterranean*

24 | 25 | 23 | $38

Babylon | 69 Deer Park Ave. (bet. Grove Pl. & Montauk Hwy.) | 631-321-1175 | www.barriquekitchenandwinebar.com
Delivering "delectable small plates" and a "serious" vino selection in a "cozy" wine cellar–style interior heavy on reclaimed wood (a barn door serves as a communal table), this "hopping" Babylon Med is a top pick for an evening "without the kids"; a staff with "knowledge and personality" "makes every night special", but since there are no rezzies, be ready to wait "over an hour" on the weekends.

Basil Leaf Cafe *Italian*

21 | 20 | 21 | $41

Locust Valley | Plaza Shoppes | 7B Birch Hill Rd. (bet. Elm St. & Underhill Rd.) | 516-676-6252 | www.thebasilleafrestaurant.com
This "neighborhood favorite" in a little shopping plaza in Locust Valley seems to have "improved" recently, offering regional Italian cuisine that's both "comforting" and "creatively prepared", delivered by an "accommodating" staff; the "quaint" surroundings open up to a "cheery terrace in the summer", attracting plenty of "ladies who lunch, local families and regulars"; P.S. reservations are recommended for the weekends.

Batata Café ☒ *Eclectic*

∇ 21 | 11 | 17 | $15

Northport | 847 Fort Salonga Rd. (bet. Layne Way & Waterside Ave.) | 631-754-4439 | www.batatacafe.com
"Well-thought-out panini", "soups with a twist" and morning burritos make this "cute", "counter-service" Eclectic Northport cafe a popular "gathering place" for breakfast or "moms' lunch out while the kids are at school"; the funky setting "showcases local artists' work", which provides a pleasant diversion when the service "takes a long time"; P.S. closes at 7 PM weekdays, 4 PM Saturdays.

Bay Burger *Burgers*

21 | 11 | 15 | $19

Sag Harbor | 1742 Bridgehampton-Sag Harbor Tpke. (Carroll St.) | 631-899-3915 | www.bayburger.com
"They keep the formula simple" at this seasonal Sag Harbor joint – "freshly ground beef burgers" from "high-quality meat" served on a house-baked bun, accompanied by "a glass of wine" (or a bottle of beer), all topped off with "amazing" housemade ice cream; there's "zero ambiance" inside, but the nice patio is a summertime draw, and a "jazz group entertains a mellow crowd" on Thursday nights.

	FOOD	DECOR	SERVICE	COST

Bayou, The Ⓜ *Cajun/Creole* — 23 | 19 | 20 | $35

North Bellmore | Omni Plaza | 2823 Jerusalem Ave. (Pea Pond Rd.) | 516-785-9263 | www.bayou4bigfun.com

It's "Mardi Gras every day" at this "funky", "festive" New Orleans outpost in North Bellmore, especially after you down one of the "signature Hurricanes" (careful, they "creep up on you") and some "spicy", "super-tasty" Cajun-Creole eats; sure, the strip-mall location "could be better", but once you get into the brazenly "tacky decor" and "party atmosphere", you "don't want to leave."

Bayview Inn & Restaurant Ⓜ *American/Continental* — 22 | 19 | 22 | $47

South Jamesport | Bayview Inn | 10 Front St. (S. Jamesport Ave.) | 631-722-2659 | www.northforkmotels.com

"Pleasant, relaxed" repasts can be found at this "out-of-the-way" American-Continental in South Jamesport where there's fireside dining in winter and a "lovely" porch for "well-prepared" summer meals; it feels "like eating at home, but you can still get dessert if you don't finish your meal", and the Sunday–Thursday prix fixe appeals to recessionaires.

Beacon *American* — 22 | 23 | 20 | $59

Sag Harbor | 8 W. Water St. (Bridge St.) | 631-725-7088 | www.beaconsagharbor.com

"Incredible sunsets" and "top-notch" New American cuisine are a "hard combination to beat" at this "exquisite" waterside "favorite" in Sag Harbor; so while the tabs are "hefty" and the no-reservations policy a "real pain", many find the wait "worthwhile" since this "hot spot actually deserves its reputation"; P.S. open seasonally.

Bella Vita City Grill *American/Italian* — 21 | 17 | 20 | $46

St. James | Colonial Shopping Ctr. | 430-16 N. Country Rd. (Clinton Ave.) | 631-862-8060 | www.bellavitacitygrill.com

"Interesting specials" from a chef-owner "who really cares" and "stops by your table" lend a bit of character to this "upscale", "reliable" Italian–New American in St. James; its newly expanded bar area accommodates martini-lovers, though the "noisy" atmosphere is a bit too Manhattan for those who say "go early if you want a quiet meal."

Bellissimo Ristorante *Italian* — ▽ 23 | 24 | 24 | $36

Deer Park | 786 Grand Blvd. (Commack Rd.) | 631-274-3378

"Wonderful Italian food" by a 60-year veteran chef impresses at this tiny, "romantic" Deer Park "staple" with just eight tables; it can be easily missed in its strip-mall location, but moderate prices and a staff that treats you like "family" ensure a loyal clientele.

Bellport, The *American/Continental* — 22 | 19 | 19 | $44

Bellport | 159 S. Country Rd. (Woodruff St.) | 631-286-7550 | www.bellport.com

Regulars say it's "always a pleasure" to dine at this "arty" New American–Continental in Bellport by the married team of Taylor

FOOD | DECOR | SERVICE | COST

Alonso and Patricia Trainor, who complement "imaginative" dishes with a "quirky", "country-house vibe"; though a few find the luster has "faded" and cite inconsistent service, it "can feel like home on the right night", and the Monday 'recession special' is a plus; P.S. closed Tuesdays year-round and Wednesdays in the winter.

NEW Bel Posto
Ristorante & Enoteca Ⓜ Italian

| - | - | - | M |

Huntington | 15 New St. (bet. Carver & Main Sts.) | 631-421-4600 | www.belpostony.com

Chef Michael Ross (ex Gabrielle's) brings a creative bent to this Huntington debut, where dishes like ricotta gnocchi with walnut sauce and porcini-rubbed sirloin stake out new terrain alongside more familiar Italian fare; the dining area's chandeliers and brickwork form a fitting backdrop to the subtle sophistication of the menu, whose moderate prices extend to many wines available by the glass and bottle.

Benihana   Japanese/Steak

| 19 | 18 | 20 | $38 |

Manhasset | Bed, Bath & Beyond Shopping Plaza | 2105 Northern Blvd. (Port Washington Blvd.) | 516-627-3400
Westbury | 920 Merchants Concourse (Privado Dr.) | 516-222-6091
www.benihana.com

"Bring on the onion volcano" clamor customers who count on an "entertaining" "show" for "all ages" (even "jaded teenagers") at this Japanese steakhouse chain in Manhasset and Westbury, where teppanyaki chefs perform tableside feats while delivering "reliable" eats, including sushi and other "updated" items; critics call it "tired", "tacky" and "overpriced", but it works as a place to "take the kids and still have an edible meal."

Benkei Japanese Ⓜ Japanese

| ∇ 23 | 19 | 21 | $31 |

Northport | 16 Woodbine Ave. (bet. Main St. & Scudder Ave.) | 631-262-7100

A "warm greeting at the door" sets the tone at this "inviting" family-owned Japanese in Northport serving "creative" sushi and sashimi, plus a range of cooked dishes, all for a "reasonable price"; it's situated in a "nice location facing the harbor", and while it's "certainly not fancy", many surveyors feel it definitely "stands out above the crowd."

Benny's Ristorante Ⓧ Italian

| 25 | 19 | 24 | $52 |

Westbury | 199 Post Ave. (Maple Ave.) | 516-997-8111 | www.bennysristorante.com

"Still the ultimate" in "fine" Northern Italian dining, this "true classic" in Westbury "always delivers" a "superb" meal in an "old-fashioned", "formal atmosphere"; the "throwback" decor is "ornate" and "elegant" to some and a bit "tired" to others, but most commend the "first-class" service, helmed by "wonderful" hosts who "treat you like royalty."

	FOOD	DECOR	SERVICE	COST

☒ Ben's Kosher Deli *Deli*

19 | 14 | 17 | $25

Carle Place | 59 Old Country Rd. (Glen Cove Rd.) | 516-742-3354
Greenvale | 140 Wheatley Plaza (bet. Glen Cove Rd. & Northern Blvd.) |
516-621-3340
Woodbury | 7971 Jericho Tpke. (S. Woods Rd.) | 516-496-4236
www.bensdeli.net

"When the craving strikes" for "flavorful" matzo ball soup, "tender" corned beef and "unbelievable pastrami on rye" surveyors tend to "never mind the cholesterol" because this "old-fashioned kosher deli" threesome "fits the bill"; customers who've "eaten here for over 20 years" say the "fair prices", "plain yet comfortable" surroundings and "loud" crowd work for "family dining", though a few lament it's "lost its vim" and wish the "brassy" staff "cared a little more."

Bertucci's *Italian*

17 | 16 | 17 | $26

Westbury | 795 Merrick Ave. (Corporate Dr.) | 516-683-8800
Hauppauge | 358 Vanderbilt Motor Pkwy. (bet. Kennedy Dr. & Marcus Blvd.) | 631-952-2100
Melville | 881 Walt Whitman Rd. (Gwynne Rd.) | 631-427-9700
www.bertuccis.com

Locals attest it's "rug-rat heaven" at this "decent" Italian family-friendly chain that's a "surefire thing" with the kids (who get to "play with dough" at the table); most just "stick with" the brick-oven pies, "hot rolls" and "nice salads" (the other selections can seem "processed"), and all agree you'll get a "predictable" meal for a "fair price."

☒ Besito *Mexican*

24 | 24 | 22 | $45

Roslyn | Harborview Shoppes | 1516 Old Northern Blvd.
(bet. Northern Blvd. & Remsen Ave.) | 516-484-3001
Huntington | 402 New York Ave. (bet. Carver & Fairview Sts.) |
631-549-0100
www.besitomex.com

Fans indulge in a "fiesta of the senses" at these "attractive" Mexican kissing cousins in Huntington and Roslyn where the "guac rocks", the "contemporary" comida is "different and delicious" and the "killer" margaritas lend extra zing to a "glowing" atmosphere that's "cool as the other side of a pillow"; though it can all add up to a "pricey night", most "shout 'arriba!'" and gladly return for more.

Best Buffet *Chinese/Eclectic*

18 | 12 | 13 | $30

Huntington Station | 179 Walt Whitman Rd. (bet. Sprucetree Ln. & Weston St.) | 631-385-0800 | www.best-buffet.com

"Eat, enjoy and diet the rest of the week" advise voracious voyagers who head to this Chinese-Eclectic buffet in Huntington Station that's a "fabulous deal if you like to stuff yourself"; there's an "astounding variety" of dishes – from the "can't-be-beat" crab legs to the "well-prepared" Peking duck – just "get there early to avoid the gluttonous crowds" and "don't look too closely at the decor."

	FOOD	DECOR	SERVICE	COST

Bevanda *Italian*

22 | 18 | 24 | $44

Great Neck | 570 Middle Neck Rd. (bet. Breuer Ave. & Brokaw Ln.) | 516-482-1510 | www.bevandarestaurant.com

"Everyone feels like a VIP" at this "gracious" Northern Italian in Great Neck dishing up "generous" plates of "consistently good", "comforting" cuisine; so even though a few tut that it's "time for some new decor", the "reasonable prices" and "complimentary biscotti" at meal's end seal the deal for "happy" regulars.

Big Daddy's *BBQ/Cajun*

24 | 18 | 21 | $33

Massapequa | 1 Park Ln. (Front St.) | 516-799-8877 | www.bigdaddysny.com

"Cajun is ragin'" at this "little bit of N'Awlins" in Massapequa that's "still spicy and going strong" with a "daily changing menu" of "sauced-up" Louisiana specialties plus "smoky BBQ" and "wild cocktails"; the staff gives "trustworthy recommendations" and the "jazzy" digs often play host to "rocking live music", though the "looong waits" and "hot" grub are "not for the faint of heart"; P.S. look out for "great deals during the week."

Bigelow's ⊘ *New England/Seafood*

24 | 9 | 20 | $23

Rockville Centre | 79 N. Long Beach Rd. (bet. Ongley St. & Sunrise Hwy.) | 516-678-3878 | www.bigelows-rvc.com

"Step back in time" at this "lovable" Cape Cod-style seafood "shack", a Rockville Centre "institution" (built in 1939) where fried-fish fans "belly up" to the original counter for battered, breaded bounty – including "some of the best Ipswich clams" around – along with "showstopper" chowders; the limited seating can get tight, but the "standing-room-only" crowd just cares about the "fresh" catch; P.S. cash only.

Bin 56 ◐⊠ *Spanish*

▽ 24 | 21 | 22 | $37

Huntington | 56 Stewart Ave. (bet. Main St. & New York Ave.) | 631-812-0060 | www.bin56.com

With "terrific" Spanish tapas – from artisanal cheeses to bacon-wrapped dates – and an "accommodating", "knowledgeable" staff, this Huntington cousin to Bistros Cassis and Citron provides a "comfy" "place to hang, sip wine and have a bite or two"; the "relaxed", low-lit setting, furnished with a communal table and couches, is "perfect for late-night", plus Tuesday tarot readings add some midweek magic.

Birchwood Tap Room *American/Polish*

▽ 20 | 13 | 21 | $30

Riverhead | 512 Pulaski St. (Hamilton Ave.) | 631-727-4449 | www.birchwoodtap.com

This "local" tavern in the heart of Riverhead's Polishtown district has been serving up "homestyle" Polish dishes (like "melt-in-your-mouth" pierogi) and American "classic pub" fare for a "good price" since 1929; while it's "kitschy", "dark and cluttered" to some, memorabilia mavens admire the tin ceiling, stained glass and "pictures of film and sports celebrities of a bygone day"; P.S. weeknight deals make it extra-affordable.

	FOOD	DECOR	SERVICE	COST

☒ **Bistro Cassis** *French*

| | 24 | 20 | 21 | $44 |

Huntington | 55B Wall St. (bet. Central & Gerard Sts.) | 631-421-4122 | www.bistrocassis.com

"Even the most discriminating Francophile approves" of this "popular" Huntington bistro (sib to Bistro Citron) turning out "magnificent mussels", "divine duck" and a "delicious" Sunday brunch, all served with "great crusty bread"; a "well-trained" staff and prices that "won't break the bank" help make up for the "cramped" setting with tables so "close together" it's "tough not to listen to other people's conversations."

Bistro Citron *French*

| | 21 | 20 | 20 | $43 |

Roslyn | 1362 Old Northern Blvd. (bet. E. B'way & Main St.) | 516-403-4400 | www.bistrocitron.com

A spin-off of Bistro Cassis, this "adorable little bistro" in Roslyn is "always a favorite" for "terrific daily specials", "reliable" French "standards" and what some call "the best burger within 50 miles"; the "lovely", "non-stuffy" setting features tables "overlooking the duck pond" and live music twice weekly, but nitpickers note "inconsistent" service, "tight seating" and slightly "pricey" fare that's "not as inventive" as it could be.

Bistro 44 *American*

| | 23 | 21 | 21 | $42 |

Northport | 44 Main St. (bet. School St. & Woodbine Ave.) | 631-262-9744 | www.bistro44.net

Fans of this "sophisticated" yet "unpretentious" Northport New American "love the food" served in a "handsome" setting designed with original 1850s woodwork and a "beautiful" heated patio; the village location works for dining "before or after a show" or taking a post-meal "stroll along the harbor", and though a few feel squeezed by the "too-small" room and moderately expensive menu, many are "impressed" by the "update" under a new owner and chef.

Bistro M ☒ *American*

| | 25 | 17 | 23 | $58 |

Glen Head | 70 Glen Head Rd. (Railroad Ave.) | 516-671-2498 | www.bistromrestaurant.com

"Fabulous" chef/co-owner Mitch SuDock "dazzles the most discerning palates" with "unique", "beautifully presented" New American dishes at this "expensive" candlelit Glen Head "winner"; a "warm" staff, outdoor patio and live music on the weekends add to the "charm" of a "special night out", though a few cite a "small" locale so close to the "train tracks" that it "shakes when the LIRR rumbles by", and "wish" the atmosphere "were as fantastic as the food."

NEW **Bistro 72** *American*

| | - | - | - | E |

Riverhead | Hotel Indigo | 1830 W. Main St. (Kroemer Ave.) | 631-369-2200 | www.indigoeastend.com

Woven-back chairs and a granite bar make for a chic setting at this newcomer in Riverhead's renovated Hotel Indigo, where a farm-to-table American menu from chef Lia Fallon (Amarelle) includes offerings such as local fish 'n' chips, with most dishes available in half or full portions; P.S. there's also outdoor poolside and fireside dining.

	FOOD	DECOR	SERVICE	COST

Bistro Toulouse *French*

	22	18	22	$39

Port Washington | 43 Main St. (bet. Bayles & Maryland Aves.) |
516-708-1852 | www.bistrotoulouserest.com

Overseen by the "lovely" Iva and Pablo Cecere, who ensure "one of
the warmest welcomes on LI", this Port Washington bistro proffers
"authentic" seasonal French fare in a "cozy" setting of "casual" "sophistication"; "generous pours" of wine are another plus, and
though some complain of "cramped" seating, the "excellent value"
helps make up for it; P.S. the three-course prix fixe is cash-only.

NEW Bistro 25 Ⓜ *Eclectic*

	-	-	-	M

Sayville | 45 Foster Ave. (bet. Middle Rd. & N. Main St.) | 631-589-7775 |
www.bistro25li.com

Twenty-five $25 bottles of wine on the list inspired the name of this
Eclectic Sayville bistro where monkfish medallions, braised short
ribs and other entrees are all priced under $20; the dining area is
decorated with white tablecloths, votive candles and paintings for sale
from a local gallery, and there's a separate section with high tables.

B.K. Sweeney's
Parkside Tavern *American*

	18	17	19	$31

Bethpage | 356 Broadway (Powell Ave.) | 516-935-9597

B.K. Sweeney's Uptown Grille *American*

Garden City | 636 Franklin Ave. (bet. 6th & 7th Sts.) | 516-746-3075
www.bksweeneys.com

Locals gather to "eat, drink and be merry" at this pub pair in Garden
City and Bethpage ("near the golf courses") turning out "hearty"
burgers, steaks and other "well-priced" American eats along with
"good tap beers"; service is generally "pleasant", even when the
crowd gets a little "raucous" on "game days" and "after work."

Black & Blue
Seafood Chophouse *Seafood/Steak*

	22	21	23	$48

Huntington | 65 Wall St. (bet. Central & Gerard Sts.) | 631-385-9255 |
www.blackandbluehuntington.com

"Super-friendly" servers who "go that extra mile" elevate this
"lively" surf 'n' turfer in Huntington, providing "innovative",
"thoughtfully presented" dishes in a supper-club setting with "big
booths" and a "beautiful" saltwater fish tank; the "classy" atmosphere gets a boost from "live music some nights", though critics
caution about the "limited" menu, adding "watch your wallet, it'll
take a hit."

Blackbirds' Grille *Cajun/Southern*

	20	15	21	$32

Sayville | 553 Old Montauk Hwy. (B'way Ave.) | 631-563-4144 |
www.blackbirdsgrille.com

"Tasty" Cajun-Southern eats (including "the best fried pickles") are
delivered by a "warm" staff at this simple, "homey" Sayville "roadhouse" decorated with a "coastal" motif; the "busy" room gets
"loud" when there's "live music on weekends", and dishes can be
"inconsistent" ("stick to basic grill fare"), but most agree it's "not
bad for a decent, casual meal."

	FOOD	DECOR	SERVICE	COST

Z Blackstone Steakhouse *Steak* — 24 | 24 | 23 | $66

Melville | 10 Pinelawn Rd. (Broad Hollow Rd.) | 631-271-7780 | www.blackstonesteakhouse.com

They're "always on top of their game" at this "see-and-be-seen" steakhouse on Melville's 110 corridor that not only offers "excellent" cuts of meat, but also "outrageous sushi rolls"; the "contemporary" lodgelike setting with "gorgeous lighting" and "professional" service attracts a "powerhouse lunch" crowd as well as a "happening bar scene", too bad "the noise level is almost as high as the prices."

Blackwells *Steak* — 23 | 25 | 24 | $51

Wading River | Great Rock Golf Club | 141 Fairway Dr. (Sound Ave.) | 631-929-1800 | www.blackwellsrestaurant.com

There's a "private country-club atmosphere" at this "elegantly decorated" steakhouse overlooking the greens of the Great Rock Golf Club in Wading River, where "you can taste the freshness" of the local ingredients in the "fine" dishes crafted by new chef Chris Gerdes; an "extensive wine list" highlighting LI vintages complements the cuisine, as does the "professional, courteous" service; P.S. the prix fixe dinners are an "excellent value", and the early-bird is a "steal."

Bliss M *American* — 22 | 19 | 21 | $46

East Setauket | 766 Rte. 25A (Nicolls Rd.) | 631-941-0430 | www.blissli.com

"High-quality" cooking shines at this "upscale" East Setauket New American, which also delivers "one of the best" happy hours around; though critics call the layout "crammed" and the dining "pricier than it should be", most report "attentive" service and a "pleasant" meal.

Blond *American* — 21 | 20 | 22 | $46

Miller Place | Aliano Shopping Ctr. | 691 Rte. 25A (Oakland Ave.) | 631-821-5969 | www.blondrestaurant.com

"Hidden in a strip mall" in Miller Place, this "swanky" "little" New American surprises with its "fresh, exciting menu" and "Manhattan" ambiance; the staff "accommodates special requests", and though a few maintain it's "expensive for the area", at least the "fried Oreo shots" ("best dessert ever") make a memorable finish.

Blue 🗑⌿ *American* — 22 | 23 | 22 | $47

Blue Point | 7 Montauk Hwy. (Nicolls Rd.) | 631-363-6666 | www.restaurantblue.com

With a clubby scene, a "South Beach"–style outdoor lounge, nightly bands and DJs, and a "tasty", "interesting" New American menu (including sushi), this "modern" Blue Pointer draws a "lively" crowd; a few guests gripe about "questionable food combinations", but most are won over by the "friendly" bar and "Lobsterfest in the summer."

NEW Blue Fish *Japanese* — - | - | - | E

Hicksville | Days Inn | 828 S. Oyster Bay Rd. (bet. Aerospace Blvd. & Meadow Ln.) | 516-605-0655 | www.bluefishli.com

Bright blue lights undulate over the onyx bar and red lights illuminate the booths at this sleek, upscale Japanese newcomer in

Hicksville; the menu goes beyond sushi and sashimi, also offering hot fare such as a tuna dumpling on guacamole and pan-seared lobster with coconut black rice.

Blue Moon *Italian/Pizza*
| 20 | 16 | 19 | $28 |

Rockville Centre | 26 N. Park Ave. (bet. Merrick Rd. & Sunrise Hwy.) | 516-763-4900 | www.bluemoonpizzeria.com

"Pizza, pasta and panini" are the main draws at this "reasonable" Rockville Centre Italian whose "terrific" coal-fired pies and "basic" "red-sauce" plates work for a "quick bite" "pre- or post-movie"; the exposed-brick walls and checkered tablecloths lend a "comfortable" feel that's "nice for families", though some argue the decor and "limited" menu "need a little zip."

Blue Parrot Bar & Grill *Tex-Mex*
| 15 | 15 | 15 | $37 |

East Hampton | 33A Main St. (Newtown Ln.) | 631-329-2583 | www.blueparroteasthampton.com

This "funky" Tex-Mex "cantina" in East Hampton was revived by "new celebrity owners" and given a "face-lift" in 2009 after a three-year hiatus, but "disappointing" food, "snooty" service and "schizo-phrenic" Western decor mar the comeback; regardless, it's a "good place to hang in the late afternoon" "slurping" a margarita, and the nightly "crowds" are "glad to have it back."

NEW Bluepoint Bar & Grill Ⓜ *American*
| – | – | – | M |

Blue Point | 154 Montauk Hwy. (Homan Ave.) | 631-419-6850 | www.bluepointbarandgrillli.com

Situated in a little house with a front porch, this Blue Point American offers a moderately priced roundup of comfort food that includes burgers and entrees such as marinated skirt steak with tempura onion rings and chicken stuffed with goat cheese; the simple room is wrapped in wood wainscoting and decorated with seasonal touches.

NEW Boathouse, The *Seafood*
| 19 | 22 | 17 | $51 |

East Hampton | Harbor Marina | 39 Gann Rd. (off Three Mile Harbor Rd.) | 631-329-3663 | www.easthamptonboathouse.com

In the former home of Bostwick's on the Harbor, this East Hampton arrival is a "pleasure" with its "open-air deck", "priceless sunset views" and "newly decorated" digs resembling a vintage yacht; the expensive seafood doesn't quite "live up to the atmosphere" ("simple entrees are the best") and service can be "amateurish", but "the young flock to it" nevertheless, keeping the "noise level at top decibel."

BobbiQue *BBQ*
| 21 | 15 | 18 | $26 |

Patchogue | 70 W. Main St. (Havens Ave.) | 631-447-7744 | www.bobbique.com

"Pull up your sleeves, loosen your belt" and get ready to "smack your lips" at this "true BBQ, blues and bourbon haven" in Patchogue offering a "fantastic" beer selection to boot; the "relaxed" atmosphere is livened up with "awesome" live music, so even if some say the "large", industrial setting has "no warmth", the "young, agile and thirsty" add heat.

	FOOD	DECOR	SERVICE	COST

Bobby's
Burger Palace *Burgers* ⎡21⎤ ⎡15⎤ ⎡18⎤ ⎡$17⎤

Lake Grove | Smith Haven Mall | 355 Smith Haven Mall
(bet. Middle Country Rd. & Nesconset Hwy.) | 631-382-9590 |
www.bobbysburgerpalace.com

Celeb chef Bobby Flay's "juicy, flavorful" burgers "cooked to order
with a wide variety of toppings", plus "crisp", "housemade fries" and
"amazing shakes" "feed your addiction" at this "upscale" Lake Grove
fast-fooder; the shopping-mall location and orange-and-lime
"McDonald's über-chic" atmosphere isn't for everyone, but the
"quick", "semi-self-serve" format ("place your order" at the counter,
"then sit") helps keep the line moving.

Bobby Van's Steakhouse *Steak* ⎡22⎤ ⎡19⎤ ⎡20⎤ ⎡$60⎤

Bridgehampton | 2393 Main St. (bet. Ocean Rd. & School St.) |
631-537-0590 | www.bobbyvans.com

This "bustling" "Bridgehampton watering hole" and meatery is
"just 'Hamptons' enough" with its "chic" yet "not intimidating"
digs, ideal for indulging in "excellent" steaks, "famous" burgers
and "generous" drinks; the service is a "cut above", catering to a
"social scene spanning multiple generations", but some doubters
disapprove of the "big tabs, long waits" and "deafening" din in the
"slightly dated" space; P.S. lunches and "midweek early dinner
deals" make it more affordable.

Bob's Place Ⓜ *American* ⎡21⎤ ⎡21⎤ ⎡20⎤ ⎡$42⎤

Floral Park | 230 Jericho Tpke. (bet. Flower Ave. & Park Pl.) |
516-354-8185 | www.bobsplacerestaurant.com

"A piece of Manhattan" in Floral Park, this "unexpected" locale cap-
tures "city quality" with its "modern yet classic styling", "creative"
cocktails and "inventive", "enjoyable" New American menu touched
by Asia and the Mediterranean; service can be "spotty" and the tabs
"a bit expensive", but the Tuesday–Thursday prix fixe is a "bargain."

Boccaccio Ⓜ *Italian* ⎡21⎤ ⎡16⎤ ⎡22⎤ ⎡$45⎤

Hicksville | 275 W. Old Country Rd. (Newbridge Rd.) | 516-433-6262 |
www.boccacciony.com

Regulars rely on this "comfortable" Northern Italian "family place"
in Hicksville for "wonderful", "accommodating" service, "very
good", if "not outstanding", fare and "reasonable prices" ("sign up
for birthday dinner discounts"); the "so-so" interior may be caught
in a bit of "time warp", but that doesn't keep it from being
a neighborhood "standby."

Bonbori Tiki *Japanese/Thai* ⎡▽ 20⎤ ⎡20⎤ ⎡20⎤ ⎡$33⎤

Huntington | 14 Elm St. (bet. Nassau Rd. & New York Ave.) |
631-673-0400

"Just off the main drag in Huntington", this "interesting" Thai-
Japanese "mainstay" is a "delight in nice weather" when those in the
know flock to the "secret garden"; the "relaxing" bi-level space, "attentive" staff and a menu that's "less expensive" than at some
nearby eateries add up to an "enjoyable experience" for most.

RESTAURANTS

	FOOD	DECOR	SERVICE	COST

Bonsai *Japanese*   22 | 16 | 20 | $31

Port Washington | 92 Main St. (bet. Evergreen & Haven Aves.) | 516-883-0103

"Always fresh", "well-presented" sushi and "excellent-value bento boxes" mean there's "usually a wait" at this "small", "popular" Port Washington Japanese; regulars recommend the "reasonable lunch specials" and appreciate the "family-friendly" service and "relaxing" vibe, "even if the decor is somewhat bland."

Bostwick's Chowder House *Seafood*   20 | 12 | 18 | $37

East Hampton | 277 Pantigo Rd. (Cross Hwy.) | 631-324-1111 | www.bostwickschowderhouse.com

A "busy" locale for real "Bonacker bites", this "casual" East Hampton roadside seafood shack (owned by the same team as Indian Wells Tavern) turns out "simple", "fresh" lobster rolls and "excellent clams and chowders" served by a "young staff that's full of energy"; it's "a little pricey" considering the "throwaway" plates, but "perfect after a day at the beach", especially if you can "snag one of the outdoor tables"; P.S. closed in the off-season.

Boulder Creek *Steak*   - | - | - | M

Franklin Square | 700 Hempstead Tpke. (Ribbon St.) | 516-564-9100 | www.bouldercreekfranklinsquare.com
Hicksville | Broadway Mall | 200 N. Broadway (Newbridge Rd.) | 516-942-4843 | www.bouldercreeksteakhouse.com
Bay Shore | 1701 Sunrise Hwy. (Redmond Ave.) | 631-968-9696 | www.bouldercreekbayshore.com
Riverhead | 1490 Old Country Rd. (Osborn Ave.) | 631-369-2900 | www.bouldercreekriverhead.com

A Rocky Mountain theme plays out at these family-friendly steakhouses with log poles, stone fireplaces and twig-style furniture as a rustic backdrop for a variety of cuts of beef, burgers and other mid-priced fare; a popular way to kick off the meal is with the Boulder Blossom – a huge, battered and deep-fried onion, served with a spicy dipping sauce.

Bozena Polish-European Restaurant ⓜ *Polish*   ▽ 23 | 14 | 21 | $27

Lindenhurst | 485 W. Montauk Hwy. (bet. 7th & 8th Sts.) | 631-226-3001 | www.polishdinner.com

"Hooked" customers heed the hankering for "comfort food, old-country style" at this "big" Polish diner in Lindenhurst delivering "incredibly good", low-priced fare (including a "winning" sampler platter); if you can look past the "catering-hall tacky" decor and "weekend parties" with "loud DJs spinning disco and polka", you'll have yourself an "amazing" meal.

⒵ Branzino *Italian*   26 | 19 | 24 | $57

Lynbrook | 152 Union Ave. (Scranton Ave.) | 516-599-6161 | www.branzinoristorante.com

"Way out" in southern Lynbrook, this "rare find" is easy to miss but hard to forget once you've indulged in its "top-notch" Northern

Italian cuisine and lengthy wine list, proffered by a "caring", "professional" staff; for such a "tiny place" it packs a "big bill" (specials can go "sky high"), but it's "worth it", even on "crowded" weekends.

Brasserie Cassis *French* | 23 | 20 | 21 | $43 |

Plainview | Plainview Ctr. | 387 S. Oyster Bay Rd. (Woodbury Rd.) | 516-653-0090 | www.brasseriecassis.com

Diners adore this "charming" "Parisian bistro" in Plainview, where the French "comfort food" is "*très bon*", particularly the "terrific" mussels and frites (a real deal on Moules Mondays); despite the view of the surrounding "strip mall", a smattering of outdoor tables allows for "people-watching" when the weather warms, a plus considering how "noisy" it can get inside.

Brasserie Persil *French* | 25 | 19 | 23 | $40 |

Oceanside | 2825 Long Beach Rd. (bet. Merle Ave. & Poole St.) | 516-992-1742 | www.persilrestaurant.com

You feel like you're "sitting on the Seine" at this "delightful" Oceanside brasserie (sister to Sage Bistro and Aperitif) that's deemed a "must-go" thanks to its "fabulous" French food and "great value"; the "close" bistro-style quarters tend to get "noisy", but a "helpful" staff deftly tends to the "crowds."

Brasserie 214 *European* | 20 | 22 | 21 | $44 |
(fka New Hyde Park Inn)

New Hyde Park | Inn at New Hyde Park | 214 Jericho Tpke. (bet. 2nd & 3rd Sts.) | 516-354-7797 | www.innatnhp.com

Sporting a fresh name to reflect its "makeover", this "stunning" European at the Inn at New Hyde Park "has come a long way" from its "dowdy" past to become a "feast for the eyes and stomach"; service is generally "very good" and the menu maintains some of the old German "standards" while incorporating hints of Belgium, France and the Mediterranean, though skeptics say the eats remain "nothing special" despite the "impressive" redo.

Brass Rail *American* | 25 | 20 | 22 | $48 |

Locust Valley | 107 Forest Ave. (bet. Birch Hill Rd. & Weir Ln.) | 516-723-9103 | www.thebrassraillocustvalley.com

"Extraordinarily creative" chef-owner Kent Monkan delivers a "home-run" menu of "scrumptious", "market-driven" American dishes ranging from bar bites to small plates to full dinners, allowing diners to order according to their appetite and budget at this Locust Valley "gem"; the service is "on track" and the "beautiful bar" enhances the "casual", "old-time tavern" feel – no wonder "reservations fill up fast."

Bravo Nader! *Italian/Seafood* | 24 | 13 | 22 | $52 |

Huntington | 9 Union Pl. (bet. New York Ave. & Wall St.) | 631-351-1200 | www.bravonader.com

Nader's Fish on the Run *Italian/Seafood*

NEW **Huntington** | 217 New York Ave. (Mill Ln.) | 631-423-6300

Chef-owner and "devoted fisherman" Nader Gebrin has earned a "loyal following" for his "amazing" crab cakes, "superb" pastas and "fantastic" specials presented by a "personable" staff at this Huntington Southern Italian; even if the tabs can be "high" and the room "tight", you'll probably "walk out with two friends from the next table"; P.S. the newly opened Nader's Fish on the Run focuses on take-out tacos and sandwiches.

Brian Scotts ⓜ *American*   ▽ | 19 | 18 | 18 | $39 |

Miller Place | 90 N. Country Rd. (Landing Rd.) | 631-331-4848 | www.brianscotts.com

Serving a "limited" New American menu inside a homey 1824 house, this "out-of-the-way" "neighborhood" eatery in Miller Place earns mixed reviews; fans insist "everything is great", from the "excellent" fare to "dining outside" in warmer weather, but foes are "disappointed" with "inconsistent" food that "doesn't match the cost" and a staff that "keeps forgetting you're there"; P.S. the Sunday-Thursday Blue Plate Special keeps tabs more affordable.

Bridgehampton Candy Kitchen ⊅ *Diner* | 15 | 12 | 17 | $20 |

Bridgehampton | Main St. (School St.) | 631-537-9885

It's a slice of "nostalgia" at this cash-only, "old-fashioned soda shop" circa 1926 in Bridgehampton where the "best" housemade ice cream, "thickest shakes" and "fast service" with a "vast tolerance" for tykes win fans; even if the "homespun ambiance" is "better" than the rest of the American eats, there's a chance to spot "celebs galore" at the "see-and-be-seen breakfasts", plus the prices leave "enough in your wallet to take the Jitney home."

Brio Ristorante Italiano *Italian* | 21 | 19 | 21 | $42 |

Port Washington | 45A Shore Rd. (bet. Mill Pond & Old Shore Rds.) | 516-767-0077 | www.brioportwashington.com

"Delicious" fare and an owner who "makes you feel like a guest in his home" are the highlights of this Northern Italian in Port Washington with an adjacent wine bar offering a "fantastic" list; the "pretty" room is suitable for "quiet dinners", while the "excellent" specials keep it a "staple on the restaurant roster" of many; P.S. Wednesday is Ladies Night, when groups of four or more women get 20% off their bill.

Broadway Beanery ⓜ *American* | 21 | 21 | 20 | $38 |

Lynbrook | 23 Atlantic Ave. (bet. Merrick Rd. & Stauderman Ave.) | 516-596-0028

Though the name shouts "coffeehouse", there's more than just java and "don't-miss" desserts at this "casual" yet "classy" Lynbrook "favorite" providing a range of "creative", "enjoyable" New American dishes in a candlelit Victorian-style setting; it's a "great place to hang" thanks to live "traditional jazz" on weekends, plus a caffeinated bar serving cups o' joe and sweets till midnight.

Brooks & Porter *Steak* | 22 | 22 | 21 | $60 |

Merrick | 16 Merrick Ave. (Sunrise Hwy.) | 516-379-9400 | www.brooksandporter.com

This Merrick steakhouse with a slick "city feel" – and the prices to match – serves up "serious", "high-quality" beef, raw bar delicacies and an after-work "scene"; the service is generally "up to par", though some doubters "don't know what the hype is about" and say that "nothing can make up for the noise level", especially on the weekends.

☑ Bryant & Cooper Steakhouse *Steak* | 26 | 21 | 23 | $69 |

Roslyn | 2 Middle Neck Rd. (Northern Blvd.) | 516-627-7270 | www.bryantandcooper.com

Serving "phenomenal" cuts of meat "aged on-site" along with "ample sides" and a "stellar wine list", this "carnivore's delight" in Roslyn "rivals Manhattan's finest" with some of the "most expertly prepared steaks in the area" (you "can't go wrong" with the seafood either); "well-trained" servers who "know their job" help justify the "pricey" tabs, though some find the pace "rushed" and the whole package "too much of a scene"; P.S. "lunch is a lot more affordable", and the adjoining butcher shop is "superb."

B. Smith's *Cajun/Southern* | 18 | 22 | 18 | $52 |

Sag Harbor | Long Wharf Promenade (Bay St.) | 631-725-5858 | www.bsmith.com

"The view is the shining star" at style guru Barbara Smith's "sleek", seasonal Sag Harbor waterfront eatery, where you can sit "outside on the deck" and ogle the "magnificent yachts and sailboats" moored in the marina while sipping a "fresh watermelon" margarita; even though the "expensive" Cajun-Southern food veers between "creative" and "so-so", and the service can be "snippy", the "priceless" locale ensures big summertime crowds.

Buccaneer Crab House *Seafood* | ▽ 23 | 19 | 23 | $45 |

Freeport | 108 W. Merrick Rd. (bet. Guy Lombardo & S. Ocean Aves.) | 516-442-1151 | www.buccaneercrabhouse.com

A "welcome addition to the Freeport seafood scene" (even though it's "not on the water"), this "warm" establishment boasts "amiable" service, a "nice atmosphere" in a Victorian house and "properly prepared" dishes including "can't be beat" all-you-can-eat crab on Thursdays; since the presiding family hails from Ukraine, the entrees take an "intriguing Russian" detour, and if you "select effectively, you won't break the bank."

Buckram Stables Cafe *American* | 19 | 18 | 19 | $36 |

Locust Valley | 31 Forest Ave. (bet. Birch Hill Rd. & Weir Ln.) | 516-671-3080

"Bigger on food than booze", this "clubby" Locust Valley pub "for the horsey set" provides "famous" burgers and other "reliable" American eats in a "friendly", "cozy" setting that "looks like a stable"; galloping gourmets say "don't expect haute cuisine", but be ready for a "busy", "noisy atmosphere" and know you'll "definitely need reservations."

Bulldog Grille, The ● *American/Continental* | - | - | - | I |

Amityville | 292 Merrick Rd. (bet. Bayview & Ocean Aves.) | 631-691-1947 | www.thebulldoggrille.com

The large bar establishes a laid-back vibe at this Amityville tavern (sibling of Babylon's Post Office Cafe) where the glass-enclosed dining area is elevated and the American-Continental menu aims to please all with options such as burgers, wings, steak and pasta; live bands entertain Saturday nights.

Buoy One *Seafood*   23 | 9 | 18 | $30

Riverhead | 1175 W. Main St. (Mill Rd.) | 631-208-9737
NEW Westhampton | 62 Montauk Hwy. (Sea Breeze Ave.) |
631-998-3808
www.buoyone.com

"Succulent", "simply prepared" seafood is the draw at this "quick", "reasonable", "no-frills" joint inside a Riverhead fish market; it's "not glamorous" and a few would "only go when you can eat outside", but "someone cooking behind the counter really knows what they're doing", so it's a real "find"; P.S. a new, more upscale Westhampton spin-off opened in January 2011.

Burton & Doyle Steakhouse *Steak*   24 | 23 | 23 | $69

Great Neck | 661 Northern Blvd. (Summer St.) | 516-487-9200 |
www.burtonanddoyle.com

"Superb", "perfectly seared" steaks and "excellent" "flexitarian" choices like sushi call for a "splurge" at this Great Neck "standout" where a "gracious" staff "pulls out all the stops to please" the "elite" North Shore set; "dark, woodsy" and "inviting", it's an "attractive date place" and frequently a "singles scene" at the bar.

☑ Butera's *Italian*   21 | 18 | 20 | $36

Seaford | 3930 Sunrise Hwy. (bet. Jackson & Washington Aves.) |
516-795-6321
Woodbury | Woodbury Village Shopping Ctr. | 7903 Jericho Tpke.
(S. Woods Rd.) | 516-496-3633
NEW Sayville | 100 S. Main St. (Collins Ave.) | 631-563-0805
Smithtown | 65 E. Main St. (Landing Ave.) | 631-979-9113
www.buteras.com

"Loyal" fans flock to this "consistent", "modern" quartet (with a new Sayville location) for its "extra-large portions" of "above-average Italian" plus "reasonable" wines; "long waits" and "hectic" surroundings are downsides, but the "accommodating" service and "solid value" make it a natural for "families" and "large groups."

Butterfields ☒ *American*   20 | 18 | 20 | $40

Hauppauge | 661 Old Willets Path (Engineers Rd.) | 631-851-1507 |
www.butterfieldsrestaurant.biz

You're "always greeted with a pleasant smile" at this "after-work hangout" in an "industrial park" in Hauppauge, offering a "diverse" New American menu ranging from "wonderful burgers" to more ambitious items, plus "fabulous" weekday prix fixe dinners; since the live music, Saturday DJs and a "good-looking" 40-ft. mahogany bar make for a "loud" scene, don't expect to easily "carry on a conversation."

☑ Cafe Baci *Italian*   22 | 17 | 20 | $34

Westbury | 1636 Old Country Rd. (Merrick Ave.) | 516-832-8888 |
www.cafebacirestaurant.com

Skip a meal and clear your schedule before visiting this Westbury stalwart where the dishes of "hearty, tasty", "super-fresh" Italian fare are so "gigantic" you "can swim in the bowl"; "there's always a wait" and the decor's a bit "tired", but a "vibrant" bar scene, "enthusiastic" service and major "bang for the buck" reward the "test of patience" for most; P.S. no reservations, except for parties of eight or more on weekdays.

Café Buenos Aires Argentinean

| 24 | 21 | 22 | $44 |

Huntington | 23 Wall St. (bet. Gerard & Main Sts.) | 631-603-3600 | www.cafebuenosaires.net

Guests "go crazy" ordering "awesome" tapas at this "festive", slightly "expensive" Huntington Argentinean (with a Spanish touch), which also dishes up "marvelous" steaks and pastas to go with "winning" wines; co-owner Hugo García, the "ultimate host", "makes you feel right at home" in a "warm" setting enhanced by a "fantastic bar", "fashionable" sidewalk dining and "entertaining tango dancers" (Friday nights and Sunday brunch), so the "only drawback" is the "long wait" for a table; P.S. reservations accepted for six or more.

Café Formaggio Italian

| 20 | 17 | 20 | $37 |

Carle Place | 307 Old Country Rd. (bet. E. Gate & Lindberg Blvds.) | 516-333-1718 | www.cafeformaggio.com

Located near Roosevelt Field, this "congenial" Carle Place trattoria gives shoppers a place to rest their feet and dig into "hot" breadbaskets before sampling an "extensive" Italian menu offering "good value for the money" (and a roster of "gluten-free delights"); weekends get "crowded" (dinnertime "valet parking is a plus"), so go midweek for a more "pleasant" repast with "great wine specials."

Cafe Havana Ⓜ Cuban

| 18 | 19 | 18 | $40 |

Smithtown | 944 W. Jericho Tpke. (bet. Ledgewood Dr. & Old Willets Path) | 631-670-6277 | www.cafehavanali.com

"Live music sets the mood" at this "hopping", "party"-ready Smithtown Cuban with a covered patio, stone fireplace, palm trees and pictures of Havana on the walls; "excellent" drinks are another plus, though some feel it's "too expensive" for food and service that are just "ok", adding it's a "great idea but not the greatest execution."

Cafe Joelle on Main St. American/Eclectic

| 22 | 17 | 20 | $35 |

Sayville | 25 Main St. (Railroad Ave.) | 631-589-4600 | www.cafejoelle.net

"Always reliable", this "petite" New American–Eclectic attracts gents and "ladies strolling through Sayville" with its "varied", "reasonably priced" menu, from "creative salads and sandwiches" to "well-prepared" pastas to "German-inspired" eats; the recently renovated, bistro-style setting is "pleasing" too, but since "no reservations" are taken, be prepared for a crowd of "BFFs" waiting for a table; P.S. the owners also run Pasta Pasta.

Cafe La Strada Italian

| 23 | 16 | 22 | $44 |

Hauppauge | 352 Wheeler Rd. (Central Ave.) | 631-234-5550 | www.cafelastradarestaurant.com

You "would never expect to find" this "exceptional" Italian in a "modest" strip-mall location in Hauppauge, but "someone is paying attention and making all the right moves", providing an "extensive" menu of "outstanding", "old-world" dishes, a "spectacular" wine list (there's a 20,000-bottle cellar) and "polite", formal service; it can get "pricey" (particularly if you order the specials) and the decor is "lacking", but fans say "that's ok" since everything else is "absolutely wonderful."

Cafe Max *American/Eclectic*
23 | 15 | 22 | $44

East Hampton | 85 Montauk Hwy. (Cove Hollow Rd.) | 631-324-2004 | www.unhampton.com

Chef-owner Max Weintraub dishes up "seasonal, locally farmed (or fished)" American-Eclectic food that's "simply prepared" and served by an "enthusiastic", "professional" staff at this "relaxed" East Hamptoner; while there's "not much decor" (apart from "knotty" cedar), the owner really "cares about his customers" and "keeps the prices fair", so no wonder locals want to keep it "their little secret"; P.S. closed Tuesdays.

Cafe Rustica *Italian/Mediterranean*
22 | 19 | 21 | $43

Great Neck | 200 Middle Neck Rd. (bet. Allenwood Rd. & Embassy Ct.) | 516-829-6464 | www.caferusticarestaurant.com

"Loyal repeat diners" frequent this Italian-Med in Great Neck for the "delicious", "hearty" dishes (including "great gluten-free" options), "comfortable" surroundings and "old-time, attentive" service; it's "a little on the expensive side", but the three-course early-bird dinner is a "bargain."

Cafe Symposio *Italian*
18 | 17 | 19 | $37

Bellmore | 2700 Sunrise Hwy. (bet. Bedford & Washington Aves.) | 516-785-6097 | www.cafesymposio.com

A "steady" Bellmore Italian, this "welcoming" place offers "no surprises" – just "huge portions" of "middle-of-the-road" fare in a "nondescript", "converted diner" setting that's more "romantic" "when the piano player is there" (Wednesday–Sunday); the grub is too "generic" for some, but the "attentive" service, "quiet" atmosphere and relatively "low cost" are pluses.

Cafe Testarossa Ⓜ *Continental*
22 | 20 | 21 | $46

Syosset | 499 Jericho Tpke. (bet. Jackson Ave. & Seaford Oyster Bay Expwy.) | 516-364-8877 | www.cafetestarossa.com

As newer models roll onto the scene, this "classic" Continental still purrs with "modern twists" on "well-prepared" fare, served in an "elegant atmosphere" that keeps Syosset locals "revving their engines"; "trendy" with an "active bar scene", it's high on decibels and dollar signs, but in terms of value, "the sunset menu can't be beat."

Cafe Toscano *Italian*
21 | 17 | 19 | $38

Massapequa | 746 North Broadway (bet. N. Manhattan & N. Richmond Aves.) | 516-799-4100 | www.cafetoscanofusion.com

"Delicious" "homemade" fare, "reasonable prices" and "wonderful service" that includes a "gracious host" make this Massapequa Italian a "reliable" "neighborhood" choice; there are "no surprises" given the "basic" menu and decor, and parking can be "a bit of a problem", but it's a "comfortable" choice that many "recommend."

Caffe Laguna *Italian*

	19	18	19	$40

Long Beach | 960 W. Beech St. (bet. New Hampshire St. & Tennessee Ave.) | 516-432-2717 | www.caffelaguna.com

Just a block from the ocean, this "romantic" Long Beach "hideaway" does "date night" right with "inviting", if slightly "expensive", Italian eats (including "standout" brick-oven pizzas) balanced by a "reasonable wine list" and NYC flair; summer brings "alfresco" seating – and the area's typically "horrendous" street parking; P.S. closed Tuesdays.

California Pizza Kitchen *Pizza*

	17	14	16	$24

Westbury | Costco Plaza | 1256 Old Country Rd. (Bert Ave.) | 516-683-3338

Huntington Station | Walt Whitman Mall | 159 Walt Whitman Rd. (Weston St.) | 631-423-7565

Lake Grove | Smith Haven Mall | 618 Smith Haven Mall (bet. Middle Country Rd. & Nesconset Hwy.) | 631-382-9610

www.cpk.com

"Clever", "unusual" pizzas (such as "BBQ chicken and Thai") and "creative" salads are the "stars" at this "gourmet" pie chain providing "something for everyone's taste"; it's "inexpensive", "prompt" and "consistent", though some complain the "wannabe eclectic offerings" have grown "tired" and the "overlit" surroundings just "don't have any charm."

Canterbury Ales
Oyster Bar & Grill *American/Seafood*

	19	18	19	$34

Oyster Bay | 46 Audrey Ave. (bet. South & Spring Sts.) | 516-922-3614 | www.canterburyalesrestaurant.com

You can "learn about Oyster Bay history" in the "vibrant", "pubby" surroundings of this rustic American with "walls covered in artifacts" and "photos of Teddy Roosevelt" (who "lived up the road at Sagamore Hill"); the "classic tavern fare" satisfies with "fresh local seafood" and "fantastic" beers, and despite sometimes "uneven" table service, the staff is full of "warmth"; P.S. it's a "bargain" Monday-Tuesday when all bottles of wine are half price with dinner.

Capriccio Family
Style Restaurant *Italian*

	24	19	25	$48

Hicksville | 294 N. Broadway (16th St.) | 516-938-0220

With a "terrific", "veteran" staff working under the "watchful eye" of chef/co-owner Elio Sobrero, the service at this "quiet", "old-style" Northern Italian in Hicksville is as "charming" as the menu – known for the "best duck with cherry sauce anywhere"; the "staid" setting doesn't come close to the rest, but the dining experience is still "first-class" (if "expensive"), especially on weekends when a pianist performs; P.S. a move is in the works.

Caracalla Ristorante ⍉ *Italian*

	23	17	24	$59

Syosset | 102 Jericho Tpke. (bet. Michael & Oak Drs.) | 516-496-3838

Customers tout the "top-of-the-line" cuisine at this Syosset Italian, a Roman-decorated palace of pasta bolstered by a 400-bottle wine list; it's a bit "stuffy" and certainly "not cheap", but some savor the "nostalgia" as well as the "elegant service", advising it's "well worth a visit."

Carnival ● *Italian*　　　　　22 | 16 | 19 | $33

Port Jefferson Station | 4900 Nesconset Hwy. (Terryville Rd.) | 631-473-9772 | www.carnivalrestaurant.net

"Don't be fooled by the strip-mall location" because this "informal", family-owned Southern Italian in Port Jefferson Station proffers an "enormous" menu of "fabulous pastas", "mouthwatering" specials and "excellent" pizza (from the front counter) in portions so "humongous" "no one leaves without leftovers"; it's "hard to get in on the weekends" and the "acoustics need improvement", but "fair prices" help soften the edges.

Carousel *Japanese*　　　　　▽ 21 | 20 | 21 | $31

Great Neck | 20 South Station Plaza (bet. Barstow & S. Middle Neck Rds.) | 516-304-5192 | www.carouselnewyork.com

This "family"-friendly Great Neck Japanese is a "cute place with an interesting concept", allowing you to "sit by a conveyor belt" and select "tempting" sushi and cold dishes, as well as order hot izakaya-style plates or "eat at the hibachi tables in back"; even if some aren't sold on the "shtick", the staff's "attentive" and most agree "you're bound to have fun."

Carrabba's Italian Grill *Italian*　　　19 | 19 | 21 | $30

Central Islip | 20 N. Research Pl. (Carleton Ave.) | 631-232-1070
Smithtown | 730 Smithtown Bypass (bet. Southern Blvd. & Terry Rd.) | 631-265-1304
www.carrabbas.com

"Outback goes to Rome" at this "energetic" sister-chain that "satisfies a craving for Italian", providing "solid", "generous" dishes amid "busy", sometimes "raucous" Central Islip and Smithtown settings tended by an "accommodating" staff; while detractors maintain it's "run-of-the-mill" and "hardly authentic", if you "keep your expectations reasonable", it's a "good-value" option.

Caruso's *Italian*　　　　　　▽ 23 | 15 | 20 | $33

Rocky Point | 41 Broadway (Rte. 25A) | 631-744-1117 | www.carusosrestaurant.com

Whether you "stop in for a quick slice" or have an "absolutely delicious" dinner in the "great outdoor area" warmed by a new fire pit, this "local" Rocky Point Italian by chef/co-owner Wayne Wadington (La Plage) is a "pleasant surprise"; the interior's "a little dull", but "affordable" tabs and a "steady" staff that "couldn't be nicer" win over most diners.

Casa Luis Ⓜ *Spanish*　　　　　22 | 13 | 21 | $38

Smithtown | 1033 Jericho Tpke. (Cornell Dr.) | 631-543-4656

Take a "mini-trip to Spain" at this "convivial", "family-owned" eatery in Smithtown, where "long waits for a table" attest to the "wonderful paellas", "best-around" green sauce dishes and "great sangria"; more than a few take jabs at the tightly packed, "tired" surroundings that look like they "haven't changed" in 20 years, but more praise owners who "outdo themselves making everyone feel welcome."

Casa Rustica *Italian*

25 | 21 | 25 | $52

Smithtown | 175 W. Main St. (bet. Edgewood Ave. & Elliot Pl.) | 631-265-9265 | www.casarustica.net

Its reputation as "one of Suffolk's best" is "well deserved" declare devotees of this Smithtown "favorite" serving "amazing" Italian "the way it should be" (the lobster in cognac butter sauce will "rock your world"); renovations two years ago "added charm" to the "old-fashioned", villa-style interior, and the "formal" service is "professional and caring", so even though it's a "tad expensive", many visit "as frequently as their budget allows."

Catfish Max *American/Seafood*

21 | 14 | 20 | $41

Seaford | 3681 Naomi St. (Ocean Ave.) | 516-679-2020 | www.catfishmax.com

A "sweet little treasure on a hot summer night", this "funky", "hard-to-find" New American seafooder is "best when you can sit by the water" "watching the boats dock" at Seaford Harbor; despite its "dumpy" looks, patrons praise the "hip", "imaginative specials" that "go a step beyond the usual" and a bar that "feels like it's served many old salts over the years."

ꆤꆤꍧ Cattlemen's Steakhouse & Saloon *Steak*

19 | 17 | 18 | $35

Port Jefferson Station | 650 Patchogue Rd. (bet. Oakland & Wykoff Aves.) | 631-509-5130 | www.cattlemenssteak.com

Lindenhurst | 127 Montauk Hwy. (S. Wellwood Ave) | 631-991-3542 | www.cattlemenssteak.com

"You're back in the Old West" at this "casual" Lindenhurst yearling (with a new Port Jefferson sidekick), a "family-friendly" beef barn where "congenial", "cowboy"-attired staffers serve "big slabs" of steak at a "low cost"; alas, more ornery wranglers brand it "quantity over quality."

ꆤꆤꍧ Cedar Creek American Bar & Grill *American*

- | - | - | M

Glen Cove | 75 Cedar Swamp Rd. (bet. 2nd & 4th Sts.) | 516-656-5656 | www.cedarcreekli.com

Small and large plates are on the midpriced menu at this Glen Cove American bistro from the owners of Bayville's Mill Creek Tavern, where dishes run the gamut from warm homemade chips with blue-cheese fondue to crispy bluefin tuna; the warm setting in walnut wood and cream tones offers booth and table seating, and there's also a bar and a large brick patio.

ꙅ Chachama Grill *American*

27 | 21 | 27 | $52

East Patchogue | Swan Nursery Commons | 655 Montauk Hwy. (S. Country Rd.) | 631-758-7640 | www.chachamagrill.com

"Star" chef Elmer Rubio crafts "marvelous" New American meals at this "exciting", "Manhattan-type restaurant in a most unlikely location" (an otherwise "dreary" strip mall) in East Patchogue; once inside, you'll "enter another world where one dish is better than the next" and they're all "beautifully served" by a "considerate" staff that "makes you feel every day is a celebration", so it's always a "winner"; P.S. the $26 three-course prix fixe is one of the "biggest bargains on LI."

Chadwicks at the Station *American/Continental*

| 22 | 21 | 23 | $41 |

Rockville Centre | 49 Front St. (bet. Clinton & N. Park Aves.) | 516-766-7800 | www.chadwicksli.com

There's "lots of competition in Rockville Centre for this style" of up-scale American-Continental cuisine, but this "underrated" stop "right across from the train station" is a "quiet", "comfortable" alternative to the bustling strip; the kitchen dishes up "something for everyone", from signature rack of lamb to "fabulous" salads, the staff "makes you feel at home" and to seal the deal, "you can always get a table."

Chalet Restaurant & Lounge ● *American/Eclectic*

| ▽ 18 | 20 | 18 | $36 |

Roslyn | 1 Railroad Ave. (bet. Roslyn Rd. & Warner Ave.) | 516-621-7975 | www.roslynchalet.com

It's a "favorite with the railroad crowd after work" and the place "to be if it's after 11 PM and you're under 40", at this loungey American-Eclectic in Roslyn known for its "upbeat" vibe and "late-night drinks"; still, the food is "surprisingly decent", especially the "great burger", and the white-toned decor has a refreshingly "un–Long Island" feel, particularly in summer when the upper deck is "the main attraction."

Chat Noir *French/Tea Room*

| 21 | 21 | 19 | $28 |

Rockville Centre | 230 Merrick Rd. (bet. S. Park & Village Aves.) | 516-208-8521 | www.chatnoirtea.com

A "nice quiet retreat" decked out in "French country" decor, this "unique" addition to the Rockville Centre scene does "decadent afternoon tea" – featuring "exquisite table settings" and "the best scones" – then transforms into a "quaint" bistro at dinnertime; though a few surveyors feel it's "overpriced" and the service "needs help", it's often the perfect brew for "girlie" groups and the "carriage crowd"; P.S. closes at 5 PM Monday–Tuesday, 8 PM Sunday.

☒ Cheesecake Factory *American*

| 20 | 19 | 18 | $30 |

Westbury | Mall at the Source | 1504 Old Country Rd. (Evelyn Ave.) | 516-222-5500 ●

Huntington Station | Walt Whitman Mall | 160 Walt Whitman Rd. (Weston St.) | 631-271-8200

Lake Grove | Smith Haven Mall | 610 Smith Haven Mall (bet. Middle Country Rd. & Nesconset Hwy.) | 631-361-6600 www.thecheesecakefactory.com

"Humongous portions and humongous lines" characterize this American chain where the "textbook"-size menu offers "lots of choices" and a "broad price spectrum" to keep families "stuffed

	FOOD	DECOR	SERVICE	COST

and happy"; the "herd 'em in, herd 'em out" feel isn't for everyone and critics knock "mass-produced" fare and "overdone" decor, but overall it's a "crowd-pleaser", especially when it comes to the "amazing" namesake dessert – even if you need to "take it home for much later."

Chefs of New York *Italian/Pizza* | 19 | 12 | 19 | $23 |

East Northport | 508 Larkfield Rd. (Clay Pitts Rd.) | 631-368-3156 | www.chefsny.com

"When you don't feel like cooking", this "little" East Northport Italian hits the spot with "consistently good" dishes and a "variety" of "delectable" pies, including a spinach pizza so memorable it was featured on the Food Network; "huge portions" at "low prices" and a "personable" staff help make up for the "typical back-of-a-pizzeria" setup.

Chequit Inn *American/Eclectic* | 19 | 18 | 19 | $42 |

Shelter Island Heights | Chequit Inn | 23 Grand Ave. (Waverly Pl.) | 631-749-0018 | www.shelterislandinns.com

The "tasty", "not outstanding" but "more than ok" American-Eclectic fare at this "historic" Shelter Island Heights inn is most enjoyable when lunching on the "flower-surrounded" patio or having dinner on the porch, where you can "watch the sun go down over the harbor"; service is "not particularly polished" but "pleasant" enough as diners take in the sights on this "beautiful little island."

Chez Kama Ⓜ *Continental/Japanese*   ▽ | 25 | 18 | 22 | $45 |

Great Neck | 77 Middle Neck Rd. (bet. Cedar Dr. & Grace Ave.) | 516-482-8360

An "unusual mix" of dishes sets apart this "small" Japanese-Continental in Great Neck, offering "superb sushi", "delicious" LI duck and other "impeccable" items; "warm, inviting" service lends a "homey" feel to the "no-frills" room, but since it often gets "packed", be sure to "make reservations."

❷ Chez Noëlle Ⓜ *French* | 27 | 19 | 25 | $55 |

Port Washington | 34 Willowdale Ave. (S. Bayles Ave.) | 516-883-3191 | www.cheznoellerestaurant.com

"Aging gracefully", this "old-fashioned French" in Port Washington is a "rare find" that "sticks to the basics and succeeds", attracting "well-dressed" guests who "appreciate" the "classic", "melt-in-your-mouth" cuisine, "gracious" greetings and the "owner's droll humor"; the "greatly improved", renovated setting boasts tables spaced out enough to "enjoy conversations", and though prices are "steep" (unless you go for the "bargain prix fixe"), it's worthy of a "special night."

Chi Ⓩ *Chinese/Eclectic*   ▽ | 25 | 23 | 24 | $47 |

Westbury | 103 Post Ave. (bet. Lexington & Madison Aves.) | 516-385-3795 | www.chidininglounge.com

"Amped-up" Chinese-Eclectic dishes go well with the signature martinis, energetic DJ sets and "sleek" decor awash in oranges and golds at this Westbury lounge that's "surprisingly" "excellent all around"; apart from the off-hours when it feels a bit "empty", it's a "great place to chill" or "meet up with a chick" if you can handle the spendy scene.

🆕 Chicken Coop *Colombian*

| - | - | - | I |

Valley Stream | 159 Rockaway Ave. (W. Valley Stream Blvd.) | 516-568-2667 | www.chickencoopny.com

Peckish patrons have lots to choose from at this affordable Colombian cafe in Valley Stream where specialty *pollo a la brasa* (rotisserie chicken) just scratches the surface of a menu offering regional classics including seafood casserole and daily specials such as meatball soup; the casual setting is decked out in ceramics and giant cutlery, and a full bar adds to the cheerful vibe.

Chicken Kebab *Greek/Turkish*

| 21 | 10 | 17 | $25 |

Roslyn Heights | 92 Mineola Ave. (Elm St.) | 516-621-6828 | www.chickenkebab.com

"Fast, tasty and cheap" Greek-Turkish eats (like a "delicious" chicken gyro) draw "lines out the door" of this Roslyn Heights "neighborhood" grill; there's "not much atmosphere", "terrible parking" and "too many kids", but "you know what you're getting" and it's a "solid value for your dining dollar."

Chipotle *Mexican*

| 20 | 12 | 16 | $13 |

Farmingdale | 901 Broad Hollow Rd. (Rte. 109) | 631-845-4598 | www.chipotle.com

"Tasty", "gut-busting" burritos "custom-made for you" are the draw at this Farmingdale link in the "fresh-Mex" chain, which earns extra "respect" for its "commitment to organic ingredients" and "well-sourced" meats; the "line moves quickly" and prices are "fair", so even if the "sparse" setting is "not too comfortable", it works for "lunch or takeout."

Chop Shop *American*

| 24 | 24 | 23 | $43 |

Smithtown | 47 E. Main St. (bet. Bank & Landing Aves.) | 631-360-3383 | www.chopshopbarandgrill.com

"Well-prepared" "quality" steaks, seafood and a "mean dirty martini" are a "pleasant surprise" at this "nice new" American addition to Smithtown, a sib to Massapequa's Hudson's Mill; the "noisy", "NYC-chic" setting features low lighting and leather booths, while the "lovely" service is capped off by a chef who visits tables "during later hours"; P.S. "go early" to save money on "half-price drinks and bar food."

Cho-Sen Island *Asian/Kosher*

| 19 | 14 | 18 | $34 |

Lawrence | 367 Central Ave. (Frost Ln.) | 516-374-1199 | www.chosengarden.com

Cho-Sen Village *Asian/Kosher*

Great Neck | 505 Middle Neck Rd. (Baker Hill Rd.) | 516-504-1199 | www.cho-senvillage.com

It's "hard to believe" the "very good" Chinese food and "requisite" sushi rolls are kosher at this "family-friendly", slightly "expensive but worth it" Asian pair in Great Neck and Lawrence, where the staff helps "accommodate" special requests; even though it could use some "new decor" and "more exotic dishes", regulars who "stay with the standards" are satisfied.; P.S. closed Friday–sundown Saturday.

Churrasqueira Bairrada Ⓜ Portuguese 25 | 15 | 22 | $34

Mineola | 144 Jericho Tpke. (Willis Ave.) | 516-739-3856 | www.churrasqueira.com

"Carnivores rejoice!" – this Mineola mecca delivers a procession of "incredible", "sizzling skewers" for a Portuguese "feast" that doesn't end "until you surrender"; the "world-class" chicken dinners also "wow", so if you don't mind the "madhouse" frenzy and "long waits", "you'll get more than you paid for" and "smooth" service to boot.

Ciao Baby Italian 20 | 18 | 19 | $37

Massapequa Park | 50-74 Sunrise Hwy. (Block Blvd.) | 516-799-5200
Commack | Mayfair Shopping Ctr. | 204 Jericho Tpke. (Harned Rd.) | 631-543-1400
www.ciaobabyrestaurant.com

You'll have to "wear elastic pants" or bring an "entire football team" to share the "monstrous plates" at this "loud", "family-style" Italian duo in Commack and Massapequa Park that's "affordable" and "decent" but otherwise draws mixed reviews; the "Sinatra-era" theme is either "cheesy" or just plain "fun" depending on the diner, and while some find the service "too chummy", it's all part of the "schtick."

Cielo Ristorante Italiano Ⓜ Italian 20 | 19 | 22 | $43

Rockville Centre | 208 Sunrise Hwy. (bet. N. Park & N. Village Aves.) | 516-678-1996 | www.cieloristorante.com

Admirers of this "enjoyable" Rockville Centre Northern Italian tout the "traditional", "beautifully presented" offerings from the old country, "professional" service and "comforting" Tuscan-inspired decor with columns and warm sunset tones; though a few feel it's "a little stuffy" and "needs more variety", it's a primo place for a "quiet dinner" by the fireplace, and early-bird and midweek specials help temper sometimes "pricey" tabs.

Cinelli's Pizzeria & Restaurant Italian 18 | 14 | 19 | $26

Franklin Square | 1195 Hempstead Tpke. (Doris Ave.) | 516-352-1745

Cinelli's Trattoria & Grill Italian

Oceanside | 156 Davison Ave. (Oceanside Rd.) | 516-678-9494
www.cinellis-ny.com

The original Franklin Square branch of this pizzeria pair turns out "consistently good" pies, pastas and panini, while the separately owned Oceanside offshoot adds rarely seen *piada* flatbreads to the "basic Italian menu"; there's "nothing fancy" to be found at either, so many opt for the "fast delivery."

Cipollini *Italian*

21 | 21 | 20 | $49

Manhasset | The Americana | 2110C Northern Blvd. (Searingtown Rd.) | 516-627-7172 | www.cipollinirestaurant.com

"Manhasset's glitterati disembark from their Maseratis" for "fabulous outdoor dining" (indoors too) at this "elegant" "see-and-be-scenester" in The Americana, where the "terrific" Italian food, including "brick-oven thin-crust pizza", often plays second fiddle to the "dressed-to-the-nines" "ladies who lunch"; the "wonderful bar" becomes a "major hook-up spot" come evening (Thursdays are a "must-see"), and even though service is mixed, the staff generally "takes care of singles" and other "blingy" "regulars."

Circa Ristorante Enoteca *Italian*

22 | 22 | 20 | $42

Mineola | Birchwood Plaza | 348 E. Jericho Tpke. (Jay Ct.) | 516-280-2234 | www.circali.com

This "beautiful" Mineola Italian with "NYC-style" sophistication shines inside its otherwise bland "strip-mall locale", attracting a "vibrant" crowd with its "tasty", sometimes "ambitious" cuisine; when "tables are tight" on busy weekends, head to the "great" granite bar to enjoy the "daily specials" and nearly 300 wines from around the globe; P.S. the prix fixe lunch offers the "best value."

Cirella's *Continental/Italian*

21 | 16 | 19 | $37

Melville | 14 Broadhollow Rd. (Arlington St.) | 631-385-7380

Cirella's at Saks
Fifth Avenue *American/Eclectic*

Huntington Station | Saks Fifth Avenue, Walt Whitman Mall | 230 Walt Whitman Rd. (Weston St.) | 631-350-1229 www.cirellarestaurant.com

"Everyone's treated like a regular" at this Melville "favorite", where "ample" servings of *fabuloso* Northern Italian and Continental "comfort food" (and sushi too) keep the room "crowded" and "noisy"; mall-walkers maintain the maki and other "tasty" American-Eclectic eats at its Saks spin-off are "the only bargains" in the store.

Ciro's Italian Restaurant *Italian*

22 | 18 | 22 | $32

Kings Park | 74 Main St. (bet. Church St. & Pulaski Rd.) | 631-269-2600 | www.ciroskingspark.com

"Accommodating" owners keep this Kings Park "neighborhood gem" full of "repeat customers" chowing down on "generous portions" of "consistent", "grandma-style" Italian food; regulars say the setting is "much improved since they moved" "up the road" to "delightful", "larger quarters", and the midweek specials are "a great buy."

cittanuova *Italian*

20 | 18 | 18 | $44

East Hampton | 29 Newtown Ln. (bet. Main St. & Park Pl.) | 631-324-6300 | www.cittanuova.com

The "burgers are applause-worthy" and the rest is "quite good" at this "cool", "Euro-style" Italian in East Hampton that's ideal for "people-watching" from "summer sidewalk tables", catching a "game at the bar" or stopping for gelato "after a movie"; so even though service can be "spotty" and the "scene" is too much for some, it's a "fairly priced" "crowd-pleaser" where you just might sit next to a celebrity.

City Cellar
| 21 | 23 | 20 | $41 |
Wine Bar & Grill *American*

Westbury | 1080 Corporate Dr. (bet. Ellison Ave. & Zeckendorf Blvd.) | 516-693-5400 | www.citycellarny.com

"Attractive" and "modern", this Westbury New American is dominated by a glass-enclosed wine cellar with 500 labels "stacked high in the sky" over the "vibrant" bar and "cavernous" dining room; the "diverse", "something-for-everyone" menu ranges from "crispy" brick-oven pizzas to steaks and seafood, and even if the "charming" service can be "inconsistent", that doesn't deter fans who "love" the lunch and vino specials.

Clam Bar at Napeague ⊅ *Seafood*
| 21 | 12 | 16 | $32 |

Amagansett | 2025 Montauk Hwy. (on Napeague Stretch) | 631-267-6348 | www.clambaronline.com

"There's something about" this "laid-back" Amagansett seasonal seafood shack on the "side of the road" that "brings you back year after year"; maybe it's the "darn wonderful lobster rolls", "fab chowders" and "fresh clams" served on "paper plates", or perhaps it's the "lively", "good-looking crowd" (with the "occasional big celeb"); whatever it is, even those who "hate the road view" say "summer wouldn't be complete without several trips" here.

Claudio's *American/Continental*
| 16 | 16 | 17 | $40 |

Greenport | 111 Main St. (bet. Front St. & Greenport Harbor) | 631-477-0627 | www.claudios.com

A Greenport "legend" (since 1870), this seasonal American-Continental "seafood shanty" offers multiple dining options, from white-tablecloth rooms to an "antique" bar to "hot" waterfront tables with "beautiful views" and "live bands" providing a "party, party on the weekends"; critics find the food "underwhelming" and "overpriced", and the service "so-so", but it's a "treat" to "bask in the sun" and soak in the "fun drinking atmosphere with a dock."

Cliff's Elbow Room *Steak*
| 22 | 11 | 19 | $38 |

Jamesport | 1549 Main Rd. (S. Jamesport Ave.) | 631-722-3292 | www.elbowroomli.com

Cliff's Elbow Too Ⓜ *Steak*

Laurel | 1085 Franklinville Rd. (off Main Rd.) | 631-298-3262 | www.elbowroomli.com

Cliff's Rendezvous *Steak*

Riverhead | 313 E. Main St. (Maple Ave.) | 631-727-6880

This "aptly named, iconic" chophouse trio offers "delish" "marinated steaks" that "cut like butta", presented with a "smile" by longtime waitresses "who know their stuff"; sure, the "closet-sized" rooms could use a "face-lift", but since they're one of the "best values" around, look out for "inevitable waits on summer Saturday nights"; P.S. reservations accepted only in Jamesport.

	FOOD	DECOR	SERVICE	COST

Clubhouse, The *Steak* `21` `17` `22` `$55`
Huntington | 320 W. Jericho Tpke. (W. Hills Rd.) | 631-423-1155 | www.clubhousesteaks.com

This "diamond in the rough" of a Huntington steakhouse is a "well-kept secret" for "fine" cuts of beef, including an "excellent porterhouse for two", served by an "unpretentious", "hospitable" staff; a few critics contend it offers "more sizzle than steak" and the "too-dark" interior "needs refurbishment", but the "terrific specials" and "late-night bar scene" help keep it "popular."

Coach Grill & Tavern *American* `22` `13` `21` `$42`
Oyster Bay | 22 Pine Hollow Rd. (bet. High St. & Lexington Ave.) | 516-624-0900 | www.coachgrillandtavern.com

A "perfect example of a great neighborhood pub" that's also a "family place", this Oyster Bay New American "consistently" turns out "good chow" with some "superb" standouts ("terrific duck"); it has a "simple" "bar-and-grill atmosphere" and a staff that's "always willing to make diners happy", along with a "friendly host" who shares "fascinating stories."

Coast Grill *American/Seafood* `22` `16` `20` `$51`
Southampton | 1109 Noyac Rd. (Turtle Pond Rd.) | 631-283-2277

New owners Brian and Stacy Cheewing have "spruced up" this Southampton American on the harbor, highlighting "wonderfully prepared" seafood in a redone "contemporary" setting that "feels more like a proper eatery and less like a fish camp"; with "welcoming" service to boot, no wonder it wins votes for "best comeback" of the year; P.S. closed Monday–Wednesday in the off-season.

Colbeh *Persian* `21` `17` `19` `$42`
Great Neck | Andrew Hotel | 75 N. Station Plaza (Barstow Rd.) | 516-466-8181
Roslyn Estates | 1 The Intervale (Warner Ave.) | 516-621-2200
www.colbeh.com

Experience an "adventure for the palate" at this kosher Persian pair (with two NYC branches) where the "amazing selection" of dishes provides a "taste of the Middle East" in "lovely, muted" surroundings (with a "more intimate", "romantic" feel in Roslyn Estates than Great Neck); it's "a little pricey" but "reasonable" considering the "plentiful" plates and "delicious freebies brought to the table" by an "amiable" staff; P.S. closes after sundown Friday and reopens Saturday night.

NEW Comtesse Thérèse *French* `-` `-` `-` `E`
Aquebogue | 739 Main Rd. (Church Ln.) | 631-779-2800 | www.comtessetherese.com

Both the tasting room for Comtesse Thérèse vineyard and a French bistro spotlighting local ingredients (some from an on-site garden) are situated in this 1830s Aquebogue house; chef Arie Pavlou turns out classics such as escargots and lamb-shank confit with Madeira sauce, and it's all served in a cozy setting complete with needlepoint rugs, a tin ceiling and local art on the walls.

☑ **Coolfish** *Seafood*   24 | 22 | 22 | $50

Syosset | North Shore Atrium | 6800 Jericho Tpke. (Michael Dr.) |
516-921-3250 | www.tomschaudel.com

Fin fans flip for the "sublime seafood" at this "casual-chic" Syosset
fish house, a "slam dunk" by chef-owner Tom Schaudel who brings
"a little glamour", "solid" service and a variety of "fabulous", "innovative" creations (including "surprising" desserts) to a "tasteful"
space buried within an office park; though it can get "costly", you
"can't beat the prix fixe", plus a lighter menu is available at the bar.

Cooperage Inn *American/Continental*   22 | 23 | 22 | $43

Baiting Hollow | 2218 Sound Ave. (bet. Edwards & National Blvds.) |
631-727-8994 | www.cooperageinn.com

Guests of this "quaint" year-rounder in Baiting Hollow "applaud" its
American-Continental cuisine that "takes advantage of the bounty
of the surrounding farms and vineyards"; a few critics feel it's
merely "ok" for the price, but most agree the "pretty" dining rooms
with an "old-world" atmosphere and "polite" service create an "inviting setting for the brunch buffet or a romantic dinner", "especially
around the holidays"; P.S. reservations recommended.

Copa Wine Bar & Tapas ● *Spanish*   ▽ 20 | 18 | 19 | $50

Bridgehampton | 95 School St. (Montauk Hwy.) | 631-613-6469 |
www.copawineandtapas.com

Offering "tasty", high-end tapas and entrees complemented by a
"large" selection of vino (and served late), this Spanish wine bar
in Bridgehampton is a "nice addition to the scene"; the "cool,
relaxed atmosphere", with a zinc-topped bar, skylights and
"friendly" service, makes it all the more "fun to go with a group and
share a bunch of dishes" – just be warned that "when it's busy, it's
an acoustic nightmare."

☑ **Country House, The** *American*   23 | 26 | 24 | $57

Stony Brook | 1175 Rte. 25A (Main St.) | 631-751-3332 |
www.countryhouserestaurant.com

The "elegant" decor at this "quaint country house" (circa 1710) in
Stony Brook "changes with the seasons" – they "really outdo themselves over the holidays" – and its status as a "romantic destination" is
enhanced by a "charming", "professional" staff; while opinions on the
"beautifully presented" New American food range from "excellent"
to merely "decent" (and "expensive for what you get"), overall most
are satisfied given the "relaxing", "special-occasion" atmosphere.

Cozymel's Mexican Grill *Mexican*   17 | 17 | 17 | $27

Westbury | 1177 Corporate Dr. (Merchants Concourse) |
516-222-7010 | www.cozymels.com

Behind the Source Mall in Westbury, this chain "cantina" offers "ample" Mexican plates, "huge frozen drinks" and "tons of chips and
salsa"; even if there are few surprises on the "off-the-rack" menu,
the "fiesta environment" attracts the young and boisterous, while
the "fast", "cheap" meals work for families and get everyone to the
movies next door with time and dollars to spare.

Crabtree's Restaurant *Continental/Mediterranean* (aka Crabtree's)

21 | 20 | 22 | $38

Floral Park | 226 Jericho Tpke. (bet. Emerson & Hinsdale Aves.) | 516-326-7769 | www.crabtreesrestaurant.com

Gather the gang at this Floral Park Continental-Med, a "find" "if you dig great seafood", bountiful brunch and "pleasant" garden dining; in keeping with the nostalgic setting that pays homage to the *Little Rascals*, the "cordial" owner and servers are "as sweet as Darla", and "you won't be stymied by the price."

NEW Crave 11025 *American/Vegetarian*

▽ 18 | 24 | 16 | $27

Great Neck | 68 Middle Neck Rd. (bet. Elm & Gussack Plaza) | 516-482-4800

A glossy "modern" interior with a black-and-white boutique look lends this Great Neck newcomer the cachet of "hip surroundings", while the meat-free American-vegetarian menu features a "simple" but "interesting" roster of omelets, salads, sandwiches and 'cravings' (which include pastas and fish); if the service can seem "a little overwhelmed", that's a small complaint.

Crew Kitchen & Bar M *American*

24 | 22 | 24 | $51

Huntington | 134 New York Ave. (Ketewomoke Dr.) | 631-549-3338 | www.crewli.com

Fans of this reconceived, "first-class" Huntingtonian (formerly Aix en-Provence, still run by the same team) return "multiple times" for the "interesting selection" of "superb" New American dishes and bar bites; further kudos are tossed to the "good-mood" staff that "never lets a water glass go empty" as well as to an "attractive" redo of the "convivial" space; P.S. the owners also run Barney's in Locust Valley.

Crossroads Cafe *American*

22 | 14 | 20 | $39

East Northport | 26 Laurel Rd. (bet. Bellerose Ave. & LIRR) | 631-754-2000 | www.thecrossroadscafe.com

Don't judge this "local" East Northport haunt by its "gruff exterior" – it will "warm your heart" with New American fare that's "fresh and tasteful"; the "cozy" confines are humble, but the "bargain" prix fixe and "lobster night" specials keep complaints in check.

Crow's Nest S M *Seafood*

▽ 19 | 17 | 17 | $44

Montauk | 4 Old West Lake Dr. (Montauk Point State Pkwy.) | 631-668-2077

Thanks to the "new ownership" of NYC hotel-bar czar Sean MacPherson, this once "dated" seasonal seafooder quartered in a Montauk inn has "turned around" with "improved" fare served by a "helpful" staff; the "relaxing, rustic atmosphere" is now juxtaposed with "pretty people to watch", all making it "worth the stop."

Cull House *Seafood*

20 | 12 | 18 | $32

Sayville | 75 Terry St. (River Rd.) | 631-563-1546 | www.cullhouse.com
Sought out for "delightful" "summer seafood", including "excellent lobster specials", this year-round mainstay with a "bare-bones" but

"beachy atmosphere" "near the Sayville Fire Island ferries" is the kind of "comfortable" "hangout" that's "perfect as is", even with "paper plates" and "plastic utensils"; true, a few find it "uninspired", but afishionados call it the "best bang for your buck" in town.

Curry Club *Indian*   20 | 16 | 20 | $30

East Setauket | 10 Woods Corner Rd. (Nicolls Rd.) | 631-751-4845 | www.curryclubli.com

Find a "true touch of India" at this "dependable" East Setauket eatery with a "terrific" $9.99 all-you-can-eat lunch buffet that's one of the "best deals" around; the "great vegetarian choices" and "courteous" service are a plus, but those who dis the "outdated decor" can just drop in for takeout; P.S. the short-lived Lake Grove spin-off is now closed.

Cuvée Bistro & Bar *French*   ▽ 22 | 17 | 18 | $50
(fka La Cuvée Wine Bar & Bistro)

Greenport | Greenporter Hotel | 326 Front St. (4th Ave.) | 631-477-0066 | www.thegreenporter.com

"Don't overlook this Greenport bistro because of its unassuming exterior", since the "tasty" upscale French dishes made from "fresh local finds" often "impress"; with "lovely" outside dining in the summer, you can "soak up" the local atmosphere over vintages from the varied by-the-glass list, and perhaps forget about the "Hamptons"-style service.

Cyril's Fish House ⊘ *Seafood*   18 | 13 | 16 | $35

Amagansett | 2167 Montauk Hwy. (on Napeague Stretch) | 631-267-7993

It's a "party on the East End" at this "casual", seasonal "local spot with character" in Amagansett that gets "packed in the evenings" with a "trendy" crowd downing "killer" "drinks in plastic" cups; owner Cyril is "a hoot" and the seafood's "fresh", but most go just to "sit outside, chill" and enjoy the "real beach feel, sans sand."

Dao *Asian*   23 | 24 | 23 | $39

Huntington | 92 E. Main St. (bet. Park Ave. & Woodhull Rd.) | 631-425-7788 | www.daorestaurant.com

Set in an "absolutely gorgeous" space that feels like a "high-end NYC cocktail lounge" with a "lovely" tropical aquarium, this Huntington arrival is a "feast for the eyes" with food to match, offering an "exceptional menu" of "attractively presented" sushi and Asian fusion dishes; also appreciating the "above-par" service and a range of price points, first-timers declare they'll "definitely return."

☑ Dario's ☒ *Italian*   26 | 17 | 26 | $59

Rockville Centre | 13 N. Village Ave. (bet. Merrick Rd. & Sunrise Hwy.) | 516-255-0535

The "outstanding" Northern Italian food is "as good as it gets" at this Rockville Centre "old-schooler", leading guests to vow that if it's "served in heaven, I'll become a better person"; while it's "on the expensive side", and decor's a bit "stodgy", "gracious" "tuxedoed waiters" who "see to every request" offer an "elegant" diversion.

NEW Dark Horse *American/Eclectic*

| – | – | – | M |

Riverhead | 1 E. Main St. (Peconic Ave.) | 631-208-0072 |
www.darkhorserestaurant.com

On a prominent corner in the heart of Riverhead, this new brasserie offers a diverse American-Eclectic menu from chef Jeffrey Trujillo, with dishes such as lentil and potato stew and braised shank of lamb; the high-ceilinged art deco setting features walls of windows facing Main Street, black leather banquettes and stainless-steel chairs.

Daruma of Tokyo *Japanese*

| 23 | 14 | 18 | $38 |

Great Neck | 95 Middle Neck Rd. (Maple Dr.) | 516-466-4180

"A 25-year-old Great Neck institution", this "consistent" Japanese presents "excellent" sushi standards as well as "off-the-beaten-path choices" for moderate prices; though the "'80s" decor (including "lots of Mets paraphernalia") "needs updating" and the uneven service could use work too, it still manages to draw a "scene" – and being next to the movie theater is an "added plus."

Da Ugo ⧄ *Italian*

| 25 | 18 | 24 | $55 |

Rockville Centre | 509 Merrick Rd. (Long Beach Rd.) | 516-764-1900

For a "divine experience" starring "uniquely varied", "first-rate" Northern Italian fare (with "exceptional daily specials"), "make a reservation far in advance" at this "high-end" Rockville Centre "jewel", an "old favorite that never changes"; service is "lovely" and "professional" inside the "tiny", "tight quarters", though some claim the closest attention is reserved for "loyal fans."

⧫ Dave's Grill *Continental/Seafood*

| 27 | 18 | 23 | $61 |

Montauk | 468 W. Lake Dr. (bet. Flamingo Ave. & Soundview Dr.) |
631-668-9190 | www.davesgrill.com

This "cozy", "pricey" Continental "right on the docks" in Montauk "rocks the East End" with its "extensive menu" of "impeccably prepared", "tremendous seafood"; while chef Dave's "gracious" wife, Julie, is the "best hostess anywhere", the "strange" "same-day reservation policy" is a "pain" for those who say "the odds" of getting a seat are akin to "winning the lottery"; P.S. closed in the off-season.

Declan Quinn's *American*

| ▽ 19 | 18 | 21 | $29 |

Bay Shore | 227 Fourth Ave. (bet. Cherry & E. Garfield Sts.) |
631-206-2006 | www.declanquinns.net

It "can get a bit rowdy at times" at this "comfortable" pub-style American in Bay Shore, where the beach "volleyball court in back" and cover bands on the weekends keep the crowd hopping, and the 1938 setting lends a little "old-time charm"; just don't expect anything beyond "well-priced" "basic" bar fare and you won't be disappointed; P.S. it gets "packed" on Thursday 'steak and brew' nights.

NEW Deco 1600 *American/Italian*

| – | – | – | E |

Plainview | Race Palace | 1600 Round Swamp Rd. (S. Service Rd.) |
516-586-6454 | www.deco1600.com

"Cool" art deco digs, "family-style" Italian dishes and an on-site OTB form a rare trifecta, but this yearling at the Race Palace in

Plainview makes it work with "very good" eats that range from traditional takes on veal, fish and pasta to casual American pub standards; the scene "leaves a little to be desired", but it's a safe bet for "large parties."

Dee Angelo's Pleasant Ave. Café *Italian* ▽ 19 | 16 | 18 | $49

Westhampton Beach | 149 Main St. (Library Ave.) | 631-288-2009

"Sit outside and people-watch" at this "cute" Westhampton Beach Italian offering "comfort food" with "delicious sauces" served by a "friendly" staff; some feel it's "pricey, even for the Hamptons", though, reporting merely "ok" eats, service and atmosphere.

Deli King *Deli* 19 | 10 | 16 | $24

New Hyde Park | Lake Success Shopping Ctr. | 1570 Union Tpke. (bet. Lakeville & New Hyde Park Rds.) | 516-437-8420

"Big portions" of "old-school" kosher eats ensure that the "tasty" sandwiches aren't the only things "overstuffed" at this New Hyde Park pastrami purveyor that's reminiscent of a "true Brooklyn deli"; the "informal" digs and "appropriately grouchy" service appeal to some, but the rest report "takeout is best."

❷ Della Femina *American* 24 | 23 | 22 | $67

East Hampton | 99 N. Main St. (Cedar St.) | 631-329-6666 | www.dellafemina.com

"Practice your air kisses" before stepping into this "standard-bearer for East Hampton fine dining" that "still has the magic touch", presenting "savory, delicate" and "surprising" New American dishes in a "delightful", "caricature-covered" room that "allows for conversation"; "professional" service adds to the "civilized" atmosphere, so while it "makes Manhattan look inexpensive", the off-season prix fixe is the "best bargain going" – and "this place rocks in any season!"

Desmond's *American* ▽ 20 | 19 | 21 | $43

Wading River | Inn at East Wind | 5720 Rte. 25A (¼ mile south of Sound Ave.) | 631-846-2335 | www.desmondsrestaurant.com

Though best known for its catered events, this dining room at the Inn at East Wind in Wading River serves a "wonderful" Sunday brunch buffet as well as other "reasonable" New American meals in a "really comfortable environment" enhanced by a pianist on weekends; lunch and dinner prix fixes are also a plus.

DiMaggio's Trattoria *Italian* 19 | 15 | 19 | $34

Port Washington | 706 Port Washington Blvd. (Davis Ave.) | 516-944-6363 | www.dimaggios.net

Fans of this "family favorite" for "home-run" pasta and pizza in Port Washington "love" the "charming" new enclosed courtyard that's "doubled the space" and "eliminated long waits for a table"; "fair prices" and a "friendly staff" that "always greets you warmly" further explain why they "do a brisk business" here.

	FOOD	DECOR	SERVICE	COST

Dish 🈂️Ⓜ️ *American*

▽ 27 | 15 | 26 | $51

Water Mill | Water Mill Shoppes | 760 Montauk Hwy., Ste. 5C (Station Rd.) | 631-726-0246

"Marvelous" and "quirky", this "tiny" BYO New American in Water Mill turns out "farm-fresh", "exciting" prix fixe menus that change "every weekend", prepared by the catering couple of Merrill Indoe and Peter Robertson; "personal service" is assured in the 12-seat space, which is "so-so" on looks but definitely one "unique experience for the Hamptons" that's "well priced" to boot; P.S. hours vary and reservations are required (and "hard to get").

Diwan *Indian*

21 | 18 | 19 | $32

Hicksville | Patel Plaza | 415 S. Broadway (Ludy St.) | 516-513-1057

Port Washington | 37 Shore Rd. (Mill Pond Rd.) | 516-439-4200

Port Washington patrons "danced in the streets" when this Indian eatery reopened after a seven-year hiatus, joining its Hicksville cousin to offer "excellent" fare delivered by a "friendly, professional" staff; the "fabulous" buffet lunch provides a "wide array of authentic dishes" at an "economical" price, and the "view of Manhasset Bay" from the second floor at PW is a plus.

Dixie's Smokehouse *BBQ*

- | - | - | I

Kings Park | 12 Indian Head Rd. (bet. E. Main St. & Meadow Rd.) | 631-292-2520 | www.dixiessmokehouse.com

Budget-friendly fare includes sliders of beef, pork, chicken and crab at this Texas BBQ joint in Kings Park, where a brick wall, cowboy art and country-western soundtrack strike a casual chord; it might be somewhat hidden in a strip mall beside the railroad tracks, but a pretty patio helps make it worth seeking out.

Dock Bar & Grill, The 🈂️Ⓜ️🚭 *Seafood*

- | - | - | M

Montauk | off West Lake Dr. (Montauk Docks) | 631-668-9778 | www.thedockmontauk.com

Funky and local, this low-key saloon near the Montauk docks is both a perch for fishermen recounting the day's adventures and for locals looking for seafood fresh from the boat; dark wood lines the small rooms and regulars know the 'rules' – no checks, no credit cards, no cell phones, no screaming children – are strictly enforced.

Dockers Waterside Restaurant & Marina *Seafood/Steak*

20 | 24 | 18 | $49

East Quogue | 94 Dune Rd. (Dolphin Ln.) | 631-653-0653 | www.dockerswaterside.com

An "incomparable" view across Shinnecock Bay showcasing "spectacular sunsets" is the draw at this "crowd-pleasing" East Quogue surf 'n' turfer whose "fresh", "unfussy" eats are served by "pleasant" (if "not always efficient") summer help; with frequent "live music" too, it's a "happening place" to "chill after a day at the beach" – and "if you arrive by yacht you won't mind the prices."

	FOOD	DECOR	SERVICE	COST

Dockside Bar & Grill *Seafood*

21	16	19	$42

Sag Harbor | American Legion Bldg. | 26 Bay St. (Ryson St.) | 631-725-7100 | www.docksidesagharbor.com

"Surprisingly delicious" seafood comes with "cheery" service at this "unpretentious" Sag Harbor eatery "tucked away" in the unlikely setting of an American Legion hall; the "loud", "cramped" interior is "nothing special", but in warm weather you can "dine under umbrellas on the patio" and take in "pretty views" of boats docked in the marina.

Dodici *Italian*

24	21	22	$43

Rockville Centre | 12 N. Park Ave. (bet. Merrick Rd. & Sunrise Hwy.) | 516-764-3000 | www.dodicirestaurant.com

This "fabulous" fixture on Rockville Centre's Restaurant Row "continues to hit the mark" with its "delicious" Italian dishes (including "guaranteed-to-please" wood-fired pizza), "awesome wine list" and "lovely" Tuscan atmosphere; when the weather warms, French doors swing open for sidewalk dining, a "nice touch" that lessens the "agita" from the "exceptional loudness" inside; P.S. it's easy to "spend a chunk of money" on vino, but there are affordable bottles too.

NEW Domo Sushi *Japanese*

21	21	22	$33

East Setauket | Stop & Shop Shopping Ctr. | 180 Rte. 25A (bet. August St. & The Hills Dr.) | 631-751-2299 | www.domosushiny.com

"Terrific sushi", "imaginative rolls", "interesting appetizers" and a "nice selection of sake" at "decent prices" are enough to win "neighborhood" loyalty at this "above-average" Japanese newcomer in an East Setauket strip mall; the "wonderful staff" and modern setting are further pluses, and while a couple of critics call it "typical", most consider it a "treat."

Dosa Diner *Indian/Vegetarian*

23	11	17	$20

Hicksville | 128 Broadway (bet. Cherry & Nicholai Sts.) | 516-681-5151 | www.dosadiner.us

Even "omnivores" "love" this vegetarian South Indian located in Hicksville, whose "fantastic", "inexpensive" buffet lunches, full Thali dinners and 20 varieties of "crispy", "crave"-able dosas make for an "incredible value"; as the room is "weather-beaten" at best, surveyors suggest "forget the ambiance" and just focus on the "rewarding" fare that keeps you "full for hours"; P.S. it's BYO only with no corkage fee.

NEW Downtown Burger at Five Points Café *American/Burgers*

-	-	-	I

Sayville | 1 Main St. (Railroad Ave.) | 631-567-5655 | www.fivepointscafe.com

Located on a five-point corner in the heart of Sayville, this burger specialist flips a variety of patties while offering inexpensive American eats including salads and sandwiches to boot; the small, casual digs feature warm rust-and-brown colors and a patio separated from the sidewalk by a low brick wall.

	FOOD	DECOR	SERVICE	COST

Duke Falcon's Global Grill *American/Eclectic*   22 | 18 | 21 | $39

Long Beach | 36 W. Park Ave. (bet. Edwards & National Blvds.) |
516-897-7000

Like a "jewel" unearthed by its namesake world-traveler, this
"engaging" Eclectic–New American in Long Beach enchants fans
with a "huge range" of "inventive", "alluring" creations and "quality
service", all for a "modest" price; sure it's "kitschy", but "unusual"
decorations from fictional journeys up the "fun" factor, while a
recent expansion "adds much needed space."

Duryea's Lobster Deck ⊄ *Seafood*   22 | 15 | 12 | $37

Montauk | 65 Tuthill Rd. (bet. Flamingo Ave. & Fleming Rd.) |
631-668-2410 | www.duryealobsters.com

With "one of the best waterside views on the East End", this "cash-
only" "seafood shack" in Montauk is "always crowded", as much for
the "beautiful sunsets" as for the "sensational" lobster and "affordable" bill (courtesy of the BYO-only policy); you'll "stand on line" to
order, then nab a "picnic table" on a deck that "could use a spruce-
up", but "never mind the minimalist digs", just enjoy the "briny
breeze" and get cracking; P.S. closed mid-October to mid-April.

Dynasty of Port Washington *Chinese*   20 | 15 | 20 | $28

Port Washington | 405 Main St. (2nd Ave.) | 516-883-4100

Standing out "in a town filled with Chinese restaurants", this
Port Washington Cantonese comes through with "tasty", "classic" fare, "pleasant" service (the owner "makes the rounds") and
a "lovely location" close enough to the water to "take a walk on
the wharf at sunset"; there's "nothing trendy" about the "dull"
decor, but the house is "always full" nonetheless, and lunch is a
particularly "good deal."

East by Northeast *American/Asian*   21 | 23 | 21 | $51

Montauk | Stone Lion Inn | 51 S. Edgemere St. (bet. Elwell St. &
S. Erie Ave.) | 631-668-2872 | www.harvest2000.com

"Perfect when you're ready to leave the flip-flops behind", this
"attractive", "trendy" sib to Harvest proffers "exciting" New
American–Pan Asian fare (the "duck tacos are a perennial favorite")
accompanied by "killer" views of Montauk's Fort Pond; even if it's
"pricey", the majority "never tires" of it – just "get there early" to
catch the "unbelievable sunset"; P.S. closed mid-February to mid-
March, and Wednesday–Thursday in the off-season.

☑ East Hampton Point *American*   19 | 26 | 18 | $61

East Hampton | 295 Three Mile Harbor-Hog Creek Rd. (4 mi. north
of Hook Windmill) | 631-329-2800 | www.easthamptonpoint.com

"You go for" the "drop-dead gorgeous views" of Three Mile Harbor
at this "lively" East Hamptoner whose "simply prepared" New
American dishes are for the most part "not special", but "decent"
and "enjoyable" nonetheless; so despite "expensive" tabs and
sometimes "slow" service, cares wash away with the "breathtaking"
sunset, and "prices are more palatable" out on the deck; P.S. closed
Labor Day to mid-April.

	FOOD	DECOR	SERVICE	COST

E. B. Elliot's ◗ *American* | 18 | 18 | 18 | $38 |

Freeport | 23 Woodcleft Ave. (Front St.) | 516-378-8776 |
www.ebelliots.com

This bi-level "Nautical Mile mainstay" in Freeport draws diners for "scenic eats" overlooking the bay or "for drinks" and "live music on the weekends"; opinions on the New American grub range from "delicious" to "pedestrian" for the price, and "service could be swifter", but regulars "go all the time" and focus on the "burgers, beers" and "views"; there's also a late-night menu served till 4 AM.

Eddie's Pizza ◗⊅ *Pizza* | 21 | 7 | 17 | $21 |

New Hyde Park | 2048 Hillside Ave. (Marcus Ave.) | 516-354-9780
The "renowned thin crusts" at this old-time New Hyde Park "pizza dive" will "rock your world" affirm admirers who dub the "addictive" signature bar pies the "best around", "bar none"; you'll get "no apologies" for the "retro decor", so you can call it "a dump, but that's part of the allure."

Edgewater ☒ *Italian* | 22 | 20 | 23 | $40 |

Hampton Bays | 295 E. Montauk Hwy. (bet. Ocean View & S. Valley Rds.) |
631-723-2323 | www.edgewaterrestaurant.com
Loyalists love the "huge", "luscious" plates of "creative" Italian at this "steady" seasonal Hampton Bays option where the "seafood is done to order" and the oysters are "fresh" for the "slurping"; the "lovely" interior and deck, offering "nice views" of Shinnecock Bay, "gets packed during the summer", but the staff "works hard" to run a tight ship, plus the midweek summertime early-bird is a "great value."

Elaine's Asian Bistro & Grill *Asian* | 22 | 23 | 21 | $38 |

Great Neck | 8 Bond St. (bet. Grace Ave. & N. Station Plaza) |
516-829-8883 | www.elainesbistro.com
"Distinctive", "delectable" Pan-Asian dishes, including "fantastic sushi", stand out at this "beautiful" Great Neck "'in' place" where "charming hostess" Elaine oversees the "quality" service in a "tastefully ornate, dramatic" setting; the "Manhattan" vibe suits an "intimate dinner or meeting a group of friends", while the "reasonable" prices keep it the local "default" for many.

Elbow East *Steak* | 19 | 12 | 19 | $38 |

Southold | 50 N. Sea Dr. (Kenney's Rd.) | 631-765-1203
"It's a little off the beaten path" and "just steps" from the beach in Southold, but the reason for bending the elbow here is the "scrumptious" steaks made with a secret marinade and paired with "local wines"; there's a "summer feeling" year-round, especially in warm weather when you can drink on the deck, and tabs are moderate, so "this is where the locals eat."

El Parral *Italian/Spanish* | 21 | 8 | 20 | $34 |

Syosset | 8 Berry Hill Rd. (Muttontown Eastwoods Rd.) | 516-921-2844 |
www.elparral.com
"If you want paella" and a pitcher of the "best" sangria – or fettuccine and a carafe of Chianti – Syosset locals say this "longtime"

Spanish-Italian combo is the "place to go" for "fresh", affordable fare that "doesn't disappoint"; meanwhile, the "hospitable" staff "makes every meal comfortable", even if the "outdated" decor "does the exact opposite."

Emilio's *Pizza*

23 | 16 | 18 | $28

Commack | Harrow's Shopping Ctr. | 2201 Jericho Tpke. (Ruth Blvd.) | 631-462-6267 | www.emiliosonlinemenu.com

It's "always busy for a reason" at this Commack "family destination" where there's "perfect", "crispy" pizza from the counter and a "huge variety" of "well-done" Italian dishes with "garlic, garlic and more garlic" available in the back dining room; a few *paesani* might take potshots at the "long lines", "noisy" setting and "iffy" service, but most are "prepared to wait" for the "affordable", "quality" eats.

Epiphany Ⓜ *Italian*

21 | 18 | 19 | $48

Glen Cove | 284 Glen St. (bet. Elm & Hendrick Aves.) | 516-759-1913 | www.epiphanyrestaurant.com

A "comfortable" "neighborhood" Italian with an "inventive, well-thought-out" menu and "excellent wine list", this "expensive" Glen Cover is further elevated by a "gracious" owner who offers a "warm welcome" and "chats it up with patrons"; the service can be uneven and the "dated" decor is an "afterthought", but regulars appreciate the "well-spaced, uncrowded" feel – when there isn't one of those "large parties" going on.

Ernesto's East Ⓜ *Italian*

22 | 16 | 23 | $48

Glen Head | 10 Railroad Ave. (bet. Glen Head Rd. & School St.) | 516-671-7828

The "out-to-please" owners and "efficient" staff "make you feel really at home" at this Glen Head "gem" near the train station serving "old-fashioned", "authentic" (and somewhat "pricey") Italian food; the "cozy" room, with tin ceilings and an oak bar, "fills up fast", however, so "make reservations."

Estia's Little Kitchen *American*

23 | 13 | 20 | $40

Sag Harbor | 1615 Bridgehampton-Sag Harbor Tpke. (bet. Carroll St. & Clay Pit Rd.) | 631-725-1045 | www.eatshampton.com

The "portions are huge" (though "not cheap") at this "peanut-sized" Sag Harbor American where "phenomenal", "garden"-fresh American dishes with an "offbeat" flair (including "amazing" breakfasts) are delivered by an "attentive" crew; local cognoscenti plead "don't tell anyone", but the crowds and the "waits" testify the word is out; P.S. dinner served weekends only.

Ethos *Greek*

21 | 20 | 18 | $45

Great Neck | 25 Middle Neck Rd. (bet. Grace Ave. & N. Station Plaza) | 516-305-4958 | www.ethosrestaurants.com

This Great Neck Greek (with two Manhattan sibs) is noted for its "superb grilled whole fish" and "lots" of "delicious" appetizers – all offered in a "pleasant atmosphere"; so while some cite "slow" service and "NY prices", the weekday early-bird is a deal.

NEW Fado *Portuguese* ▽ 21 | 19 | 21 | $34

Huntington | 10 New St. (Main St.) | 631-351-1010 | www.fadohuntington.com

Early word on this "small" Portuguese newcomer in Huntington commends an "interesting" menu featuring the "freshest calamari", grilled octopus, *bacalhau a bras* (shredded cod) and other "winners"; lined with photos of the old country, the "attractive" space can be "quite filled", especially since fans declare they'll "definitely be back."

Famous Dave's *BBQ* 19 | 16 | 18 | $27

Westbury | 1060 Corporate Dr. (bet. Ellison Ave. & Zeckendorf Blvd.) | 516-832-7300
Smithtown | 716 Smithtown Bypass (Terry Rd.) | 631-360-6490
www.famousdaves.com

The "mouthwatering" brisket and other "lightly smoky" specialties are a "joy" at these "above-average" BBQ chain links in Smithtown and Westbury, so "don't let the fact that some of the food is served on trash-can lids turn you off"; though naysayers call them "nothing special" and knock their "kitschy" looks ("like a movie set of a Texas" joint), the "chipper" service and "fair" prices keep them a "favorite."

Fanatico *Italian* 20 | 18 | 19 | $29

Jericho | Waldbaum's Shopping Ctr. | 336 N. Broadway (bet. Burke & Scott Aves.) | 516-932-5080

"Freshly made" pastas, "super-thin pizza" and other "consistently good" Italian fare at "moderate" prices make for a "crowded" scene full of "families" at this Jericho strip-mall eatery; there's a "bright, comfortable" setting and "friendly" service, but a handful isn't sure it's worth the "long" weekend waits since they only "take reservations for seven or more people."

Farm Country Kitchen *American* 23 | 14 | 20 | $29

Riverhead | 513 W. Main St. (bet. Marcy & Sweezy Aves.) | 631-369-6311 | www.farmcountrykitchen.net

"Overlooking the beautiful Peconic River with paddlers" floating by, this "little old house" in Riverhead offers a "peaceful" setting for enjoying "splendid" New American dishes served by an engaging, sometimes "kooky" staff that "makes you laugh"; it's "hard to find", "parking is terrible" and the "decor needs help", but the prices are "bargain-basement" and you "feel as though you're cruising down the river"; P.S. it's BYO only.

NEW Farmhouse *American* ▽ 26 | 21 | 22 | $53

Greenport | 45 Front St. (bet. 1st & Main Sts.) | 631-477-6788

"A refreshing addition to Greenport", this "tiny" New American offers "imaginative" dishes created by "talented chef" Richard Lanza, who pays "attention to detail" and sources "local and organic" for a weekly changing menu that's not inexpensive but "doesn't break the bank"; "beautifully decorated, simple" surroundings and "gracious, enthusiastic" service complete the picture, making it one of the "best new restaurants on the North Fork"; P.S. closed Monday-Tuesday in the off-season.

	FOOD	DECOR	SERVICE	COST

fatfish Wine
Bar & Bistro *Mediterranean/Seafood* | 21 | 20 | 19 | $43 |

Bay Shore | 28 Cottage Ave. (Clinton Ave.) | 631-666-2899 |
www.fatfish.info

It's "all about the water views" from the patio of this Bay Shore Med-
seafooder that's "perfect on a beautiful summer night" when the two
bars are "packed" and acoustic rock is playing; the "enjoyable" fin
fare pleases many, but those annoyed by "long waits" and a "fat bill"
feel the "run-of-the-mill" menu "doesn't do justice" to the "sparkling"
Great South Bay location; P.S. no reservations; closed in the winter.

Fatty Fish *Japanese* | 22 | 15 | 18 | $38 |

Glen Cove | 2 Glen St. (Bridge St.) | 516-676-1823 | www.fattyfishsushi.com
Customers commend this Glen Cove Japanese for its "creative",
"high-quality" sushi, "aromatic" dishes and "bargain bento boxes",
all served with an "upscale presentation"; a few frown on the "narrow" space that's "not much to look at", but most are won over by
the "exciting" food, "hip" feel and sidewalk dining in the summer.

F.H. Riley's Ⓜ *American* | 23 | 18 | 22 | $32 |

Huntington | 400 New York Ave. (bet. Carver & Fairview Sts.) |
631-271-7600 | www.fhrileys.com

Benefitting from "good word-of-mouth", this usually "crowded"
Huntington "local hangout" serves "ridiculously large" portions of
"excellent" "pub fare" (the "best" meatloaf and fish 'n' chips) as well
as refined American bistro bites including "wonderful salads" and
"fantastic" gumbo; there are "no complaints" about the "pleasant"
service, solid "bar scene" or "pricing" that works "for families", either, so patrons predict "you'll become a regular"; P.S. the $14 all-
you-can-eat Sunday pasta special is a "nice treat."

Fifth Season, The *American* | 26 | 23 | 23 | $48 |

Port Jefferson | 34 E. Broadway (bet. Main St. & Mariners Way) |
631-477-8500 | www.thefifth-season.com

"Top-notch all around", this Port Jefferson standout presents "artful", "locavore" New American cuisine served by a "caring" staff; the
"warm" dining room has "beautiful" harbor views, so "sit by the windows" or "on the veranda" in summer, and offset the "high prices"
with a BYO bottle – there's "no corkage fee" if it's from Long Island;
P.S. closed on Mondays in winter.

56th Fighter Group *American* | 16 | 20 | 17 | $36 |

Farmingdale | 7160 Republic Airport (Rte. 110) | 631-694-8280 |
www.56thfgrestaurant.com

"Nostalgia" seekers have a soft spot for this "World War II-themed"
American eatery at Farmingdale's Republic Airport, where they can
"watch the planes take off", listen to "old-time radio broadcasts"
and peruse lots of "flight memorabilia"; while "families" love the
"something-for-everyone" Sunday brunch buffet ("make reservations early"), modernists dis "mediocre" "airline fare" and "spotty"
service, declaring it a "kitschy", "trip back to the '40s" that's "had its
day – and it's just not today."

Fishbar on the Lake *Seafood*
▽ 18 | 13 | 16 | $45

Montauk | Gone Fishing Marina | 467 E. Lake Dr. (opp. Montauk Airport) |
631-668-6600 | www.freshlocalfish.com

"Fresh seafood shines" at this seasonal Montauker, largely a "rustic"
covered deck with tables "overlooking the water"; though a few find
it "disappointing", an "anything-to-please" attitude, "fair prices"
and "breathtaking views" ensure it's "crowded on weekends";
P.S. reservations taken for groups of eight or more only.

Fisherman's Catch *Seafood*
20 | 18 | 20 | $41

Point Lookout | 111 Bayside Dr. (Hewlett Ave.) | 516-670-9717 |
www.fishermanscatchrestaurant.com

"Watch the boats" bring home the day's catch at this "upbeat" Point
Lookout seafooder overlooking Reynolds Channel and dishing a
"tasty" (if "not special") variety of marine treats; prices are modest
considering the "gorgeous" waterside view, though some wish
they'd upgrade the "blah" interior.

Fishery, The *Seafood*
19 | 15 | 19 | $35

East Rockaway | 1 Main St. (Atlantic Ave.) | 516-256-7117 |
www.thefishery1.com

Just as popular for "meeting friends" as it is for cracking shells, this
East Rockaway joint dishes out "great chowders" and other "decent
seafood" at "favorable prices"; while some say it's "hit-or-miss", few
take issue with the "outdoor scene", a "delight" in summer when the
"lovely" canalside patio "rocks" with live music and a "hopping" bar.

NEW Fish Store, The Ⓜ *Seafood*
- | - | - | I

Bayport | 836 Montauk Hwy. (Bayport Ave.) | 631-472-3018 |
www.thefishstoreonline.com

Open since 1978, this Bayport fish store has added two small blue-
and-white dining rooms with table service and decorated with
coastal photos as a bright-and-airy setting for digging into an inexpensive lineup of fresh-from-the-counter seafood (fried, broiled or grilled)
plus specialties like Blue Claw crab cakes; outdoor seating is planned.

Ⓩ Five Guys *Burgers*
21 | 9 | 15 | $12

Levittown | 3497 Hempstead Tpke. (bet. Jerusalem & Wantagh Aves.) |
516-796-1237
Long Beach | 2 W. Park Ave. (Edwards Blvd.) | 516-431-1999
Merrick | 2099 Merrick Rd. (Hewlett Ave.) | 516-208-8601
NEW Hicksville | 265 N. Broadway (bet. Nevada & Princess Sts.) |
516-822-8022
Amityville | Bay Village Plaza | 35 Merrick Rd. (Ketcham Ave.) |
631-691-6800
NEW Deer Park | 1942 Deer Park Ave. (bet. Long Island Ave. &
Nicolls Rd.) | 631-243-4447
Hauppauge | 601 Veterans Hwy. (Wheeler Rd.) | 631-265-0335
Huntington Station | 350 Rte. 110 (bet. Norwich St. & Schwab Rd.) |
631-271-4144
www.fiveguys.com

What fans call "the best burgers on the planet" are the "big, fat, juicy"
specimens "with all the trimmings" at LI's No. 1 Bang for the Buck, an

FOOD   DECOR   SERVICE   COST

Obama favorite also praised for fries that are "potato perfection" and free "peanuts while waiting" for your order; so even if doubters pooh-pooh "all the fuss", devotees of this "no-frills" but "fast and friendly" franchise "don't know why anyone would go to another chain."

Foody's BBQ/Pizza

▽ | 21 | 9 | 18 | $30

Water Mill | Water Mill Shoppes | 760 Montauk Hwy. (Station Rd.) | 631-726-3663

The wood-burning grill lends a distinctive bit of "smoke" to "comfort food", including "great pizza" and BBQ selections, at this Water Mill eatery by chef/co-owner Bryan Futerman (ex Nick & Toni's); "it is what it is" say some, noting an "unappealing, poorly lit" space with outdoor seating that's "almost in the parking lot", but on the plus side it's a low-cost, easy place for "families with young children."

Fork & Vine American

23 | 19 | 23 | $51

Glen Head | 32 Railroad Ave. (bet. Prospect & School Sts.) | 516-656-3266 | www.forkandvineny.com

"Creative" "small-plate tastings" paired with "extensive wine offerings" "impress" at this "reinvented" American (fka On 3) near the Glen Head train station, geared toward a kid-free crowd; though the surroundings can get "cramped" and "loud", they're "attractive enough" with changing displays of local artwork, Wednesday night jazz and "professional" service, plus there's a "romantic backyard garden."

Fortune Wheel Chinese

22 | 10 | 15 | $26

Levittown | Nassau Mall | 3601 Hempstead Tpke. (Wantaugh Ave.) | 516-579-4700

If you want "authentic dim sum" that makes you feel like "you're halfway across the globe", this "hard-to-find" Levittown Chinese in the Nassau Mall is a "must-visit", though if you don't "go with someone who speaks Cantonese", "be prepared to point"; there's "absolutely no atmosphere", the service can be downright "surly" and the "always-crowded" weekends mean "long lines", but regulars insist it "rivals Chinatown" for "very respectable" eats.

Four Food Studio 🅂 American

21 | 24 | 19 | $50

Melville | 515 Broadhollow Rd. (Baylis Rd.) | 631-577-4444 | www.fourfoodstudio.com

"Modern", "eye-catching" digs, boasting four "unique" rooms representing "each season" plus a "slick", "jaw-dropping bar scene", define this "NYC-chic" Melville "hangout" for "happening" "young professionals"; the "seasonally changing" New American menu puts a "different twist on some standard fare" (plus the "cotton candy with the check" is a "perfect ending"), but the "cheeky" staff and "deafening roar" from revelers prompt some patrons to wonder if they "want to be a club or a restaurant."

NEW 490 West 🅜 American

- | - | - | E

Carle Place | 490 Westbury Ave. (bet. Cherry Ln. & Rushmore Ave.) | 516-338-0848 | www.490west.com

Situated in the Carle Place space that was long home to Camille's, this newcomer is turning out New American fare with an eye toward local products (e.g. Long Island duck breast); the white-tablecloth setting has gold-colored walls, and a three-course early-bird is available Tuesday–Thursday and all day Sunday.

Franina Ristorante ⓜ *Italian*   26 | 22 | 24 | $60

Syosset | 58 W. Jericho Tpke. (bet. Haskett & Oak Drs.) | 516-496-9770 | www.franina.com

"Exquisite" Italian fare sets apart this Syosset "winner" serving "classic" dishes, "intriguing specials" and "exotic" game for more adventurous types in an "inviting" Tuscan setting ("you're no longer in a little strip mall" once you step inside); as the staff is "committed to excellence and personal attention", indulging in such a "superior" experience is worth the "splurge."

Frank-N-Burger *Burgers/Hot Dogs*   ▽ 19 | 12 | 17 | $14

St. James | 739 Middle Country Rd. (Sunny Rd.) | 631-780-5693 | www.franknburger.com

"A hidden freak of a hit!" howl fans of this "unique fast-food haunt" in St. James with a Frankenstein theme, serving burgers and franks "based on monster movies" (the Swamp, the Wolf Dog), along with spicy chili and fries; opinions on the grub range from "decent" to "scary-great", and though a few call the setting – with murals of bats clutching hot dogs – "fun", since there's not much seating it's "geared toward takeout and teens."

Frank's Steaks *Steak*   21 | 18 | 21 | $51

Jericho | Jericho Shopping Plaza | 4 Jericho Tpke. (Aintree Rd.) | 516-338-4595
Rockville Centre | 54 Lincoln Ave. (S. Village Ave.) | 516-536-1500
www.frankssteaks.com

Known for "melt-in-your-mouth" Romanian skirt steak, this "refreshingly unpretentious" duo is proof "you don't need to go to the bigger-name steakhouses" for a "good" cut of beef; the "old-school" Rockville Centre outpost is "much less noisy" than the "busy", newly renovated Jericho branch, but both offer the same "courteous" service, "crayons on the tables for closet artists" and "upscale" yet "reasonable" tabs.

Frederick's ⓩ *Continental*   23 | 17 | 23 | $48

Melville | 1117 Walt Whitman Rd. (bet. Arlington St. & Old Country Rd.) | 631-673-8550 | www.fredericksofli.com

The "congenial", "aim-to-please" staff "welcomes regulars and first-timers" like they're "old friends" at this Melville Continental that offers plenty of "cozy" comfort for "power lunches" (i.e. "expense account dining in your grandparents' house"); most find the "classic", "consistent" menu (beef Wellington, stuffed fillet of sole) "fantastic", even if it "hasn't changed in 25 years", but customers "bored" by the "same old" eats and "blah" decor feel a "refurbish" is in order.

Fresco Crêperie & Café ⋈ *French*   23 | 14 | 20 | $18

Long Beach | 150A E. Park Ave. (bet. Long Beach & Riverside Blvds.) | 516-897-8097

(continued)

Fresco Crêperie & Café
NEW **Williston Park** | 72 Hillside Ave. (bet. Broad & Cross Sts.) | 516-280-6630
www.frescocreperie.com

Turning out "marvelous" French crêpes for "any craving", this "cute, little" Long Beach cafe is perfect for a "light bite" near the boardwalk, whether it's a "sweet" dessert or more "savory" stuffing you seek; factor in "wonderful salads", some of the "best soups in town" and a full coffee bar, and it's a good thing the "charming respite" takes cash only, otherwise fans fear they'd "max out" their credit cards; P.S. a Williston Park offshoot opened post-Survey.

Fresno *American*
22 | 19 | 22 | $56

East Hampton | 8 Fresno Pl. (bet. Gingerbread Ln. & Railroad Ave.) | 631-324-8700 | www.fresnorestaurant.com

"As homey as it gets" in East Hampton, this "perennial favorite" (related to Beacon and red bar) offers "excellent" New American cuisine (particularly when it comes to "local fish"), "snappy" service and a "warm, clubby atmosphere" enlivened by a "hopping" bar and a "beautiful" garden with a fountain and fire pit; "fair prices" and prix fixe options are another plus, making it a "class act" all around; P.S. closed Monday–Tuesday in the off-season.

Frisky Oyster *Eclectic*
25 | 20 | 23 | $57

Greenport | 27 Front St. (bet. 1st & Main Sts.) | 631-477-4265 | www.thefriskyoyster.com

New owner Robert Beaver (chef here since 2008) crafts an "inspired" Eclectic menu that changes daily at this Greenport "hipster joint", incorporating "local ingredients" into "bright", "exceptional" dishes, while holding service to a "high standard"; so though a few diners dis the "noise" and "expensive" tabs, most praise the "chic" room with a "dynamite" atmosphere, affirming that the whole package will "wow you"; P.S. no children under the age of six permitted; closed Monday–Tuesday in the off-season.

Fulton & Prime Fish
and Steakhouse *Seafood/Steak*
23 | 20 | 22 | $56

Syosset | 352 Jericho Tpke. (bet. Bruce St. & Seaford-Oyster Bay Rd.) | 516-921-1690

One of the more "understated" North Shore steakhouses, this "secret" Syosset chop shop camouflaged by a strip mall "excels" at both the surf and the turf – especially the signature porterhouse for two – setting a "relaxing" vibe that's ideal for "couples" or "the whole family"; the service is "accommodating" too, and while it's not cheap, most feel the "generous" "prime" cuts are "priced right."

Galangal *Japanese/Thai*
23 | 23 | 22 | $31

Syosset | 140 Jericho Tpke. (Underhill Blvd.) | 516-682-0688 | www.galangal2.com

Surveyors are smitten with this "delightful" Syosset Thai-Japanese that boasts "superb", "artistic" dishes (including "excellent" sushi), all served with "smiles from the staff" at "inexpensive" prices; the stylish room "dazzles" with an indoor waterfall and pool guarded over by a large Buddha statue, a perfectly "tranquil" reward for those maddened by the "hard-to-find" location behind a real-estate building.

Galleria Dominick *Italian*   26 | 20 | 25 | $55

Westbury | 238 Post Ave. (bet. Drexel & Winthrop Aves.) |
516-997-7373 | www.galleriadominick.com

"Devoted patrons" can't get enough of the "wonderful" Northern Italian specialties at this "upscale" Westbury veteran, a "beautiful" escape into "old-world elegance" and a "perennial favorite" for "special occasions"; the "European feel" is enhanced by "first-class service", live piano on weekends and "personal attention" so "pleasant" that "Dominick should run a charm school."

Garden Grill *American*   21 | 23 | 22 | $40

Smithtown | 64 N. Country Rd. (bet. Judges Ln. & Main St.) |
631-265-8771 | www.thegardengrill.com

The "lovely ambiance" in a "delightful" old Victorian house with several "beautiful rooms", a fireplace and lots of "lace and candles" is the highlight of this "soothing" Smithtown American, though the "reliable", "welcoming" service runs a close second; even if the menu offers "no surprises", the dishes are "very good" and there are "fine choices" at the three-course early-bird dinners.

Gasho of Japan *Japanese/Steak*   20 | 17 | 19 | $35

Hauppauge | 356 Vanderbilt Motor Pkwy. (bet. Kennedy Dr. & Marcus Blvd.) | 631-231-3400 | www.gasho.com

"You go for the show" at this hibachi house in Hauppauge, where "the chefs try their best to make you laugh" as they "toss around pieces of shrimp" and "cook in front of you"; it's "great for family parties" and the "kids love it", but spoilsports snap that the Japanese steakhouse fare is "nothing special" and the "tired" room "needs a makeover."

George Martin *American*   22 | 19 | 21 | $43

Rockville Centre | 65 N. Park Ave. (bet. Front St. & Sunrise Hwy.) |
516-678-7272 | www.georgemartingroup.com

The patriarch of the George Martin Group, this Rockville Centre "classic" ("the original and still the best") combines "creativity with quality" as it turns out "delicious" New American "comfort food" in a "convivial" setting; on weekends, expect "long waits" and a "noisy" bar scene, so visit during the week for a more "enjoyable ambiance" (and discounts on Wine Down Wednesdays).

George Martin's Grillfire *Burgers*   20 | 19 | 19 | $33

Long Beach | 152 W. Park Ave. (bet. Magnolia & National Blvds.) |
516-889-3366
Merrick | 33 W. Sunrise Hwy. (Merrick Ave.) | 516-379-2222
Rockville Centre | 13 N. Park Ave. (bet. Merrick Rd. & Sunrise Hwy.) |
516-678-1290
www.georgemartingroup.com

There's "always something appealing on the menu" at this "friendly" trio grilling up a "great burger" and an assortment of "surefire" pub standards; kids of all ages "can't resist" the "pretzels with mustard to start" and "cotton candy at the end" (like eating "at the ballpark"), while adults delight in "moderate prices" and a "jumping" social scene.

NEW George Martin's Strip Steak *Steak* — | — | — | VE

Great River | 60 River Rd. (Woodhollow Rd.) | 631-650-6777 | www.georgemartingroup.com

Situated on a country road in a shingled cottage complete with a front porch, this Great River addition to the George Martin family offers high-end steakhouse fare in a classy setting featuring leather upholstery, fireplaces and a large mural evocative of the 1920s; a large wine display at the entrance hints at house selections.

Georgica *American* 18 | 16 | 16 | $67

Wainscott | 108 Wainscott Stone Rd. (Montauk Hwy.) | 631-537-5603 | www.georgicarestaurant.com

Earning mixed reviews, this seasonal Wainscott New American, headed by "Hell's Kitchen graduates" Robert Hesse and Seth Levine, pleases some reviewers with its "quality" fare and "fabulous bargain" of a prix fixe (served till 7 PM on weekends), but disappoints others who find "rude" service, "outrageous" drink prices and "more of a lounge/disco than a restaurant", given the "trendy club" scene; the "exquisite" location overlooking Georgica Pond remains a powerful lure, but be warned: "it's not for mature types."

Giaccone's Pizzeria & Restaurant *Pizza* — | — | — | I

Mineola | 124 Old Country Rd. (Willis Ave.) | 516-877-7790 | www.giaccones.com

Popular with the lunch crowd from the nearby county courthouse, this Mineola pizzeria offers a huge selection of pies on a menu that branches out with sandwiches, burgers, pastas and such; the casual, smallish room is geared more to takeout than eating in and parking's limited, but prices are reasonable and lines are out the door.

Giulio Cesare Ristorante 🖂 *Italian* 25 | 17 | 24 | $56

Westbury | 18 Ellison Ave. (Old Country Rd.) | 516-334-2982

"Some things never change", and this "outstanding" "old favorite" in Westbury is one of them, which is fine with "regulars" who dub its "authentic" Northern Italian delicacies (including "delectable" seafood and osso buco) the "best around"; the staff ensures all are "happy and content", but beware tabs that "add up quickly" and decor as "dated" as the Roman Empire.

Golden Pear Café, The *American/Coffeehouse* 18 | 11 | 14 | $21

Bridgehampton | 2426 Montauk Hwy.
(bet. Bridgehampton-Sag Harbor Tpke. & Corwith Ave.) | 631-537-1100
East Hampton | 34 Newtown Ln. (bet. Main St. & Osborne Ln.) | 631-329-1600
Sag Harbor | 111 Main St. (Spring St.) | 631-725-2270
Southampton | 99 Main St. (Nugent St.) | 631-283-8900
www.goldenpearcafe.com

This quartet of East End American coffeehouses serves an "eclectic selection" of "attractive beverages and sandwiches", "decent" baked goods and soups that "hit the spot" (basically "yuppie equivalents of luncheonette" items); the spaces are "cramped" as the "subway", and the prices could leave you feeling "mugged in the Hamptons", but "superior people-watching" means "it's the scene that's golden here."

Goldmine Mexican Grill *Mexican*
∇ 21 | 10 | 15 | $14

Greenlawn | 99 Broadway (bet. Central St. & Pulaski Rd.) | 631-262-1775

Burrito fans make a beeline for "top-tier", "inexpensive" Mexican food at this Greenlawn counter-service joint with just "a few tables for eat-in"; some report "attitude" and contend that it's squandering "so much potential", but admirers consider it the "best" nonetheless.

Gonzalo's American Café *American*
∇ 21 | 13 | 19 | $26

Glen Cove | 5 School St. (Highland Rd.) | 516-656-0003

Loyalists "love" the "home-away-from-home comfort food" at this Glen Cove American "next to the movie theater" – from "always-made-fresh" soups to "kid"-friendly fare like "excellent" burgers and mac 'n' cheese; the "drab, crowded" interior "has seen better days", but the service is "friendly", it's a good "value" and there's "enough variety to make every member of the family happy."

Gosman's Dock *Seafood*
19 | 19 | 17 | $43

Montauk | 500 W. Lake Dr. (Soundview Dr.) | 631-668-5330 | www.gosmans.com

You "can see the fishing boats from your table" at this "huge" "Montauk landmark" that draws "both day-trippers and local families" for "abundant, tasty" seafood served in four dining areas, including an outdoor deck; sure, you're "paying for" the location and "it's always a wait" with no reservations and "amateur" service, but "one scrumptious bite" of those "steamed lobsters" while taking in "knockout views" and it's "worth it"; P.S. closed November–May.

Graffiti *American*
20 | 17 | 19 | $33

Woodbury | Woodbury Common | 8285 Jericho Tpke. (bet. Juneau Blvd. & Woodbury Rd.) | 516-367-1340 | www.graffitiamericangrill.com

Newly lodged in a remodeled space next door to its original digs, this "lively" Woodbury New American is a "dependable" "standby" for a "ladies lunch" or "family get-together" with "well-prepared" "salads galore", "hearty burgers" and other "fairly priced" bites from a "speedy" staff; now that it's in "expanded" quarters, the "high decibels" may even subside; P.S. the Decor score does not reflect a post-Survey move.

Grand Lux Cafe *Eclectic*
19 | 21 | 18 | $32

Garden City | Roosevelt Field Mall | 630 Old Country Rd. (bet. Clinton Rd. & Meadowbrook Pkwy.) | 516-741-0096 | www.grandluxcafe.com

Offering "pages and pages of options" for Garden City guests, this "classier counterpart" to the Cheesecake Factory serves "nicely done" Eclectic dishes in a "loud", somewhat "over-the-top" "high-ceilinged" setting inspired by European grand cafes; portions are as "ridiculously large" as the original's (but a bit "more expensive"), so there's still "no room" for the "decadent" desserts.

Grasso's *American*   24 | 21 | 23 | $52
Cold Spring Harbor | 134 Main St. (bet. Elm & Poplar Pls.) | 631-367-6060 | www.grassosrestaurant.com
A "sophisticated crowd" coos over this Cold Spring Harbor "gem" for its "amazing", "creative" New American fare, "top-notch" staff and "romantic" setting with "terrace tables for hot nights"; more things to "love" include live jazz, a bar that's "easy to hang out in" and the "charming" location in a "seaside village" – just be ready for "expensive" tabs on par with the "affluent neighborhood."

Greek Village *Greek*   19 | 12 | 19 | $25
Commack | Macy's Plaza | 44 Veterans Memorial Hwy. (bet. Jericho Tpke. & Sunken Meadows Pkwy. S.) | 631-499-6590 | www.greekvillagecommack.com
"Go for the regular standbys and you won't be disappointed" at this Greek staple that's been around "forever" (since 1980), dishing up "hearty" salads and spanakopita in a Commack shopping center; there's "no decor" in the "glorified-diner" setting, but "efficient" service and "good-value" pricing make that easy to ignore.

Green Cactus Grill *Mexican*   20 | 10 | 15 | $15
Garden City Park | 2441 Jericho Tpke. (bet. Herricks Rd. & Marcus Ave.) | 516-248-0090
Plainview | Plainview Ctr. | 397B S. Oyster Bay Rd. (Woodbury Rd.) | 516-937-3444
Rockville Centre | 288 Sunrise Hwy. (Park Ave.) | 516-536-0700
Roslyn Heights | 215 Mineola Ave. (bet. MacGregor Ave. & Powerhouse Rd.) | 516-626-3100
Wantagh | Cherrywood Shopping Ctr. | 1194 Wantagh Ave. (Jerusalem Ave.) | 516-781-4900
North Babylon | 1209 Deer Park Ave. (Woods Rd.) | 631-242-2008
Huntington | 1273 E. Jericho Tpke. (Manor Rd.) | 631-673-1010
Huntington | 318 Main St. (bet. Green & Prospect Sts.) | 631-271-8900
Oakdale | 1274 Montauk Hwy. (Oakdale-Bohemia Rd.) | 631-567-8226
Stony Brook | 1099 Rte. 25A (bet. Cedar St. & Hawkins Rd.) | 631-751-0700
www.greencactusgrill.com
Additional locations throughout the Long Island area
Considering the "always-fresh" ingredients, "awesome fish tacos" and a fixin's free-for-all at the "self-serve" salsa bar, "what's not to like?" ask amigos of this local Mexican chain; since the "brisk" counter service and "no-frills" atmosphere lack even a hint of spice, many say it's best to take your "cheap" eats "on the go."

Greenport Tea Company *Tea Room*   21 | 22 | 21 | $26
Greenport | 119A Main St. (bet. E. Front St. & Greenport Harbor) | 631-477-8744 | www.greenportteacompany.com
"An exotic selection of teas from around the world" complements the "well-prepared" lunch items and "Brit" food – "finger sandwiches" and "scones with clotted cream" – at this "sweet place" in Greenport that "looks like your grandmother did the decorating";

"unpretentious and relaxing", it's a pleasant choice for "getting away from the hustle and bustle of life", as "the world changes a little slower here"; P.S. closes at 5 PM (hours vary by season).

Grey Horse Tavern ⓂAmerican | 23 | 23 | 25 | $40 |

Bayport | 291 Bayport Ave. (Railroad St.) | 631-472-1868 | www.greyhorsetavern.com

"Put your money on this horse" cheer fans of this Bayport New American, a "locavore's delight" turning "organic ingredients" from LI farms into "inventive", "stylish" dishes in a 140-year-old bi-level space (a former stagecoach stop) with a "quaint bar" and "outstanding" live music on weekends; the service is "wonderful" too, so even if some dub it "pricey" for tavern fare, the rest maintains it's "completely worth every penny"; P.S. check out the family-style dinners on Sundays.

NEW Grill on Pantigo American | 21 | 21 | 19 | $52 |

East Hampton | 203 Pantigo Rd. (bet. Maple Ln. & Patingo Pl.) | 631-329-2600 | www.thegrillonpantigo.com

Under the same owners as 1770 House, this "terrific addition to East Hampton" (in the former Wei Fun space) offers an "attractive", "dependable" New American menu in a "crisp", "pretty" setting; so while the service varies (maybe it's still "shaking out the start-up kinks") and pricing's on the "fancy" side, there's universal appeal in the "bargain" prix fixe (offered every night but Saturday).

Grill Room ⊠American | 21 | 19 | 21 | $41 |

Hauppauge | 160 Adams Ave. (bet. Arkay & Commerce Drs.) | 631-436-7330 | www.thegrillroomrestaurant.com

"Use your GPS" to find this "off-the-beaten-path" New American in a Hauppauge office park, and you'll be treated to "surprisingly good" seasonal fare delivered by a "helpful" staff to a "business-casual" crowd; the "beautiful", "modern" setting sports an outdoor patio, "lively bar scene" and "music on the weekends" (it can get "loud"), but a few are "not overly impressed", remarking it "tries to be a city place" but only "gets as far as Queens."

Grimaldi's Pizza | 23 | 15 | 19 | $23 |

Garden City | 980 Franklin Ave. (bet. 9th & 10th Sts.) | 516-294-6565 | www.grimaldisrestaurant.com

No need to stand on line in Brooklyn – the "outstanding" pies that put the famous original on the map might make you "weep" at this Garden City parlor, a bastion of brick-oven pizza fired to "pure perfection"; "red-checkered tablecloths" and a bridge-and-skyline mural color a dining room that's "nothing special" otherwise, while "lots of kids" and plenty of "big parties" keep it "bustling."

Gulf Coast Kitchen American | ▽ 21 | 23 | 22 | $55 |

Montauk | Montauk Yacht Club Resort & Marina | 32 Star Island Rd. (W. Lake Dr.) | 631-668-3100 | www.montaukyachtclub.com

The jury's still out on this New American newcomer at the Montauk Yacht Club: proponents praise the "fantastic" local seafood served in a "relaxing" space featuring frequent live jazz and a "great view" of the lake; a few are "disappointed" by the pricey cuisine, however, and feel it hasn't fulfilled its initial "promise"; P.S. closed December–March.

Haiku *Japanese* | - | - | - | M |

Riverhead | 40 E. Main St. (bet. East & Roanoke Aves.) | 631-727-7778
Japanese fare from sushi to hot dishes is served in a snazzy surround featuring an arched beamed ceiling, black leather chairs and a large fish tank at this midpriced Riverhead newcomer where a wall of windows looks out on Main Street; no alcohol is served, but you're welcome to BYO.

Haiku Asian Bistro & Sushi Bar *Asian* | 24 | 19 | 22 | $34 |

Woodbury | Woodbury Town Plaza | 8025 Jericho Tpke. (bet. S. Woods & Woodbury Rds.) | 516-584-6782 | www.haikuasianbistro.com
"They know what they're doing" at this "modern" Woodbury standout that's "worth hunting down" for its "amazing sushi" and "lots of different things to try" on a menu that veers from Japanese to Chinese to Malaysian and Thai; the "beautiful setting" (bamboo, waterfall, hanging lanterns), "helpful" service and "bargain" lunch special are further reasons its fans swing by "all the time."

Hampton Chutney Co. *Indian* | 22 | 9 | 15 | $19 |

Amagansett | Amagansett Sq. | Main St. (Hedges Ln.) | 631-267-3131 | www.hamptonchutney.com
Dosa doyens descend on this "wholesome" counter-service "gem" in Amagansett for "tasty", "fast" and "plentiful" Indian fare wrapped up in a "shabby-chic" "take-out" setting (the outdoor picnic tables are a "nice touch"); "wildly popular with the yoga set", it's the type of "addictive" place "you obsess about" later.

Hampton Coffee Company *Coffeehouse* | 19 | 13 | 18 | $19 |

Water Mill | 869 Montauk Hwy. (Davids Ln.) | 631-726-2633
Westhampton Beach | 194 Mill Rd. (Oak St.) | 631-288-4480
www.hamptoncoffeecompany.com
A "nice break from Starbucks", this East End duo proffers "high-quality" coffee ("roasted on premises") to go with "rustic" sandwiches, "delicious" scones and other sweets; the "tiny" Westhampton Beach location is the place to "catch up on village gossip", while the larger, full-service Water Mill branch is the "place to be seen on Saturday or Sunday mornings in the summer", when you can "eat in the lovely garden."

Harbor Bistro *American* | 21 | 19 | 19 | $49 |

East Hampton | Maidstone Harbor Marina | 313 Three Mile Harbor-Hog Creek Rd. (4 mi. north of Hook Windmill) | 631-324-7300 | www.harborbistro.net

Harbor Grill *American*

NEW **East Hampton** | 367 Three Mile Harbor Rd. (Squaw Rd.) | 631-604-5290 | www.harborgrill.net
"Members of the clean-plate club" laud the "solid" New American cuisine (with some "unusual combinations") at this seasonal East Hamptoner offering "mesmerizing views" of the harbor, especially "at sunset from the terrace"; sealing the deal, the "early dinner spe-

cials" are an "incredible bargain"; P.S. Harbor Grill, a year-round, more casual branch, opened just down the street in the fall of 2010.

Harbor Crab *Seafood*

| 18 | 16 | 19 | $37 |

Patchogue | 116 Division St. (bet. River & West Aves.) | 631-687-2722 | www.harborcrab.com

Champions of this Patchogue seafooder "love" sitting on the "floating dock" enjoying "well-prepared" catches and "awesome drinks", especially during the "packed happy hour"; "reasonable" prices are another plus, though crabs complain the tiki-style decor "needs some help" and the fare is just "so-so", adding "you go for the outdoor deck, live entertainment" and "views"; P.S. "it's locally known for having the most flattering mirror in the world in the ladies' room."

NEW Harbor Mist *American*

| ∇ 19 | 22 | 19 | $43 |

Cold Spring Harbor | 105 Harbor Rd. (off Lawrence Hill Rd.) | 631-659-3888 | www.harbormistrestaurant.com

"Breathtaking views of Cold Spring Harbor at sunset" draw diners to this two-floor newcomer where the "accommodating" kitchen turns out "good" New American fare, plus appealing "specials on Sundays and Mondays"; despite a hard-working staff, surveyors say the food and service sometimes "miss" and the restaurant is going through "growing pains" while the management tries to "get it together."

Harbor-Q *BBQ*

| 21 | 14 | 21 | $26 |

Port Washington | 84 Old Shore Rd. (Shore Rd.) | 516-883-4227 | www.harborq.com

Chef-owner "Keith [Dorman] is a welcome addition" to Port Washington say 'cue fans "craving the ribs", "melt-in-your-mouth" steaks and "phenomenal" housemade potato chips (plus "custom salads") at this "real-deal" BBQ "destination"; the "bare-bones", "college bar–like setting" in an old metal-shipping building is "questionable", but the "kid-friendly" service and "fast, efficient takeout" for "weekend football parties" is "right on the money."

Z Harvest on Fort Pond *Italian/Mediterranean*

| 26 | 22 | 22 | $53 |

Montauk | 11 S. Emery St. (Euclid Ave.) | 631-668-5574 | www.harvest2000.com

Remember that "one entree feeds two", so be ready to "share" at this "sensational" Tuscan-Med serving "simply wonderful" dishes that some call "the best on the South Fork"; it's ideal for "alfresco dining on a summer evening", with a "gorgeous garden" for watching the sunset over Fort Pond, but "long waits" for a table "even with reservations" make some yearn for the "off-season"; P.S. half-portions are now available.

Heart of Portugal *Portuguese*

| 20 | 16 | 20 | $39 |

Mineola | 241 Mineola Blvd. (bet. Jackson & Jefferson Aves.) | 516-742-9797 | www.heartofportugalrestaurant.com

So "authentic" it's "like eating in Lisbon", this "unpretentious" Mineola Portuguese turns out "perfect paella", "good sangria" and some excellent "wine values" to "satisfy" diners in the know; the "competent" staff is "accommodating", and while "a little change" would give the decor a lift, the "pleasant courtyard" and piano player on Saturdays "add a nice touch."

Hellenic Snack Bar & Restaurant *Greek* | 20 | 11 | 17 | $31 |

East Marion | 5145 Main Rd. (bet. Maple & Shipyard Lns.) | 631-477-0138 | www.thehellenic.com

"Zorba would be proud" of this "go-to Greek" in East Marion where the "fabulous broiled fish", "divine lemonade" and other specialties are all "fresh and appetizing"; so despite the "dated" digs, the covered patio "can't be beat in the summer", and "generous" plates make it a "great value for the money"; P.S. reservations taken only for large groups; closed mid-November to mid-January.

Hemingway's *American* | 19 | 19 | 19 | $35 |

Wantagh | 1885 Wantagh Ave. (bet. Brooktree Ln. & Park Ave.) | 516-781-2700 | www.hemingwaysgrill.com

Offering exactly what you'd expect from a "neighborhood pub", this "comfortable" Wantagh fixture provides a "solid" mix of New American fare so there's "something for everyone when you go with a group", complemented by "aim-to-please" service (though it can be "a tad green") and "TVs at the bar" to "watch the game"; it's "not spectacular" by any means, but comes through with "reasonable prices" and a "great" Sunday brunch buffet.

Hideaway, The *Eclectic* | 19 | 17 | 17 | $39 |

Ocean Beach | Housers Hotel, Fire Island | 785 Evergreen Walk (Bay Walk) | 631-583-8900

Sunsets seen from outdoor tables "overlooking the Great South Bay" are "breathtaking" at this seasonal spot in a "hidden" Ocean Beach hotel; its "upbeat" service and Eclectic lineup of "basic but fresh" seafood are "better than most" on Fire Island, but the "scenic view" remains the real bait.

Hildebrandt's Ⓜ *American* | 19 | 13 | 19 | $21 |

Williston Park | 84 Hillside Ave. (bet. Roslyn Rd. & Willis Ave.) | 516-741-0608 | www.hildebrandtsrestaurant.com

Bringing back "fond memories", this seriously "old-school" soda shop in Williston Park harbors "no pretenses", just some of the "best" housemade ice cream, shakes and fountain drinks on the Island; there's "regular" American "luncheonette" grub as well, but do yourself a favor and order the "hot fudge sundae" with "real whipped cream" because "life's too short to waste on anything else."

Hinata *Japanese* | 23 | 18 | 22 | $41 |

Great Neck | 6 Bond St. (Grace Ave.) | 516-829-3811

"Unique rolls" and other "excellent creations" are delivered by "efficient" servers in a "calm, quiet atmosphere" at this slightly expensive Great Neck sushi bar with an "Asian fusion" touch; add the ministrations of a "hospitable owner" (offering up the occasional "sake bomb") and a recent decor face-lift, and it's evident why diners dub it a "neighborhood favorite."

	FOOD	DECOR	SERVICE	COST

Homura Sushi *Japanese* ▽ 23 | 11 | 20 | $35

Williston Park | 636 Willis Ave. (bet. Fordham & Harvard Sts.) |
516-877-8128 | www.homurasushi.com

"Super-fresh, delicious" sushi – and "don't forget" the tuna pizza –
at "modest prices" make this "friendly", "consistent" Williston Park
Japanese a "true find" for many; there's "never a long wait", but the
"semi-divey" setting means it's "best for takeout."

Honu Kitchen & Cocktails Ⓜ *American* 22 | 25 | 22 | $49

Huntington | 363 New York Ave. (bet. E. Carver & Elm Sts.) |
631-421-6900 | www.honukitchen.com

It "still has what it takes" report regulars of this "electric"
Huntington New American with "beautiful, Manhattan-style" looks
and a "fun bar" boasting "lots of pretty people" partaking in a "boisterous pickup scene"; it's "hard to keep up" with the "constantly
changing menu", but the dishes are "tasty" (if "pricey") and the
drinks "amazing", all served by a "knowledgeable", "sexy" staff;
P.S. under new ownership post-Survey.

Horace & Sylvia's 20 | 18 | 20 | $34
Publick House *American*

Babylon | 100 Deer Park Ave. (bet. Grove Pl. & Main St.) | 631-587-5081 |
www.horaceandsylvia.com

"Regulars" see real improvement at this "homey" Babylon bistro
where "new owners have introduced a seasonal" New American
menu with "local ingredients" and are paying "attention to the
ambiance" in a "gastropub" kind of way; the "bar is pretty lively
on weekends", and despite some complaints of "inconsistent"
quality, most feel it's a "cut above" and appreciate the range of
"price levels" too.

Hotoke Sushi & 21 | 22 | 20 | $36
Steakhouse *Japanese/Steak*

Smithtown | Village Ctr. | 41 Rte. 111 (E. Main St.) | 631-979-9222 |
www.hotokejapanese.com

A "citified" space is the backdrop for "beautiful" sushi, "distinctive" rolls and "bursts of flame from hibachis" at this "busy" midpriced Smithtown Japanese steakhouse where locals "bring the
kids and let them enjoy a free show", or else go later on for "date
night"; the "noisy" atmosphere and uneven service are sore points
for some, but others swear by the "awesome" martinis for a
"rocking" good time.

House of Dosas *Indian/Vegetarian* 25 | 9 | 20 | $19

Hicksville | 416 S. Broadway (Boehme St.) | 516-938-7517 |
www.houseofdosas.com

"Eat like a king and you'll never break the bank" at this Hicksville
South Indian offering "exceptional" dosas in sizes "you wouldn't believe", as well as other "spicy" vegetarian dishes "so rich and flavorful" you'll "forget there isn't any meat"; the "spartan interior limits
the appeal", but fortunately the "owner and staff go out of their way
to make you feel at home."

	FOOD	DECOR	SERVICE	COST

House of India *Indian*
21 | 15 | 20 | $30

Huntington | 256B Main St. (New York Ave.) | 631-271-0059 | www.houseofindiarestaurant.com

"Flavorful", "filling" Indian food "prepared as hot or as mild as you want" wins over customers of this "family-run", "accommodating" subcontinental on Huntington's main drag; though the "old-fashioned" decor "lacks imagination", the "freshly made", moderately priced dishes "won't disappoint."

Houston's *American*
22 | 20 | 21 | $35

Garden City | Roosevelt Field Mall | 630 Old Country Rd. (bet. Clinton Rd. & Meadowbrook Pkwy.) | 516-873-1454 | www.hillstone.com

The "crème de la crème" of "grill chains", this "stylish, adult" place in Garden City delivers "properly done", midpriced American eats in a "fern bar" setting with a "happening" after-work scene; "well-informed, efficient" servers add to the "welcoming" vibe, but "long" weekend waits for a table are a drawback.

H.R. Singleton's *American*
18 | 18 | 19 | $33

Bethpage | 150 Hicksville Rd. (Hempstead Tpke.) | 516-731-7065 | www.hrsingletonsrestaurant.com

Offering a "decent", "pub-style" American menu served by a "well-trained" staff, this "comfortable", "family-friendly" "neighborhood place" in Bethpage does the "basics" well, and can even be "fun on the weekends"; the meals are fairly "predictable", but the lunch prix fixe is a "great value."

H2O Seafood Grill *Seafood*
23 | 21 | 21 | $53

Smithtown | 215 W. Main St. (Edgewood Ave.) | 631-361-6464 | www.h2oseafoodgrill.com

Veteran LI chef Michael Meehan offers both "classic" and "imaginative" dishes – from "stellar sushi" to "must-have" seafood crêpes – at this "charming, beachy" Smithtowner specializing in "carefully prepared" fish; there's "accommodating" service, patio seating (though "Jericho Turnpike is not very scenic") and "entertainment some nights in the bar", but some are put off by the "Hamptons"-level tabs.

Hudson & McCoy *Seafood*
18 | 19 | 16 | $43

Freeport | 340 Woodcleft Ave. (bet. Manhattan & Suffolk Sts.) | 516-868-3411 | www.hudsonmccoy.com

"With a young crowd more interested in drinking" than dining, this seasonal seafooder on Freeport's Nautical Mile gets "packed" on summer weekends when "overpowering" live bands play on the patio; upstairs, there's a "balcony view and quieter seating", but some find it "overpriced" for "just ok" eats and "spotty" service; P.S. closed October–May.

Hudson's Mill *American*
22 | 22 | 21 | $43

Massapequa | 5599 Merrick Rd. (Carman Mill Rd.) | 516-799-5394 | www.hudsonsmill.com

Massapequans high on this "inviting" New American commend its "Manhattan-quality" offerings, especially the "sensational steaks and wines" (hit the bar for "recommendations from the 'wine guy'"); its "relaxing", bistro-style interior benefits from "excellent" service and weekly live guitar, and while the prices are slightly upscale, regulars call it "reasonable" all around.

Hunan Taste *Chinese*
22 | 16 | 19 | $35

Greenvale | 3 Northern Blvd. (Wellington Rd.) | 516-621-6616 | www.hunantasterestaurant.com

"Once you go" to this "winning" Hunan "haunt" in Greenvale "you'll definitely go back" declare devotees of its "fairly priced" Chinese cuisine, including "terrific" Peking duck, "delicate" dumplings and "noteworthy" seafood; it's "noisy" and "crowded most of the time" and service can feel "rushed", but most affirm it's "worth the effort to get in" (especially if you "go early").

Iavarone Cafe *Italian*
21 | 14 | 19 | $33

(fka Fratelli Iavarone Cafe)

New Hyde Park | Lake Success Shopping Ctr. | 1534 Union Tpke. (bet. Lakeville & New Hyde Park Rds.) | 516-488-4500 | www.iavaronecafe.com

"Home-cooked" Italian that's "always spot-on" is the attraction at this "family-run" New Hyde Park trattoria, a "definite winner" thanks to "nicely prepared" entrees and "crisp" pizza with "first-rate" toppings; situated in a "shopping center", the "busy", "diner"-esque room (behind the pizzeria) could use an "update", but service from a "cheery staff" is a plus, and so is the gourmet retail store next door.

Il Capuccino Ristorante *Italian*
19 | 17 | 20 | $42

Sag Harbor | 30 Madison St. (bet. Main & Sage Sts.) | 631-725-2747 | www.ilcapuccino.com

"Trustworthy" Italian classics (complemented by "irresistible", "deadly" garlic knots) are served in a "casual" setting decorated with traditional "trappings" like "cute checkered tablecloths and Chianti bottles hanging from the ceiling" at this "old Sag Harbor fave"; even if the room "could be more pleasing", it's a "good family" place where the staff "remembers you" and prices are "decent" as well, so most guests leave "smiling."

Il Classico 🅼 *Italian*
23 | 19 | 22 | $47

Massapequa Park | 4857 Merrick Rd. (bet. Cartwright & Park Blvds.) | 516-798-8496 | www.ilclassico.net

This "fabulous Northern Italian should be in NYC" praise Massapequa Park *paesani* who call it an "outstanding eatery masquerading as a simple neighborhood restaurant"; "personal service", "beautiful" surroundings and live music on Thursdays further elevate the upscale experience, particularly for "special dinners and celebrations."

🆉 Il Mulino New York *Italian*
27 | 23 | 25 | $77

Roslyn Estates | 1042 Northern Blvd. (bet. Cedar Path & Searingtown Rd.) | 516-621-1870 | www.ilmulino.com

"Exceptional", "abundant" Northern Italian cuisine, "delivered with panache" by a "superb" staff, creates an "exquisite" (if "over-the-top") experience at this "romantic" Roslyn branch of the Manhattan classic, geared toward the "LI elite"; while some patrons pout about "dim" lighting and "too much of everything" for "shockingly expensive" tabs, most don't mind splurging on the "amazing" "feast"; P.S. the Sunday prix fixe is a more "reasonable" option.

Il Villagio Trattoria *Italian*   ▽ 24 | 22 | 24 | $44

Malverne | 366 Hempstead Ave. (Arlington Ave.) | 516-792-6336

Shoehorned into a tiny "strip-mall" storefront, this "cozy" Italian arrival brings "delicious" food, "upscale ambiance" and "top-notch" service to Malverne; convenient to the train station, it's quickly become a "go-to place" for locals, though some "just wish the space were bigger."

NEW Imperial Seoul *Japanese/Korean*   - | - | - | E

New Hyde Park | 3365 Hillside Ave. (bet. Herricks Rd. & Moore St.) | 516-741-2340

Waitresses dressed in traditional Korean billowy skirts and embroidered tops greet guests at this classy New Hyde Park newcomer where the menu ranges from Japanese sushi and sashimi to Korean BBQ; the red-and-white tiled rooms are divided by bamboo stalks, with shoji screens creating small, private dining areas.

Indian Cove *American/Seafood*   18 | 19 | 18 | $43

Hampton Bays | 258 E. Montauk Hwy. (off Canoe Place Rd.) | 631-728-5366 | www.indiancoverestaurantmarina.com

An "extraordinary view with ordinary food" is one take on this Hampton Bays American seafooder that's best in summer for live music and "wonderful drinks" "upstairs on the deck" watching the passing boats; while it's "pleasant" enough for some, others feel the "haphazard" service and "hit-or-miss" fare land it in "tourist-trap" territory; P.S. closed Tuesday–Wednesday in the off-season.

Indian Wells Tavern *American*   17 | 15 | 18 | $34

Amagansett | 177 Main St. (bet. Cozzins & Windmill Lns.) | 631-267-0400 | www.indianwellstavern.com

A "lively", "family-oriented" "locals' hangout" in Amagansett, this year-round East Ender offers "standard" but "satisfying" American tavern grub with service that some find "more consistent" at lunch; even if it's a fairly "typical bar" (with "acoustics that could use some adjusting"), the "unpretentious atmosphere" and "good prices" make it a "nice change from the chichi" competition; P.S. BYO welcome, with a $10 corkage fee.

Inlet Seafood *Seafood*   21 | 19 | 20 | $48

Montauk | 541 E. Lake Dr. (opp. Montauk Airport) | 631-668-4272 | www.inletseafood.com

"Right on the inlet", this "casual" (yet slightly "pricey") two-floor Montauk seafooder boasts "amazing" sunset views to accompany the "limited menu" of fin fare (including "great sushi") that's fresh "off the boats" of the "fishermen owners"; there's a "lovely wine list, especially from local vineyards", though "long waits" and no reservations are a drawback; P.S. closed January–March.

Inn Spot on the Bay ◑ *Eclectic/Seafood*

19 | 21 | 19 | $53

Hampton Bays | 32 Lighthouse Rd. (Foster Ave.) | 631-728-1200 | www.theinnspot.com

Bringing together "spectacular" views of the bay and "tasty" seafood-centric Eclectic fare, this "gorgeous" Hampton Bays charmer in a Victorian beach house is fit for a "romantic sunset dinner"; some critics complain of "inconsistent" food that's "not worth the price", but more are pleased with the "accommodating" kitchen and "enjoyable" setting; P.S. in winter, it's open for Thursday–Sunday dinner and weekend brunch.

Intermezzo *Italian*

23 | 18 | 21 | $34

Fort Salonga | Village Plaza | 10 Fort Salonga Rd. (Bread & Cheese Hollow Rd.) | 631-261-4840 | www.intermezzorestaurantny.com

The pizza is "thin-crusted" and "delicious" but there are other "fine Italian dishes" too at this "little gem tucked away in a shopping center" in the "restaurant desert of Fort Salonga"; "affordable prices" and service that "makes you feel so welcome" help offset the "small", "somewhat noisy" surroundings.

International Delight Cafe ⇗ *Diner*

18 | 9 | 17 | $20

Bellmore | 322 Bedford Ave. (Wilson Ave.) | 516-409-5772
Rockville Centre | 241 Sunrise Hwy. (bet. N. Park & N. Village Aves.) | 516-766-7557 ◑
www.internationaldelightcafe.com

"Leave room for dessert" advise sweet-toothed surveyors who frequent these Bellmore and Rockville Centre diners for good old American "comfort food" and "heavenly" gelato (enough flavors to "make your head spin") scooped high on "terrific" Belgian waffles; beyond that they're just plain vanilla in menu and atmosphere, but still do the trick for a "quick, cheap" bite; P.S. cash-only; open late on the weekends.

Irish Coffee Pub *Continental/Irish*

23 | 22 | 23 | $41

East Islip | 131 Carleton Ave. (bet. Stewart & Wall Sts.) | 631-277-0007 | www.irishcoffeepub.com

"Calling it a pub is a misnomer" report regulars of this "huge" East Islip "icon" with several "warm, comfortable" dining rooms providing the "best potato soup in NY" as well as other "excellent" Continental and Irish dishes; a "well-dressed", "congenial" crowd and frequent live Irish folk music create a "party atmosphere", while "top-shelf service" ("usually with a brogue") completes the "night out in the old country"; P.S. it's a popular venue for "catered events."

Island Mermaid *American/Seafood*

20 | 20 | 19 | $48

Ocean Beach | Fire Island | 780 Bay Walk (Evergreen Walk) | 631-583-8088 | www.islandmermaid.com

A "real summer tradition" for "breathtaking" sunset drinks and "creative" New American fare enjoyed on a "wonderful deck", this Ocean Beach seafooder next to the ferry basin is still a "great place to gather" after 20 years; the "friendly" "island feel" is just right for a "daycation", though a couple of patrons pooh-pooh the food as merely "ok"; P.S. there's a $39 prix fixe "Taste of Fire Island" special that includes a ferry ticket and parking.

Ivy Cottage *American*

| 23 | 19 | 21 | $46 |

Williston Park | 38 Hillside Ave. (Nassau Blvd.) | 516-877-2343 | www.ivycottagerestaurant.com

"Succulent", high-end American dishes are served in "hearty" portions at this "delightful little place" "nestled in the quaint village" of Williston Park; service is "above average" and the "snug" setting is "lovely for small gatherings", though perhaps not ideal for "accommodating large ones"; P.S. "reserve about a month in advance."

Izumi Ⓜ *Asian*

| ∇ 23 | 23 | 24 | $35 |

Bethpage | Bethpage Mktpl. | 440 N. Wantagh Ave. (Carson St.) | 516-933-7225 | www.izumifood.com

"Kudos" go to this Asian eatery in a Bethpage strip mall that "doesn't look like much from the outside" but puts forth "impressively presented", "outstanding sushi" and "unique appetizers" among an array of Thai, Chinese and Japanese dishes; a "hip", "city" feel and "warm, efficient" service also help "separate it" from the competition.

🆕 Jack Halyards
American Bar & Grill *American/Seafood*
(fka Fiddleheads)

| 23 | 17 | 22 | $40 |

Oyster Bay | 62 South St. (Hamilton Ave.) | 516-922-2999 | www.jackhalyards.com

"A refreshing change" from "its previous life as Fiddleheads", this "new kid on the block" in Oyster Bay serves "inventive", "seafood-oriented" American fare in a "fixed-up" space with a nautical theme and a "neighborhood feel"; add an "attentive staff", "affordable" tabs and live music three nights per week, and most "can't wait to go back."

🆕 Jackson Hall
American Bar & Grille *American*

| - | - | - | M |

East Islip | 335 E. Main St. (Overlook Dr.) | 631-277-7100 | www.jacksonhallbarandgrille.com

Airy and handsomely designed with mahogany woods, white tablecloths and a stacked stone wall, this East Islip New American offers an extensive menu, from salads, pastas and seafood to stonecooked pizza, as well as gluten-free items; live music on Fridays and a snazzy lineup of martinis (there's even a PB&J rendition) tempt tipplers to stay at the inviting bar to sip and nibble on classic apps.

Jaiya *Thai*

| 19 | 13 | 17 | $30 |

Hicksville | 46 W. Old Country Rd. (bet. Jerusalem Ave. & S. B'way) | 516-681-3400 | www.jaiya.com

"They don't kid around when it comes to spiciness" at this Hicksville Thai (with a Manhattan sib) that serves "authentic, elegant" dishes "full of flavor" and "heat" (so "make sure to clarify" how much you can take); the "coffee-shop digs" have "seen better days", though, and the staff gets mixed reviews, which might explain why it's "never crowded"; P.S. closed Tuesdays.

Jamesport Country Kitchen *American*   23 | 17 | 22 | $38

Jamesport | 1601 Main Rd. (Manor Ln.) | 631-722-3537 |
www.northfork.com

"Relying on local produce and seafood", chef-owner Matthew Kar prepares "inspired", "sophisticated" New American dishes paired with a "wonderful selection of Long Island wines" at this "quaint" "farmhouse setting" in Jamesport; add in "pleasant" service and "reasonable" prices, and you have a "true country kitchen experience" with a bit of "big-city" expertise.

☑ Jamesport Manor Inn *American*   23 | 25 | 22 | $56

Jamesport | 370 Manor Ln. (bet. Main Rd. & Sound Ave.) | 631-722-0500 |
www.jamesportmanorinn.com

Inside a "beautifully reconstructed old" Jamesport manor, this "first-rate" New American by owner Matthew Kar (Jamesport Country Kitchen) provides "high-end", "delicious" dishes with "unexpected" touches and a "good choice of local wines" served by a generally "courteous, competent" staff; though it's a bit "out-of-the-way", most guests agree it's "worth loading the GPS for", plus the "second-floor art gallery makes for an interesting diversion after your meal"; P.S. closed Tuesdays.

NEW J&C 68 *Asian*   - | - | - | M

Farmingville | 654 Horseblock Rd. (Pommer Ave.) | 631-736-6688

Handling a hat trick of cuisines – Japanese, Chinese and Thai – this casual new Farmingville Pan-Asian plies a midpriced menu running the gamut from spicy basil beef to Hunan lamb, with the owner turning out impressive rolls at a two-seater sushi bar; the unfussy setting sports compact booths and a koi-filled fish tank.

NEW Janine's *American*   - | - | - | E

Hauppauge | 470 Wheeler Rd. (Rabro Dr.) | 631-761-5602 |
www.janine470.com

Named for the owner's daughter, this Hauppauge newcomer offers American fare along the lines of crispy wild salmon and filet mignon with bordelaise sauce in a setting decorated with mirrors, posters and a variety of wooden chairs; P.S. there's a weekday happy hour with drink specials at the roomy bar and live music on Friday nights.

NEW JD Steakhouse Ⓜ *Steak*   ∇ 19 | 13 | 19 | $45

Southold | 62375 Main Rd. (Old Main Rd.) | 631-876-5101

Just outside of Southold, this new "house of beef" across from Port of Egypt (in the former Cimino's space) offers "large portions" of "decent food at a decent price", with a focus on "melt-in-your-mouth" steaks; so while some customers "could do without the old-time" decor, it's a "consistent", "simple" choice for "family dinners and larger groups."

Jean Marie Patisserie & Bistro *American*   ∇ 22 | 12 | 20 | $20

Great Neck | 66 Middle Neck Rd. (bet. Elm St. & Gussack Plaza) |
516-304-5439 | www.jeanmariepatisserie.com

After a recent move to roomier digs in the heart of Great Neck, this "casual" bakery/cafe now underpins its "superb" pastries and "inventive sandwiches" with American bistro fare to furnish "well-prepared" "light" bites for lunch or dinner; "friendly" servers and "reasonable" prices round out a "delightful surprise", even if it's "far from real French"; P.S. the Decor score does not reflect the relocation.

Jeff's Seafood & Galley *Seafood*

∇ 20	9	17	$30

East Northport | Elwood Plaza | 1965 Jericho Tpke. (Elwood Rd.) | 631-858-2393

Expect nothing less than "fresh seafood" at this "takeout"-geared East Northport eatery that's simply a "fish store with a few tables on the side", dressed up with murals and an ocean of teal and sea blue; kids get a kick out of kitschy maritime effects like barrels and netting, and for adults, "BYO is always fun", even if a few feel it's "a little pricey" for the portions.

Jimmy Hays *Steak*

25	21	23	$62

Island Park | 4310 Austin Blvd. (Kingston Blvd.) | 516-432-5155 | www.jimmyhayssteakhouse.com

"Don't waste gas to go to a North Shore steakhouse" when this handsome "carnivore's delight" near the beach in Island Park "delivers on all fronts", with a "professional" team serving "top-grade", "properly cooked" beef and lobster, along with "kick-ass" cocktails; a "premium price" comes with the "buzzing" "NYC ambiance", but filet fanatics don't mind forking it over for a "superb" meal.

John Harvard's
Brew House ❶ *Pub Food*

16	15	17	$29

Lake Grove | Smith Haven Mall | 2093 Smith Haven Mall (Moriches Rd.) | 631-979-2739 | www.johnharvards.com

"Terrific beer" is all you need to know about this "casual" brewpub branch in Lake Grove dispensing a "wide selection" of "craft-brewed" suds to wash down "ok" American "comfort food"; though it can "feel like a frat house" ("expect a drinking crowd"), it's perfectly "adequate" as an "after-work hangout" with "reasonable prices."

Jolly Fisherman &
Steak House Ⓜ *Seafood/Steak*

21	16	20	$48

Roslyn | 25 Main St. (bet. E. B'way & Old Northern Blvd.) | 516-621-0055 | www.jollyfishermanrestaurant.com

Longtime loyalists of this "family-oriented" Roslyn "landmark" laud its "rock-solid seafood", "reliable" steaks and "specialty breads", saying it's "still great after all these years" with "helpful" service and a "bargain" lunch deal; though some patrons ponder "what's older, the menu or the crowd?" and deride "downer" decor, the gist is "nothing ever changes, and you either love that or hate it."

Jonathan's *American*

20	20	21	$39

Garden City Park | 3000 Jericho Tpke. (Herricks Rd.) | 516-742-7300 | www.jonathansrestaurant.net

"Always dependable", this Garden City Park standby comes through with a "moderately priced", "extensive" New American menu offering "something to please everyone's palate"; the spacious, "attractive" dining rooms and "hospitable" service are a hit with "families and large parties", while the bar is a "better experience" for intimate meals, though the whole package is a little "boring" for some.

Jonathan's Ristorante *Italian* | 24 | 22 | 23 | $50 |

Huntington | 15 Wall St. (bet. Gerard & Main Sts.) | 631-549-0055 | www.jonathansristorante.com

"Refined" Italian dishes, "lovely specials" and an "impressive" wine list draw diners to this "high-end" standout in the "crowded food hamlet of Huntington village"; the staff "makes you feel like you're the only table in the place" while the "charming atmosphere" is enhanced by French doors and a "cute little patio", so forget the "up-scale price tags" and "enjoy."

JT's Corner Cafe *American* | 23 | 14 | 18 | $25 |

Nesconset | 204 Smithtown Blvd. (bet. Joseph Pl. & Lake Ave. S.) | 631-265-5267 | www.jtscornercafe.com

It's "like News 12 – local as local gets" remark regulars of this "little diner-style" American "storefront" in Nesconset turning out "top-quality", "eclectic" breakfast and lunch items all day (including "all different types of pancakes and French toast"); service can be "spotty" and it may "not be worth a special trip", but it's a "satisfy-ing" choice for most; P.S. closes at 8 PM (3 PM Sundays).

Kabul Afghani Cuisine *Afghan* | 23 | 16 | 21 | $31 |

Huntington | 1153 E. Jericho Tpke. (bet. Dix Hills Rd. & Park Ave.) | 631-549-5506 | www.kabulny.com

"Tender" kebabs and "terrific vegetarian" eats have the power to "awaken new taste buds" at this Huntington Afghan "mainstay in a strip mall" that's been "consistently" "wonderful" "for many years"; though it's "time to change the decor", the "affordable" fare, "excel-lent" service and "entertaining belly dancing on Fridays" make din-ing here a "treat."

Kawasaki Japanese Steakhouse Ⓜ *Japanese* | ▽ 19 | 17 | 22 | $32 |

Long Beach | 22 E. Park Ave. (bet. Edwards & Riverside Blvds.) | 516-889-6699

"If you want fancy, this may not be the place", but if you want a "show", the hibachi grill at this Long Beach Japanese is "always en-tertaining" for "tweens" and others who like to see their meats and veggies tossed and sizzled before their eyes (sushi is also available); a few feel the space needs more upkeep and the food could be "bet-ter", but the "friendly" service is a hit.

King Umberto *Italian* | 23 | 15 | 22 | $38 |

Elmont | 1343 Hempstead Tpke. (Meacham Ave.) | 516-352-3232 | www.kingumberto.com

The distinctive "aroma of garlic" and red sauce wafts through the air at this "popular", "slightly upscale" Elmont "throwback" where the "masses" assemble for "standout" pizza, Italian dishes "done right" and a "value-filled wine list"; "cheerful banter with the staff" is an-other plus, and "you'll be pleasantly surprised at the results" if you "ask for suggestions"; P.S. "reservations are a must."

	FOOD	DECOR	SERVICE	COST

NEW Kinha Sushi *Japanese*

-	-	-	M

Garden City | 988 Franklin Ave. (bet. 9th & 10th Sts.) | 516-877-0888 | www.kinhasushi.com

Some 30 sakes are on hand at this midpriced Japanese newcomer in Garden City where a fusion influence can be found in dishes such as lobster mango ceviche and Peking duck crêpe with pickled plum and mentaiko butter sauce; chairs and banquettes are covered in black leather and red fabric in a setting illuminated by seductive lighting.

Kiraku *Japanese*

∇ 26	20	22	$37

Glen Head | 127 Glen Head Rd. (bet. Benjamin & Wall Sts.) | 516-676-3686 | www.kirakurestaurant.com

The "innovative sushi" at this "gracious" Glen Head Japanese looks "too pretty to eat", but once you do "you're in heaven" sigh loyalists who laud a menu with "so many different rolls, it's hard to decide"; though often "busy", the setting is "romantic" enough for "date night", while "nice" tatami booths, an array of cocktails and "reasonable" prices pull in larger groups.

Kiran Palace *Indian*

24	14	23	$26

Hicksville | Delco Plaza | 67-75 E. Old Country Rd. (S. B'way) | 516-932-5191 | www.kiranpalacehicksville.net
Levittown | Dunkin Donuts Plaza | 2934 Hempstead Tpke. (bet. Center Ln. & Division Ave.) | 516-796-2600 | www.kiranpalacelevittown.com
Commack | Commack Corners | 6092 Jericho Tpke. (Commack Rd.) | 631-462-0003 | www.kiranpalace.net

"Fabulous, authentic" Indian fare, including a "bargain lunch buffet" with plenty of "interesting choices" and "subtly spicy" dishes, makes diners "happy" at this subcontinental trio with "helpful" service; though calling it a palace may be a stretch given the "hole-in-the-wall" surroundings, it's "popular" nonetheless – and there's always takeout.

Kiss'o *Japanese*

21	16	19	$36

New Hyde Park | Lake Success Shopping Ctr. | 1532 Union Tpke. (bet. Lakeville & New Hyde Park Rds.) | 516-355-0587 | www.kisso-sushi.com

Make a day of sushi, sake and shopping at this New Hyde Park strip-mall "oasis" where the "special rolls are delicious" and the bento-box "lunch deals are not to be missed"; "for those not into raw fish, there's plenty" to enjoy, all at a "decent price" and served "without attitude."

☒ Kitchen A Bistro ✍ *French*

27	19	23	$51

St. James | 404 N. Country Rd. (Edgewood Ave.) | 631-862-0151 | www.kitchenabistro.com

It "doesn't get any better" declare devotees of this "super-relaxed" "rare find" in St. James, where "outstanding" chef-owner Eric Lomando crafts "awesome" French bistro dishes (including "unique" seafood specials) with "novel twists and turns"; it's a touch "less crowded" now that it's in "the old Mirabelle space", and the staff provides "helpful" service, plus it's a "bargain with BYO and no corkage charge"; P.S. cash-only and "reservations are a must", so "plan in advance."

FOOD | DECOR | SERVICE | COST

⧉ Kitchen A Trattoria Ⓜ⌿ *Italian* · 28 | 16 | 25 | $42

St. James | 532 N. Country Rd. (Lake Ave.) | 631-584-3518 |
www.kitchenatrattoria.com

It's even "better than Kitchen A Bistro" marvel guests of this "exciting" St. James spin-off from chef-owner Eric Lomando, a "foodies' haven" proffering "inspired seasonal Italian dishes" you "dream about", served by a "terrific" staff; the "shockingly small" space is "still a bit rough" and it "takes a while to get a reservation" (required on weekends), but it's "worth adjusting your schedule to eat here"; P.S. the BYO policy and prix fixe specials "make it a steal."

Koenig's *Continental/German* · 19 | 14 | 19 | $36

Floral Park | 86 S. Tyson Ave. (Mayflower Pl.) | 516-354-2300 |
www.koenigsrestaurant.com

"Still going strong", this moderately priced Floral Park "institution" "hits the spot" when only "roast beef on that fabulous rye" or "sauerbraten you can eat without a knife" will quiet a German-Continental craving; it's a "sentimental favorite" for "older" customers who take comfort in the familiarity and "amicable" service, and don't mind being "transported back to 1950" to enjoy it.

⧉ Kotobuki Ⓜ *Japanese* · 27 | 18 | 20 | $41

Roslyn | Harborview Shoppes | 1530 Old Northern Blvd.
(bet. Northern Blvd. & Skillman St.) | 516-621-5312
Babylon | 86 Deer Park Ave. (Main St.) | 631-321-8387
Hauppauge | 377 Nesconset Hwy. (bet. Brooksite Dr. & Hauppauge Rd.) |
631-360-3969
www.kotobukinewyork.com

"Best. sushi. ever." declare diners in awe of this "phenomenal" Japanese trio, "Long Island's answer to Nobu" serving fish so "sumptuous" it's worth getting in line and "waiting for the doors to open"; the "highly skilled chefs" create other "inventive" dishes as well, and the value's "amazing", but remember that variable service and "cramped" settings (apart from the Roslyn patio) are part of the deal; P.S. no reservations.

Kumo Sushi *Japanese* · 25 | 18 | 19 | $37

Plainview | Manetto Hill Mall | 18 Manetto Hill Rd. (bet. Old Country Rd. &
Washington Ave.) | 516-681-8881 | www.kumosushi.net

Reviewers "rave" about the "delectable" sushi creations, e.g. a "unique" spicy-tuna "pizza sandwich", at this Japanese "hidden treasure" "in a Plainview strip mall"; though service varies and the "packed" crowd can be "ear-numbing", most agree it's a "top-notch" place to "spend an evening with friends" when you "don't want to spend a fortune."

Kurabarn Ⓜ *Japanese* · 24 | 17 | 21 | $37

Huntington | 479 New York Ave. (bet. High & Hillcrest Sts.) |
631-673-0060 | www.kurabarn.com

Serving "fresh, inventive sushi", this "charming" Japanese that's "been in Huntington forever" (since 1978) is a "popular" choice with moderate prices; the "peaceful interior" and "efficient service" are further draws, attracting regulars who say it "feels like home"; P.S. reservations taken for groups of five or more.

Kurofune *Japanese*

| 23 | 16 | 22 | $34 |

Commack | 77 Commack Rd. (Jericho Tpke.) | 631-499-1075 | www.kurofunerestaurant.com

"Excellent" sushi and other "authentic" Japanese eats served by a "marvelous staff" are the calling cards of this Commack veteran that's been a "neighborhood" staple "for many years"; "there are more attractive" settings than the "modest" space here, but given the "unpretentious", "comfortable" vibe and "consistently fresh" offerings, most believe it "should be busier than it is."

La Bottega *Italian*

| 21 | 15 | 18 | $22 |

Floral Park | 49 Covert Ave. (Drew Ave.) | 516-216-5177
Garden City | 147 Nassau Blvd. (bet. Newmarket Rd. & Stratford Ave.) | 516-486-0935
Massapequa Park | 4883 Merrick Rd. (bet. Cartwright & Park Blvds.) | 516-799-4444
Oceanside | 3216 Long Beach Rd. (Montgomery Ave.) | 516-543-4540
NEW **Plainview** | Plainview Ctr. | 397A S. Oyster Bay Rd. (Woodbury Rd.) | 516-605-1280
NEW **Port Washington** | 138 Shore Rd. (off Fairway Dr.) | 516-439-5165
Rockville Centre | 234C Merrick Rd. (Village Ave.) | 516-593-4930
Roslyn | 1424 Old Northern Blvd. (Remsen Ave.) | 516-621-2685
Huntington | 9 Wall St. (bet. Gerard & Main Sts.) | 631-271-3540
www.labottegagourmet.com
Additional locations throughout the Long Island area

Caffe Barocco *Italian*

Garden City | 143 Nassau Blvd. S. (7th St.) | 516-292-0144 | www.caffebarocco.com

"Panini paradise" can be found at this "expanding" Italian chain that's "taken LI by storm" with its "dizzying" array of "flavor-packed" sandwiches and "inventive" salads; detractors denounce "slow service", "cramped quarters" and "largely absent" decor, but takeout is always an option for "one of the best bargains" around; P.S. Caffe Barocco features a "creative" tapas-style menu and 400-bottle wine list.

La Bussola *Italian*

| 23 | 18 | 22 | $54 |

Glen Cove | 40 School St. (bet. Glen St. & Highland Rd.) | 516-671-2100 | www.labussolaristorante.com

It's "been there forever" for a reason say fans of this "real keeper" (the parent of Piccola Bussola) that dishes out "hefty" portions of "robust", upscale Italian in Glen Cove; the "on-point" staff is always "willing to please" ("if something is not on the menu, they'll make it"), so even if the "dark", "old-fashioned" interior seems a bit "dated" to some, the majority maintains "you won't be disappointed."

La Cocina de Marcia Ⓜ *American/Spanish*

| - | - | - | I |

Freeport | 77B W. Merrick Rd. (bet. Church St. & Guy Lombardo Ave.) | 516-986-5222 | www.lacocinademarcia.com

Located in a storefront in Freeport, this new Spanish-American serves affordable fare such as Dominican chicken soup and mofongo (mashed plantains), chopped roast pork and barbecued chicken in warmly hued quarters hung with brightly colored paintings; it's named for one of the owners, whose mom is also in the kitchen.

La Coquille *French*
24 | 22 | 24 | $61

Manhasset | 1669 Northern Blvd. (Manhasset Woods Rd.) | 516-365-8422 | www.la-coquille-manhasset.com

The "quintessential go-to place for any special occasion", this "upper-class" Manhasset "tradition" has "stood the test of time", with its "meticulously prepared", "*magnifique*" French dinners enhanced by "white-glove" service, "fine wines" and a "delightful rolling table of desserts"; the setting is full of "old-world charm" "reminiscent of Paris", though a few just "wish it were open for lunch"; P.S. the "prix fixe during the week is a plus."

La Famiglia Ⓜ *Italian*
22 | 16 | 21 | $35

Plainview | 641 Old Country Rd. (bet. Barnum & Belmont Aves.) | 516-938-2050
Smithtown | 250 W. Main St. (Brookside Dr.) | 631-382-9454
www.lafamiglia-ny.com

As the name suggests, "family-style" dining rules at these "nice-value" Plainview and Smithtown Italians that are "better with lots of friends" since you "never leave without leftovers"; they're "not fancy" and sometimes "crowded", but they're both made more "comfortable" by a "thoughtful" staff and "homey" food that's "worth returning for"; P.S. reservations accepted for parties of six or more.

La Ginestra *Italian*
25 | 18 | 23 | $56

Glen Cove | 50 Forest Ave. (bet. Elliott Pl. & Walnut Rd.) | 516-674-2244 | www.laginestrarestaurant.com

"Innovative specials", "unforgettable" homemade pastas, "out-of-this-world" seafood and "excellent desserts" all shine at this "outstanding" Sicilian in Glen Cove staffed by a "personable", "professional" crew; though it's "expensive" and a handful says the "homey" room could use some "updating", "you always feel welcome" and know you'll be treated to "traditional Italian at its best."

La Gioconda Ⓜ *Continental/Italian*
21 | 17 | 24 | $40

Great Neck | 21 N. Station Plaza (bet. Bond & Park Sts.) | 516-466-2004 | www.lagiocondarestaurant.com

"Exceptional" hospitality marks this "small", "family-owned" trattoria near the Great Neck train station, where an "attentive" team serves "hearty" portions of "classic" Continental-Southern Italian cooking "done right"; it's "a bit old-fashioned", but the "consistent" quality and appealing "price point" (especially for the Tuesday-Thursday and Sunday prix fixe) ensure "many repeat" customers – and they "remember you when you return."

Laguna Grille *Nuevo Latino*
20 | 17 | 19 | $30

Woodbury | Woodbury Village Shopping Ctr. | 7927 Jericho Tpke. (S. Woods Rd.) | 516-682-8000 | www.lagunagrille.com

Loyalists "love to take the family" to this "vibrant" Nuevo Latino in a Woodbury shopping center where "kids eat free" (up to two per party, age 10 and under) and the "huge menu", including "delicious fried plantains" and "tasty, filling salads" with "Caribbean flair", has "something for everyone"; the servers are "friendly", so even when it's "busy" and "noisy", fans don't mind soaking up the "amazing energy" and "sipping a margarita."

Z Lake House 🅼 *American* | 28 | 24 | 26 | $60 |

Bay Shore | 240 W. Main St. (bet. Garner Ln. & Lawrence Ave.) | 631-666-0995 | www.thelakehouserest.com

"Spectacular meals" deliver "pure bliss in every aspect" at this Bay Shore "beauty" where co-owners Eileen and Matthew (a "true artist" chef) Connors provide "exquisite" New American dining accompanied by "gorgeous views" of the lake; the outdoor fire pit is "perfect for a romantic occasion" and the "exceptional" staff pulls it all together, so it's "well worth the cost" and the "drive" to experience "one of the best restaurants on Long Island."

NEW La Maison *American* ∇ | 18 | 20 | 19 | $55 |

Sag Harbor | 16 Main St. (bet. Nassau & Water Sts.) | 631-899-4609

A "new kid on the block" occupying the former JLX Bistro space in Sag Harbor, this New American bistro (under the aegis of the Trata team) is a "welcome" arrival with "utterly charming" decor flaunting chocolate banquettes, a golden ceiling and "well-placed" seating "both inside and out"; the upmarket menu takes an "innovative", seafood-centric tack, though hedgers hint it's "not quite there yet."

La Marmite *French/Italian* | 24 | 21 | 24 | $56 |

Williston Park | 234 Hillside Ave. (bet. Campbell Ave. & Mineola Blvd.) | 516-746-1243 | www.lamarmiterestaurant.com

"Fantastic" French–Northern Italian dishes are served by a longtime "first-class" staff ("they watched my kids grow up") at this "tasteful" Williston Park veteran, an "elegant" choice for "celebrating major events"; the room is "traditional" and a bit "sedate", but most can't get enough of its "old-world atmosphere."

La Nonna Bella Ristorante 🅼 *Italian* ∇ | 21 | 20 | 22 | $41 |

Garden City | 660 Franklin Ave. (7th St.) | 516-248-0366 | www.lanonnabella.com

Grandma would be proud of the "classic" homestyle cooking and meatballs "to die for" at this "well-run" Italian, an "underappreciated player" on the Garden City scene that's "getting more popular" as new ownership under chef Lino De Vivo (who has always cooked there) takes a somewhat more refined turn; "bring the family" and settle into plush banquettes while the "efficient" staff sees to your needs, or get "comfortable" at the large bar.

La Novella Ristorante 🅼 *Italian* ∇ | 19 | 12 | 22 | $41 |

East Meadow | 364 E. Meadow Ave. (Prospect Ave.) | 516-794-6248 | www.lanovella.com

A "home away from home" for East Meadow neighbors, this "charming family place" earns props for its "well-prepared" Northern Italian specialties, "warm" greetings from the owner and live guitar during the week; the lunch prix fixe is a further draw, though a few dissenters call it just "ok" with "outdated" digs.

La Pace with Chef Michael M *Italian* — 25 | 22 | 25 | $60

Glen Cove | 51 Cedar Swamp Rd. (3rd St.) | 516-671-2970 | www.lapaceglencove.com

Glen Covers commend this "top" Tuscan that's been an "excellent choice for years" with its "superb", high-end menu, "interesting specials" and "fine service" (chef Michael Mossallam himself "likes to walk around and meet patrons"); there are "lovely private areas for parties or romance" as well as a "vibrant" bar, and if it all feels "antiquated" to some, others simply label it "classic."

La Panchita *Mexican/Spanish* — ▽ 22 | 16 | 22 | $27

Smithtown | 67 W. Main St. (bet. Karl & Maple Aves.) | 631-360-0627

It's "always festive" at this Smithtowner serving "well-done" Spanish and Mexican dishes and "pitchers of homemade sangria" for "reasonable prices"; though the interior doesn't dazzle, the "wonderful" staff and "sweet serenades" from occasional mariachi bands make it a "favorite" for many.

☒ La Parma *Italian* — 23 | 15 | 20 | $42

Oceanside | 410 Merrick Rd. (Saratoga St.) | 516-763-1815
Port Washington | 415 Main St. (2nd Ave.) | 516-439-4960
Williston Park | 707 Willis Ave. (Henry St.) | 516-294-6610 M
Huntington | 452 Jericho Tpke. (bet. Chickory & Sheppard Lns.) | 631-367-6360 M
www.laparma.com

"Expect to wait" or "go on a weekday to avoid the crowds" at this Italian quartet that's best for "large groups" given the "abundant" plates of "tasty", "family-style" fare with "garlic, garlic, garlic"; critics complain that service is "rushed", prices are "a little steep for the style" and the decor "leaves a lot to be desired", but others shrug it's "no frills – just a great meal."

La Parmigiana M *Italian* — 22 | 10 | 17 | $32

Southampton | 48 Hampton Rd. (bet. Main & Pine Sts.) | 631-283-8030

"Still going strong" after 37 years and counting, this "*famiglia*"-run Southampton joint slings "delicious" "red-gravy" Italian in "humongous portions" ("you need two doggy bags") served "family-style" by folks "who make you feel right at home"; the "great value" keeps the "casual" quarters "packed and noisy" with "lots of kids", so touchy types tend to "prefer the takeout."

La Piazza *Pizza* — 21 | 14 | 17 | $27

Merrick | 2191 Merrick Rd. (bet. Frankel & Lincoln Blvds.) | 516-546-2500
Plainview | Crossroads Shopping Ctr. | 1137 Old Country Rd. (Manetto Hill Rd.) | 516-938-0800
NEW Melville | 512 Walt Whitman Rd. (Holland St.) | 631-425-0500
www.lapiazzaonline.com

Pie partisans brave lines "out the door" and "loud" crowds to dig into "delicious" brick-oven pizza and "flavorful" pasta at this affordable, "family-oriented" trio; "decor and service are secondary" and "all

FOOD | DECOR | SERVICE | COST

the commotion could be a turnoff" to some, but most agree that these joints "get it right."

☑ La Piccola Liguria ⓂItalian   27 | 21 | 27 | $59

Port Washington | 47 Shore Rd. (bet. Mill Pond & Old Shore Rds.) | 516-767-6490

A "loyal cadre of regulars" "loves to hear" the "highly experienced" waiters recite a "mind-boggling" list of specials in "succulent detail" at this "outstanding" Port Washington Northern Italian where the "brilliantly executed" dishes are among "the best on the Island"; the "minimally decorated", "sweet setting" fills up fast, so it's "hard to get a reservation" (and "not cheap"), but you're treated "like royalty."

La Pizzetta Ⓜ Italian   21 | 14 | 20 | $34

East Norwich | 1008 Oyster Bay Rd. (bet. Hawthorne Rd. & Northern Blvd.) | 516-624-7800

Marinara mavens get their Italian "comfort-food" fix at this East Norwich "neighborhood joint", the "perfect venue for an easy meal", whether it's "great pasta and pizza" or other "well-prepared" dishes; though some say there's "no ambiance" to speak of, others call it "upscale casual", adding the "everyone-knows-everyone" vibe goes well with the "steady" "home cooking."

☑ La Plage Eclectic   27 | 19 | 24 | $59

Wading River | 131 Creek Rd. (Sound Rd.) | 631-744-9200 | www.laplagerestaurant.net

Though it's an "unlikely location" for "truly inventive" cuisine, this "beachy" "oasis" sited well "out of the way" in Wading River is a "special" "find" for "exuberant cooking" from chef-owner Wayne Wadington, whose "elegantly prepared", "beautifully presented" Eclectic dishes are matched with "knowledgeable" service; the "small" "cottage" setting may seem at odds with the "steep" tabs, but most maintain it's "totally charming" and "so worth the trip" (use "the GPS"); P.S. "reservations are a must" on weekends.

La P'tite Framboise French   22 | 19 | 20 | $40

Port Washington | 294 Main St. (bet. Bank & Jackson Sts.) | 516-767-7164 | www.reststarinc.com

Admirers "appreciate" this "romantic little bistro hiding in Port Washington" (sister to Bistros Cassis and Citron) that's a "pleasant" choice for "solid" French fare served in a simple setting with a "nice buzz"; the service and value are generally "good", so even though there's "room for improvement", most feel it's "worth" tolerating the "lousy parking" situation.

Lareira Portuguese   ∇ 20 | 14 | 19 | $40

Mineola | 66 E. Jericho Tpke. (Columbus Pkwy.) | 516-248-2004 | www.lareira.kpsearch.com

It's "Portugal without a passport" at this Mineola mainstay, "a must for fish lovers" and anyone who relishes "authentic" Iberian eats in a "quiet", congenial setting; "marvelous sangria" is a sweet complement to the food, but due to an interior that "needs serious dusting off", some critics say it only rates as a "back-up place."

	FOOD	DECOR	SERVICE	COST

La Rotonda *Pizza* ▽ 19 | 15 | 19 | $29

Great Neck | 8 Bond St. (bet. Grace Ave. & N. Station Plaza) | 516-466-9596 | www.larotondarestaurant.com

"It's all about the pizza" at this "brick-oven" pie palace in Great Neck, which also turns out "decent" "homestyle" pastas and such in "very casual" but "friendly" surroundings; it's viewed as a "local staple" that's "satisfying" "if you're in the nabe", but "not a destination."

La Spada *Italian* 21 | 17 | 23 | $48

Huntington Station | 315 Walt Whitman Rd. (bet. Old Walt Whitman & Schwab Rds.) | 631-549-3033 | www.laspadarestaurant.com

"You can always count on" this Southern Italian in Huntington Station for a "warm" greeting and "superb pasta" amid "lots of regulars"; what the simple, burgundy-toned space "lacks in decor", it "makes up for" with "top-notch" service and "quality", upscale fare.

La Strada *Italian* 20 | 20 | 21 | $36

Merrick | 2100 Merrick Ave. (bet. Miller Pl. & Smith St.) | 516-867-5488 | www.lastradaofmerrick.com

"Satisfied" customers chow down on "tasty" Italian cuisine at this moderately priced Merrick trattoria that some report has "much improved since it opened" a few years ago, serving wood-fired pizzas and other "solid" fare in "accommodating" style; though a few feel the meals are "nothing special", the "beautiful", brick-floored setting, reminiscent of a courtyard in Italy, is a draw in itself.

La Tavola *Italian* 22 | 21 | 21 | $42

Sayville | 183 W. Main St. (bet. Greeley & Greene Aves.) | 631-750-6900 | www.latavolasayville.com

"Not your usual spaghetti-and-meatballs Italian", this "happening", "new-wave" Sayville trattoria (from the brothers behind Ruvo) offers "wonderfully different", slightly "expensive" seasonal dishes in "rustic" environs furnished with farm-wood tables; since you "can't beat the happy hour", the bar's popular for "refreshing cocktails" after work, while the "outside patio is great" for hanging out on "summer evenings."

La Terrazza Ⓜ *Italian* ▽ 22 | 17 | 21 | $50

Cedarhurst | 142 Spruce St. (bet. Chestnut St. & Willow Ave.) | 516-374-4949

Just steps from the Cedarhurst train station, this "intimate" Italian pleases with its "varied", "well-prepared" cuisine (including specials worth "paying attention" to) and "professional" service; it's often "noisy" and a bit "pricey", but that doesn't deter diners who appreciate the "welcoming" atmosphere.

La Viola *Italian* 20 | 15 | 21 | $40

Cedarhurst | 499 Chestnut St. (bet. Cedarhurst Ave. & Spruce St.) | 516-569-6020 | www.laviolarestaurant.com

"Family-style dining excels" at this Cedarhurst "fixture" that delivers "traditional red-sauce" Italian and sends diners home happy "with a doggy bag in hand"; though the room is "starting to look frayed", it's "relaxed" and "friendly" "whether you're a regular or a first-timer", and gets a boost from live "opera songs" or Broadway tunes on the first Friday of the month.

La Volpe Ristorante Ⓜ *Italian*   23 | 22 | 23 | $43

Center Moriches | 611 Montauk Hwy. (Brookfield Ave.) | 631-874-3819 | www.lavolperestaurant.net

"Impressed" eaters praise the brick-oven pizza, "delicious" dishes and "creative" specials at this slightly "upscale" Center Moriches Italian run by a "hands-on" family that "clearly loves its business" and "knows what good food is"; the "attractive" setting with a Tuscan "farmhouse look" benefits from "expert" service, live weekly music and patio seating, and the three-course lunch deal enhances the "value."

Le Chef *Continental/French*   22 | 17 | 21 | $49

Southampton | 75 Jobs Ln. (bet. Main St. & Windmill Ln.) | 631-283-8581 | www.lechefbistro.com

"A longtimer in Southampton" (since 1980), this "pretty little" French-Continental bistro reliably provides "nicely prepared" "old-line" dishes and "personal" service in a "cozy" setting that "feels like the French countryside"; despite "nothing new to offer", it draws "steady patrons" who promise you get your "money's worth", especially when opting for the all-night prix fixe.

Legal Sea Foods *Seafood*   20 | 18 | 19 | $41

Garden City | Roosevelt Field Mall | 630 Old Country Rd. (bet. Clinton Rd. & Meadowbrook Pkwy.) | 516-248-4600
Huntington Station | Walt Whitman Mall | 160 Walt Whitman Rd. (Weston St.) | 631-271-9777
www.legalseafoods.com

Enjoy some of "Boston's best seafood in your backyard" via these "high-quality" chain links in Garden City and Huntington Station that are "deservedly popular" for their "always fresh" offerings, including "legendary New England clam chowder"; though they're a bit "basic" for the "upscale" prices and the "modern" decor isn't for everyone, the servers are "accommodating" and the gluten-free menu earns it "huge props."

Legends *Eclectic*   23 | 20 | 21 | $44

New Suffolk | 835 First St. (bet. King & Main Sts.) | 631-734-5123 | www.legends-restaurant.com

"The best of both worlds" awaits at this "welcoming" "find" in "the quiet village of New Suffolk", where a "robust" "sports bar" adjoins a "sedate dining room" serving "generous" portions of "surprisingly creative" Eclectic fare prepared with "flair and finesse" and conveyed by a "caring" staff; also offering "200-plus bottled beers", it's a legendary "local" fave that's "well worth seeking out" despite tabs inclined to be "a little steep."

Lemonleaf Grill Ⓜ *Thai*   22 | 12 | 19 | $24

Hicksville | Compare Food Shopping Ctr. | 536 S. Broadway (bet. Farm Ln. & Lewis St.) | 516-939-2288

(continued)

(continued)

Lemonleaf Grill

Port Jefferson Station | 208 Rte. 112 (bet. Cherub Dr. & Dayton Ave.) | 631-928-8880

www.lemonleafgrill.com

"Terrific", "gently seasoned" Thai food "pleases the entire family" at these "reliable" Hicksville and Port Jefferson eateries that "aren't fancy" but offer "good value"; even those who call the "quiet" settings a "step above a take-out kitchen" and service merely "adequate" are "never disappointed in the food", but heat-seekers be warned that "nothing will set your mouth on fire" here.

Lemon Leaf Thai Restaurant *Thai*   20 | 11 | 17 | $25

Carle Place | 227 Old Country Rd. (bet. Glen Cove Rd. & Meadowbrook State Pkwy.) | 516-739-3666

Mineola | 197 Mineola Blvd. (Grant Ave.) | 516-877-1899

www.lemonleafthairestaurant.com

The cooks deliver "flavorful" standards – and "they don't stumble with the drunken noodles, either" – at this Thai twosome catering to the "not-too-spicy" set; the newer Mineola branch is more "charming" than the rather "run-down" original in Carle Place, but both come through with "real bang for the buck."

☑ Le Soir Ⓜ *French*   27 | 21 | 25 | $52

Bayport | 825 Montauk Hwy. (Bayport Ave.) | 631-472-9090 | www.lesoirbayport.com

It's "getting better with age" report regulars who've gone "for years" to Michael Kaziewicz's "outstanding" French destination in Bayport proffering "exquisitely prepared" dinners; the service is "amazing" too, so even if the "slightly fussy" room "could use a spruce-up", it's still a "nice place for date night" and a "favorite during the week" for the "bargain" prix fixe.

Library Cafe ➊ *American*   18 | 21 | 19 | $29

Farmingdale | 274 Main St. (Conklin St.) | 516-752-7678 | www.thelibrarycafe.com

"Ironically, it's one of the loudest places you can go" remark guests of this "adorable", "neighborhood pub" set in a former Farmingdale library (sib to Babylon's Post Office Cafe), where "scrumptious" burgers and other "comforting" New American grub bolster "one of the best happy hours around"; the staff "makes you feel welcome" and the martinis "actually have a kick", so it's "enjoyable" if you're into the "scene."

☑ Limani *Mediterranean/Seafood*   26 | 27 | 24 | $71

Roslyn | 1043 Northern Blvd. (bet. Middle Neck Rd. & Port Washington Blvd.) | 516-869-8989 | www.limaniny.com

There's a "beautiful atmosphere for beautiful people" at this "gorgeous" Roslyn Mediterranean with teak floors, mosaic tiles and a "bar scene that's a bit of a show", and it also "wows" in the kitchen, providing "incredible" fare ("fabulous" seafood "cooked to perfection") matched by a "formidable" wine list; "extremely accommodating" service is another plus, but just be ready for a "noise level that's off-the-charts" and tabs so "expensive", it might be "cheaper to go to Greece."

Living Room, The American   25 | 25 | 22 | $68

East Hampton | c/o The Maidstone | 207 Main St. (Mill Hill Ln.) | 631-324-5006 | www.themaidstone.com

"We should all have a living room like this" gush "impressed" patrons at this "high-end" East Hamptonite in the c/o The Maidstone Hotel, where chef James Carpenter (ex Della Femina) does a "terrific take on Slow Food" showcasing "local" ingredients via "sophisticated", "Scandinavian-inspired" New American dishes; bright, "elegant decor" and "superb" service add to the "amazing" experience, and though such "quality doesn't come cheap", epicures "with deep pockets and refined taste buds" shrug "we only live once."

Livorno ◪ Italian   ▽ 21 | 18 | 21 | $46

Port Washington | 95-97 Manorhaven Blvd. (Edgewood Rd.) | 516-944-2730

Those who've tried this Port Washington eatery serving "traditional" Sicilian food appreciate the "old-fashioned home cooking" and "love the backyard" brick courtyard for alfresco meals; inside, French doors and fresh flowers lend a breezy touch to the upscale meal.

LL Dent ◪ Southern   23 | 13 | 20 | $31

Carle Place | 221 Old Country Rd. (bet. Glen Cove Rd. & Meadowbrook Pkwy.) | 516-742-0940 | www.lldent.com

From the "chicken and catfish to die for" to the "mouthwatering desserts", the "good ol' Southern cuisine" at this Carle Place "gem" is the "real thing" (and not for "calorie-counters"); "sweetheart" owners put their "personal touch" on the affordable meal – daughter Leisa Dent works the kitchen while mother Lillian provides "great hospitality" up front – though the small, "simple" space lacks the "flair" of the fare.

Lobster Inn Seafood   19 | 13 | 17 | $45

Southampton | 162 Inlet Rd. (Sunrise Hwy.) | 631-283-1525 | www.thelobsterinn.com

"Don't dare dress up" for this "unchic" Southampton "staple", an oversized "seafood shack" that "remains above average" after 40-plus years for "moist and juicy" steamed lobster and the "famous 'splat'" (a heaping shellfish platter); while the "no-frills" interior "looks like a shipwreck", the "open-air" deck's "waterfront view" of Cold Spring Pond keeps it "crowded all summer."

Lobster Roll Seafood   19 | 12 | 17 | $33

Amagansett | 1980 Montauk Hwy. (on Napeague Stretch) | 631-267-3740 | www.lobsterroll.com

"Once you've been here, you're hooked" claim fin fans about this seasonal Amagansett "shack" (nicknamed 'Lunch' for its sign) that's been a lure since the '60s for its "delicious lobster rolls", "fried puffers" and the like; "it's the antithesis of elegant" and some call it "overpriced", but the "beachy atmosphere" and homemade desserts by the owner enhance the appeal for a "local, lively crowd."

	FOOD	DECOR	SERVICE	COST

Lobster Roll Northside Ⓜ *Seafood* — `20` `16` `18` `$35`

Baiting Hollow | 3225 Sound Ave. (Roanoke Ave.) | 631-369-3039 | www.lobsterroll.com

Fans "love the lobster rolls" and "awesome puffers" at this seasonal Baiting Hollow "favorite" (which originated as an offshoot of the Amagansett locale); with "weekend music in the summer" and a "pretty", kid-friendly setting in a plaza with "interesting shops", it's a "traveling staple" for many, despite the rather "pricey platters."

Lola Ⓜ *Eclectic* — `24` `23` `23` `$54`

Great Neck | 113A Middle Neck Rd. (Maple Dr.) | 516-466-5666 | www.restaurantlola.com

"Truly gifted" chef-owner Michael Ginor (Tel Aviv) "is beyond an artist" at this "top-flight" Great Neck "destination", where the "thrilling" lineup of "remarkably" "imaginative" Eclectic "delights" – many enhanced with "decadent foie gras" from his own farm – includes an "extensive small plate" selection ("go hungry and try lots"); "attentive" servers oversee a "vibrant and sexy" setting with a "marvelous" "glowing red bar", and while you can "expect quality rather than quantity", "the 'wow' factor" is "well worth the money."

Lola's Kitchen & Wine Bar *American* — `20` `21` `21` `$36`

Long Beach | 180 W. Park Ave. (Magnolia Blvd.) | 516-442-1090

The "cool" "Key West" vibe "enlivens" this "relaxing" Long Beach "crowd-pleaser", where merrymakers escape the daily grind with "enticing" New American fare and an "excellent" vino lineup; inside it "can get a bit loud", but a "cute outdoor area" furthers the "vacation" feel and "nightly specials" mean it's both "happening" and "affordable" ("a recipe for success").

Lombardi's on the Bay *Seafood/Steak* — `23` `24` `21` `$48`

Patchogue | 600 S. Ocean Ave. (Masket Dock) | 631-654-8970 | www.lombardisonthebay.com

"A view to relish" from a "multilevel deck with lots of tables" is a part of the package at this Patchogue special-occasion destination (related to Lombardi's on the Sound and Mamma Lombardi's) serving "abundant" portions of "quality" surf 'n' turf, with a few Italian accents; the interior is "gracious" too, however, it's not cheap and some critics contend it's all a bit "too much" – "a catering hall should not try to be a restaurant also."

Lombardi's on the Sound *Italian* — `21` `23` `20` `$45`

Port Jefferson | Port Jefferson Country Club at Harbor Hills | 44 Fairway Dr. (Village Beach Rd.) | 631-473-1440 | www.lombardisonthesound.com

"Unbeatable views" of Long Island Sound along with "enormous portions" of "sumptuous" Italian food make this Lombardi's family player "enjoyable for special events", big catered affairs and a "Sunday brunch buffet like no other"; a few consider it "overpriced" with variable service, but lunch offers a more "affordable" option for soaking in the "beautiful" scenery.

RESTAURANTS

	FOOD	DECOR	SERVICE	COST

Long River *Asian* ▽ 21 | 15 | 20 | $23
Kings Park | 4 Main St. (Indian Head Rd.) | 631-544-4666

"Solid" selections of "well-done" Chinese and Indonesian dishes (including "wonderful" fried dumplings) are served by a "fast, friendly" staff that "works hard" at this veteran Pan-Asian near the train station in Kings Park; given the so-so setting, though, some say it's "best for takeout" – especially since it's always "ready on time and right, no matter how much you order."

Los Compadres *Mexican* ▽ 23 | 6 | 19 | $18
Huntington Station | 243 Old Walt Whitman Rd. (bet. Chichester Rd. & Livingston St.) | 631-351-8384

"Everything is homemade and fresh, right down to the corn chips" and "dreamy chimichangas" at this "authentic" Huntington Station Mex where "you can tell" the owner "takes pride in his food"; since it's a "terrific value", no one's complaining about "paper plates and plastic utensils" or the "bare-bones" setting; P.S. no alcohol served.

Lotus East *Chinese* 21 | 14 | 19 | $27
Mount Sinai | 331 Rte. 25A (Rte. 347) | 631-331-6688
St. James | 416 N. Country Rd. (Edgewood Ave.) | 631-862-6030

There's a "wide variety" of Chinese at these "mainstays" in Mt. Sinai and St. James turning out "consistently excellent", "classic" dishes for a "reasonable" price; still, some find the fare "pedestrian" and the "bland" settings in need of an "extreme makeover."

Louie's Oyster Bar & Grille *Seafood* 17 | 20 | 18 | $46
Port Washington | 395 Main St. (Prospect St.) | 516-883-4242 | www.louiesoysterbarandgrille.com

"Spectacular" sunset views are the draw at this "landmark" (circa-1905) Port Washington seafooder with an "extensive" outdoor deck for watching "the boats go by" and an "attractive" nautical-themed interior; the lobster's "delicious", but with service that's just "average" and "above-average prices", some just go for "drinks and apps"; P.S. look out for "Frank Sinatra nights" on Mondays with a live band.

Love Lane Kitchen *American* 23 | 15 | 19 | $34
Mattituck | 240 Love Ln. (bet. Main Rd. & Pike St.) | 631-298-8989 | www.lovelanekitchen.com

"Upscale", locally sourced "comfort food" from an "ambitious", "ever-evolving" New American menu is "well executed" and served in "unpretentious style" at this "super-casual" Mattituck "gem", which is also beloved for its "wonderful" "house-roasted coffee"; the pace "can be slow" when it's "busy", but "reasonable" prices and a staff "so sweet you could swear they've been spun from sugar" make it "easy to stroll in" for breakfast, lunch or dinner.

NEW LT Burger Ⓜ *Burgers* 16 | 15 | 13 | $30
Sag Harbor | 62 Main St. (bet. Garden & Spring Sts.) | 631-899-4646 | www.ltburger.com

Co-owned by celeb chef Laurent Tourondel, this "very casual" new "addition to the Sag Harbor eating scene" serves up "all kinds of burgers" (classic, Tex-Mex, turkey, veggie, et al.) in a "white-tiled" retro-industrial space; critics beef about "just ok" food, "clueless" service and "lots of hype", but "it's kid-friendly" and "won't break the bank" so be ready for "massive lines in summer."

Lucé 🅼 *Italian* | 22 | 21 | 23 | $60 |

East Norwich | 1053 Oyster Bay Rd. (bet. Johnson Ct. & Northern Blvd.) | 516-624-8330

"Elegant in every way" from the white tablecloths to the colorful mosaics, this "upscale" East Norwich Italian "makes you feel special" indulging in the "delicious" likes of potato-wrapped halibut and grilled veal paillard set down by an "attentive" staff; but while "they really take pride in the food", they also attach a "hefty price tag", leading some to prefer "lunch when it's quiet" – and lighter on the wallet.

🆉 Luce & Hawkins *American* | 25 | 27 | 26 | $65 |

Jamesport | Jedediah Hawkins Inn | 400 S. Jamesport Ave. (bet. Main Rd. & Peconic Bay Blvd.) | 631-722-2900 | www.jedediahhawkinsinn.com

If you "like to be surprised and challenged", "run, don't walk" to this New American in the "gorgeous restored" Victorian home that's now Jamesport's "magnificent" Jedediah Hawkins Inn, where chef/co-owner Keith Luce "loves to tantalize" by "coaxing wonderful flavors" out of the "farm-to-table" "local ingredients" (many from his own "garden in the back") showcased in his "inspired" dishes; with a "terrific" team staffing an "elegant" yet "comfortable" venue, it's a "gourmet" experience to "savor."

Lucy's Café & Bistro 🆂🅼 *American* | ▽ 25 | 18 | 23 | $39 |

Babylon | 135 Deer Park Ave. (James St.) | 631-669-1640 | www.lucysbistro.com

The "talented" new chef-owner pays "attention to detail" at this "fabulous" "little" Babylon Village "gem", where the "up-to-date" New American menu is prepared "to perfection" with "top-of-the-line ingredients" and served by an "attentive" staff; the "charmingly casual" (if "tight") quarters are secreted down a "brick-lined alleyway", but it's "well worth finding" and tolerating the occasional "wait."

Ludlow Bistro 🅼 *American* | 24 | 19 | 23 | $47 |

Deer Park | 1945 Deer Park Ave. (Schwartz Pl.) | 631-667-9595 | www.ludlowbistro.com

Once you "get past the fluorescent orange exterior", this Deer Park New American is liable to "surprise" with "innovative" "twists" on a "fantastic" seasonal menu and service from a "first-rate" crew; the "convivial atmosphere" fostered by a "very present" owner and "funky" interior sporting "cool artwork" further prompt patrons to observe you can "never judge a book by its cover."

Luigi Q 🆂 *Italian* | 23 | 18 | 20 | $56 |

Hicksville | 400B S. Oyster Bay Rd. (Woodbury Rd.) | 516-932-7450

Admirers of chef-owner Luigi Quarta's "charming" "old-school Italian" in Hicksville attest that the "excellent" "traditional" cuisine and "warm, personable service" are "a perfect delight" "for that special occasion or just because"; those low on lire object that it's "over-priced", but "when it's on, it's on."

Luso *Portuguese*

22 | 17 | 22 | $33

Smithtown | 101 E. Main St. (bet. Bellemeade & Landing Aves.) | 631-406-6820 | www.lusorestaurant.com

Indulge the "carnivore in you" with "never-ending meats" "smoking hot from the grill" at this Portuguese BBQ joint in Smithtown, where "efficient" servers bring on the "wonderful" rodizio specialty in a "flavorful" "parade" that "stops only when you say so"; prices are "reasonable" and the "small space" expands with a "bonus" patio in summer, but "plan on skipping breakfast the day after."

Mac's Steakhouse *Steak*

23 | 23 | 22 | $60

Huntington | 12 Gerard St. (bet. New York & Stewart Aves.) | 631-549-5300 | www.macssteakhouse.com

"An emphatic wow", this Huntington meatery "powerhouse" presents "excellent" prime cuts, "delicious sides" and a "terrific", 350-vintage vino list ferried by "gracious" staffers who "bend over backward for you"; the "impressive digs" brandish "beautiful" "dark wood" and a glassed-in private wine cellar, and though the "high prices" are "not for every day", "if you're up for a special meal" and have "deep pockets" it's "solid" to the max; P.S. it hosts live music on Fridays.

Madras Woodlands
Exotic Tastes of India *Indian/Vegetarian*

▽ 22 | 14 | 24 | $23

New Hyde Park | 1627 Hillside Ave. (New Hyde Park Rd.) | 516-326-8900 | www.exotictastesofindia.com

Dosas are "made to perfection" and "authentic South Indian" spices "dance in your mouth" at this New Hyde Park subcontinental standout, where the "top-notch" kosher vegetarian cooking brings out "flavors so complex" that even card-carrying carnivores "never miss the meat"; the prices are as "light" and "satisfying" as the food, and the "excellent" staffers will gladly "give advice" to neophytes.

Maguire's *American*

19 | 19 | 19 | $45

Ocean Beach | Fire Island | 1 Bay Walk (Ocean Rd.) | 631-583-8800 | www.maguiresbayfrontrestaurant.com

"Beautiful sunset views" from a "delightful" deck "right on the bay" are a "popular" draw at this seasonal New American in Ocean Beach, an "old-time Fire Island" stalwart with a "simple" menu of "tried-and-true favorites" ("Thursday night lobsterpalooza" is "the best value"); though it offers "no surprises" foodwise, the "alfresco" scenery alone is "worth the price of the meal"; P.S. the $45 'Taste of Fire Island' includes parking, a three-course dinner and round-trip ferry service from Bay Shore.

Main St. Bakery & Café *Bakery/Sandwiches*

▬ | ▬ | ▬ | I

Port Washington | 170 Main St. (bet. Madison & Monroe Sts.) | 516-304-5214

Breakfast, brunch and lunch are offered at this bakery/sandwich shop in Port Washington where savory items include a turkey and avocado baguette and eggs Benedict with fingerling-potato hash; among the numerous treats in a huge glass pastry case is the decadent house specialty – a multilayered candy bar meant to be eaten either sliced or with a knife and fork.

Majors Steak House *Steak*   19 | 16 | 20 | $39

East Meadow | 284 E. Meadow Ave. (Fairhaven Rd.) | 516-794-6600
Woodbury | 8289 Jericho Tpke. (bet. Juneau Blvd. & Woodbury Rd.) | 516-367-7300

"When funds are tight", these "busy" East Meadow and Woodbury beef barns cater to the "budget-minded" "masses" with "fantastic" burgers and "basic but passable" steaks for a price you "can't beat"; they're "nothing elegant", but supporters say "enough has rubbed off" from parent Bryant & Cooper "to make it worthwhile" when you want to "bring the family" and leave "full."

Mama's *Italian*   21 | 14 | 20 | $32

Centereach | Centereach Mall | 605 Middle Country Rd. (Holbrook Rd.) | 631-585-1498
Holbrook | 1057 Main St. (bet. Furrows Rd. & Railroad Ave.) | 631-981-6262
Oakdale | LaSalle Commons | 587 Montauk Hwy. (Dale Dr.) | 631-589-9640
www.theoriginalmamas.com

This "red-sauce" threesome wins support from "local" families seeking "reliable" Italian "standards" (think pastas and pizza) in "big portions" "for the buck"; though the food and generic decor are "not particularly memorable", they're "trustworthy" enough to attract "long lines at peak times"; P.S. the Centereach and Oakdale outlets' $13.95 Wednesday prix fixe is "a very good deal."

Mamma Lombardi's *Italian*   23 | 19 | 21 | $41

Holbrook | 400 Furrows Rd. (Patchogue-Holbrook Rd.) | 631-737-0774 | www.mammalombardis.com

Beloved "through the years" for "humongous portions" of "mouth-watering" Southern Italian fare "like you wish your mamma could make", this Holbrook vet is a "wonderful family-style" "mainstay"; though the "old-fashioned" setting "could use a makeover" and "there's always a wait" owing to the "no-reservations policy", "spot-on" service and a "doggy bag" that "can last for days" render "every visit" "satisfying"; P.S. the owners also run a nearby gourmet market, as well as Lombardi's on the Sound and Lombardi's on the Bay.

Manucci's *Italian/Pizza*   ∇ 19 | 15 | 17 | $37

Montauk | Kenny's Tipperary Inn | 432 W. Lake Dr. (Flamingo Ave.) | 631-668-4455 | www.manuccis.com

Now settled in new quarters at Kenny's Tipperary Inn, this Montauk Italian is dishing out "old-school" staples and brick-oven pizzas that "can be quite tasty", with the Sunday buffet breakfast and Monday pasta night adding "family value"; less satisfied sojourners say it's "inconsistent" but "ok" "in a pinch" if you "stick to the basics"; P.S. hours vary by season.

RESTAURANTS

	FOOD	DECOR	SERVICE	COST

NEW Marco Polo's *Asian/Italian* — | — | — | M

Westbury | Viana Hotel & Spa | 3998 Brush Hollow Rd. (Montrose Rd.) | 516-338-7777 | www.marcopolos.weebly.com

East meets West at Westbury's Viana Hotel and Spa, where the midpriced Asian and Italian menu offers not only the likes of truffle ravioli and grilled salmon with sweet Chinese mustard, but also a fusion-style chicken française egg roll; the feng shui-inspired, eco-friendly decor features a dramatic entryway with a fireplace and a compass floor design, black granite dining tables and a red under-lighted bar.

Mario *Italian* 25 | 21 | 25 | $44

Hauppauge | 644 Vanderbilt Motor Pkwy. (bet. Marcus Blvd. & Washington Ave.) | 631-273-9407 | www.restaurantmario.com

"Still going strong" after 30 years, this "old-style" Hauppauge Northern Italian remains a "fave" for "terrific" cuisine set down by "pleasant and professional" staffers who'll "change anything you wish" to suit your palate; even if spoilers suggest the "deep-red" "flashback decor" could use some "updating", for a "consistently excellent" meal that "won't break the bank", "you can't miss."

☑ Maroni Cuisine ⊠Ⓜ⇄ *Eclectic/Italian* 28 | 18 | 26 | $109

Northport | 18 Woodbine Ave. (bet. Main St. & Scudder Ave.) | 631-757-4500 | www.maronicuisine.com

"Inventive is an understatement" for chef-owner and "genial genius" Michael Maroni's "phenomenal" Eclectic-Italian tasting menu, which makes dining at his cash-only Northport standout an "exciting" "event" as "personable" servers convey course after course of "perfectly executed" "delicacies" (like those "famous" "tender" meatballs in "lush red sauce") till you "need help getting up"; it's "always worth" the "splurge" to be "wowed" by a "dream meal" "you'll never forget", but "reservations are a must" for a spot in the "shoebox" space; P.S. there's also a fair-weather courtyard and a party room.

Massa's Ⓜ *Pizza* 23 | 10 | 17 | $20

Huntington Station | 146 W. Jericho Tpke. (bet. Collins Pl. & Pine Tree Rd.) | 631-935-0200 | www.massaspizzeria.com

"For those who know the true virtues of coal-oven pies", this Huntington Station parlor's "amazing" pizza – featuring a "crisp", "paper-thin crust", "fresh mozzarella" and just the "right amount" of "delicious" sauce – is "one of the best" "ever"; sure, the "decor is slim to nonexistent" and service isn't stellar, but with rounds like these, "who cares?"

Matsulin *Asian* 22 | 18 | 20 | $39

Hampton Bays | 131 W. Montauk Hwy. (Springville Rd.) | 631-728-8838 | www.matsulin.com

With an "extensive" menu of "surprisingly high quality" – whether Thai, Chinese, Malaysian, Vietnamese or "fresh sushi" – this Hampton Bays Pan-Asian is "a real find" "in an unexpected place" (i.e. "a former bank"); regulars rely on the "reasonable prices" and "efficient service" to outweigh any lack of "luster."

	FOOD	DECOR	SERVICE	COST

Matsuya *Asian* | 21 | 19 | 20 | $36

Great Neck | Gardens Mall | 6 Great Neck Rd. (bet. Brompton & Middle Neck Rds.) | 516-773-4411 | www.matsuyasushi.com

With a "stepped-up menu" providing "more Pan-Asian choices" and cooked dishes to complement the "top-notch" sushi "creations" from a "chef who works magic", this "unpretentious" Great Neck "go-to" "keeps getting better with age"; "gracious and accommodating" service and a "colorful", wall-length "tank of tropical fish" ("like going to a real aquarium") also ensure it "stands out" in the area.

❏ Matteo's *Italian* | 23 | 16 | 20 | $44

Bellmore | 416 Bedford Ave. (Wilson Ave.) | 516-409-1779
Long Beach | 777 W. Beech St. (New York Ave.) | 516-432-8101
Roslyn Heights | 88 Mineola Ave. (bet. Elm & Willow Sts.) | 516-484-0555
Huntington Station | 300 W. Jericho Tpke. (West Hills Rd.) | 631-421-6001
www.matteosristorante.com

"Those who love lots of garlic" "count on" this "family-style" Italian quartet, where "helpful" staffers deliver "oversized" platters of "well-prepared" "comfort" fare; dissenters are distracted by the "loud", "tacky" settings, but they're "busy, busy" with "a happy crowd" that's willing to "wait on line", so "they must be doing something right."

Matthew's *Seafood* | ▽ 22 | 19 | 21 | $43

Ocean Beach | Fire Island | 935 Bay Walk (bet. Evergreen & Surfview Walks) | 631-583-8016 | www.matthewsseafood.com

This seasonal Ocean Beach vet "packs" in Fire Island fin fans lured by "tasty" seafood – there's a featured catch of the day – and "beautiful water views" from the deck and "private dock" overlooking the Great South Bay; though the food is "fine", the open-air "atmosphere is why you pay the price"; P.S. shoppers can also net fresh fish from the adjacent market.

Maureen & Daughters' Kitchen 🏴 *American* | 25 | 20 | 22 | $20

Smithtown | 108 Terry Rd. (Larsen Ave.) | 631-360-9227

"Holy cow!", this "bustling", "cash-only" morning "nirvana" in Smithtown "takes care of you for the day" with "bountiful" "homemade" breakfasts built on "phenomenal pancakes", "fabulous French toast" and "too-good-to-be-true" baked oatmeal (the lunchtime "sandwiches are interesting and tasty too"); the bovine-themed interior is "adorable" and the "lightning-fast" service is the "sweetest around", just "be prepared" to "brave the lines."

Maxwell's ◑ *American* | - | - | - | M

Islip | 501 Main St. (bet. Grant & Locust Aves.) | 631-210-0011 | www.lessings.com

Conviviality reigns at this Islip saloon (sibling of Post Office Cafe) where a huge wood bar and raised dining area with booths and tables beckon locals for drinks and moderately priced American grub such as burgers and babyback ribs; prancing carousel horses divide the eating and drinking areas, and a tin ceiling gleams in the stylishly casual setting; P.S. weeknights bring happy hours.

	FOOD	DECOR	SERVICE	COST

Mediterranean Grill-Kebab *Mediterranean*

▽ 21 | 12 | 20 | $27

Hewlett | 10-12 Franklin Ave. (bet. B'way & W. B'way) | 516-374-4203 | www.mygrillkebab.com

"Value"-seekers cite "large portions" and "unbelievably cheap" tabs at this Med "local" near the Hewlett train station, where a "friendly" if "laid-back" crew serves up "very good" kebabs, gyros, Greek salad and the like; naysayers skewer a "dreary" space in need of "a little sprucing up" but concede it's "ok to run in" for takeout.

Mediterranean Snack Bar ⊄ *Greek/Mediterranean*

22 | 8 | 18 | $27

Huntington | 360 New York Ave. (bet. E. Carver & Elm Sts.) | 631-423-8982 | www.medsnackbar.com

"Excellent since the day it opened" 37 years ago, this "popular" Huntington Village "fixture" serves "super-delicious" Med staples including "fantastic Greek salads", "quality gyros", "moussaka like mom's" and owner Steve Souellis' "fresh-caught seafood"; it's a "great value", but you'll have to ignore the "tight", "no-frills" setting or opt for "takeout"; P.S "beware: no credit cards."

Meeting House, The *American/Mediterranean*

20 | 18 | 18 | $44

Amagansett | Amagansett Sq. | 4 Amagansett Square Dr. (Montauk Hwy.) | 631-267-2764 | www.meetinghouseamagansett.com

Recently reopened with spiffed-up decor and a New American–Med menu that's strong on small plates, this Amagansett Square standby appeals to "neighborhood" types seeking "well-prepared", "sensibly priced" bites; everything's "amicably served" in a "lively" space with an "active bar" and a predictably vigorous "noise level"; P.S. the Food and Decor scores do not reflect the recent renovation and menu change.

Melting Pot *Fondue*

18 | 20 | 20 | $45

Farmingdale | 2377 Broadhollow Rd. (Smith St.) | 631-752-4242 | www.meltingpot.com

"It's all about sharing" and "cooking your own food" at this Farmingdale chain link serving "every kind of fondue", including "delicious" chocolate pots; while it's a "romantic" "treat" for "younger couples" and "fun to do with a group", critics contend it's "overpriced" and "pretentious", and would prefer a "more casual" setup; P.S. go with a large party if you want "two burners."

Mercato Kitchen & Cocktails *American/Italian*

20 | 20 | 21 | $32

Massapequa Park | Southgate Shopping Ctr. | 4958 Merrick Rd. (Whitewood Dr.) | 516-308-3582 | www.mercatokitchen.com

Fast becoming a "favorite" in Massapequa Park, this "inviting" American-Italian is "better than your average" "neighborhood joint" for "unpretentious" bites like its "delicious" specialty flatbreads ("think pizza without the guilt") at a "reasonable" cost; the "gregarious", "welcoming" staff is "trying hard", and the "lively bar" is a "popular" draw "just for drinks and appetizers."

Meritage 🅂Ⓜ *American/Asian*

▽ 25 | 21 | 21 | $44

Bellport | 14 Station Rd. (S. Country Rd.) | 631-286-3300

A "fabulous" "mix" of "outstanding" New American and Pan-Asian dishes – as well as a sushi bar that "deserves a spotlight" – merits a visit to this "Bellport hideaway", as do "charming" quarters with a pressed-tin ceiling and "comfy seats outside"; "personable" service contributes to the "warm and cozy" atmosphere, though a few fuss it's "pricey" "for what you're getting"; P.S. dinner only.

Meson Iberia *Continental/Spanish*

22 | 14 | 22 | $34

Island Park | 4335 Austin Blvd. (bet. Kingston Blvd. & Sagamore Rd.) | 516-897-4911

The paella "loaded with seafood" and "homemade sangria" "are *muy bueno*" at this "warm", "family-owned" Island Parker, a fallback for "authentic", "flavorful" Spanish-Continental "standards" presented with a personal touch; maybe the "dated" room's "in need of a makeover", but it's "not too expensive" and "you always feel at home."

NEW Metropolitan Bistro *American*

▽ 22 | 22 | 19 | $39

Sea Cliff | 39 Roslyn Ave. (10th Ave.) | 516-801-4500 | www.themetropolitanbistro.com

Locals laud this "wonderful new addition to Sea Cliff" for its concise menu of midrange New American fare – including a "smoky, juicy burger" – delivered by "unobtrusive" staffers in a "relaxed" setting sporting French doors and a patio; a hedger or two hints they're "still finding their way", but it's becoming a "neighborhood" "favorite."

Michael Anthony's Food Bar *Eclectic*

24 | 16 | 21 | $48

Wading River | 2925 N. Wading River Rd. (bet. Hulse Ave. & Hulse Landing Rd.) | 631-929-8800 | www.michaelanthonysfoodbar.com

An "inventive menu" of "awesome" Eclectic dishes in "picturesque" presentations marks this Wading River "hideaway", where the "talented" eponymous chef is "likely to arrive at your table at any moment to see how you're enjoying his masterpieces"; "friendly" servers tend the "comfortable", "recently redecorated" space, so while "it's not easy to find", it's "worth the effort" and "the price of admission"; P.S. closed Tuesdays.

Michaels' at Maidstone Beach *American*

18 | 15 | 21 | $45

East Hampton | 28 Maidstone Park Rd. (off Three Mile Harbor Rd.) | 631-324-0725 | www.michaelsofmaidstone.com

"Hidden away" "off the beaten track" in East Hampton, this "old-timer" is "known by the locals" for its "good, honest" American fare (crab cakes, Long Island duck) and "very un-Hamptons" atmosphere; true, a few feel the well-worn digs "need a makeover", but regulars who prize it as a "best-kept secret" still plead "don't tell anyone!"

Milk & Sugar Café *American*

21 | 24 | 19 | $30

Bay Shore | 49 W. Main St. (Park Ave.) | 631-969-3655 | www.milkandsugarcafe.com

"Meet the girls for a catch-up lunch" at this "cute" Bay Shore "rendezvous", a "quaint and offbeat" setup akin to "a friend's house" with "cozy couches" to "just melt into" while enjoying "comforting" American eats and "delectable desserts" served day and night "at affordable prices"; it's a "sweet" spot to "relax and chat", but go with "time to linger" since the staff sometimes shows "the attentiveness of a bad ex."

Mill Creek Tavern ☑ Seafood/Steak | 21 | 20 | 21 | $39 |

Bayville | 275 Bayville Ave. (Pine Park Ave.) | 516-628-2000 | www.millcreekny.com

Everyone from "grandma to grandchild will be happy" with the "huge menu" at this Bayville "sister restaurant of Mim's", which "lures you back like a magnet" with "reliable" surf 'n' turf (e.g. "huge buckets of mussels") and "warm" atmospherics kindled by a "very personable" owner who "hops tables" to "get the party going"; it's "popular" for "everyday casual dining" and the "consistency shows why."

Milleridge Inn American | 16 | 22 | 19 | $40 |

Jericho | 585 N. Broadway (bet. Jericho Tpke. & Market St.) | 516-931-2201 | www.milleridge.com

"History surrounds you" at this Jericho "standby" for "family celebrations" set in a "grand" Colonial home with 14 fireplaces and a neighboring "village" of "cute" "little shoppes", which is at its best "during the holidays when everything's decorated" and "carolers in 1700s costume" roam the rooms; for many, the prix fixe–only menu's "Traditional American" fare is "mediocre" and the service merely "satisfactory", but it stays "busy" with stalwart supporters who come "for old time's sake"; P.S. a separate cottage and carriage house are available for private events.

Mill Pond House Seafood/Steak | 25 | 23 | 23 | $54 |

Centerport | 437 E. Main St. (bet. Centershore & Little Neck Rds.) | 631-261-7663 | www.millpondrestaurant.com

"Amazing views" of the eponymous pond, especially from "the terrace in summer", combine with "top-notch steaks and seafood" ("surprisingly" "excellent" sushi included) and "unbeatable service" to make this "lovely" Centerport "cousin to Piccolo" "a special-occasion magnet"; warm weather also brings on a "jumping" "tiki bar scene", and though dinner's admittedly "pricey", the prix fixe lunch "is an incredible value."

Mim's American | 20 | 17 | 19 | $36 |

Roslyn Heights | 235 Roslyn Rd. (bet. Jane & Thelma Sts.) | 516-625-7305
Syosset | 33 Berry Hill Rd. (bet. Church St. & Muttontown Eastwoods Rd.) | 516-364-2144
www.mimsny.com

Mum's certainly not the word on these "always-busy" "standbys" in Roslyn Heights and Syosset, where the "mind-boggling" variety of "well-prepared", "substantially portioned" New American faves sends patrons home hauling "big doggy bags"; they can "get a little hectic" and "deafening", but with "accommodating" service and a "terrific" early-bird deal, they're "convenient" for "comfort-type" dining "without having to take out a loan."

	FOOD	DECOR	SERVICE	COST

Minado *Japanese*
| 21 | 13 | 16 | $34 |

Carle Place | 219 Glen Cove Rd. (bet. Old Country Rd. & Westbury Ave.) | 516-294-9541 | www.minado.com

"Fresh and plentiful" sushi is only the highlight among "endless choices" at this "mother of all buffets" in Carle Place, a "cavernous all-you-can-eat" "wonderland" for Japanophiles "gorging on" "tasty" seafood, salads and teppanyaki till they "roll out of the place"; despite the "mass-produced" feel, it's "a fun indulgence" and "family favorite" "for the price of admission" ("they charge kids by height").

Minami *Japanese*
| ∇ 26 | 18 | 22 | $34 |

Massapequa | 12 Central Ave. (bet. Grand Ave. & Veterans Blvd.) | 516-799-4799 | www.minamijapaneserestaurant.com

Afishionados favor this "Japanese gem" in Massapequa for "consistently" "delectable" sushi that's "not the same old, same old", served "fresh" "from the ocean right to your plate" and "reasonably priced" to boot; a "caring staff" that "greets repeat customers" helps explain why its "loyal clientele" is "willing to bypass" the competition.

Mirabelle, Restaurant Ⓜ *French*
| 25 | 23 | 24 | $67 |

Stony Brook | Three Village Inn | 150 Main St. (Shore Rd.) | 631-751-0555 | www.lessings.com

"Another winner" for "top chef" Guy Reuge, his "extraordinary" French flagship (relocated from St. James) now occupies a "refined", fireplace-equipped space in Stony Brook's "venerable" Three Village Inn, where "superior" cuisine is prepared with "inventive" "subtlety" and matched with "marvelous" service; a few nostalgists "miss the old" locale, but most declare they'll "follow this Guy wherever he goes"; P.S. for those put off by "high prices", the more affordable Mirabelle Tavern awaits under the same roof.

Mirabelle Tavern *American*
| 21 | 22 | 21 | $47 |

Stony Brook | Three Village Inn | 150 Main St. (Shore Rd.) | 631-751-0555 | www.threevillageinn.com

For a "more relaxed" taste of "culinary impresario" Guy Reuge's "creative" cooking, try this "inviting" sidekick in a "delightful" tavern space "mere feet away" from Stony Brook's Restaurant Mirabelle; applying the same "meticulous preparation" to a more affordable, "small plates"–centric New American menu, it "raises the bar for casual dining", though some are miffed by "noise" and "occasional slow service"; P.S. the $26 prix fixe lunch is a "great deal."

NEW Miraj
Healthy Grill *Mediterranean/Persian*
| - | - | - | M |

Williston Park | 171 Hillside Ave. (bet. Park & Willis Aves.) | 516-747-3181 | www.mirajhealthygrill.com

Focusing on healthy fare, this midpriced Med-Persian cafe in Williston Park offers salads and grilled vegetables and meats (e.g. charbroiled Cornish hen), plus more complex dishes such as a chicken stew with walnuts in a pomegranate sauce; the simple setting features wood paneling and burgundy tablecloths.

	FOOD	DECOR	SERVICE	COST

☑ Mirko's Ⓜ *Eclectic* — 26 | 22 | 24 | $79

Water Mill | Water Mill Sq. | 670 Montauk Hwy. (bet. Cobb & Old Mill Rds.) | 631-726-4444 | www.mirkosrestaurant.com

"Absolutely exquisite" Eclectic fare via a chef who "really knows how to cook" and "clubby" service led by his co-owner/hostess wife lure a "loyal" clientele to this Water Mill class act set in a "lovely", country-style space with a fireplace and seasonal patio; even with "high prices" it's "often tough to get in", though a few opine "it helps to be known here"; P.S. closed January to mid-February.

Mitsui *Japanese* — ▽ 24 | 19 | 22 | $38

Bay Shore | 1 W. Main St. (4th Ave.) | 631-630-9890 | www.mitsuisushi.com

Jonesing sushiphiles can get their mitts on "fantastic", "super-fresh" fish – including "creatively presented" rolls that "send your palate soaring" – at this "true hidden gem in Bay Shore"; with "pleasant" service, "competitive prices" and a setting where "you can actually have a conversation", it's a local "go-to" for Japanese.

MoCa Asian Bistro *Asian* — 18 | 22 | 19 | $40

Hewlett | 1300 Peninsula Blvd. (bet. Gibson Blvd. & Mill Rd.) | 516-295-8888

"Sexy" and "swanky", this neon-lit Hewlett Pan-Asian lures Five Towners seeking "Manhattan"-style scenery to "meet friends" over "creatively presented" fusion fare and cocktails; but the buzz doesn't sway skeptics who charge it's "overpriced" given the "small portions", "noise level" and focus on the "chic interior" "rather than the food."

Modern Snack Bar Ⓜ *American* — 18 | 11 | 19 | $28

Aquebogue | 628 Main Rd. (bet. Church Ln. & Edgar Ave.) | 631-722-3655 | www.modernsnackbar.com

"Torn from the 1950s", this "popular" Aquebogue "fixture" has earned a "well-deserved" rep for "reliable" American "home cookin'" à la "delicious mashed turnips" and "insanely good" "slabs of pie" ("save room") served by "friendly" waitresses in retro "uniforms"; while "nothing fancy", it's a "bargain" and "you won't go hungry" so there may be a "line at the door"; P.S. closed December–April.

Montebello *Italian* — ▽ 21 | 17 | 21 | $43

Port Washington | 14 Haven Ave. (bet. Franklin Ave. & Main St.) | 516-767-7828 | www.montebellorestaurant.com

Sited "close to the LIRR" in Port Washington, this "local" "standby" sometimes "falls under the radar" despite its "many years" of dishing up "generous" "family-style" "platters" of "well-prepared" Northern Italian fare; given the "reasonable prices" and "above-average service", loyalists are inclined to overlook the "dated" decor.

☑ Morton's The Steakhouse *Steak* — 25 | 23 | 24 | $70

Great Neck | 777 Northern Blvd. (Susquehanna Ave.) | 516-498-2950 | www.mortons.com

A steakhouse "standard-bearer", this "big-ticket" chain offers "excellently prepared" cuts of beef and "grand sides" "served professionally" amid an "ambiance of wealth and class" in Great Neck; some find it a bit "staid" and wish they'd "lose the raw-meat presentation" and "high" wine pricing, but the many who love its "traditional" ways consider it "one of the best."

⊠ Mosaic ⊠ Ⓜ American   28 | 21 | 27 | $64

St. James | 418 N. Country Rd. (Edgewood Ave.) | 631-584-2058 | www.eatmosaic.com

The "spectacular" "ever-changing, five-course tasting menu" via "geniuses in the kitchen" Tate Morris and Jonathan Contes "never fails to please" at this petite St. James "gem", where "adventurous diners" are drawn to the "inspired" New American fare "paired with exquisite wines"; with "cheerful" servers who "never miss a beat" and a "cozy", "quiet" space, it's an "unexpected treat for the palate."

Mother Kelly's American/Italian   21 | 12 | 18 | $30

Cedarhurst | 490 Chestnut St. (bet. Cedarhurst Ave. & Spruce St.) | 516-295-5421

Syosset | Long Island Industrial | 575 Underhill Blvd. (Jericho Tpke.) | 516-802-0333

www.motherkellysli.com

"Dress down" at this "boisterous" Cedarhurst "staple", where the "ginormous" portions of "awesome" Italian-American "comfort food" and pizza will bust your belt but not your budget; the "casual" quarters "resemble a mess hall", but a "loyal following" attests it's "tough to go wrong" here; P.S. the Syosset spin-off offers takeout only.

Moules et Frites Belgian/French   19 | 18 | 19 | $41

Syosset | 4 Berry Hill Rd. (Cold Spring Harbor Rd.) | 516-802-0713 | www.moulessyosset.com

Downtown Syosset's more "lively" thanks to the "welcome addition" of this "busy" Belgian-French offshoot from the Bistro Cassis clan, which fills a "void" with "mussels galore" in "mouthwatering" broths – ranging from the signature white wine and garlic to more "offbeat" options – plus "crisp" frites; with a "smart" staff and 20 taps to "delight" "beer lovers" ("ask for the flight"), it's "off to a good start."

Mumon ⊠ Japanese   ▽ 22 | 25 | 21 | $48

Garden City | 1300 Franklin Ave. (bet. 13th & 14th Sts.) | 516-747-3388 | www.mumonrestaurant.com

"All-around classy", this Garden City stunner is a fantasy come to life for sushi savants savoring "lovely presentations" of the "best quality" fish – along with "excellent" cooked dishes – in an "upscale", "modern Asian" milieu with "wonderful" "Zen" decor and "topnotch" service; it aims to impress "much like a Manhattan hot spot", leaving a few to yen only for "more affordable" prices.

Muse Restaurant &   23 | 23 | 22 | $54
Aquatic Lounge American/Eclectic

Water Mill | Water Mill Shoppes | 760 Montauk Hwy. (Station Rd.) | 631-726-2606 | www.musehampton.com

"Unique all the way around", this "hidden" Water Mill charmer features "enthusiastic" chef-owner Matthew Guiffrida's "complex" menu of "creatively delicious" New American–Eclectic fare and a "cozy yet sophisticated" setting with a saltwater "fish tank as a bar top" so imbibers can "watch the aquatic life"; an "excellent" staff and weekly "live music" help earn it "return visits"; P.S. closed Monday–Wednesday in the off-season.

☑ Nagahama *Japanese*
28 | 15 | 22 | $37

Long Beach | 169 E. Park Ave. (bet. Long Beach & Riverside Blvds.) | 516-432-6446 | www.nagahamasushi.com

For "real quality", "you just can't beat" "inventive" chef-owner Hide Yamamoto's "pristine sushi" at this "reliable" Japanese, where the "incredibly fresh" fish and "warm" service have the natives feeling "lucky to live in Long Beach"; the renovated space is still "as small as a bento box" and "packed" to the gills, so dragon-roll disciples either get their "fix during the week" or "have them on speed dial" for delivery.

Nagashima ☒ *Japanese*
24 | 13 | 19 | $35

Jericho | Jericho Office & Shopping Plaza | 12A-1 Jericho Tpke. (Brush Hollow Rd.) | 516-338-0022 | www.nagashimali.com

"It doesn't look like much", but this Japanese "hole-in-the-wall" in a Jericho "strip mall" is a "proven" "treasure" for sushi-seekers who praise its "terrific variety" of "consistently fresh" fish, notably the "innovative" "specialty rolls"; touchy types nag the "service is not the nicest", but it's "quick" enough that "your cup of green tea never goes low."

Nanking *Chinese/Thai*
∇ 19 | 20 | 16 | $34

New Hyde Park | 2056 Hillside Ave. (bet. Aster Dr. & Marcus Ave.) | 516-352-0009 | www.nankingrestaurantgroup.com

Representing the "diversity of Asian cuisine", this New Hyde Park branch of a regional chainlet is a "reasonably consistent" source of midpriced Chinese-Thai fare served in eye-pleasing environs equipped with plush banquettes, copper-top tables and a "huge Buddha"; it strives to be something "different", though doubters declare they're "trying for fusion" but producing "mostly confusion."

Nautilus Cafe *Seafood/Steak*
24 | 17 | 23 | $46

Freeport | 46 Woodcleft Ave. (bet. Adams & Front Sts.) | 516-379-2566 | www.nautiluscafe.com

"Whether it's surf or turf", this Freeport "fixture" is "a winner" among "ever so many" rivals "on the Nautical Mile" thanks to its "super seafood", "wonderful" steaks and "right-on" service from a "courteous staff"; the interior is "nothing fancy", but there are views "across the street to the waterside" and the early-bird deal is "one of the best" going.

NEW Navy Beach *American*
19 | 20 | 17 | $49

Montauk | Port Royal | 16 Navy Rd. (off Industrial & 2nd House Rds.) | 631-668-6868 | www.navybeach.com

"Beautiful sunsets" snare shorebirds at this new seasonal "'in' spot" on Montauk's Fort Pond Bay, where "picnic tables" on the sand and a "nautical" dining room set the "beachy" scene for a "limited" but "surprisingly tasty" American menu of seafood and burgers; snipers

	FOOD	DECOR	SERVICE	COST

say the service is "amateurish" given the "expense", but that doesn't lower the "buzz" that draws "weekend crowds" despite the "hard-to-find location."

Nello Summertimes *Italian*   ▽ 16 | 21 | 13 | $116

Southampton | Nello Summertimes | 136 Main St. (bet. Hampton Rd. & Post Crossing) | 631-287-5500

If you're "just people-watching", this seasonal Southamptoner (via an Upper East Side original) is a "showstopper" with "gorgeous surroundings", a "lively bar" and an especially sceney "outdoor terrace"; but given merely "average" Northern Italian food and lacking service, it's "hard to justify" "absurdly expensive" tabs that are "enough to even make a longtime Hamptonite gasp."

New Chilli & Curry Restaurant *Indian*   ▽ 26 | 15 | 24 | $27

Hicksville | 106 Woodbury Rd. (bet. Charles & Max Aves.) | 516-932-9180

"Hot means hot" at this "tiny" Hicksville hideaway, where "spectacular" Northern Indian dishes – along with "innovative" Chinese and Thai "fusion" fare – are prepared "as spicy as you can stand it" even if you need "a fire extinguisher at meal's end"; "incredibly friendly" staffers welcome all "like long-lost family", and the "cozy digs" are often "bustling" now that "the locals have discovered it"; P.S. "you can't beat" the $7.95 lunch buffet.

New Paradise Cafe *American/Eclectic*   22 | 17 | 21 | $56

Sag Harbor | 126 Main St. (bet. Nassau & Spring Sts.) | 631-725-6080 | www.newparadisecafe.net

"It's a keeper" confirm "the locals" at this "solid" Sag Harbor "favorite" (under the same ownership as Robert's in Water Mill), "one of the better" area options for "tasty and innovative" New American-Eclectic eats and "welcoming" service with "no attitude"; the "neighborhood vibe" extends to the "attractive bar" and summertime deck, and the "dependable" performance brings the faithful "back on a regular basis."

Nicholas James Bistro Ⓜ *American*   22 | 17 | 21 | $37

Merrick | 2057 Merrick Rd. (bet. Hewlett & Merrick Aves.) | 516-546-4805 | www.njbistro.com

Regulars relish the "creative menu" at this "shining star in Merrick", a "neighborhood eatery" where the New American fare and "accommodating service" are "consistently" "a cut above"; penny-pinchers protest it's "on the pricey side", but the "understated" yet "appealing" space is "almost always crowded."

Nichol's *American*   17 | 12 | 19 | $38

East Hampton | 100 Montauk Hwy. (Cove Hollow Rd.) | 631-324-3939

Like "the *Cheers* of East Hampton", this "unpretentious", "very local" "hangout" is an "easy" option for "decent" burgers and other "simple" American grub served in "friendly, pub-type" surroundings; "bargain" prices boost its "popularity", and come summer "you can sit outdoors" if you don't mind "cars whizzing by."

	FOOD	DECOR	SERVICE	COST

☑ Nick & Toni's *Italian/Mediterranean* | 24 | 22 | 22 | $69

East Hampton | 136 N. Main St. (bet. Cedar St. & Miller Terrace) | 631-324-3550 | www.nickandtonis.com

"Classy and consistent", this "legendary" East Hampton "standout" is still "bustling" with "the 'in' crowd" drawn to its "first-rate" Italian-Med plates (some via a "wood-burning oven"), "spot-on" service and "celebrity aura"; though "wallet pain" may set in, it "hasn't lost its touch" for "memorable" dining – if "you can get a reservation."

Nick's *Pizza* | 23 | 16 | 21 | $26

Rockville Centre | 272 Sunrise Hwy. (bet. Morris & N. Park Aves.) | 516-763-3278 | www.nicksrvc.com

Pizzaphiles hail this "family-friendly" Rockville Centre Italian (with sibs in Manhattan and Forest Hills) as a "step above the rest" for its "superb thin-crust" pies ("they don't sell slices"), but "bring an appetite" for the "plentiful" portions of *delizioso* pastas, salads and calzones too; add "fair prices", "great service" and "Sinatra singing to you in the background", and "what more do you want?"

Nick's Tuscan Grill Ⓜ *Italian* | 21 | 21 | 21 | $39

Long Beach | 40 E. Park Ave. (bet. Edwards & Riverside Blvds.) | 516-432-2690 | www.georgemartingroup.com

After a "transformation" from the seafood-centric Coastal Grill, this "feel-good" Long Beach eatery is now the George Martin chain's link to Northern Italy, upholding the same "even-keeled" "standards" with its "hearty", "quite tasty" "traditional" menu and "smooth" service; lodged in a "warm setting" with Tuscany brick and earth tones, it "knows how to please" even if have-nots nix it as "too highly priced."

Nisen *Japanese* | 25 | 24 | 20 | $49

Commack | 5032 Jericho Tpke. (Larkfield Rd.) | 631-462-1000

Nisen Sushi *Japanese*

Woodbury | Woodbury Village Shopping Ctr. | 7967 Jericho Tpke. (S. Woods Rd.) | 516-496-7000
www.nisensushi.com

"Awesome sushi" "the way it should be", as well as "perfect" Japanese dishes presented like "art on a plate" in "beautiful" "modern" settings catapult this "pricey" Commack and Woodbury duo to "winner" status among its "good-looking", "lively" crowd; a handful gripes about a staff with "attitude", but most like the "trendy" "Manhattan feel"; P.S. there's a DJ in Woodbury Thursday and Friday nights.

☑ Noah's *American* | 26 | 18 | 21 | $50

Greenport | 136 Front St. (bet. 1st & 3rd Sts.) | 631-477-6720 | www.chefnoahschwartz.com

"Adventuresome" chef/co-owner Noah Schwartz (formerly of Southold's now-defunct Seafood Barge) lends his "highly imaginative" flair to this "welcome addition to Greenport", where the New American menu showcases "inspired", seafood-centric small plates alongside full entrees and a raw bar; the "professional" staff is "helpful", and despite a "stark", "too-noisy" setting that's "more SoHo than NoFo", the "fabulous" "grazing" ensures it's "always hoppin'."

Nonnina ⓜ *Italian* — 25 | 24 | 23 | $53

West Islip | 999 Montauk Hwy. (bet. Gladstone Ave. & Oak Neck Rd.) | 631-321-8717 | www.nonninarestaurant.com

Count on "terrific" "interpretations of the classics" at this "upscale" West Islip Italian, where the "fabulous food", "stellar service" and "beautiful" but "comfortable" surroundings are "perfect for a romantic" "special occasion" or a "wonderful" "night out with friends"; devotees who "are never disappointed" deem it "so worth" "the trip and the price."

ⓩ North Fork Table & Inn *American* — 29 | 25 | 27 | $77

Southold | North Fork Table & Inn | 57225 Main Rd./Rte. 25 (bet. Boisseau & Laurel Aves.) | 631-765-0177 | www.northforktableandinn.com

Chef Gerry Hayden (ex Aureole) "has reached new heights" at this "stellar" Southold "destination", which secures the No. 1 rating for Food in this Survey with "a constantly evolving, brilliantly realized" New American menu crafted from "the freshest local ingredients" and matched with "gold-standard" desserts from Claudia Fleming (ex Gramercy Tavern); "impeccable, gracious" service that's also rated No. 1 on Long Island and a "civilized" "rural setting" round out an experience as "unforgettable" "as anything in NYC, period"; P.S. this year saw the arrival of the Lunch Truck planted out back, where midday lobster rolls, artisan hot dogs and such come at gentle prices.

Novitá Wine Bar and Trattoria *Italian* — 23 | 22 | 22 | $41

Garden City | 860 Franklin Ave. (bet. 9th St. & Stewart Ave.) | 516-739-7660 | www.novita-ny.com

"Inventive", "trendy" and a "wine lover's dream", this stylishly "modern" Garden City spot pairs its "wonderful" Italian bites with 100 "fantastic" vinos by the glass dispensed from a state-of-the-art system by an "educated" staff; while "totally worth" "every penny", it's "definitely a scene" "for singles looking to mingle" so "eat early or bring earplugs" if you're "over the age of 35."

Oak Chalet ⓜ *Continental/German* — 19 | 19 | 20 | $37

Bellmore | 1940 Bellmore Ave. (bet. Beltagh Ave. & Natta Blvd.) | 516-826-1700 | www.oakchalet.net

Home to Continental-German dishes "done right", this "old standby" in Bellmore proffers a "meat-and-potatoes" menu and a "wide variety" of *bier* in "homey", "inviting" quarters tended by "friendly people"; detractors who discern "nothing spaetzle" contend it "needs updating", but fans of the "change of scenery" and "homemade taste" counter "who really cares?"

Oakland's *American/Seafood* — 18 | 21 | 18 | $49

Hampton Bays | Dune Rd. (Rd. H, at Shinnecock Inlet) | 631-728-6900

Sundays on the Bay *Seafood*

NEW **Hampton Bays** | 369 Dune Rd. (Rd. H, at Shinnecock Inlet) | 631-728-2611
www.oaklandsrestaurant.com

"Go just before sunset" for "unbeatable views" from the "waterfront" deck "on Shinnecock Inlet" (a "boat-watcher's dream") that draw "crowds galore" to this seasonal Hampton Bays American (the new Sundays is open year-round); those who find the seafood-leaning menu and "undertrained" service merely "adequate" for the price prefer it for the "ocean breeze", "live music" and "enjoyable" open-air bar.

Oar Steak & Seafood Grill *Seafood/Steak*   21 | 19 | 20 | $38

Patchogue | Sun Dek Marina | 264 West Ave. (Mulford St.) | 631-654-8266 | www.theoar.com

As it's "accessible by boat", seafarers and landlubbers alike can enjoy "alfresco" "dockside dining" on "solid" fish and steaks at this "funky" "warm-weather" "favorite" in Patchogue's Sun Dek Marina; the "casual" interior's walls are aptly "covered in paddles", and "live bands" on summer weekends ensure there's a "good time to be had by all."

Oasis Waterfront   24 | 23 | 23 | $60
Restaurant & Bar *American*

Sag Harbor | Mill Creek Marina | 3253 Noyac Rd. (bet. Burkeshire Dr. & Ruggs Path) | 631-725-7110 | www.oasishamptons.com

Like "a breath of fresh air", this "family-run" Sag Harbor New American with "waterfront views" of the Mill Creek Marina is a "welcoming" oasis with "excellent" seafood-leaning specialties and "exceptionally nice" service from folks "who care"; occupying a "lovely, serene" space, it's "not as trendy as some" but still "reliably" "worth the price"; P.S. closed Monday–Wednesday in the winter.

Oaxaca Mexican Food Treasure *Mexican*   23 | 10 | 22 | $24

Huntington | 385 New York Ave. (bet. Main & W. Carver Sts.) | 631-547-1232

"Don't tell anyone" plead "in-the-know" compadres "blown away" by this Huntington "joint", whose "amazing", "super-cheap" "peasant food" delivers "homemade" "Mexican authenticity at its best"; the "lovely" staff "makes you feel like a regular", and "don't be fooled by" the "divey" digs – it's an "unpolished gem" that "really is a treasure"; P.S. serves beer and wine only.

Ocean Grill Ⓜ *American/Seafood*   ▽ 23 | 18 | 22 | $50

Freeport | Al Grover High & Dry Marina | 499 S. Main St. (Laurel Rd.) | 516-208-9604 | www.oceangrillfreeport.com

Fans find "fresh" seafood, "modestly priced burgers" and other American and Italian eats at this family-oriented Freeporter; there's patio seating in the summer, and a simple, red-accented, white-tableclothed interior completes the setting.

Oevo Ⓜ *Italian*   ▽ 21 | 21 | 20 | $53

Great Neck | 421 Northern Blvd. (bet. Lakeview & Merrivale Rds.) | 516-504-9690 | www.oevoristorante.com

The Great Neck sib of Manhattan's Da Ciro, this upmarket Italian features a "wood-burning oven" turning out the "tasty" likes of personal pizza and its signature "focaccia made with robiola cheese"; the "attractive" surroundings are manned by "a professional staff", but brace yourself for a "pricey" tab and "deafening loudness on a busy" night.

	FOOD	DECOR	SERVICE	COST

NEW Old Fields 🚫Ⓜ *American/Steak* — — — M

Greenlawn | 81 Broadway (Railroad St.) | 631-754-9868

New owners John Tunney (Besito) and his wife, Christine, renovated this vintage Greenlawn American steakhouse while keeping period details including a fireplace, wooden booths, tin ceiling and knotty-pine paneling; a midpriced menu offers both the house strip steak – marinated according to a 55-year-old recipe – and new items like a beef patty nestled between two grilled cheddar cheese sandwiches.

Old Mill Inn *American/Seafood* 20 20 20 $44

Mattituck | 5775 W. Mill Rd. (Naugles Rd.) | 631-298-8080 | www.theoldmillinn.net

Although "really off the beaten path", this "waterfront" New American in a restored mill with a "pretty view" of Mattituck Inlet is a "charming" "surprise" where "friendly" staffers serve a "well-prepared" menu focused on local seafood; with an interior sporting "polished wood" that "evokes an old yacht" and an "excellent" "deck" for summer, it's worth using "a GPS to find"; P.S. closed November–April.

Olive Oils *Italian* 20 16 18 $29

Point Lookout | 28 Lido Blvd. (Bellmore Ave.) | 516-432-0000 | www.oliveoilsrestaurant.com

For a "decent" fix of pizza, panini or "something parmigiana", Point Lookout denizens turn to this "little" "local Italian" at the foot of the Loop Parkway; though some find it "very ordinary", others say its "casual" bites and Monday prix fixe pasta nights are "surprisingly good" for the price, and there's seating "outside in the summer."

O'Mally's ❶ *Pub Food* 18 15 20 $31

Southold | 44780 North Rd. (bet. Horton Ln. & Youngs Ave.) | 631-765-2111

"You'd be amazed how many ways" they can prepare a burger (30 or so are on the menu) at this Southold "standby" for "solid" American pub fare delivered by "cheerful" staffers in "comfortable", "kid-friendly" digs; "fair prices" and service "until midnight" keep "locals and weekenders" alike "coming back" for more.

1 North Steakhouse Ⓜ *Steak* 22 18 21 $48

Hampton Bays | 1 North Rd. (bet. Montauk & Sunrise Hwys.) | 631-594-3419 | www.1northsteakhouse.com

Most diners are "proud to bring friends" to this upscale Hampton Bays "tavern" boasting a porterhouse that's "soft as silk", "excellent" sides and "creative" options like a lobster mac 'n' cheese; service is generally "pleasant" and there's live music Friday nights, but despite a double-sided fireplace, few warm up to the "bland" decor with a bit of a "shopping-mall" feel.

NEW Onsen Sushi *Japanese* — — — M

Oakdale | 597 Montauk Hwy. (bet. Dale Dr. & La Salle Pl.) | 631-567-1688

Chef/co-owner Jason Chen (ex Nisen in Commack) is luring sushi enthusiasts to this tiny, moderately priced Japanese newcomer in

Oakdale for creations such as the Kenny Special roll – seared tuna wrapped with chopped shrimp; hot dishes from chef-partner Eric Wu include an eggplant sandwich stuffed with seafood and wasabi, and add further incentive to look past the simple storefront setting.

Onzon Thai House Ⓜ *Thai* 　　24 | 12 | 21 | $27

Bellmore | 2618 Merrick Rd. (bet. Centre & St. Marks Aves.) | 516-409-6113

"First-rate" Siamese specialties with "authentic", "delicate" spicing "always satisfy" at this Bellmore "neighborhood" "benchmark"; the "welcoming" staff and "reasonable prices" (with a BYO policy that "adds to the value") lead its "loyal following" to forgive the "small", "bland" space.

Orchid *Chinese* 　　23 | 20 | 22 | $35

Garden City | 730 Franklin Ave. (bet. 7th St. & Stewart Ave.) | 516-742-1116

"Below street level" but way "above standard" Chinese, this Garden City "institution" is "always jumping" with longtime loyalists relishing the "subtle flavors" of "upscale Cantonese" specialties ("Peking duck is a must") "prepared to perfection" and "artfully served" by a "cheerful" staff; decor featuring a mirrored ceiling and colorful flora is "a real blast from the past" that lends '80s-era "class" to the "basement location."

Ⓩ Orient, The *Chinese* 　　27 | 9 | 19 | $27

Bethpage | 623 Hicksville Rd. (bet. Courtney & Fiddler Lns.) | 516-822-1010

As "authentic as going to Chinatown", this "famously unfancy" Bethpage Chinese is "the real thing" for "phenomenal", "richly flavored" Cantonese and "wonderful dim sum" that "can't be beat for quality and value"; "welcoming" owner Tommy Tan leads a team of "skilled waiters" who can "suggest terrific off-menu specials", and though it "gets completely packed" (on weekends particularly), "it's definitely worth the lines" and "blah decor."

Osaka Ⓢ *Japanese* 　　▽ 24 | 16 | 22 | $31

Huntington | 328 W. Main St. (bet. Green & Prospect Sts.) | 631-673-7271

"Amazing" sushi and "excellent" cooked dishes qualify this fairly priced Huntington Japanese as an unsung "favorite" in the nabe; staffed by a chef-owner and his "friendly" crew, the small, spare setup tends to be "quiet" – and the regulars say "let's keep it that way"; P.S. serves beer and wine only.

O's Food & Wine Bar ● *French* 　　22 | 21 | 21 | $44

St. James | 552 N. Country Rd. (bet. Acron Rd. & Lake Ave.) | 631-584-4600 | www.osfoodandwinebar.com

A "terrific" "way to explore different dishes", this "creative" St. James French from chef-owner Philippe Corbet (ex Bouley) specializes in an "exciting" "tapas menu" that "highlights foods from a different country each month"; it's "fun for a light or full dinner" with "eager" service in "comfy beach house" environs enhanced by two fireplaces, live music Wednesday–Friday and a "hopping" "bar scene."

	FOOD	DECOR	SERVICE	COST

RESTAURANTS

Osteria da Nino *Italian* | 24 | 19 | 23 | $46 |

Huntington | 292 Main St. (bet. Green & New Sts.) | 631-425-0820 | www.ninosrusticitalian.com

"Compliments to the chef" cheer champions of this "homey" Huntington Italian (sibling to nearby Red), which "never misses" with "authentic pastas" and other "fabulous" "rustic" dishes "made with love and care" "at a reasonable price"; "professional service" and a "warm", "comfortable setting" further explain why it's a former "secret" "that's becoming more and more popular."

Osteria Toscana *Italian* | 23 | 19 | 21 | $50 |

Huntington | 69 Wall St. (Central St.) | 631-549-7074 | www.osteriatoscana.com

"Italian with flair" draws applause for this "Huntington find", which joins "freshly made pasta" and other "delicious" Tuscan-style classics with "wonderful service" led by a chef-owner who "treats you like a regular"; split into a brick-lined ground floor and a "prettier" upstairs "anchored by a lovely fireplace", it's considered "a keeper" notwithstanding "noisy" acoustics and "expensive" tabs.

Ozumo Japanese Restaurant *Japanese* | 23 | 17 | 20 | $34 |

Bethpage | 164 Hicksville Rd. (Hempstead Tpke.) | 516-731-8989

This Bethpage Japanese remains a fish fancier's "favorite" thanks to "superb sushi" professionally served in either a dining area bedecked with photos of sumo wrestlers (Ozumo being the sport's Super Bowl) or a tatami room; but while "the quality hasn't waned" foodwise, foes wrestling with the "run-down feel" suggest "they need to update."

Pace's Steak House *Steak* | 22 | 20 | 22 | $59 |

Hauppauge | 325 Nesconset Hwy. (bet. Brooksite Dr. & Hauppauge Rd.) | 631-979-7676

Port Jefferson | 318 Wynn Ln. (Main St.) | 631-331-9200 www.pacessteakhouse.com

Reminiscent of "NYC without the drive", this fast-paced Hauppauge and Port Jefferson pair plies "humongous" cuts of meat "cooked to perfection" (plus "fresh and delicious seafood") and matched with "fine service" amid "classy" "traditional" atmospherics; they're "busy" and "loud" and it's easy to "run up your tab", but carnivores who call it a "first local choice" "still come back for more."

Paddy McGees *Seafood* | 18 | 18 | 18 | $40 |

Island Park | 6 Waterview Rd. (Pettit Pl.) | 516-431-8700

Diners from land and sea ("ample boat parking" is available) wash up at this "rustic" Island Park stalwart, where the deck's "water views" of Reynolds Channel give a "Jimmy Buffett–like" boost to the "average" fish and very "relaxed" service; there's also a "mean" Sunday brunch "spread", and on weekends a "massive" "summertime bar crowd" "takes over" for "loud", "rowdy" revelry; P.S. closed to the public November through mid-March.

| | FOOD | DECOR | SERVICE | COST |

Page One *American/Eclectic*
22 | 18 | 22 | $41

Glen Cove | 90 School St. (bet. Highland Rd. & North Ln.) | 516-676-2800 | www.pageonerestaurant.com

Glen Cove converts are "totally seduced" by "talented", "personable" chef/co-owner Jeanine Dimenna's "creative cooking" at this "welcoming" American-Eclectic "treasure", where the "fabulous" fare is "presented artistically" and served "with a smile" by an "excellent" staff; "reasonable" prices (including a "budget-friendly" prix fixe) make it one "amazing treat", so "don't miss out."

Painters' Ⓜ *Eclectic*
20 | 20 | 19 | $36

Brookhaven Hamlet | 416 S. Country Rd. (Montauk Hwy.) | 631-286-6264 | www.paintersrestaurant.com

About the "coolest place" in Brookhaven Hamlet (and beyond), this "offbeat" Eclectic is a "relaxed" "change of pace" with "spot-on food, tables you can draw on" and "changing artwork displayed" wall-to-wall; as a "casual" "hangout" it lures legions of "locals" who come to "mingle" above "the din" and catch live bands on weekends.

🏆 Palm, The *Seafood/Steak*
26 | 20 | 23 | $71

East Hampton | Huntting Inn | 94 Main St. (Huntting Ln.) | 631-324-0411 | www.thepalm.com

"Perfect" lobster, "superb" steaks and "hefty" cocktails are the signatures of this "bustling", "special-occasion" chophouse chain link in The Huntting Inn, with a "dark men's-club" look and "wonderful atmosphere" enhanced by "caricatures of celebs" (and "locals") covering the walls; "impeccable", "old-school" service seals the deal, so while it's "not cheap", most conclude it's "worth it."

🏆 Palm Court at the Carltun Ⓜ *American/Continental*
24 | 28 | 25 | $61

East Meadow | The Carltun | Eisenhower Park (Merrick Ave.) | 516-542-0700 | www.thecarltun.com

"Get pampered" like "a member of an upscale club" at this "lovely" Continental-New American set in a mansion in East Meadow's Eisenhower Park, which oozes "class all the way" with "beautiful surroundings" rated No. 1 for Decor in this Survey (look for paintings of flying monkeys overhead) and "spectacular" presentations of "inventive" cuisine complemented by "extraordinary" wines and "gracious" service; "they charge you accordingly", but "it all works" "if you want to make an impression" or "feel special" – and lunch is "truly a bargain."

Palmer's American Grille *Continental*
21 | 19 | 21 | $41

Farmingdale | 123 Fulton St. (Hempstead Tpke.) | 516-420-0609 | www.palmersamericangrille.com

A "nice surprise" in Farmingdale, this onetime pub now "looks great all around" with a tastefully "comfortable" dining room lined with historic photos, an "inviting" bar area with live music on the weekends and a sizable terrace; "accommodating" staffers serve an "excellent" Continental menu (including a $22 prix fixe Sunday–Friday), so most sum it up as "a winner."

Panama Hatties *American*

25 | 23 | 24 | $66

Huntington Station | Post Plaza | 872 E. Jericho Tpke. (bet. Cooper Ave. & Emerald Ln.) | 631-351-1727 | www.panamahatties.com

Restaurateur George Echeverría (formerly of Woodmere's Soigné) recently assumed ownership of this "truly top-drawer" New American "hidden" in a Huntington Station "strip mall", which "never fails to impress" with an "inspired menu" of "sensational" seasonal dishes presented by "experienced, unobtrusive" servers in "classy" quarters; it's "costly" but "worth the splurge", and on weekdays there's a "bargain" prix fixe lunch; P.S. a post-Survey chef change and renovation are not reflected in the Food and Decor ratings.

Pancho's Border Grill *Tex-Mex*

19 | 15 | 19 | $28

Great Neck | 10 Grace Ave. (bet. Bond St. & Middle Neck Rd.) | 516-829-5305

Pancho's Cantina *Tex-Mex*

Island Park | 4245 Austin Blvd. (Audubon Blvd.) | 516-897-8300 www.panchostexmex.com

"When a fajita fix is needed", this "busy" Tex-Mex twosome in Great Neck and Island Park "caters to families" with "tasty" staples served in "easygoing" environs with "crayons on the tables"; they're "loud" and "very informal", but "plentiful" portions, "obliging" service and "decent prices" are reason enough to "*ándale!*"

Panini Café
at Diane's *Sandwiches*

▽ 23 | 15 | 16 | $22

Roslyn | 23 Bryant Ave. (bet. Roosevelt Ave. & Skillman St.) | 516-621-2522 | www.trattoriadiane.com

"Pick up a quick lunch or delicious dessert" "on the cheap" at this "casual cafe" annexed to Diane's Bakery in Roslyn, where "very appetizing" panini, salads and "hot dishes" are prepared "fresh daily" along with the expected "out-of-this-world" baked goods; the "cozy, homey" locale with second-floor seating and a terrace is a midday "favorite."

Papa Razzi *Italian*

18 | 18 | 19 | $35

Westbury | 1500 Jericho Tpke. (Glen Cove Rd.) | 516-877-7744 | www.paparazzitrattoria.com

For "hearty Italian" fare in a "casual", "kid-friendly" setting that's "spacious" enough for a "large group", this Westbury "staple" from a regional chain is a "decent" choice; "quick service", an "engaging atmosphere" and "reasonable prices" help make it a "popular place."

NEW Park Place *American/Seafood*

- | - | - | M

Floral Park | 41 Covert Ave. (bet. Beverly & Marshall Aves.) | 516-775-9004 | www.parkplacefp.com

Earthy colors and a grandly arched, stained-glass window are the backdrop for seafood-centric American small plates such as a lobster BLT at this midpriced Floral Park gastropub; live bands perform Friday and Saturday nights.

	FOOD	DECOR	SERVICE	COST

Pasta-eria *Italian* | 23 | 13 | 17 | $27 |

Hicksville | Woodbury Shopping Ctr. | 440 S. Oyster Bay Rd. (Woodbury Rd.) | 516-938-1555

It's a "very casual" setup at the rear of a strip-center pizzeria, but this Hicksville Italian is a "local favorite" offering "all kinds of" "tasty" pastas and pies "on the cheap"; but since it's a "busy" go-to with "slow" service and "tables on top of each other", some suggest it's "way better for takeout."

Pasta Pasta *Italian* | 25 | 20 | 23 | $41 |

Port Jefferson | 234 E. Main St. (Prospect St.) | 631-331-5335 | www.pastapasta.net

Paesani proclaim this "charming" Port Jefferson Italian (sister to Sayville's Cafe Joelle) "one of the best" for "top-of-the-line" renderings of its namesake and other "excellent" dishes ("it ain't just pasta"), all served by a "wonderful" staff at an "affordable" price; housed in the "cutest little" space, it has "a huge following", so "be sure to make a reservation" on weekends.

Pasta Vino Italian Bistro *Italian* | 22 | 19 | 23 | $36 |

Mineola | 149 Mineola Blvd. (Harrison Ave.) | 516-294-1715 | www.pastavinobistro.com

True to its name, this "local Italian" "keeper" in Mineola dishes up "delish", "nonna"-style standards accompanied by "decent wines" from an affordable, 50-label list; "agreeable" servers maintain the "comfortable" bistro ambiance and help ensure the regulars "keep coming back for more."

Pastrami King Ⓜ *Deli* | 20 | 11 | 16 | $24 |

Merrick | 196 Merrick Rd. (bet. Bernard St. & Meadowbrook Pkwy.) | 516-377-4300 | www.pastramiking.com

"If pastrami's your thing", you "can't do much better" hereabouts than this Merrick deli "standby", where "overstuffed sandwiches" lead an "enjoyable" lineup of Jewish ("but not kosher") staples and Eclectic eats; the "decor is somewhat tacky" and service can be "sluggish", but it's a "cheap" "fix" "when you're in the mood."

Patio at 54 Main, The *American* | 19 | 16 | 20 | $52 |

Westhampton Beach | 54 Main St. (bet. Potunk & Sunset Lns.) | 631-288-0100 | www.thepatiowhb.com

The "reliable" roster of meat and fish renders this Westhampton Beach New American a "solid" "local" pick for "upscale comfort food" served by "attentive" types in a space featuring a glass-encased patio; while "nothing novel", it's an "enjoyable" fallback with live music on weekends and a $25 prix fixe to temper tabs that may seem "pricey for what you get."

Pearl East *Chinese* | 23 | 20 | 19 | $37 |

Manhasset | 1191 Northern Blvd. (bet. Maple St. & Norgate Rd.) | 516-365-9898

"Not your run-of-the-mill Chinese", this Manhasset "bastion of quality" boasts an "imaginative and fresh" "gourmet" menu that its "steady customers" "can depend on" (and sushi is an "added plus"); with a "gracious owner" who's "always on hand" to "oversee" the "lovely", antiques-filled setting, it's something "really special", though it "does tend to crowd up."

Pentimento Italian   22 | 20 | 22 | $48

Stony Brook | Stony Brook Village Ctr. | 93 Main St. (bet. Christian Ave. & Rte. 25A) | 631-689-7755 | www.pentimentorestaurant.net

A "dedicated clientele" touts this "charming", "little" Stony Brook Italian as "a great find" for "sophisticated" seasonal fare from an "upbeat" staff that "doesn't rush you out the door"; installed in "cozy", "comfortable" digs with "delightful" "garden seating in the back", it's a "reliably" "memorable experience" albeit one priced at the "high end for the area."

NEW Pepe Rosso 24 Italian   - | - | - | M

Port Washington | 24 Manorhaven Blvd. (bet. Ashwood & Boxwood Rds.) | 516-944-9477 | www.peperosso24.com

Pizza comes in round, square, ultrathin and stuffed variations at this midpriced Port Washington newcomer that also serves pastas, panini and Italian entrees; painted murals on the walls add a fanciful touch to the casual setting with a take-out section on one side and a dining room with a tile floor and wood tables on the other; P.S. a pianist performs Wednesday nights.

Peppercorns Continental   19 | 16 | 19 | $35

Hicksville | 25 E. Marie St. (B'way) | 516-931-4002 | www.peppercornsny.com

"Tucked away in Hicksville", this "long-term" "local" "staple" is "inviting" enough for "ample" helpings of "consistently good" steaks and Continental fare served by a "friendly and competent" crew; it's "convenient" for "a quick bite", and though nitpickers may knock the "bar atmosphere", at least the "price is right."

PeraBell Food Bar American/Eclectic   26 | - | 23 | $40

Patchogue | 69 E. Main St. (bet. Maple & N. Ocean Aves.) | 631-447-7766

Now relocated "down the street" next to the Patchogue Theatre, this "delightful" "neighborhood find" continues to shine thanks to the "scrumptious", "artfully prepared" dishes on "terrific chef" John Peragine's "oh-so-comforting" American-Eclectic menu; add an "attentive" staff and "larger digs" that "should help with crowd control", and its admirers simply "can't rave enough"; P.S. it moved post-Survey.

NEW Perfecto Mundo   ∇ 24 | 21 | 26 | $34
Latin Fusion Bistro Ⓜ Pan-Latin

Commack | Northgate Shopping Ctr. | 1141-1 Jericho Tpke. (Kings Park Rd.) | 631-864-2777 | www.perfectomundony.com

"Forget about the location" in a strip mall and the modest decor, 'cause this "wonderful new" Commack Pan-Latin shows "a lot of promise" when it comes to "amazing" fusion fare from chef Steven Del Lima (ex Black & Blue); with such "unique and delicious" dishes as chipotle-dusted salmon and hickory-spiced steak, "pleasantly surprised" early arrivers promise they'll "definitely be back."

Per Un Angelo *Italian*

22 | 17 | 22 | $43

Wantagh | Jones Beach Hotel | 3275 Byron St. (bet. Atlantic Blvd. & Willow St.) | 516-783-6484

Sited "off the beaten path" in Wantagh's Jones Beach Hotel, this "old-world" Northern Italian is a haven for "consistent" cuisine from a "professional" staff led by "personable" owners who "greet visitors with open arms"; a keyboardist performs three nights a week, and though modernists insist the "dated" setting "needs a makeover", that doesn't deter backers who've "been going here for years."

☑ Peter Luger ⌦ *Steak*

27 | 17 | 21 | $71

Great Neck | 255 Northern Blvd. (bet. Jayson Ave. & Tain Dr.) | 516-487-8800 | www.peterluger.com

"Xanadu for steak", this Great Neck offshoot of the "iconic" Williamsburg meatery extends its run as Long Island's Most Popular restaurant for an 18th year by regaling "ravenous carnivores" in "traditional" style with "succulent, buttery beef" set down by "brusque" but "professional" "old-school waiters"; even loyalists concede the tabs are "gargantuan" and "cash will go out of existence before they accept credit cards", but it's still "the platinum standard": "calling them a steakhouse is like calling a Ferrari a car."

P.F. Chang's China Bistro *Chinese*

20 | 21 | 18 | $34

Westbury | Mall at the Source | 1504 Old Country Rd. (Merchants Concourse) | 516-222-9200 | www.pfchangs.com

"Light, delicious", "Americanized" Chinese food keeps fans "coming back" – especially for the "standout" lettuce wraps – to this "trendy", "stylish" chain link in Westbury; though not everyone is convinced ("overpriced", "ordinary", "loud"), the "consistent" service is a plus, as is the "smart" menu "catering to people with allergies" and other needs.

PG Steakhouse *Steak*

22 | 13 | 21 | $66

Huntington | 1745 E. Jericho Tpke. (Ware Ave.) | 631-499-1005 | www.pgsteakhouse.com

It's "not elegant", but this durable Huntington meatery does a "pretty decent" job providing "very good" cuts of beef and "attentive" service; maybe the "worn", "old-style" room "needs upgrading", but if you can "forget the decor", it's "all a steakhouse needs to be."

Phao Thai Kitchen Ⓜ *Thai*

21 | 16 | 20 | $45

Sag Harbor | 29 Main St. (bet. Bay & Washington Sts.) | 631-725-0101 | www.phaorestaurant.com

"Thai done right" makes this latest next-door neighbor to "sister restaurant Sen" a "welcome" "surprise" in Sag Harbor for fans of its "beautifully spiced and aromatic" cooking, "great cocktails" and "cool" dishabille vibe; others opine the "price is a little high" and note that after 11 PM on weekends it "turns into more of a club."

	FOOD	DECOR	SERVICE	COST

Philippe East ◐ *Chinese* — 24 | 22 | 22 | $70

East Hampton | Lily Pond | 44 Three Mile Harbor Rd. (Oakview Hwy.) | 631-907-0250

🆕 **Philippe** ⧆ Ⓜ *Chinese*

Jericho | 399 Jericho Tpke. (Merry Ln.) | 516-605-2555
www.philippechow.com

Trendy Manhattan chef Philippe Chow "never fails to please the palate" with "exquisite" "gourmet Chinese" dishes – "the Peking duck is phenomenal" – delivered in a "gorgeous" two-toned setting at this seasonal East Hamptonite; a few foes fume at "the pretentiousness and astronomical prices", but for its "upscale" clientele it's "worth every penny"; P.S. the Jericho branch opened post-Survey.

Piccola Bussola *Italian* — 23 | 17 | 22 | $41

Mineola | 159 Jericho Tpke. (bet. Mineola Blvd. & Willis Ave.) | 516-294-4620

Huntington | 970 W. Jericho Tpke. (bet. Round Swamp Rd. & Sheppard Ln.) | 631-692-6300
www.piccolabussolarestaurant.com

"Go hungry" and "mangia" on "superior family-style Italian" at this "popular" pair in Huntington and Mineola, where the "substantial servings" of "garlicky" "red-sauce" "standards" and "accommodating" service are "always satisfying"; a few feel the "homey" settings could use "a pick-me-up", but most don't mind as long as "the price is right."

⧉ **Piccolo** *American/Italian* — 27 | 20 | 25 | $56

Huntington | Southdown Shopping Ctr. | 215 Wall St. (bet. Mill Ln. & Southdown Rd.) | 631-424-5592 | www.piccolorestaurant.net

A "faithful crowd" stays true to this "upscale" New American–Italian in Huntington, which "deserves its reputation" for "superb cuisine" spanning "delicious pastas" to "phenomenal meat and fish"; the "top-notch" service and "intimate" setting with a pianist Sunday–Thursday will "make any occasion special", but "close quarters" lead to "long waits on weekends" so reserve ahead.

Piccolo's Ⓜ *Italian* — 24 | 18 | 22 | $39

Mineola | 150 E. Jericho Tpke. (Congress Ave.) | 516-248-8110 | www.piccolosny.com

"Anyone who eats here knows" you "must try" the signature chicken zingarella and "wonderful" varieties of "homemade ravioli" to understand why this "nothing-fancy" Northern Italian is a long-running fixture in Mineola; given the "homey" backdrop, it's no surprise the "owner greets you" "like you're part of the family."

Pie, The *Pizza* — 21 | 17 | 20 | $25

Port Jefferson | 216 Main St. (Arden Pl.) | 631-331-4646 | www.thepieofportjeff.com

Serving "many varieties" of "fabulous" thin-crust, brick-oven pies with "unique toppings" plus "decent pasta dishes" in "casual" digs, this Port Jefferson pizzeria weighs in as an "inexpensive", "family-friendly" choice; a "personable" staff and "big booths" add to the attraction, but be prepared to "wait" because it's "often crowded."

	FOOD	DECOR	SERVICE	COST

Pier 95 Ⓜ *Mediterranean* — 24 | 21 | 23 | $47

Freeport | 95 Hudson Ave. (bet. Norton & Overton Sts.) |
516-867-9632 | www.pier95.com
A somewhat "hidden pearl" "close to Freeport's Nautical Mile", this
"first-class" Portuguese-leaning waterfront Med offers "marvelous"
seafood and an "excellent wine list" brought by a "knowledgeable",
"charming" staff; the "out-of-the-way" location means it's "quiet
enough" to "hear your partner's conversation" and feels "less
rushed" than others in town, plus the "beautiful views" and "lovely"
live music on weekends make it suitable for "intimate" dinners.

Pierre's *French* — 21 | 19 | 17 | $58

Bridgehampton | 2468 Main St. (bet. Bridgehampton-Sag Harbor Tpke. &
Hull Ln.) | 631-537-5110 | www.pierresbridgehampton.com
Francophiles favor this Bridgehampton bistro for "outstanding" fare
with an "emphasis on seafood" in a "cozy", "charming" setting with a
patisserie up front that "feels like France"; most find chef-owner
Pierre Weber to be a "wonderful", "friendly host", and though a few
have encountered "attitude", that doesn't stop the multitudes from
"waiting"; P.S. there's live jazz Tuesday and Sunday nights.

Pine Island Grill *American* — 18 | 25 | 16 | $52

Bayville | Crescent Beach Club | 333 Bayville Ave. (bet. Ships Ln. &
Sound Beach Ave.) | 516-628-3000 | www.thecrescentbeachclub.com
"It's all about" the "breathtaking view of Long Island Sound" that's
especially "enchanting" "as the sun sets" at this New American
"right on the water" in Bayville's Crescent Beach Club; if some say
the "so-so" food is "overpriced" and the service "slow", it still "feels
like a mini-vacation" if you "relax with cocktails" "on the deck" and
enjoy the "heavenly real estate."

Pita House *Mediterranean/Turkish* — 22 | 16 | 20 | $30

East Setauket | Heritage Sq. | 100-27 S. Jersey Ave. (Rte. 25A) |
631-675-9051
Patchogue | 680 Rte. 112 (bet. E. Woodside & Old Medford Aves.) |
631-289-2262
www.pita-house.com
"Authentic", "well-prepared" Mediterranean-Turkish offerings –
"amazing" red lentil soup, kebabs "to love" – make this "consistent"
pita pair a "unique" choice; service is "friendly", and though the decor in Patchogue "needs a makeover" and the East Setauket spot is
"buried behind a shopping center", "reasonable" prices more than
make up for any shortcomings.

Pizza Place ⊘ *Pizza* — ▽ 24 | 10 | 19 | $16

Bridgehampton | 2123 Montauk Hwy. (Hildreth Ln.) | 631-537-7865
It's the "best pizza around" proclaim local fans of the "remarkable"
thin-crust pies at this Bridgehampton joint where some 30 different
toppings are offered (try the bacon cheeseburger); beer and wine
plus cheap tabs compensate for a "charmless" setting, and day-
trippers declare it's always the "first stop" on a trip out East or their
perfect "snack before the ride home."

RESTAURANTS

	FOOD	DECOR	SERVICE	COST

Planet Bliss *Eclectic/New World*
▽ 20 | 16 | 21 | $43

Shelter Island | 23 N. Ferry Rd. (Duvall Rd.) | 631-749-0053 | www.planet-bliss.com

"Dining pleasure" awaits at this "offbeat" Shelter Islander, where "warm and welcoming" staffers serve "creative" Eclectic–New World cuisine crafted using ingredients sourced from "local" "farm-stands and fishermen"; the converted Victorian quarters harbor a "low-key" "hippie vibe" and a porch that's "lovely in the summer"; P.S. open weekends only in the off-season.

☒ Plaza Cafe *Seafood*
26 | 22 | 24 | $70

Southampton | 61 Hill St. (bet. 1st Neck & Windmill Lns.) | 631-283-9323 | www.plazacafe.us

"They set the bar really high" at this "civilized" "Southampton gem", where chef/co-owner and "real pro" Douglas Gulija's "superb" seafood is prepared "with care" and "presented to perfection", paired with "unusual wines"; the "courteous staff" oversees a "cozy", "quiet" setting with "high ceilings and a fireplace", and while it's "a bit expensive", it offers "adult dining" "in a class by itself."

Poco Loco *Mexican*
17 | 14 | 17 | $31

Roslyn | 1431 Old Northern Blvd. (bet. E. B'way & Skillman St.) | 516-621-5626 | www.pocolocorestaurant.net

"*Delicioso*" Mexican offerings – from "chips, salsa and guac" to "wonderful margaritas" – at "cheap enough" prices make this "old standby" in Roslyn "popular" for a "not-too-fancy" outing; the staff is "friendly and efficient", and though the decor's a little "worn", there's always the "outdoor patio" for a "warm summer evening."

Pollo Rico Latin Bistro *Pan-Latin*
20 | 16 | 19 | $30

Centereach | 2435 Middle Country Rd. (bet. Hammond Ln. & Oak St.) | 631-471-0585
Patchogue | Rent Ctr. | 350-12 E. Main St. (bet. Case & Evergreen Aves.) | 631-475-4200 Ⓜ
www.polloricolatinbistro.com

"Unique", "tasty" Pan-Latin dishes draw fans to this "lovely" "family-run" Centereach "bang for the buck" (with a take-out counter in Patchogue), where the arroz con pollo is a must and the sangria is "wonderful"; service is "accommodating", and the "bistro" setting is sweetened with a trompe l'oeil mural of a garden courtyard – though it's not the place for "quiet conversation."

Pomodorino *Italian*
19 | 15 | 18 | $33

Seaford | 3915 Merrick Rd. (bet. Jackson Ave. & Smith Ln.) | 516-826-1555
NEW Babylon | 90 W. Main St. (bet. Carll & Deer Park Aves.) | 631-321-0763
Hauppauge | 160 Adams Ave. (bet. Arkay & Commerce Drs.) | 631-951-0026
Huntington | 326 W. Jericho Tpke. (bet. Jones St. & Oakwood Rd.) | 631-425-1196
www.pomodorino.com

While this quartet of "checkered-tablecloth" Italians is "pretty predictable", it delivers "satisfying portions" of "tasty" pasta and pizza

FOOD DECOR SERVICE COST

at "reasonable prices" in "pleasant" quarters where carafes of "house wine" are on the table and you're "charged by the glass"; service is generally "reliable", and even if the decor's "ho-hum", it's still a "solid choice."

Porters on the Lane *Seafood/Steak*   20 | 21 | 20 | $46

Bellport | 19 Bellport Ln. (bet. Bell St. & S. Country Rd.) | 631-803-6067 | www.portersonthelane.com

Whether "on the porch in summer" or in the "cozy back room with a fireplace" in winter, fans of this three-year-old Bellport surf 'n' turfer enjoy "delicious" pastas, "fresh" fish and a "fantastic" wine list; pressed-tin ceilings and wood floors add character to the decor, but it can get "noisy", as there's an "active bar" scene and live music Fridays and Saturdays.

NEW Portly Grape *American*   – | – | – | E

Greenport | Portly Grape Inn | 305 North Rd. (Sound Rd.) | 631-477-4500 | www.theportlygrape.com

The nearby North Fork vineyards inspire this Greenport newcomer in the Portly Grape Inn that offers a trio of New American dining options – a small, elegant Victorian dining room, a casual pub with a bar and booth seating, and a living room-like lounge for small plates, dessert, coffee and drinks; P.S. occasional live entertainment and a small patio add to the allure.

Porto Bello *Italian*   ▽ 22 | 21 | 22 | $45

Greenport | Stirling Harbor Marina | 1410 Manhanset Ave. (bet. Beach Rd. & Champlain Pl.) | 631-477-1515 | www.portobellonorthfork.com

"Set right on the water" in the Stirling Harbor Marina, this Greenport seasonal Italian's bright surroundings and dockside "window views" provide a "lovely" backdrop for "big portions" of "well-done" "traditional" dishes; with "friendly" service led by an "owner who mixes with patrons", it's a "dependable" performer that typically draws a "lively crowd."

Porto Vivo ● *Italian*   22 | 25 | 20 | $59

Huntington | 7 Gerard St. (Stewart Ave.) | 631-385-8486 | www.porto-vivo.com

"NYC style" comes to Huntington via this tri-level "hot spot", where an "intimate" dining room features a fireplace on the top floor and a "sexy bar" attracts "major crowds" of the "young and beautiful", adding to the "happening" scene; yes, it's "expensive", and reviews are mixed on "inconsistent" service ranging from "outstanding" to "inattentive", but the "inventive" Italian menu wins praise.

Post Office Cafe ● *American*   19 | 20 | 19 | $31

Babylon | 130 W. Main St. (bet. Carll & Deer Park Aves.) | 631-669-9224 | www.thepostofficecafe.com

Situated in a "cute" former post office with "eclectic" touches (carousel horses, a fake chicken hanging from the ceiling), this "upbeat", "friendly" Babylon "fixture" (sibling to Farmingdale's Library Cafe) draws fans for American "favorites" like "Buffalo wings" or "a burger

FOOD | DECOR | SERVICE | COST

and beer" while catching "the game" with the "young crowd"; "cool happy hours", "live music"and DJ nights amp up the "noise level."

Post Stop Cafe *American*

17 | 16 | 17 | $35

Westhampton Beach | 144 Main St. (bet. Mill Rd. & Sunset Ave.) | 631-288-9777

If you're "lucky enough to get a table outside", this Westhampton Beacher is a "picturesque", "people-watching" spot serving "reliable" midpriced American fare ("burgers, salads, soups") that's "decent for lunch" if "a bit frumpy for dinner"; the vintage post office interior is "quaint", but some suggest the "slow" staff may be mailing it in.

NEW Press 195 *Sandwiches*

- | - | - | I

Rockville Centre | 22 N. Park Ave. (bet. Merrick Rd. & Sunrise Hwy.) | 516-536-1950 | www.press195.com

Hot off the presses are panini at this affordable Rockville Centre sandwich specialist (with siblings in Queens and Brooklyn) offering some 40 varieties plus accompaniments including crispy Belgian fries; a long black granite bar leads to a dining room with dramatic arches and colorful backlit glass tiles; P.S. there's live music Wednesday nights.

Z Prime *American*

23 | 27 | 22 | $67

Huntington | 117 New York Ave. (bet. Ketewomoke Dr. & Youngs Hill Rd.) | 631-385-1515 | www.restaurantprime.com

"Beautiful" "both inside and out", this "amazing" waterfront New American (from the owners of H2O and Tellers) with floor-to-ceiling windows is even more "prime" in summer when outdoor seating affords "amazing views" of Huntington Harbor and "fabulous people-watching"; "excellent" if "expensive" fare, including "first-rate steaks" and a "fantastic Sunday brunch", plus generally "gracious" service make this one a "special-occasion" standout; P.S. boat docking is available.

NEW Prime Catch *Seafood*

- | - | - | E

Rockville Centre | 41 S. Park Ave. (Lenox Rd.) | 516-705-5340

Fin fanciers are already hooked on this loungelike new seafooder in Rockville Centre, where chef Axell Urrutia is turning out upscale creations such as crab-stuffed salmon with sambuca-laced Dijonaise sauce; the room is saturated in red – from the walls to a glittery divider screen – and floor-to-ceiling windows in the bar area open to the sidewalk, providing additional fair-weather seating; P.S. there's live entertainment on weekends.

Public House 49 *American*

20 | 17 | 19 | $37

Patchogue | 49 E. Main St. (bet. Maple & Ocean Aves.) | 631-569-2767 | www.publichouse49.com

It's "worth adding to your rotation" report regulars of this midpriced Patchogue New American where "singing" chef Richard Desmond (ex Bliss) offers a "creative take" on pub fare from "simple" Kobe beef franks to "sophisticated" roast pork belly with Bing cherry sauce; "good" service is a plus, and a large bar with a dance floor and weekend DJs keeps things "lively."

NEW Puglia's of
Garden City **M** *Italian*

-	-	-	E

Garden City | 987 Stewart Ave. (bet. Selfridge Ave. & South St.) | 516-222-1421 | www.pugliascitycafe.com

A supper club with upscale Italian food and retro music acts on the menu, this sizable newcomer in Garden City's former City Café space offers a lively alternative to quiet neighborhood establishments; the front evokes a village cafe in Puglia, with umbrella-topped sidewalk tables, while the crisp beige-and-brown interior features two carpeted dining rooms – one with a fireplace, one bi-level – plus a spacious bar and a small dance floor.

Pumpernickels *German*

21	17	21	$38

Northport | 640 Main St. (Fort Salonga Rd.) | 631-757-7959

"Loyal local" followers find "rib-sticking" "traditional" German dishes, including "tender" sauerbraten, at this midpriced Northport "old-timer" that "works hard to get it right"; decor that hasn't "changed in years" and "friendly" "waitresses who dress the part" assure a "vintage feel" for a "satisfying meal."

Quetzalcoatl *Mexican*

20	17	19	$33

Huntington | 296 Main St. (bet. Green & New Sts.) | 631-427-7834 | www.quetzalcoatlmexrest.com

Mole mavens maintain there's "better than average" Mexican fare served in "huge" portions at this bi-level Huntington sibling to nearby Oaxaca, where the "colorful", "quirky" decor includes a rainforest mural and Mayan sculptures; "hospitable" service and "pitchers of margaritas keep the festivities going", and the lunch prix fixe is an even better "deal."

NEW Race Lane *American*

19	19	19	$53

East Hampton | 31 Race Ln. (bet. Gingerbread Ln. & Railroad Ave.) | 631-324-5022 | www.racelanerestaurant.com

Newly installed in digs once occupied by The Lodge and longtime favorite The Laundry, this "welcome addition" to East Hampton now "looks much spiffier" with its "freshened decor", freestanding fireplace and brick courtyard; there's "something for everyone" on the "surprisingly good" New American menu and service is "pleasant and helpful", so though it's "still learning", early admirers "will be back."

Rachel's Cafe *Italian*

22	15	21	$38

Syosset | 57 Berry Hill Rd. (bet. Church & East Sts.) | 516-921-0303 | www.rachelscafe.net

"Quaint", "cozy" and "full of warm smiles", this "sweet" Syosset "neighborhood standby" stands out with "fabulous", "inventive takes" on "homemade pastas" and other "classic Italian fare" followed by "amazing" desserts that "are worth saving room for"; however, the "tight quarters" tend to be "busy" "with the locals" "so be prepared to wait."

	FOOD	DECOR	SERVICE	COST

Rachel's Waterside Grill *American/Seafood* | 20 | 15 | 18 | $37 |

Freeport | 281 Woodcleft Ave. (bet. Manhattan & Suffolk Sts.) |
516-546-0050 | www.rachelswatersidegrill.com

Go "for the views" of the "boats passing by" say patrons who've "never
had a bad meal" (but "never had a great" one) at this waterfront seafooder on Freeport's Nautical Mile; weekly live music and "lively" terrace dining add appeal, and while some call for a decor "revamp",
fans dub the staff "solicitous" and the specials "a pleasant surprise."

Ram's Head Inn *American/Eclectic* | 20 | 24 | 20 | $62 |

Shelter Island | Ram's Head Inn | 108 Ram Island Dr. (N. Ram Island Dr.) |
631-749-0811 | www.shelterislandinns.com

A "quintessential summer spot", this seasonal "classic" in a circa-
1929 Shelter Island "country inn" turns on the "romantic" "charm",
especially when you head for the "beautiful terrace" to "watch the
sun set" over Coecles Harbor; the American-Eclectic dishes are
"well prepared" and service is "accommodating", but it's a location
"right out of *The Great Gatsby*" that merits the "ferry ride."

Rangmahal Ⓜ *Indian* | 23 | 15 | 23 | $36 |

Hicksville | 355 S. Broadway (Lawnview Ave.) | 516-942-7256

Run with "passion and energy" by a "charming husband-and-wife
team", this Hicksville veteran is a "favorite" for its "adventurous",
"modern interpretations of Indian cuisine"; an "attentive" staff
ascertains your "tolerance for spice", and though there's not much
decor, weekly live sitar music guarantees a "lively crowd."

Rare 650 *American/Steak* | 24 | 24 | 22 | $68 |

Syosset | 650 Jericho Tpke. (Cedar St.) | 516-496-8000 | www.rare650.com

As a "hipper" "reinvention of the former Sagamore Steakhouse", this
classed-up Syosset New American is "a rare find" with a "superb"
menu focused on "thick" steaks and sushi and an "iPad" "wine list to
make your head spin", plus an "outstanding" staff; with a "beautiful"
layout including "outdoor dining" and a "noisy" bar "singles scene", it
appeals to "designer" types who advise "don't forget your wallet."

Ravagh *Persian* | ▽ 22 | 13 | 21 | $36 |

Roslyn Heights | 210 Mineola Ave. (bet. High St. & Powerhouse Rd.) |
516-484-7100

NEW **Huntington** | 335 Main St. (bet. Clinton Ave. & West Neck Rd.) |
631-923-2050 Ⓜ

"Lots of interesting" "real Persian" dishes get kudos at this Roslyn
Heights eatery (with a Huntington sibling) where "excellent" kebabs
and "amazing" stews are delivered by a "pleasant" staff; it may not
be much to look at, but that doesn't faze fans who "love" it for
"tasty", "large portions" at "reasonable" prices.

red bar brasserie *American/French* | 22 | 19 | 21 | $62 |

Southampton | 210 Hampton Rd. (bet. Lewis St. & Old Town Rd.) |
631-283-0704 | www.redbarbrasserie.com

With its "consistently superior" New American-French fare, "glowing ambiance" and "excellent service", this "sophisticated" "fave"

	FOOD	DECOR	SERVICE	COST

earns "a thumbs-up" as "one of Southampton's better choices"; many maintain the "deafening" "noise level" makes it harder to "share the rapture with tablemates", but "once you've eaten here you'll understand" why it's a "popular" draw despite the price.

Red Fish Grille *American/Seafood*

| 23 | 17 | 20 | $43 |

Plainview | Woodbuy Row Plainview Ctr. | 430 Woodbury Rd. (S. Oyster Bay Rd.) | 516-932-8460 | www.redfishgrille.com

A "dependable local" "favorite" that most outsiders "don't know about", this Plainview New American "in an innocuous strip-mall setting" surprises with "an innovative menu" featuring "an excellent variety of fresh fish" served "with a smile" "for a decent price"; but it's apt to be "jumping" with regulars and so "noisy" you'll risk "returning home with laryngitis."

Red Restaurant & Bar *American*

| 25 | 22 | 25 | $49 |

Huntington | 417 New York Ave. (bet. High & W. Carver Sts.) | 631-673-0304 | www.redrestaurantli.com

Café Red M *American*

NEW Kings Park | 107 Main St. (Pulaski Rd.) | 631-544-4500

You'll "taste heaven" sigh worshipers of the "creative" New American fare and "phenomenal wine list" at this "highly" recommended Huntington "prize"; a "gracious", "well-trained" staff works the "attractive", red-accented space that includes a zinc bar, velvet lounge chairs and an "amazing" "secret" "garden in summer"; P.S. the Kings Park cafe opened post-Survey.

Red Rooster Bistro *American*

| ∇ 16 | 20 | 17 | $37 |

Cutchogue | 4805 Depot Ln. (bet. Main & Middle Rds.) | 631-734-8267

"Burgers, ribs" and "old-fashioned dinners" are the kinds of plates that make this midpriced American bistro a "homestyle heaven" for Cutchogue comfort-food seekers; sometimes "inattentive" service might be nothing to crow about, but the place is decked out in "cute" "rooster-theme decor" that makes for a "lovely setting."

Rein *American*

| 23 | 24 | 24 | $53 |

Garden City | Garden City Hotel | 45 Seventh St. (bet. Cathedral & Hilton Aves.) | 516-877-9385 | www.gardencityhotel.com

"If you just feel like spoiling yourself", this "posh" New American in the Garden City Hotel flaunts an "elegant" interior (think burnished wood, paintings and a fireplace) and "fabulous service" that add a "touch of class" whether for a "high-end" meal, afternoon tea or Sunday brunch; sophistos say it's "like being in NYC", complete with the "big price."

Restaurant at The Inn *American*

| ∇ 21 | 22 | 21 | $51 |

Quogue | The Inn at Quogue | 47 Quogue St. (Jessup Ave.) | 631-653-6800

This "latest edition" of the The Inn at Quogue's eatery "is a solid performer", matching a diverse New American menu with "surprisingly good service" and traditionally "elegant" environs equipped with twin fireplaces; it offers an affordable prix fixe, and diners disinclined to "drive home" from the remote locale can always book a room; P.S. in winter, open weekends only.

Rialto ☑ *Italian*

| 26 | 20 | 25 | $57 |

Carle Place | 588 Westbury Ave. (bet. Glen Cove Rd. & Post Ave.) | 516-997-5283 | www.rialtorestaurantli.com

"Top-notch" "each and every time", this "small" Carle Place Italian attracts adoring *amici* willing to go "out of the way" for "heavenly" "old-line" cuisine (including "wonderful whole fish") "served with style" by "warm hosts" who look after you like "their only customer"; it's "pretty pricey" and "worth every penny", but "they don't have room for a crowd" so "don't tell."

Ristorante Gemelli ☑ *Italian*

| 24 | 24 | 23 | $51 |

Babylon | 175 E. Main St. (bet. Cooper St. & Totten Pl.) | 631-321-6392 | www.gemellirestaurant.com

Paesani praise this Babylonian for its "top-shelf" Italian cuisine – "decadent lobster risotto", "phenomenal" osso buco – and "warm", "romantic" setting that's "like dining in a small village piazza"; a staff that goes "overboard" (including owners who always "visit your table") further justifies the "pricey" tabs; P.S. the family's fine-food market is down the street.

Ristorante Italiano Toscanini *Italian*

| ▽ 24 | 18 | 26 | $39 |

Port Washington | 179 Main St. (bet. Madison & Monroe Sts.) | 516-944-0755 | www.toscaninipw.com

"Friendly service" starts with a "warm and gracious" owner at this Port Washingtonian where the midpriced Italian fare includes "outstanding specials" and "amazing desserts"; the "attractive setting" features murals of the Tuscan countryside, adding to the "welcoming" vibe.

Ritz Cafe, The *Continental*

| 19 | 12 | 17 | $34 |

Northport | 42 Woodbine Ave. (bet. 5th & Scudder Aves.) | 631-754-6348

Surveyors say this "unassuming little bar" near the Northport waterfront "packs a wallop" with "tasty" Continental fare at "sane prices"; it's "definitely not ritzy" – "loud and "crowded" is more accurate – and the service is "so-so", but when you "gaze out at the bay" you "forget all your stress"; P.S. the $12 brunch prix fixe "can cure whatever ails you."

☑ Riverbay Seafood Bar & Grill *Seafood*

| 23 | 19 | 21 | $50 |

Williston Park | 700 Willis Ave. (bet. Charles & Henry Sts.) | 516-742-9191 | www.riverbayrestaurant.com

"Incredibly fresh seafood" – including a "vast" selection at the "fabulous raw bar" – plus a "knockout Sunday brunch" lures fans to this Williston Park "favorite" from the owner of the Central Park Boathouse; the "vibrant" scene in a nautically decorated former Masonic Hall can get "loud", but service is generally "accommodating" – just expect it to cost "an arm and a leg"; P.S. it's "always crowded", so "be prepared to wait, even with a reservation."

	FOOD	DECOR	SERVICE	COST

Riviera Grill *Italian* — ∇ 26 | 17 | 24 | $49

Glen Cove | 274 Glen St. (bet. Elm & Hendrick Aves.) | 516-674-9370 | www.rivieragrillrestaurant.com

"Terrific" Italian fare including "plentiful" specials and "homemade limoncello" at meal's end wins "repeat customers" for this Glen Cove "charmer"; even if the dining room, with paintings of the Italian Riviera, is "not extravagant", a "superb", "gracious host" and a staff that treats you "like one of the family" make the setting feel "perfect."

Robata of Tokyo *Japanese* — ∇ 20 | 11 | 18 | $32

Plainview | 1163 Old Country Rd. (Manetto Hill Rd.) | 516-433-5333 | www.robatasushi.com

With a "dizzying array" of "drool-worthy" "fresh sushi" and "grilled Japanese" fare from the namesake robata, this Plainview strip-center spot aims to please every palate; the "outdated" "interior is nothing to look at", but given the "unpretentious service and decent prices", its area advocates shrug "no matter."

Robert's *Italian* — 25 | 21 | 23 | $69

Water Mill | 755 Montauk Hwy. (bet. Nowedonah Ave. & Station Rd.) | 631-726-7171 | www.robertshamptons.com

"Outstanding", "beautifully presented" Italian cuisine that's as "imaginative" as it is "delicious" is proffered at Robert Durkin's Water Mill "respite" from the "happening Hamptons scene", set in a "lovely old farmhouse" with summer patio seating; service is "serious" and "professional", and if the tabs are a bit "pricey", that doesn't keep it from rising to "the head of the class"; P.S. hours vary by season.

Robinson's Tea Room Ⓜ *Tearoom* — 23 | 22 | 22 | $23

Stony Brook | Stony Brook Village Ctr. | 97 Main St. (bet. Christian Ave. & Rte. 25A) | 631-751-1232

"Genuine high tea" is "beautifully served" – complete with "delicious" brews, "luscious scones", "homemade" cream, "fresh jams" and "finger sandwiches" – at this "cozy", lace-curtained and antiques-filled Stony Brook teahouse that's perfect for a "ladies' day out" or a treat with your "granddaughter"; with "wonderful quiches" and salads and a "pleasant" staff, you could "have lunch instead", just "reserve early."

Rock 'n Sake *Japanese* — 22 | 19 | 16 | $37

Port Washington | 90 Main St. (bet. Evergreen & Haven Aves.) | 516-883-7253 | www.rocknsakeny.com

A "hip, NYC-style" scene draws partyers who want to "combine dinner with clubbing" at this "loud" PW Japanese offering "inventive" sushi and "fairly priced" hot dishes plus "bold music" from a DJ booth; it's "always upbeat and full of beautiful people" and even if some sniff the staff "needs to get over itself", the "dark" setting is "appealing."

Rockwell's Bar & Grill *American* — ∇ 22 | 18 | 21 | $30

Smithtown | 60 Terry Rd. (bet. Middle Country Rd. & Nesconset Hwy.) | 631-360-8900 | www.rockwellsbarandgrill.com

Sports fans and a "local après-work crowd" keep this Smithtown pub "humming", especially around the "huge bar" at Friday happy hour;

for diners, there's a midpriced menu of "standard" American fare "with a twist" (e.g. baked clam casserole) and a "friendly" staff in a setting with lots of flat-screen TVs, plus outdoor seating; P.S. live bands play on Saturdays.

Roe's Casa Dolce *Bakery/Italian*   ▽ 24 | 11 | 19 | $20

Rockville Centre | 486 Sunrise Hwy. (bet. Forest Ave. & Long Beach Rd.) | 516-536-2253

"Heaven on earth" for sweet tooths, this pint-sized Italian bakery/ cafe in Rockville Centre is favored "mainly for" its pastries and other "sinfully delicious" desserts, though the lineup of breakfast and lunch fare is also "obviously prepared with care"; it's now under the "new ownership" of its former head baker, "but the quality is still top-notch" and their "casa is your casa."

Roots 🅂🅼 *American*   ▽ 26 | 23 | 23 | $48

Sea Cliff | 242 Sea Cliff Ave. (bet. Central & Roslyn Aves.) | 516-671-7668

"You won't even feel like you're on Long Island" at this "funky" Sea Cliff "farm-to-table" "find" with "delicious", "unique" American "home cooking" via chef-owner David Santoro; further "oh-so-inviting" aspects include "warm, familial service" and an "eclectic" space boasting recycled wood furnishings and a wine rack hanging from a 100-year-old chestnut ceiling, but "don't ask to alter a menu item" as they prefer no "substitutions."

🅉 Rothmann's Steakhouse *Steak*   25 | 22 | 23 | $66

East Norwich | 6319 Northern Blvd. (Oyster Bay Rd.) | 516-922-2500 | www.chasrothmanns.com

Meat eaters "dine like kings" at this "exceptional" East Norwich cow palace, which has the chops to "compete with any" of its "high-end" North Shore rivals and "all the bells and whistles you'd expect" of a "classy" "carnivore's lair"; the "fabulous" steaks, "professional ser-vice" and "attractive setting" are "well worth the expense", but be-ware of "noise" and "the real feeding frenzy" when "cruising cougars" hit the "hopping bar"; P.S. it's also known for its Sunday brunch.

Rowdy Hall *Pub Food*   20 | 16 | 19 | $36

East Hampton | Parrish Mews | 10 Main St. (bet. Fithian Ln. & The Circle) | 631-324-8555 | www.rowdyhall.com

Ever a "steady" "backup", this "convivial" member of "the Nick & Toni's family" "hidden" in an East Hampton village mews is "satisfying" for "basic", Gallic-accented pub fare ("can't beat those burgers") served by "spirited" sorts who "greet you with a smile"; the "reason-able prices" and "party atmosphere" make it "popular" with "rowdy" patrons "of all ages" who agree it "feels like home."

Royal Bukhara Grill *Indian*   ▽ 22 | 18 | 21 | $31

Hicksville | 70 Broadway (bet. Herzog Pl. & W. Marie St.) | 516-822-2400 | www.royalbukharagrill.com

Fans of the "vibrant flavors" of Indian cuisine head for this Hicksville spin-off of Manhattan's Bukhara Grill (under different ownership) for the "outstanding breads", "excellent dal" and chicken tikka

	FOOD	DECOR	SERVICE	COST

masala that "has a kick to it"; a simple, "dimly lit" setting, and "warm", "efficient service" complete the experience.

RS Jones ⓜ *Southwestern*

| 22 | 21 | 24 | $34 |

Merrick | 153 Merrick Ave. (bet. Miller Pl. & W. Loines Ave.) | 516-378-7177 | www.rsjones.com

For a "loud", "stompin' good time", Merrick wranglers recommend this "colorful local hangout" with the "friendliest" staff in town, where "kitschy", "Texas-rodeo decor" and "people-watching taken to a new level" create a "quirky" backdrop for "spicy", "imaginative" mid-priced Southwestern fare including "delicious" chicken-fried steak and "so-o good cheese grits"; P.S. there's "live music" some nights.

Rugosa *American*

| 21 | 18 | 21 | $54 |

Wainscott | 290 Montauk Hwy. (Daniels Hole Rd.) | 631-604-1550 | www.rugosarestaurant.com

It's "not yet a Hamptons hot spot", but with "lovely" presentations of "farm-fresh", "creative" New American fare and "warm", "accommodating" service in a "pleasant", simple setting, this East Ender is a "keeper"; it's run by a CIA grad chef and his wife – who "know how to treat customers" – and most agree you'll be "glad you came."

Runyon's *American*

| 18 | 16 | 19 | $31 |

Seaford | 3928 Merrick Rd. (bet. Jackson Ave. & Smith Ln.) | 516-221-2112 | www.runyons.com

A "busy local pub" with "standard" American fare, this Seaford "mainstay" offers "friendly" service and "inexpensive" eats including a "decent" "burger and beer"; dissenters dis "dated" decor that "needs work", but fans call it "comfortable."

ⓩ Ruth's Chris Steak House *Steak*

| 25 | 21 | 24 | $66 |

Garden City | 600 Old Country Rd. (Clinton Rd.) | 516-222-0220 | www.ruthschris.com

Loyalists "love the sizzling platters" of "oh-so-good buttery steaks" at this "top-quality" chophouse chain link in Garden City that comes through with "winning" sides too; delivering "old-style service" in a "traditional" setting, it's "expensive" (and "not for the dieter"), but "utterly reliable", especially for "entertaining friends and clients."

Ruvo *Italian*

| 22 | 20 | 21 | $42 |

Greenlawn | 63 Broadway (Smith St.) | 631-261-7700
Port Jefferson | 105 Wynn Ln. (Main St.) | 631-476-3800
www.ruvorestaurant.com

Red-sauce fans go for the "amazing pastas" and other "artfully prepared" "rustic Italian standards" at this "homey" North Shore duo where a "lovely" staff "goes out of its way to be nice"; both offer "bargain prix fixe" options at lunch and dinner, and the Greenlawn location has an attached butcher shop and market.

Sabai Thai Bistro *Thai*

| ▽ 22 | 22 | 19 | $29 |

Miller Place | 825 Rte. 25A (bet. Harrison & Tyler Aves.) | 631-821-1780

The "lovely", "restful" setting – with granite-topped tables, gold walls and gongs – rivals the "delicious" fare at this Miller Place Thai where BYO with no corkage keeps tabs low; time-crunched critics say "service is on the slow side" but admit that's just "more time to enjoy" the "beautiful decor."

NEW Sabor a Colombia *Colombian* — | — | — | M
Levittown | 26 Division Ave. (Hempstead Tpke. & Schoolhouse Rd.) | 516-513-1520
Tucked behind a Levittown gym, this midpriced Colombian new-comer serves breakfast, lunch (including savory crêpes until 3 PM) and dinner entrees such as salmon with salsa and fried plantains; the decor makes a colorful statement with a tile floor and canary-yellow walls hung with parrot sculptures.

Sage Bistro *French* 24 | 20 | 22 | $43
Bellmore | 2620 Merrick Rd. (bet. Centre & St. Marks Aves.) | 516-679-8928 | www.bistrosage.com

Sage Bistro Moderne *French*
Woodbury | Woodbury Village Shopping Ctr. | 7955 Jericho Tpke. (S. Woods Rd.) | 516-584-6804 | www.sagebistrogroup.com
"Fabulous" French fare that "tickles your taste buds" – from "excellent mussels" to "steak tartare" and "wonderful boeuf bourguignon" – draws Francophiles to this duo from the owner of Oceanside's Brasserie Persil; the newer Woodbury location has a "more formal feel" than the Bellmore original, but both get "crowded and noisy" on weekends and benefit from an "attentive" staff and an extensive martini list.

NEW Sakaya ⑤Ⓜ *Japanese* — | — | — | E
Albertson | 1162 Willis Ave. (Netz Pl.) | 516-621-1887
Blue LED lights and illuminated crystals add pizzazz to this upscale Japanese newcomer in the Albertson space that was formerly Hokkaido, while a soothing waterfall wall separates the main dining room from an area filled with hibachi tables; sushi fans have copious choices, with hot entrees on the menu too.

Salamander's General Store *Eclectic* ▽ 24 | 15 | 17 | $26
Greenport | 414 First St. (bet. Center & South Sts.) | 631-477-3711
Akin to a mini "local version of Zabar's", this seasonal "gourmet" grocer in Greenport concocts an "amazingly good" array of Eclectic prepared dishes – notably the "legendary fried chicken" – to eat in at its two tables or on an "inviting" patio; "excellent salads", "zesty" "homemade soups" and plenty more also provide "terrific takeout" on "those lazy I-don't-want-to-cook days."

Salsa Salsa *Californian/Mexican* 23 | 11 | 19 | $17
Bayport | 893 Montauk Hwy. (bet. Barrett & Sylvan Aves.) | 631-419-6464
Port Jefferson | 142 Main St. (bet. Mill Creek Rd. & Wynn Ln.) | 631-473-9700
Smithtown | Maple Commons Shopping Ctr. | 320 Maple Ave. (Rte. 111) | 631-360-8080
www.salsasalsa.net
Burrito-boosters bet on these "exceptional" Cal-Mex fast-fooders for "consistently" fresh, "reasonably priced" "quick" meals; there's

a "friendly staff", but the "take-out" settings with "limited seating" are "a bit primitive" for eating in, so put it on "speed dial" and pick it up "to go."

Salvatore's ☑⇱ *Pizza* | 25 | 13 | 20 | $21 |

Port Washington | 124 Shore Rd. (bet. Manhasset Ave. & Soundview Dr.) | 516-883-8457

Pie at Salvatore's, The ⇱ *Pizza*

Bay Shore | 120 E. Main St. (bet. 1st & 2nd Aves.) | 631-206-1060 | www.salvatorescoalfiredpizza.com

"Just the right amount of sauce and cheese" grace the "awesome" brick-oven pies "made right in front of you", while the "ginormous" calzones "are a treat" too, at this family-owned duo of pizza-and-pasta joints in Port Washington and Bay Shore that "stand above the rest"; the "delicious" fixin's are served in "always-crowded", "lively" "hole-in-the-wall" settings by a "friendly" staff, and though "take-out" is an option, the "crisp crusts" taste best when you "eat in"; P.S. remember it's "cash only."

Sam's *Italian/Pizza* | 18 | 11 | 18 | $33 |

East Hampton | 36 Newtown Ln. (bet. Main St. & Osborne Ln.) | 631-324-5900

Known for "thin-crust pizza" that'll "satisfy any appetite", this enduring East Hampton "staple" also slings "not-bad" "basic Italian" in "plentiful" portions; maybe there's "no atmosphere" in the "old-fashioned" "bar-and-grill" digs, but those with "kids in tow" appreciate an "informal" option that's "as local as it gets."

Samurai ☑ *Japanese* | ∇ 24 | 21 | 20 | $45 |

Huntington | 46A Gerard St. (Wall St.) | 631-271-2588 | www.samuraihibachi.com

"Perfect for families" or "a group" looking for an "entertaining night out", this "always crowded" Huntington Japanese sibling to nearby Tomo is "just what you'd expect" from a "noisy" hibachi steakhouse; the "cute" "show is the same every time", and though it's a bit "pricey", the "kids love it" and the adults appreciate a "breathtaking Asian-inspired interior" and "surprisingly good sushi."

⛾ San Marco *Italian* | 26 | 21 | 26 | $46 |

Hauppauge | 658 Motor Pkwy. (bet. Kennedy Dr. & Marcus Blvd.) | 631-273-0088 | www.sanmarcoristorante.com

"Everyone is treated like a VIP" by a "top-notch", "black tie"-clad staff wheeling "carts with appetizers and desserts" at this "tried-and-true" Hauppauge "special-occasion" "favorite" serving "some of the best" Northern Italian on the Island; although some suggest the decor "needs a bit of updating", "you can't go wrong" here, even "after all these years" – and it "won't break the bank" either.

Sant Ambroeus *Italian* | 24 | 20 | 22 | $70 |

Southampton | 30 Main St. (bet. Meetinghouse Ln. & Wall St.) | 631-283-1233 | www.santambroeus.com

The "beautifully prepared" Milanese cuisine and "caring service" are "a cut above" at this "civilized" seasonal Southamptonite (with sibs in

Manhattan and Milan), a "wonderful European" enclave that's also favored for its "terrific" espresso bar ("don't miss their cappuccino") and "fantastic" gelato and desserts; granted, it's so "insanely expensive" you may need "to take out another mortgage", but it's always "heavenly" "to sit on the patio" and scope the passing "parade."

Sapporo   *Japanese*   23 | 19 | 23 | $35

Wantagh | 3266 Merrick Rd. (1 block east of Wantagh Pkwy.) | 516-785-3853

This longtime midpriced "staple for sushi" in Wantagh, offering "amazing hand rolls", "creative" Japanese dishes and a "nice assortment of sake" served by a "pleasant, prompt" staff, makes an "outstanding choice" for dining, with improved scores to prove it; the "quiet" setting – including a traditional tatami room where patrons "sit on the floor" – is "suitable for talking", leaving some saying now if they'd just "update" the decor, "it would be perfect."

NEW Sapsuckers Hops & Grub   *American*   - | - | - | I

Huntington | 287 Main St. (bet. Green & Wall Sts.) | 631-683-4945

Artisanal and farm-fresh ingredients are spotlighted on the affordable American menu at this slim-lined Huntington sibling of Café Red (Kings Park) and Osteria da Nino (Huntington); mirrors on the walls give the narrow quarters an illusion of space, and a copper ceiling and oak floor add warmth.

Sarabeth's   *American*   20 | 16 | 18 | $28

Garden City | Lord & Taylor | 1200 Franklin Ave. (bet. 12th & 13th Sts.) | 516-742-7000 | www.sarabeth.com

"Serious shoppers" at the Garden City Lord & Taylor "recharge" their browsing batteries at this "convenient" branch of the Manhattan-based cafe chain, which "fits the bill" for "casual" lunching with a "surprisingly good" American menu of salads, sandwiches and desserts; it's a "pleasant" "respite" if "not the classiest place", and though it doesn't open until 11 AM, breakfast bites are served all day.

Sarin Thai   *Thai*   24 | 18 | 22 | $33

Greenvale | 43 Glen Cove Rd. (Wellington Rd.) | 516-484-5873
NEW **Kings Park** | 25 Main St. (Henry St.) | 631-269-4130 Ⓜ
www.sarinthaicuisine.com

You "can count on" this "longtime" Greenvale "favorite" for "amazing" Thai with a "sophisticated twist", from "wonderful" curry and "spicy duck" to "excellent pad Thai", accompanied by a "respectable wine list"; the staff "tries hard to please" in the "relaxed", "elegant" space, so admirers admit they'd "eat here more often" if not for the "parking problem"; P.S. a new outpost in Kings Park opened post-Survey.

Savanna's   *American*   20 | 18 | 17 | $67

Southampton | 268 Elm St. (Powell Ave.) | 631-283-0202 | www.savannassouthampton.com

"One of the 'in' places" in Southampton, this "glammy" seasonal hot spot appeals to "strivers" with "ambitious" New American fare and "great people-watching" "if you don't mind the prices"; critics complain of the "ear-throbbing" "noise factor", but there's a "peaceful" "garden in the rear" "if you want to have a conversation."

Schooner *Seafood/Steak* | 17 | 17 | 18 | $43 |

Freeport | 435 Woodcleft Ave. (Richmond St.) | 516-378-7575 | www.theschooner.com

"Lovely" "waterside views" in a "lively" setting with indoor and outdoor tables and an option to "come by boat and tie up" have kept this surf 'n' turfer on Freeport's Nautical Mile "around forever"; some say the rest – from "so-so" fare to an interior that reminds you of "your grandparents' place" – "needs a makeover", though the "staff couldn't be nicer."

Scotto's *Italian/Pizza* | 20 | 19 | 18 | $32 |

Westbury | Roosevelt Raceway Ctr. | 1195 Corporate Dr. (Merchants Concourse) | 516-222-1042

Pizzaphiles plug this "welcome addition" to Westbury from the Scotto Brothers hospitality team for the wood-fired, "ultra-thin-crust" pies leading an "enjoyable" mix that also includes pastas and other Italian staples; however, critics claim the "cavernous", multiroom space "loses any intimacy" and the service "could use upgrading."

Scrimshaw *American* | 23 | 20 | 19 | $56 |

Greenport | Preston's Wharf | 102 Main St. (bet. Front St. & Greenport Harbor) | 631-477-8882 | www.scrimshawrestaurant.com

Chef-owner Rosa Ross' "unpretentious" Greenport New American "never fails to satisfy" with "wonderful" dishes featuring "fresh local ingredients", a "focus on seafood" and a "melding of Asian" influences; outdoor seating "on the wharf" affords "beautiful waterfront views" of Greenport Harbor and Shelter Island that distract from the "high prices"; P.S. open Thursday–Sunday in the winter.

Sea Basin *Italian/Seafood* | 19 | 18 | 22 | $34 |

Rocky Point | 642 Rte. 25A (bet. B'way & Polk St.) | 631-744-1643 | www.seabasin.com

A "local standby", this Italian seafooder in Rocky Point dishes up "reliable" "traditional" fare at "reasonable" prices, especially via "prix fixe lunches and dinners"; though "you won't get gourmet" here and the "tired decor" "hasn't been updated in many years", "excellent service" and "big portions" have regulars leaving "satisfied and happy."

Sea Grille *American/Italian* | ∇ 21 | 21 | 21 | $48 |

Montauk | Gurney's Inn | 290 Old Montauk Hwy. (bet. Fir Ln. & Maple St.) | 631-668-2345 | www.gurneysinn.com

The "view of the beach and ocean can't be beat" at this American-Italian in Gurney's Inn that serves up "excellent seafood" in a "relaxing" setting that works "even in winter" (Friday–Saturday DJs and Thursday-night karaoke are year-round); though the service gets mixed marks and the tab can "add up quickly", fans dub it a Montauk "must."

	FOOD	DECOR	SERVICE	COST

Sea Levels ⑤Ⓜ *American/Seafood* ▽ 22 | 19 | 21 | $43

Brightwaters | 391 N. Windsor Ave. (Orinoco Dr.) | 631-665-8300 | www.sealevelsrestaurant.com

"A great place to start out a Saturday night", this Brightwaters New American "pleases" with its "amazing" seafood and "cowboy steaks" by chef-owner John Peter Montgomery; though the "large" mahogany bar is a "raucous" "gathering place on weekends" when there's live acoustic music, the "separate", "quiet" dining room is buffered from the "noise"; P.S. there's a "terrific" prix fixe dinner special and monthly cooking and wine classes.

Second House Tavern *American* ▽ 19 | 17 | 17 | $42

Montauk | 161 Second House Rd. (bet. Industrial Rd. & S. Dewey Pl.) | 631-668-2877 | www.secondhousetavern.com

This Montauk American is "pub"-style in the Grill Room and "more sophisticated" in the Tavern Room with "great happy-hour specials" and a "cozy" setting with artisan-crafted farm tables, warm lighting and views over Fort Pond; the food is "decent", but service can be "a little off", so patrons "hope they get it together."

Seeda Thai *Thai* 23 | 17 | 21 | $31

Valley Stream | 28 N. Central Ave. (Merrick Rd.) | 516-561-2626 | www.seedathai.com

Valley Streamers "regularly" Thai one on at this "cozy", "relaxing" yet, a "reliable" fallback for "palatable" standards and also some "authentic" specialties (e.g. "more frogs' legs' dishes than most"); even if the decor's "not so fancy", the "flavorful food" brings followers "back again and again" – especially once they seeda "reasonable prices."

❷ Sempre Vivolo *Italian* 27 | 24 | 27 | $56

Hauppauge | 696 Vanderbilt Motor Pkwy. (Old Willets Path) | 631-435-1737

"Always a pleasure", this "refined" Hauppauge Italian is a "long-standing" source of "delectable" cuisine presented by "impeccable", "tuxedo-clad" pros; with "jackets required on Saturday night", it's a "fabulous" chance to "slow down" and "carry on a conversation" in a pleasant "old-world" atmosphere.

Sen *Japanese* 21 | 17 | 18 | $54

Sag Harbor | 23 Main St. (bet. Bay & Madison Sts.) | 631-725-1774 | www.senrestaurant.com

"Raw fish aplenty" and a "lively" vibe add up to "sushi à la Hamptons" at this Sag Harbor Japanese, a "rather excellent" source of "orthodox as well as nouvelle rolls" served by "polite" staffers; it's "clearly a hot spot" with "long waits on weekends", and wallet-watchers are sensitive to the "high price", but "if you're recession-proof, go for it."

Ⓝⓔⓦ Sensasian ⑤ *Asian* - | - | - | M

Levittown | 636D Wantagh Ave. (bet. Sprucewood Dr. & Stony Ln.) | 516-520-8811 | www.sensasianbistro.com

Offering a respite from its Levittown mall surroundings, this Asian newcomer serves Chinese and Japanese fare with a few Thai dishes also in the mix; moody blue, red and orange neon lighting and dark walls add atmosphere, and moderate prices complete the package.

NEW Serafina ● *Italian* | 18 | 16 | 16 | $47 |

East Hampton | 104 N. Main St. (Cedar St.) | 631-267-3500 | www.serafinarestaurant.com

"Young, hip and single" sorts nosh on pizza, pasta and other Italian bites while "people-watching" "on the patio" at this "casual but chic" arrival, the East Hampton outpost of a Manhattan-based chain; some complain that you'll pay "city prices" for merely "adequate" food "served by amateurs", but it's already a "big scene" so "expect a wait."

☑ 1770 House | 25 | 25 | 24 | $66 |
Restaurant & Inn *American*

East Hampton | 1770 House | 143 Main St. (Dayton Ln.) | 631-324-1770 | www.1770house.com

From the "thoughtfully prepared", "delectable" American fare to the "elegant, old Colonial" setting with a "peaceful" patio and "blazing fireplaces", this "charming", "expensive" East Hampton eatery in an 18th-century inn is "first-rate" all around; the "ever-obliging service" extends to a "less formal" "downstairs tavern" offering a "reasonably priced" pub menu, so it's "cozy" and "civilized" even if you're not "East End–endowed."

Seventh St. Cafe *Italian* | 20 | 19 | 20 | $39 |

Garden City | 126 Seventh St. (bet. Franklin & Hilton Aves.) | 516-747-7575 | www.seventhstreetcafe.com

"After shopping" "in the heart of Garden City", this "cute", "consistent" Northern Italian "works" for "above-average" "standards" "at a reasonable price"; knockers feel the "ho-hum" menu "needs a little pick-me-up" and say the "noise level might be off-putting", but in warm weather there's always "alfresco dining" on the tree-lined Seventh Street strip.

75 Main ● *Italian* | 18 | 19 | 17 | $49 |

Southampton | 75 Main St. (bet. Jobs Ln. & Nugent St.) | 631-283-7575 | www.75main.com

New ownership "finally seems to be getting it right" at this Southampton Italian where the sidewalk tables offer "beautiful" "people-watching" and the redecorated interior sports a "cool, unpretentious ambiance"; opinions of the food range from "tasty" to "so-so", and service can be "choppy", but it's a "happening place with the under-30 crowd and those who wish they were", especially when the beat picks up with live music and DJs late-night.

Shagwong *American/Seafood* | 18 | 14 | 15 | $37 |

Montauk | 774 Main St. (bet. Edgemere & Essex Sts.) | 631-668-3050 | www.shagwong.com

"Salty character" defines this "old-school Montauk" "mainstay", which supplies "simple" seafood and other "decent" American eats in a "tavern" setting with "home-grown" regulars "hunched over the bar"; service is "spotty" and the digs have "seen better days", but

FOOD DECOR SERVICE COST

"natives" and "weekenders" keep it "thriving" "and they stay open all year."

Shang Hai Pavilion *Chinese* ▽ 21 | 12 | 19 | $26
Port Washington | 46 Main St. (bet. Bayles & Maryland Aves.) | 516-883-3368

Shang Hai Pavilion II *Chinese*
Bellmore | 2725 Merrick Rd. (bet. Centre & St. Marks Aves.) | 516-221-2332

"The most amazing soup dumplings east of Chinatown" "can cure anything" at these "Shanghai-style" Chinese storefronts in Bellmore and Port Washington; but beyond the "tasty" potstickers, the "mainstream" menu and "standard neighborhood" setups are "nothing special."

Shiki *Japanese* ▽ 24 | 19 | 22 | $36
Babylon | 233 E. Main St. (Cooper St.) | 631-669-5404 | www.shiki-longisland.com

"Repeat customers" are hooked on the "fantastic" fish at this "affordable" Japanese in Babylon, which specializes in "exquisite" presentations of "super-fresh" sushi bolstered by "delicious" "non-raw" items; it's "not a Nobu, but gaining", and the "low-key" milieu means "you won't be waiting for a table."

Shiki *Japanese* - | - | - | E
East Hampton | 47 Montauk Hwy. (bet. Baiting Hollow & Cove Hollow Rds.) | 631-329-9821 | www.shikihamptons.com

This upscale Asian-Japanese newcomer to the East Hampton scene moved into the space that was Bamboo, and sports a fresh coat of paint in the former occupant's shadowy, sexy colors; there's a new sushi bar for a variety of raw fish, and hot dishes include the likes of grilled Mongolian beef; P.S. a garden patio is poised to be a popular summer perch.

Shiro of Japan *Japanese* 22 | 20 | 22 | $38
Carle Place | 401 Old Country Rd. (Carle Rd.) | 516-997-4770 | www.shiroofjapan.com

The "show never gets old" declare fans of this "delightful" Carle Place Japanese, long known for "hibachi done right" with "plentiful" helpings of "yum-o" food and a "fiery" "performance" that's "a real treat" for "kids" and "groups"; the "amazingly fresh sushi" also wins applause, and though it gets "a bit pricey", it's still "way better" than some competitors.

Shogi ⓜ *Japanese* ▽ 25 | 9 | 28 | $33
Westbury | 584 Old Country Rd. (bet. Longfellow & Tennyson Aves.) | 516-338-8768

All feel "well treated and special" at this Westbury "neighborhood" Japanese, where the "terrific" hostess "makes the place come to life" and the chef crafts "wonderful", "exceptionally authentic" sushi (including "variations by request") featuring fish "so fresh" it's "practically flopping"; it's a humble setup, but it's "guaranteed to make you feel at home."

	FOOD	DECOR	SERVICE	COST

Show Win *Japanese* | 20 | 15 | 19 | $35

Amagansett | 40 Montauk Hwy. (bet. Cross & Indian Wells Plain Hwys.) |
631-267-7600 | www.showwinsushi.com
Northport | 325 Fort Salonga Rd. (bet. Reservoir & Woodbine Aves.) |
631-261-6622 | www.sushishowwin.com
Admirers of this "dependable", "good-value" sushi duo say they "go
into withdrawal when it's been too long" since they've had their "inventive" rolls and other Japanese fare; the Amagansett location's
semi-private tatami room is a "big plus" for small groups, but
Northport gets knocked by some for "needing an update."

☑ Siam Lotus Thai Ⓜ *Thai* | 28 | 16 | 26 | $35

Bay Shore | 1664 Union Blvd. (bet. 4th & Park Aves.) | 631-968-8196
A local "must" for a taste of "Bangkok at its best", this "exceptional"
Bay Shore Thai brings you "all the classics" plus "delectable" daily
specials, prepared "to a T" and "beautifully presented" courtesy of
a kitchen that's "not afraid to use spice"; the "personal attention" is
likewise "a cut above", so if the room's "nondescript", keep in mind
"you don't go here for the decor."

Silver's *Eclectic* | 23 | 16 | 16 | $46

Southampton | 15 Main St. (bet. Jobs Ln. & Nugent St.) |
631-283-6443 | www.silversrestaurant.com
They elevate "lunch into an art form" at this "sweet, little"
Southampton "favorite", where the Eclectic midday fare runs to
"delicious" BLTs, lobster rolls, "homemade soups" and more served
in a "sunny" space that's been in chef-owner Garrett Wellins' family
since 1923; it'll cost you "some moola", but "everything they do,
they do well"; P.S. dinner may now be offered on summer weekends.

Simply Fondue *Fondue* | 17 | 19 | 18 | $44

Great Neck | The Gdns. | 24 Great Neck Rd. (bet. Brompton &
Middle Neck Rds.) | 516-466-4900 | www.simplyfondelongisland.com
Dip it yourself at this upstairs "find" in a Great Neck shopping center, where prix fixe fondue deals have "attentive" staffers bringing
on "tasty tidbits" you cook "in the style of your choice" on tabletop
burners, from "main-course meats and fish" to "dreamy" chocolate
desserts; "it's not cheap" and can be a "slow meal", but after a few
"signature martinis", it's "lots of fun", especially "for groups."

Simply Thai *Thai* | 21 | 13 | 19 | $27

Rockville Centre | 274 Merrick Rd. (N. Park Ave.) | 516-255-9340
This "no-frills" Rockville Centre nook earns support with "solid
Thai" favorites made all the more "tantalizing" by some of the "best
value" around; the "small", "simple setting" is "not much to look at",
but service is "quick" and you can always "take it to go."

NEW Sip City *Eclectic* | - | - | - | E

Great Neck | 16 Middle Neck Rd. (Cutter Mill Rd.) | 516-482-1500 |
www.sipcity.net
Equal parts dining room and lounge, this Eclectic rookie provides a
glitzy alternative to more staid Great Neck spots with arty decor

touches like red walls and cylindrical lights, plus tall windows that open to the street in warm weather; the menu includes the likes of Chilean sea bass with mushroom and cauliflower risotto, and live entertainment most nights plus dancing on Saturdays add to the scene.

☒ Smokin' Al's Famous BBQ Joint *BBQ*

23 | 17 | 19 | $31

Massapequa Park | 4847 Merrick Rd. (bet. Harbor Ln. & Park Blvd.) | 516-799-4900
Bay Shore | 19 W. Main St. (bet. 4th & 5th Aves.) | 631-206-3000
www.smokinals.com

"Wave goodbye to your diet" and "pig out" on "scrumptious" "Southern BBQ done right" at this "roll-up-your-sleeves" Bay Shore "mmmmeat" mecca and its Massapequa Park follow-up, "informal" outlets for "unbelievable" ribs, "tender brisket" and "awesome pulled pork" in "*Flintstone*-sized" portions "slathered" with "sloppy" sauce; the "raucous", "smoky" quarters are perpetually "mobbed" despite "insane" "waits" and "the trip to the dry cleaner" afterward.

Snapper Inn Ⓜ *Seafood*

18 | 19 | 19 | $42

Oakdale | 500 Shore Dr. (½ mi. west of Vanderbilt Blvd.) | 631-589-0248 | www.thesnapperinn.com

Ever a "fixture" for "summertime dining" thanks to a "lovely location" overlooking the Connetquot River, this "old favorite" in Oakdale "takes you away" with its "relaxed atmosphere" and "really pretty" view; nonfans who cite "so-so seafood" and "indifferent service" snap it's "living on its earlier legend", but loyal habitués say the "charm" "makes up for" everything.

☒ Snaps American Bistro Ⓜ *American*

26 | 19 | 23 | $39

Wantagh | 2010 Wantagh Ave. (Sunrise Hwy.) | 516-221-0029 | www.snapsrestaurant.com

It's easy to "pass this diamond-in-the-rough" hidden in a Wantagh "strip of stores", but that would be a shame since "talented" chef/co-owner Scott Bradley creates an "ever-changing menu" of "extraordinary" New American dishes, including specials that "keep you coming back"; service is "excellent" and a recent "face-lift greatly improved" the "cool" space, plus the daily prix fixe and tasting menus make it such a "great value" you can't get in without "a reservation on weekends"; P.S. closed Monday–Tuesday.

Solé *Italian*

26 | 15 | 21 | $40

Oceanside | 2752 Oceanside Rd. (Merle Ave.) | 516-764-3218 | www.soleny.com

"Despite its simple exterior", this "Italian gem" in Oceanside is a "terrific little spot" where a "marvelous" menu is served "with good humor" in a "bright", butter-hued space; the sole "drawback" is "large turnouts" that lead to "cramped and noisy" conditions and major "waits", but "top-notch" food at "moderate prices" easily outweighs "the negatives"; P.S. reservations accepted for five or more only.

Southampton Publick House *Pub Food*

18 | 17 | 19 | $38

Southampton | 40 Bowden Sq. (N. Main St. & N. Sea Rd.) |
631-283-2800 | www.publick.com

"Fresh beer's always on tap" to wash down "standard American" pub grub at this roomy Southampton microbrewery, where the house-brand suds are "the big attraction"; it's a "friendly" enough "local hangout" "if you can handle" "the loud bar scene."

NEW South Edison *American*

∇ 22 | 21 | 22 | $50

Montauk | 17 S. Edison St. (S. Etna Ave.) | 631-668-4200 |
www.southedison.com

Making waves in Montauk, this seasonal newcomer in the heart of the village "hit the deck running" with chef-owner Todd Mitgang (of NYC's Cascabel Taqueria) showing his "creativity" via seafood-leaning American fare backed up by a "great raw bar"; sporting an "attractive" "beach feel", it's already gaining fans who "can't wait" for summer.

NEW Southfork Kitchen *Seafood*

– | – | – | VE

Bridgehampton | 203 Bridgehampton-Sag Harbor Tpke. (bet. Narrow Ln. & Sawasett Ave.) | 631-537-4700 | www.southforkkitchen.com

An "outstanding" "gourmet addition" to Bridgehampton, this newcomer offers "inventive takes on seafood" as a "talented chef" "artfully draws" "subtle flavors" from "mostly local fish and produce" matched with wines from area vineyards; "attentive" servers oversee a rustic space with a "warm", "woodsy" vibe, so all in all diners with deep pockets "expect great things"; P.S. prix fixe only, with a separate bar bites menu; closed Tuesday and Wednesday.

Southside Fish & Clam *Seafood*

20 | 8 | 12 | $27

Lindenhurst | 395 W. Montauk Hwy. (bet. 4th & 5th Sts.) |
631-226-3322 | www.southsidefishandclam.com

In spite of the "plastic utensils", "self service" and "rudimentary decor", this '30s-era Lindenhurst seafooder remains a "mainstay" for "fresh fish" "on the cheap" including a "twin lobster deal" that "can't be beat"; still, those who expect "a bit more class" claim it's "much better" for retail fin fare at the on-site market.

Souvlaki Palace *Greek*

∇ 24 | 8 | 18 | $22

Commack | 57 Commack Rd. (Jericho Tpke.) | 631-858-1482

A "hole-in-the-wall" "family operation", this "unpretentious" Commack Greek serves "huge" plates of "honest, well-prepared" standards, from the "best souvlaki" to "fresh whole fish", at "reasonable prices"; there's not much to the "modest" surroundings, but if your "priority is food" and "nothing else", it works.

Spare Rib, The *BBQ*

18 | 14 | 18 | $29

Hicksville | 600 W. Old Country Rd. (bet. Charlotte St. &
E. Wantagh State Pkwy.) | 516-433-5252
Commack | 2098 Jericho Tpke. (Indian Head Rd.) |
631-543-5050
www.spareribonline.com

"For those who like a little body to their baby-backs", this Commack and Hicksville duo is "the place to go for BBQ ribs, chicken" and other "satisfying", "economical" eats; but some have a bone to pick over "varying service", digs that "could use a makeover" and "interminable" weekend waits for what they dub "nothing-special" grub.

Spice Village Grill *Pakistani/Persian* ▽ 20 | 13 | 19 | $28

Huntington | 281 Main St. (Wall St.) | 631-271-4800 |
www.spicevillagegrill.com

When you're looking for something "a bit different", this Pakistani-Persian in Huntington is "surprisingly good considering its outer appearance"; the staff makes "helpful" recommendations while the BYO policy "keeps a night out within your budget", so the "simple", "cramped" space is easy to overlook.

Spicy's Barbecue *BBQ* 20 | 5 | 13 | $18

Bellport | 501 Station Rd. (bet Atlantic & Patchogue Aves.) |
631-286-2755
Riverhead | 225 W. Main St. (bet. Griffing & Osborn Aves.) |
631-727-2781

Take a "quick trip to the Deep South" at these way "retro" BBQ joints in Bellport and Riverhead, where the "killer ribs" and "fabulous chicken wings" are a "delicious" "reward" at a "minuscule" price; just know that the "broken-down diner" settings make "takeout better than eating in."

Squiretown *American* ▽ 20 | 19 | 20 | $45

Hampton Bays | 26 W. Montauk Hwy. (bet. Ponquogue Ave. &
Springville Rd.) | 631-723-2626 | www.squiretown.com

"Yay for Hampton Bays!" cheer natives giddy over the arrival of this "delightful" American bistro, a "surprise" "hit" "in an unlikely location"; its "locally sourced" lineup of midpriced steaks and seafood complements an "airy", "serene setting" with a "modern" look defined by hardwood floors, earth tones and drum chandeliers.

Sripraphai *Thai* 25 | 16 | 18 | $29

Williston Park | 280 Hillside Ave. (Collins Ave.) | 516-280-3779 |
www.sripraphairestaurant.com

The "best Thai food in Queens is now the best on LI" since this "vibrant" new branch that's "just a tiny notch below" the Woodside original opened, bringing a "massive menu" of "amazing", "memorable", "hot and spicy" dishes to Williston Park; even if the "bright lime decor can be off-putting" to some and the "crowds on weekends" mean "long waits", it's a mighty "fine" purveyor of "authentic", "inexpensive" chow – and you don't need to "brave the LIE"; P.S. closed Wednesdays.

Sri Thai *Thai* 22 | 15 | 21 | $28

Huntington | 14 New St. (bet. Main & W. Carver Sts.) |
631-424-3422

Fans "can't wait to go back" to this "hidden" yet "popular" Huntington Thai where the "fantastic" dishes have a "subtlety of flavor not found in run-of-the-mill" recipes elsewhere; the staff is "pleasant", and while there's "limited seating" and "no ambiance", you "don't go for the setting" but for the "wonderful", "fairly priced" food.

Star Confectionery ⊄ *Diner/American* ▽ 22 | 19 | 22 | $17

Riverhead | 4 E. Main St. (Roanoke Ave.) | 631-727-9873

Dating to the 1920s, this "classic" "mom-and-pop" luncheonette in the heart of Riverhead is "perfect" for all-American breakfast and lunch fare in "suitable" vintage surroundings with wooden booths and a black-and-white checked floor; sweet tooths can count on "great ice cream" too, since they still make their own.

☒ Starr Boggs *American/Seafood* 26 | 23 | 22 | $62

Westhampton Beach | 6 Parlato Dr. (Library Ave.) | 631-288-3500 | www.starrboggsrestaurant.com

A perpetual Westhampton Beach "'in' spot", this "upbeat" New American shines bright with an "absolutely delicious" menu starring the eponymous chef-owner's "outstanding" seafood, served by a "terrific" team in "first-class" quarters flaunting original Warhols and a "gorgeous patio"; it provides "insanely sceney" "people-watching" on weekends, but if evading "pricey" tabs takes priority, there's a "wonderful" lobster bake deal on Mondays; P.S. closed mid-October to May.

Stella Ristorante ☒ *Italian* 24 | 18 | 22 | $41

Floral Park | 152 Jericho Tpke. (bet. Belmont & N. Tyson Aves.) | 516-775-2202 | www.stellaristorante.com

This circa-1960 "family favorite" in Floral Park "never gets old" as it reliably indulges its followers with "magnificent" "old-fashioned" Italian fare" and "top-notch" hospitality headed up by the "namesake" "matriarch"; the "warm" if "dated" digs are "always busy", so "reservations are a must on weekends" (and there still may be "a long wait").

Steve's Piccola Bussola *Italian* 24 | 16 | 22 | $42

Westbury | 649 Old Country Rd. (Tennyson Ave.) | 516-333-1335

Steve's Piccola Bussola II *Italian*

Syosset | 41 Jackson Ave. (Underhill Blvd.) | 516-364-8383 www.stevespiccolabussola.com

"Go with a group" and share "fabulous family-style" fare at these "jovial" "belly-busters" located in Westbury and Syosset, where accolytes assure that there's "joy in every bite" of the Italian "classics" that are doused in "garlic-laden" "red gravy" and "served promptly" at a "very reasonable" price; claustrophobes may wish for "more elbow room" to "sop up the sauce", but they're "popular" "so be prepared to wait."

☒ Stone Creek Inn *French/Mediterranean* 26 | 24 | 24 | $64

East Quogue | 405 Montauk Hwy. (bet. Carter Ln. & Wedgewood Rd.) | 631-653-6770 | www.stonecreekinn.com

There's "first-class" dining "nestled deep" in East Quogue at this "culinary tour de force", where the "adventurous" seasonal menu of "superior" French-Med cuisine shows off "fantastic variations and flavors" in discreetly "sophisticated" environs overseen by a "gracious" staff; the "noise level is certainly robust" and you may need to "negotiate a line of credit" to pay, but it's the stuff that "great memories" are made of; P.S. closed January–March.

NEW Stone Turtle *American/Eclectic*　21 | 19 | 20 | $39

Island Park | 4160 Austin Blvd. (Trafalgar Blvd.) | 516-431-6570 | www.thestoneturtlerestaurant.com

Chef-owner Gregory Baumel's "creativity" makes this Island Park debut a "fantastic find" for "exciting" New American–Eclectic dishes that show off "unusual flavor combinations", embracing the likes of rabbit pot pie, antelope burgers and wild boar lasagna; the "cool" space with "dark-wood and black-leather" accents plays host to live music on weekends, and despite sporadic service slips, most see "a lot of potential" here.

Stonewalls *American/French*　23 | 21 | 23 | $52

Riverhead | Woods at Cherry Creek Golf Club | 967 Reeves Ave. (bet. Doctors Path & Roanoke Ave.) | 631-506-0777 | www.stonewalls-restaurant.com

"Fantastic chef" Guy Peuch "works wonders" with his "beautifully prepared and presented" specialties at this New American–French "find", which follows through with "outstanding" service and "lovely surroundings" overlooking Riverhead's Woods at Cherry Creek golf course; sated surveyors applaud a "refreshingly consistent" performance that "should be more widely appreciated."

Strawberry's ● *American/Italian*　18 | 18 | 19 | $32

Huntington | 279 Main St. (bet. New York Ave. & Wall St.) | 631-427-0999 | www.strawbar.com

Even if it's a "glorified sports bar" with huge TV screens, the "dedicated owners", "great live music" and entertainment that ranges from karaoke and comedy to murder mystery nights make this "loud" Huntington arrival a "fun find"; the Italian-American fare is "well prepared" say some, "hit-or-miss" according to others, but the "drink specials" and desserts are a plus.

Stresa *Italian*　25 | 21 | 23 | $61

Manhasset | 1524 Northern Blvd. (¼ mi. east of Shelter Rock Rd.) | 516-365-6956 | www.stresarestaurant.com

"Marvelous", "high-end" Italian food "prepared with finesse" continues to lure a "who's who of Nassau County" to this "longtime favorite" where an "efficient, formal" staff enhances the "elegant" setting; still, some Manhasset-ites maintain "it helps to be a regular on the weekend unless you have plenty of time to wait", "even with a reservation."

NEW Sugar Dining Den & Social Club ⓈⓂ *American/Asian*　- | - | - | M

Carle Place | Staples Ctr. | 246 Voice Rd. (Glen Cove Rd.) | 516-248-7600 | www.sugarli.com

Glitzy and sexy, this lively new restaurant and lounge located in a less-than-glam retail mall in Carle Place offers a spectacular setting – a vaulted ceiling glowing with lights, tree branches in glass cases lining the walls and whimsical murals – as a backdrop for midpriced Asian-American small plates designed for sharing; P.S. there's a DJ and dancing Thursdays, Fridays and Saturdays.

Sugo *American*

23 | 20 | 20 | $41

Long Beach | 62 W. Park Ave. (bet. Edwards & National Blvds.) | 516-431-7846 | www.sugocafe.com

"One of Long Beach's hidden treasures", this "cute, colorful" "local place" "stands out" with a "delightfully" "different" American lineup offering "inventive apps" and "excellent specials" alongside burgers and brick-oven pizza; the "arty interior" is staffed by "down-to-earth" types helmed by a "hands-on" owner who "makes you feel right at home"; P.S. the Food rating may not reflect a recent chef change.

Suki Zuki *Japanese*

24 | 13 | 17 | $41

Water Mill | 688 Montauk Hwy. (Old Mill Rd.) | 631-726-4600

"The size of the crowds" "testifies to the quality" at this Water Mill Japanese "favorite", "a real keeper" for "excellent sushi" ("try the 'tuna sandwich'") and "robata-grill" specialties "at moderate prices"; the "humble storefront setting" is apt to be "noisy and cramped" and the "no-reservations policy" means you'll "often have to wait", but it's "well worth it."

Sullivan's Quay *Pub Food*

18 | 20 | 22 | $32

Port Washington | 541 Port Washington Blvd. (Revere Rd.) | 516-883-3122 | www.sullivansquay.com

There'll be "no disappointments" if you "stick to the basics" – "burgers, chops, steaks" – at this "typical Irish pub" in Port Washington with a "nice staff" serving up Traditional American fare and some "tasty" old-country specialties; it's a "comfortable" place to "watch the game" and a real "scene" Thursday nights for trivia and late-night karaoke.

Sundried Tomato Cafe *Italian/Pizza*

21 | 13 | 20 | $26

Nesconset | Nesconset Plaza | 127-3 Smithtown Blvd. (bet. Mayfair Rd. & Southern Blvd.) | 631-366-6310 | www.lisundriedtomato.com

"Huge portions" of "old-fashioned Italian" please patrons at this Nesconset "neighborhood" pizzeria/restaurant that sureveyors deem "worthy of a revisit" despite its being "not much to look at"; a "friendly" staff and "bargain lunches" are further reasons there's "always a crowd."

Sunset Beach *Asian/French*

18 | 24 | 16 | $59

Shelter Island Heights | Sunset Beach Hotel | 35 Shore Rd. (Sunnyside Dr.) | 631-749-2001 | www.sunsetbeachli.com

It's like you've "landed in the South of France" at this seasonal beachfront "hangout" on Shelter Island, where the "bikinis, boats" and "people-sighting" are "a bit like a party" whether you "sit upstairs" "watching the sunset" or surfside "with your toes in the sand"; meanwhile, malcontents moan about "hit-or-miss" Pan-Asian and French bistro fare, service that caters to "the 'in' crowd" and "sky-high prices for what you get."

Surf Lodge *American*

▽ 19 | 23 | 16 | $59

Montauk | Surf Lodge | 183 Edgemere St. (bet. Elwell St. & Industrial Rd.) | 631-238-5216 | www.thesurflodge.com

Once the sun sets over Montauk's Fort Pond, this "swingin'", beach-themed New American becomes a "trendy scene" fueled by cock-tails and "fresh seafood" from *Top Chef* vet Sam Talbot; it's "a blast" if you're willing to shell out "city prices", but the deluge of "hipsters" "dressing like surfers" makes it "hard to get in" and "score a table"; P.S. closed October–May.

Surf 'N Turf Mediterranean Grill *Greek/Turkish*

▽ 24 | 17 | 24 | $34

Merrick | 2205 Merrick Rd. (bet. Fox & Lincoln Blvds.) | 516-992-0918 | www.surfnturfgrill.com

It's a toss-up as to which is better at this Greek-Turkish Grill in Merrick – the "old-world-style" staff that treats you "like royalty" or the menu of "perfectly cooked" fish and other "simple, well-prepared" turf selections; tabs are moderate, so the "only draw-back" is that the "tight" space – decorated with an oak bar and polished mahogany floors – easily gets "crowded" and "noisy."

Surfside Inn *Continental/Seafood*

▽ 18 | 20 | 18 | $46

Montauk | Surfside Inn | 685 Old Montauk Hwy. (bet. School Ln. & Washington Dr.) | 631-668-5958

With its panorama "of the ocean surf", this longtime Continental seafooder is a "low-key" "summer pleasure" in Montauk that's extra "dreamy" if you manage to snag a spot "on the deck"; the "well-prepared" food may be "a little pricey", but at least there are "no big surprises" to distract from the "gorgeous view"; P.S. closed December to mid-March.

Surf's Out *Italian/Seafood*

▽ 17 | 19 | 18 | $45

Kismet | Fire Island | 1 Bay Walk (E. Lighthouse Walk) | 631-583-7400 | www.surfsoutfireisland.com

"Everyone meets and greets" at this waterfront hub in Kismet, where Fire Island denizens fraternize with Great South Bay types while the sounds of live bands serve as backdrop; meanwhile, the "decent" Italian-and-seafood menu is "trying to be all things" but wipes out with critics who contend it's "expensive for what it is"; P.S. closed October to mid-April.

Sushi Palace *Japanese*

▽ 24 | 16 | 21 | $30

Great Neck | 148 Middle Neck Rd. (Linden Blvd.) | 516-487-8460

The "all-you-can-eat offer" is "an all-out bargain" at this Great Neck Japanese, where for a fixed price patrons can "check off the quan-tity" desired from a "wide range" of "very good" "specialty rolls, sushi and sashimi" as well as "hot food", all served "with a smile"; the "value" alone is "worth the visit", but it's also "lots of fun."

Sushi Ya *Japanese*

21 | 15 | 19 | $36

Garden City | 949 Franklin Ave. (bet. 9th & 10th Sts.) | 516-873-8818

(continued)

Sushi Ya

New Hyde Park | 2311 Jericho Tpke. (Nassau Blvd.) | 516-741-2288
www.sushiyagc.com

For "steady" sushi, regulars report ya can't go wrong at these mid-priced Japanese eateries in Garden City and New Hyde Park, which do double duty with "hibachi grills" joining their "consistently fresh" fish; they also put together "great bento boxes", though a few aesthetes train their sights on the "unimpressive decor."

NEW Swallow ⑤ American — | — | — | M

Huntington | 366 New York Ave. (bet. Carver & Elm Sts.) |
631-547-5388 | www.swallowrestaurant.com

Nested in a tiny space, this Huntington New American turns out midpriced small plates that update homey favorites, e.g. butternut squash cappuccino and mac 'n' cheese with orzo, bacon and peas; the decor stokes a comfort vibe with exposed brick, butcher-block tables illuminated by votive candles and – what else? – birdcages.

Sweet Mama's Diner 19 | 17 | 19 | $23

Northport | 9 Alsace Pl. (Fort Salonga Rd.) | 631-261-6262 |
www.sweetmamaskitchen.net

"Still one of the best breakfast places around", this "real treat" in Northport attracts a "brunch scene to rival anything in the city" and serves "solid, generous" American plates for lunch and dinner as well; the staff is "conscientious", but those not so sweet on the retro setting say it's "a little too plain" and "you can't hear yourself think" when it "gets overcrowded with families on weekends."

Swingbelly's Beachside BBQ ● BBQ 23 | 15 | 19 | $29

Long Beach | 909 W. Beech St. (Wisconsin St.) | 516-431-3464 |
www.swingbellysbbq.com

"Chow down" on "dynamite" BBQ till your belly's "swinging low" at this ultra-"casual" Long Beach "joint", where "hefty" helpings of brisket and ribs chased with "a couple of brewskis" make for an "excellent" "pig out" at a "reasonable price"; it entails braving a "noisy bar crowd" with "sports blasting", but then 'cue fans don't mind.

Table 9 Ⓜ American/Italian 22 | 22 | 20 | $55

East Hills | 290 Glen Cove Rd. (Red Ground Rd.) | 516-625-9099 |
www.table9reservations.com

Following a recent transfer to "new ownership", this East Hills American-Italian remains an "upscale" haven for "first-rate food" enhanced by "excellent service" and dolled-up decor that "feels like you're dining in the city"; it's predictably "expensive", but the daily prix fixe (offered till 6 PM only on Saturdays) is a "best buy" "with enough choices to appeal to many tastes."

Taiko Ⓜ Asian 24 | 17 | 23 | $37

Rockville Centre | 15 S. Village Ave. (bet. Lincoln Ave. & Merrick Rd.) |
516-678-6149 | www.taikorestaurant.com

"Reliable" "for decades", this "local" "find" in Rockville Centre "never fails to impress" with "heavenly", "swimmingly fresh" sushi and "outstanding" Asian fusion fare courtesy of a "terrific" staff led by the family owners; maybe the space is "not much to look at", but it's usually "humming" since the "price and quality" "cannot be beat."

Tai-Show *Japanese* | 23 | 18 | 22 | $34 |

Levittown | 170 Gardiners Ave. (Hempstead Tpke.) | 516-731-1188
Massapequa | 4318 Merrick Rd. (Harrison Ave.) | 516-798-1119
Massapequa | 4320 Merrick Rd. (Harrison Ave.) | 516-798-3958
East Setauket | 316 Main St. (bet. Deering St. & Shore Rd.) | 631-751-2848
www.taishow.com

Tai-Show East *Japanese*

Oakdale | 1543 Montauk Hwy. (Vanderbilt Ave.) | 631-218-0808 | www.taishoweast.com

"Superior sushi" and "Japanese steakhouse cooking" come with "fantastic" service at this "good-value" Long Island chainlet; there's a "rockin' hibachi grill" tended in "high-style" at some locations, and though the "small" spaces at other outposts aren't particularly memorable, patrons do recall that the "sake bombs" are a blast.

Takara *Japanese* | ∇ 28 | 19 | 23 | $44 |

Islandia | Islandia Shopping Plaza | 1708 Veterans Memorial Hwy. (Blydenburg Rd.) | 631-348-9470 | www.takara-sushi.com

The "fresh-off-the-boat" fish gives all rivals "a run for their money" at this "excellent" Islandia Japanese, where skilled sushi chefs ("including the owner") slice a "super" "array of exotic rolls"; with a "sweetheart" hostess and "personal attention" from the servers to "make the experience even better", boosters urge "don't miss this one."

Taste 99 *American* | ∇ 18 | 21 | 21 | $46 |

Farmingdale | Carlyle on the Green, Bethpage State Park | 99 Quaker Meeting House Rd. (Round Swamp Rd.) | 516-501-9700 | www.carlyleonthegreen.net

"You won't meet anyone you know" at this "quiet rendezvous spot" insist incognito eaters who savor both the "beautiful" updated room, decorated with mahogany tables and chandeliers, and outdoor patio with "views of the famed" Bethpage Black golf course; less impressive is the "ok" menu, which includes upscale American entrees as well as grilled pizzas and small-plate options, but some say the vista is "worth it."

Tasty Crepes *Crêpes* | 18 | 7 | 14 | $14 |

Carle Place | Country Glen Shopping Ctr. | 55 Old Country Rd. (bet. Glen Cove Rd. & Vanderbilt Dr.) | 516-747-8278
NEW **Rockville Centre** | 2 N. Park Ave. (Merrick Rd.) | 516-442-0233
www.tastycrepes.com

"Tasty" "choices galore" confront lunchers at this Carle Place crêperie, where numerous "sweet and savory selections" ("the dessert ones are to die for!") are "freshly made to order"; skeptics shrug "nothing fabulous", but as an "affordable" "change of pace" it's "more than adequate"; P.S. the Rockville Centre location opened post-Survey.

	FOOD	DECOR	SERVICE	COST

NEW Tate's Ⓜ⇗ *American/Italian*   ▽ 26 | 15 | 21 | $32
Nesconset | 292 Smithtown Blvd. (Chestnut St.) | 631-676-3283 |
www.tatesrestaurant.com
Early fans of this "busy" family-run Nesconset arrival praise its
"amazing" New American–Italian eats, including housemade pastas
and "great cookies and baked goods", served by an "excellent" staff
in a cozy, white-tablecloth setting; the three-course prix fixe dinner
deal and "awesome" BYO-only policy (with no corkage fee) help
keep prices reasonable, but plastic's not accepted so "bring cash."

Tava *Turkish*   18 | 18 | 19 | $38
Port Washington | 166 Main St. (Monroe St.) | 516-767-3400 |
www.tavarestaurantandbar.com
One side of this split locale in Port Washington is devoted to
"delicious", "different" Turkish food "with flair" in a "cool Manhattan"-
style space decked out with "intimate" velvet couches and cande-
light, while the other is a "low-key" "burger-and-shakes" spot that
some "love" but critics would rather "skip"; luckily, they both feature
"good service" and "reasonable" prices; P.S. there's frequent live
guitar and piano and a low-cost weekday lunch deal.

Tel Aviv *Israeli*   22 | 12 | 18 | $38
(aka TLV)
Great Neck | 613 Middle Neck Rd. (bet. Beach Rd. & Fairview Ave.) |
516-466-6136 | www.tlvrestaurant.com
"Simple but amazing", this Great Neck niche is "a rare find" for "excellent and authentic" Israeli specialties – "fab" meze, "hummus
concoctions", "pita sandwiches", etc. – delivered by "servers who
give excellent suggestions"; though the "small" space has "no ambi-
ence", partisans who are "extremely pleased with the food" "return
again and again"; P.S. it's no longer certified kosher.

🡨 Tellers American Chophouse *Steak*   26 | 27 | 25 | $70
Islip | 605 Main St. (bet. Locust & Nassau Aves.) | 631-277-7070 |
www.tellerschophouse.com
Set in a "stately" "former bank building", this "high-class" Islip
chophouse is "a cut above the rest" according to South Shore carnivores savoring "signature rib-eyes" (like "something out of *The
Flintstones*") and other "superb" strips "done to perfection" and
matched with wines from an "impressive" cellar in the former vault;
you'll "drop a mortgage payment", but diners with "deep pockets"
are happy to be "treated royally."

Tequila Jacks *Caribbean/Seafood*   ▽ 18 | 21 | 20 | $41
Port Jefferson | 201 Main St. (entrance on Arden Pl.) | 631-331-0960
"Get lost in the Caribbean feel" at this "cheery" Downtown Port Jeff
seafooder – from the "knock-your-socks-off" mojitos to the somewhat upscale plates including "some favorites from Key West"; the
staff is "happy to talk you through the menu", but a few guests dub
the food "mediocre" and just go for the energetic bar scene and "live
bands on weekends"; P.S. "when the music starts" be prepared to
"read lips" since "no one will hear a word you're saying."

	FOOD	DECOR	SERVICE	COST

Tesoro Ristorante Ⓜ *Italian*
`23` `17` `22` `$47`

Westbury | 967 Old Country Rd. (bet. New York Ave. & Sylvester St.) | 516-334-0022 | www.tesorosrestaurant.com

They "make you feel like family" at this Westbury "oldie but goodie", treasured by legions of "repeat customers" who "count on" its "*delizioso*" traditional Italian fare and "eager-to-please" service; maybe the "outdated" room "needs a makeover", but the "satisfying" comestibles and "moderate cost" more than compensate.

Thai Gourmet Ⓜ⌿ *Thai*
`26` `14` `19` `$24`

Port Jefferson Station | Common Plaza | 4747-24 Nesconset Hwy. (bet. Terryville Rd. & Woodhull Ave.) | 631-474-0663

Boosters feel "blessed" by the "best Thai food this side of Bangkok" at this strip-mall "treasure" in Port Jefferson Station where the "tempting" dishes "burst with flavor" and "prices are dirt-cheap"; just "hit the cash machine" first and "bring your own bottle and patience", since "you may have to wait for a seat" in the "kitschy" digs; P.S. there's a "substantial take-out business" as well.

Thai Green Leaf *Thai*
`21` `10` `18` `$25`

Copiague | 47 Merrick Rd. (bet. Baylawn & Jarvis Aves.) | 631-789-8866
East Northport | 1969 Jericho Tpke. (bet. Daly & Elwood Rds.) | 631-462-8666
www.thai.netau.net

Fit for both "Thai beginners" and vets who cry "bring on the hot sauce", the "tasty" dishes at these "everyday-type" Siamese "standbys" in Copiague and East Northport are "well executed", nicely spiced and "efficiently served"; the digs are "sparsely" appointed, but the tabs "won't break your wallet" and diners "leave satisfied" so "who cares?"

Thai House *Thai*
`24` `19` `23` `$30`

Smithtown | 53 W. Main St. (Maple Ave.) | 631-979-5242 | www.thaihousesmithtown.com

Admirers of this "surprising" Smithtowner say its "reputation is spreading" for "amazing, authentic" Thai, including "light, healthy" selections prepared "to your taste", from "mild to spicy"; the "personalized" service makes you feel "appreciated", and fans even "love" the "simple" look with warm tones and "decorations from Thailand", adding to an "enjoyable experience" for a "reasonable" price.

Thai Table *Thai*
`23` `19` `21` `$27`

Rockville Centre | 88A N. Village Ave. (Sunrise Hwy.) | 516-678-0886

"Locals" laud this Rockville Centre "diamond in the rough", a "reliable" choice for "terrific Thai" seasoned with "plenty of spice" and served by a "fast, attentive" staff "at giveaway prices"; the brick-lined digs are sparsely adorned but "relaxed" enough for "an enjoyable meal."

Thai USA *Thai*
`23` `17` `19` `$34`

Huntington | 273 New York Ave. (bet. Gerard St. & Union Pl.) | 631-427-8464

"The food is always good and cooked to your liking" at this "consistent" Huntington Thai that draws a "regular following" for its "fresh, delicious", moderately priced fare; the "newly decorated" space is "cool" and the staff "attentive", so it's both a "family favorite" and a "great date spot" that's "perfect before a movie."

34 New Street ☒ *Eclectic* | 18 | 14 | 20 | $33 |

Huntington | 34 New St. (bet. Main & W. Carver Sts.) | 631-427-3434 | www.34newstreet.com

A "wide array" of "innovative" pizzas and other affordable Eclectic eats keeps this Huntington "standby" a "decent" choice "for the family"; though some say it's "not a star" given the "awkwardly constructed" space (pizza counter up front, bistro-style dining room in back) and a menu that "needs Ritalin to focus", it wins points for "value" and "warm greetings" at the door.

Thomas's Ham & Eggery Diner ⊅ *Diner* | 22 | 10 | 19 | $17 |

Carle Place | 325 Old Country Rd. (bet. E. Gate Blvd. & Mitchell Ave.) | 516-333-3060

"Things in skillets really do taste better" attest early-risers who "leave smiling" from this "old-fashioned" Carle Place diner, a "distinctive" "breakfast stop" since 1946 specializing in "super omelets" served "in the frying pan", "pancakes light as clouds" and other "usual suspects"; the "brisk" pace doesn't prevent "lineups out the door on weekends", but for "plentiful" helpings "priced right" it's "worth any wait you have to endure."

Thom Thom *Seafood/Steak* | 20 | 19 | 20 | $41 |

Wantagh | 3340 Park Ave. (bet. Beech St. & Wantagh Ave.) | 516-221-8022 | www.thomthomrestaurant.com

With a "unique" Asian-accented menu ranging from "steak to sushi and all sorts of eclectic plates", this "refined" yet "comfortable" Wantagh place attracts a "good crowd"; the service varies a bit, though, and a few feel that it's "expensive for the neighborhood" and "trying too hard to create a Manhattan feel."

NEW 388 Restaurant *American/Italian* | 20 | 20 | 21 | $47 |

Roslyn Heights | 388 Willis Ave. (Cambridge St.) | 516-621-3888 | www.388restaurant.com

This "neat newcomer" to Roslyn Heights (from ex-members of the "Matteo's gang") is attracting "a following" with the "flair and flavor" of an American-Italian menu, served up in "plentiful" portions by a "friendly, attentive" staff; the atmosphere in the sizable, Tuscan-esque space is "enjoyable" "all around", if sometimes "a little noisy."

Thyme Restaurant & Café Bar ☒ *American* | 21 | 19 | 20 | $46 |

Roslyn | 8 Tower Pl. (bet. Main St. & Old Northern Blvd.) | 516-625-2566 | www.thymenewyork.com

"Refreshing, tasty" dishes and a "pretty ambiance" attract Roslynites to this "romantic" bi-level New American with a "beautiful" outdoor dining area "overlooking the pond"; the staff "always makes you feel welcome" and you can "sit at the bar" on weekends" "listening to live music", but a few find it all just "a little basic" for the price; P.S. the prix fixe dinner is a "best buy" alternative.

	FOOD	DECOR	SERVICE	COST

Tide Runners *American* ▽ 16 | 18 | 16 | $36

Hampton Bays | 7 North Rd. (bet. Montauk & Sunrise Hwys.) |
631-728-7373 | www.tiderunners.com

Sit "on the deck" and "see the boats pass by" at this Hampton Bays
joint "right on the Shinnecock Canal", where the "waterfront views"
and "live bands" are "the top draws"; the seafood-centric American
menu is deemed "run-of-the-mill" and slightly "pricey", but "location,
location, location" keeps it "popular"; P.S. closed October–May.

Toast *Eclectic* 24 | 18 | 21 | $22

Port Jefferson | 242 E. Main St. (Thompson St.) | 631-331-6860 |
www.toastcoffeehouse.com

Breakfast's "a treat" at this "quirky", "jumpin'" Port Jeff Eclectic serving "creative" eats like "graham cracker French toast" ("a must"),
along with "perfectly brewed" java and "fabulous" lunch items; it stays
open for tapas and "late-night fondues" on Friday and Saturday nights,
dished up by a "cute", "hipster" staff; P.S. expect weekend waits.

Toast & Co. *American* 18 | 15 | 17 | $23

Huntington | 62 Stewart Ave. (bet. Main St. & New York Ave.) |
631-812-0056

There's a "good range of comfort-style options and caloric splurges"
at this Huntington American specializing in "cut-above" omelets,
pancakes and other breakfast items; a "hardworking staff" makes
the "retro" space "buzz", though some critics crack the service
"needs improvement" and the rest is "nothing to get eggcited over."

⦿ Toku *Asian* 25 | 26 | 23 | $60

Manhasset | The Americana | 2014C Northern Blvd. (Searingtown Rd.) |
516-627-8658 | www.tokumodernasian.com

"Lots of fancy cars parked out front" hint at the "swanky", "over-the-
top" scene inside this "beautiful" Asian fusion player on Manhasset's
Miracle Mile with a "spectacular ambiance" and a staff that treats
everyone "as a somebody"; luckily, it's "worth going" for the "sensational" food and cocktails alone, so "take out a mortgage", "treat
yourself" and have a "sublime" time; P.S. the "singles crowd" comes
out in full force on "Thursday nights."

Tokyo *Japanese/Korean* ▽ 24 | 14 | 24 | $33

East Northport | Laurelwood Ctr. | 192 Laurel Rd. (bet. Bellerose &
Dickinson Aves.) | 631-754-8411

"Although off the beaten path", this "tiny" East Northport fixture
"saves the day" for natives craving the "freshest sushi", tempura
and other "fantastic" Japanese fare augmented by Korean specialties; it "doesn't charge crazy prices" and the "sweet" staffers "really
care", which helps explain why the "tight space" is often "jammed."

Tomo Hibachi Steak House *Japanese* 20 | 18 | 20 | $39

Huntington | 286 Main St. (New St.) | 631-271-6666 |
www.tomohibachi.com

"You get a show and a decent meal for a fairly reasonable price"
at this Huntington hibachi house that's a "favorite among the

	FOOD	DECOR	SERVICE	COST

kids" even if the performance "is the same every time"; it's "loud and smoky", but many enjoy the "communal" atmosphere as well as the "good" steak and sushi, and recommend it for "fun with the family."

Tony's Asian Fusion *Asian*

| 19 | 14 | 17 | $33 |

East Quogue | 337 Montauk Hwy. (Seashore Ave.) | 631-728-8850 | www.tonysasianfusion.com

Tony's Fusion Express *Asian*

Hampton Bays | 1 W. Main St. (Squiretown Rd.) | 631-728-1799 | www.tonysasianfusion.com

Tony's Fusion West *Asian*

Westhampton Beach | 23 Sunset Ave. (bet. Hanson Pl. & Main St.) | 631-288-8880 | www.tonysfusionwest.com

Tony's Sushi *Asian*

East Moriches | 466 E. Main St. (Atlantic Ave.) | 631-878-9575 | www.tonyssushi.net

There's a "wide array" "to choose from or mix" together at these East End Asian foursome, which proffers a "solid" selection of Chinese, Japanese and Thai with the addition of a "hibachi show" in East Quogue; the casual quarters are "not relaxing", but "your dollar goes a long way"; P.S. the Hampton Bays branch is a "grab-and-go" counter only.

Top of the Bay *American*

| - | - | - | E |

Cherry Grove | Fire Island | 1 Dock Walk (Bayview Walk) | 631-597-6028

"The views are incredible" at this seasonal New American overlooking the Cherry Grove "ferry dock", a prime spot for summer sojourners to take in the "wonderful" sights of the Great South Bay, "especially at sunset"; offering dishes like crab cakes and rack of lamb in airy quarters sporting ceiling fans and banks of windows, it's top-of-the-line for Fire Island and priced accordingly.

Torcellos *Italian*

| 21 | 15 | 20 | $27 |

East Northport | Elwood Shopping Ctr. | 1932 Jericho Tpke. (Elwood Rd.) | 631-499-8792 | www.torcellos.com

A "hometown" "favorite" since 1988, this "little Italian joint" in East Northport "always draws a crowd" with "traditional pizzas" and "generous" portions of "well-prepared" "staples"; "seating may be tight", but it's so "family-friendly" and "light on the wallet" that few mind that it's "not fine dining."

Townline BBQ *BBQ*

| 19 | 15 | 15 | $27 |

Sagaponack | 3593 Montauk Hwy. (Townline Rd.) | 631-537-2271 | www.townlinebbq.com

The "smoky" aroma will "transport you to the South" at this Sagaponack "roadhouse" from the Nick & Toni's team, where the "Texas BBQ" is "up to par" for "cheap eats" if you "stick to the basics"; the rough-hewn, "counter-service" setup offers "a minimum of creature comforts", but it's "child-friendly" and "the bar scene is fun"; P.S. closed Tuesday and Wednesday.

	FOOD	DECOR	SERVICE	COST

Trata *Greek/Seafood* 22 | 23 | 19 | $70

Roslyn | 1446 Old Northern Blvd. (Remsen Ave.) | 516-625-2600
Trata East ☽ *Greek/Seafood*
Water Mill | 1020 Montauk Hwy. (bet. Deerfield & Scuttle Hole Rds.) |
631-726-6200
www.trata.com

"A well-heeled crowd" delights in "extraordinarily fresh" seafood
and other "outstanding" "upscale Greek" fare at this "classy" couple
in Water Mill and Roslyn, whose "gorgeous" environs are "definitely
the place to be seen"; they "live up to" their "reputation for high
quality", but be ready for "noise" and "attitude galore" and "bring
your drachmas" to cover the "over-the-top" tabs; P.S. the Water Mill
location is closed October–March.

NEW Trattachino Ⓜ *American*  - | - | - | M

Wantagh | Wantagh Plaza | 753 Wantagh Ave. (bet. Hunt Rd. &
Sprucewood Dr.) | 516-735-6500 | www.trattachino.com
This casual newcomer in a little shopping plaza in Wantagh offers
midpriced New American fare with an Italian bent in a modern cafe
setting featuring a painted cement floor, red-cushioned banquettes
and industrial-chic exposed pipes overhead; P.S. a DJ spins Friday
and Saturday nights.

Trattoria Diane Ⓜ *Italian* 25 | 21 | 23 | $56

Roslyn | 21 Bryant Ave. (bet. Roosevelt Ave. & Skillman St.) |
516-621-2591
A "relaxing" Roslyn respite for "delightful" Northern Italian fare and
"scrumptious" desserts (it's affiliated with Diane's Bakery next
door), this "elegant, unpretentious" spot is "lovely for a special occasion" or a "romantic" date; "artful presentations", "professional
service" and an "unreal" Sunday night deal ensure it's the "absolute
favorite" of many.

Trattoria Di Meo *Italian* 21 | 15 | 20 | $48

Roslyn Heights | 183 Roslyn Rd. (Donald St.) | 516-621-4895 |
www.trattoriadimeo.com
"Warm greetings" abound at this "neighborhood go-to" in Roslyn
Heights that's celebrating 40-plus years serving "solid" Italian
fare – including the "best red sauce east of the city" – with a
"personal touch"; despite the "high prices", it's "homey" enough
to feel like "grandma's kitchen", and they "never rush you"
through the meal.

Trattoria Lucia *Italian* ▽ 22 | 19 | 24 | $40

East Meadow | 2485 N. Jerusalem Rd. (bet. Sterling & Taft Sts.) |
516-785-8808 | www.trattorialuciarestaurant.com
This "charming" East Meadow trattoria (with an adjunct in
Bellerose) is "an unexpected treat" for "delicious and plentiful"
Italian "home cooking" prepared and served "with love" by its
"wonderful" husband-and-wife owners; once you add in "alfresco"
seating and daily early-bird deals, it earns "a big shout-out" from
the "neighborhood" faithful.

	FOOD	DECOR	SERVICE	COST

Tricia's Café Ⓜ *American* — 23 | 16 | 20 | $20

Babylon | 26 E. Main St. (Fire Island Ave.) | 631-422-7879 |
www.triciascafe.com

"You could easily walk right past" this "small", "family-owned" "local joint" in Babylon, but you'd miss out on its "decently priced" lineup of "super" American fare, notably the "inventive burgers"; service can "take awhile" when it's "busy", but that leaves more time to admire the walls full of '50s "memorabilia."

Trio *American* — ▽ 21 | 15 | 20 | $35

Holbrook | Holbrook Country Club | 700 Patchogue-Holbrook Rd.
(Smith Ave.) | 631-585-4433 | www.triofinefood.com

Golfers gravitate to this "comfortable" New American that moved from its original Patchogue location to a "peaceful" setting with patio seating and views of the greens in the Holbrook Country Club; the interior is "nothing fancy", but there are "some excellent dishes" and early-bird specials; P.S. closed Tuesdays.

ⓩ Trumpets on the Bay *American/Continental* — 22 | 25 | 22 | $52

Eastport | 58 S. Bay Ave. (south of Montauk Hwy.) | 631-325-2900 |
www.trumpetsonthebay.com

"Pure romance" is in the air at this "lovely" American-Continental in Eastport, where the "breathtaking" views of Moriches Bay ("ask for a window seat") and "warm and attractive" setting manned by staffers who "can't do enough for you" will make "stress melt away"; though the "amazing" seascape is undeniably "their trump card", the "fine" cuisine is "always a safe bet" too.

Tsubo Ⓜ *Japanese* — ▽ 23 | 13 | 22 | $32

Syosset | 18 Cold Spring Rd. (Jackson Ave.) | 516-921-8154

It's "not for the trendy", but "locals love" this long-running Syosset Japanese for "finely cut" "traditional" sushi that couldn't be "fresher" "except in the ocean" and "sweet, unassuming service"; it's "not inventive" and the "no-frills" "decor could be better", but it's "one of the best buys around" and "you can always get a table."

Tula Kitchen *Eclectic* — 24 | 25 | 25 | $33

Bay Shore | 41 E. Main St. (bet. 3rd & 4th Aves.) | 631-539-7183 |
www.tulakitchen.com

Chef-owner Jackie Sharlup's "tip-top" Eclectic "gem" in Bay Shore is a "healthier" alternative that's "noteworthy" for "surprisingly" "delightful" "vegan- and vegetarian-friendly" choices, though "omnivores" "will be just as pleased" with the poultry and fish; with "red, velvety digs" and "lovely service", it's a "soothing" "bohemian" enclave that channels "a little bit of Manhattan" "without being pretentious."

Tulip Bar & Grill *Mediterranean/Turkish* — 19 | 15 | 20 | $36

Great Neck | 4 Welwyn Rd. (Shoreward Dr.) | 516-487-1070 |
www.tulipbarandgrill.com

Great Neckers turn to this "neighborhood" joint for a "consistently" "solid" Turkish-Med menu (now with "a selection of Indian as well") served by "friendly" types at a "reasonable price"; faultfinders feel the decor's "a little tired", but it gets a fez-tive boost with "fun, fun, fun belly dancing" on Saturday nights.

Turquoise *Seafood*
| 21 | 12 | 19 | $43 |

Great Neck | 33 N. Station Plaza (bet. Bond St. & Park Pl.) | 516-487-3737
"Plain" looks aside, this "local" seafooder near the Great Neck train station is "a real find" for "the freshest" "whole grilled fish" and "wonderful starters" like Israeli salad; quarters can be "too close for comfort", but the daily early-bird's "always a good buy."

Turtle Crossing *American/BBQ*
| 22 | 11 | 16 | $36 |

East Hampton | 221 Pantigo Rd./Rte. 27 (bet. Maple Ln. & Pantigo Pl.) | 631-324-7166 | www.turtlecrossing.com
"If you hanker for BBQ", this seasonal in East Hamptonite supplies "irresistible" ribs in a "down-and-dirty setting" that's "kind of like a roadside joint" with "live music" and "picnic tables outside"; critics grow cross over service that "could be a little more accommodating", but between "lots of families" and a "noisy" "bar scene" it's "constantly busy"; P.S. a new menu includes more health-minded American fare.

Tuscan House *Italian*
| ▽ 22 | 18 | 22 | $52 |

Southampton | 10 Windmill Ln. (Jobs Ln.) | 631-287-8703 | www.tuscanhouse.us
"The real McCoy" for "fresh, homemade" Italian, this "lesser-known" Southamptonite features "huge portions" of "well-presented" specialties "timely delivered" in "warm", Tuscan-esque surroundings; *ciao*-hounds who acknowledge it's "expensive but oh-so-good" pay compliments to "a worthwhile visit."

Tutto Il Giorno Ⓜ *Italian*
| 25 | 19 | 20 | $62 |

Sag Harbor | 6 Bay St. (Rector St.) | 631-725-7009
"*Perfetto!*" cry partisans of the "absolutely amazing" cuisine and "warm service" that qualify this "creative" Italian as "a must-try" in Sag Harbor; the "cozy quarters" and "wonderful" warm-weather terrace maintain an insidery vibe boosted by a "parade of celebrities", but be prepared for an "expensive" tab and a "queue to get in" ("wish they would take reservations").

Tutto Pazzo *Italian*
| 20 | 21 | 21 | $42 |

Huntington | 84 New York Ave. (bet. Ketewomoke Dr. & Youngs Hill Rd.) | 631-271-2253 | www.tuttopazzo.com
Regulars relish the "reliable red-sauce" dishes at this "local" Huntington Italian that's "especially nice in warm weather when the windows are open to the harbor breeze" and the patio fills up; a "super-nice" staff helps makes it "great for groups" and "family celebrations."

Tweeds Restaurant & Buffalo Bar *American*
| 21 | 21 | 21 | $44 |

Riverhead | J.J. Sullivan Hotel | 17 E. Main St. (bet. East & Roanoke Aves.) | 631-208-3151 | www.tweedsrestaurant.com
Bison steaks and burgers are "the house specialty" heading a "well-prepared" New American lineup at this "relaxed" Riverhead retreat

in a "historic building", which adopts a "charming" "saloon look" down to the "buffalo head on the wall" over the "antique bar"; with "cozy" atmospherics and a "piano player" on weekends, it "really grows on you."

21 Main *Steak*
| 23 | 22 | 23 | $59 |

West Sayville | 21 Montauk Hwy. (Cherry Ave.) | 631-567-0900 | www.21main.com

It's "hard to beat" this "classy", "pricey" West Sayville chophouse delivering "huge", "tender" steaks along with "two-pound baked potatoes" and other "terrific sides"; the "on-point" staff and "cool", "convivial" surroundings, boasting several fireplaces and frequent live piano music, make it "awesome for date night"; P.S. "go for Wine Down Wednesdays", when specially priced vinos are served with cheeses from around the world.

☒ Two Steak & Sushi Den *Japanese/Steak*
| 24 | 26 | 22 | $66 |

New Hyde Park | 1270 Union Tpke. (bet. Lakeville & New Hyde Park Rds.) | 516-358-2222 | www.twoonline.com

With a "comfortable yet futuristic" design likened to "the *Jetsons'* living room", this "drop-dead gorgeous" New Hyde Park yearling combines a "striking" setting and "swinging" vibe with a "superlative" "take on steak and sushi" served by a "solicitous staff"; it's a "trendy" destination for the area "who's who", and big spenders affirm it's "so worth the money" for "all the bells and whistles."

Umberto's *Italian/Pizza*
| 22 | 15 | 19 | $29 |

Garden City | 361 Nassau Blvd. S. (bet. Cambridge Ave. & Princeton Rd. S.) | 516-481-1279 | www.originalumbertos.com
New Hyde Park | 633 Jericho Tpke. (Lakeville Rd.) | 516-437-9424 | www.originalumbertos.com
Wantagh | Cherrywood Shopping Ctr. | 1180 Wantagh Ave. (Jerusalem Ave.) | 516-221-5696 | www.originalumbertos.com
Huntington | 138 E. Main St. (Loma Pl.) | 631-935-1391

Angoletto Café *Italian/Pizza*
New Hyde Park | 1598 Hillside Ave. (New Hyde Park Rd.) | 516-358-2010

Village Pizzeria ⌽ *Italian/Pizza*
Floral Park | 169 Tulip Ave. (bet. Iris & Plainfield Aves.) | 516-775-0612

"Awesome" pizza "is the thing" at this family of parlors known for its "sensational" slices (like the grandma and Sicilian) that are "worth traveling for", and sauce that "reminds you of Sundays at nonna's"; the otherwise "typical" sit-down menu and "long waits" don't faze fans; P.S. the original Umberto's ("Napoli in New Hyde Park") is praised as a "step above the rest", and the Huntington branch is separately owned.

Uncle Bacala's *Italian/Seafood*
| 21 | 18 | 21 | $35 |

Garden City Park | 2370 Jericho Tpke. (bet. Herricks Rd. & Marcus Ave.) | 516-739-0505 | www.unclebacala.com

"You'll never leave hungry" from this "family-style" Garden City Park "standby" where a "high-energy" staff delivers "decently priced", "generous portions" of Southern Italian "staples" including seafood;

gratis cotton candy is even sweeter if you "go during the week", when the package doesn't include "deafening" decibels.

Uncle Dai *Chinese*

| 18 | 11 | 18 | $26 |

Glen Cove | 26 School St. (bet. Glen St. & Highland Rd.) | 516-671-1144 | www.uncledais.com

"The menu doesn't change often" at this "inexpensive", "child-friendly" Glen Cove Chinese "but you don't want it to" given the "always dependable" Hunan selections; the staff is "fast and pleasant", but the "unappealing decor" leads many to opt for "takeout."

Upper Crust Café ⓜ *American*

| - | - | - | E |

Garden City | 931 Franklin Ave. (bet. 9th & 10th Sts.) | 516-248-5677 | www.uppercrustgc.com

Red walls, a tile floor and slanted wood-plank room dividers lend rustic warmth to this Garden City American where the menu leans toward updated comfort favorites like chicken with polenta and crab mac 'n' cheese; P.S. there's a patio for alfresco dining.

Varney's ⓢ *American/Seafood*

| 23 | 9 | 19 | $29 |

Brookhaven | 2109 Montauk Hwy. (Westminster Ave.) | 631-286-9569 | www.varneysrestaurant.com

Known to "the local crowd" for 30 years, this "tiny" "shack" tucked "out of the way" in Brookhaven is "an old reliable" for "palate-pleasing" American "home cooking" focused on "fresh seafood"; it's "not much to look at" and the pace is "leisurely" "when busy", but the payoff is "satisfying grub" that "doesn't break the bank."

Venere Ristorante *Italian*

| 20 | 14 | 20 | $33 |

Westbury | 841 Carman Ave. (bet. Lake & Land Lns.) | 516-333-2332 | www.ristorantevenere.com

"Mamma would approve" of this Westbury "joint", "a longtime favorite" that plies the "locals" with "reliable" "homestyle Italian" till their "pants won't fit"; holdouts huff the food's "nothing spectacular" and the decor's "seen better days", but with "friendly service" and "reasonable prices", it remains a "neighborhood go-to."

☑ Verace *Italian*

| 26 | 26 | 25 | $47 |

Islip | 599 Main St. (bet. Locust & Willow Aves.) | 631-277-3800 | www.veracerestaurant.com

"Another winner" from the owners of next-door neighbor Tellers, this "sophisticated" Islip newcomer's takes an "inspired" approach to Italian, showcasing "mouthwatering" "small-plate servings" (plus full portions) presented by "professional" staffers tending the "stunning" interior and "cobblestone" patio; to sweeten the already "reasonable" cost, "they offer everything half-price" for the last two hours of the night and the "Monday wine dinner is a steal."

NEW Vero *Italian*

| - | - | - | M |

Amityville | 192 Broadway (bet. Greene Ave. & W. Oak St.) | 631-608-4340 | www.verorestaurant.biz

Chef Massimo Fedozzi (of the shuttered Palio) has resurfaced at this midpriced Amityville newcomer, serving small, sharable plates of salumi and nonna's meatball sliders plus heartier dishes such as grilled-to-order veal lollipops; the stylish design includes a bar area with chandeliers and a more formal dining room with a cathedral ceiling and Murano-glass sconces.

Vespa Cibobuono *Italian*   22 | 18 | 20 | $49

Great Neck | 96 Northern Blvd. (bet. Buttonwood & Westminster Rds.) | 516-829-0005 | www.vespany.com

"When you need a break from red sauce", this "cute" Great Neck Northern Italian offers a "terrific take" on "regional" fare from the top of "The Boot" with its "delicious" renditions of Tuscan and Milanese specialties; "service is pleasant" if "slow at busy times", and even with highish prices, there's plenty of reason "it's caught on."

View *American/Continental*   22 | 23 | 19 | $51
(fka Riverview)

Oakdale | 3 Consuelo Pl. (Shore Dr.) | 631-589-2694 | www.viewoakdale.com

Thanks to new owner Lessing's Hospitality, this renamed and "re-modeled" Oakdale American-Continental "finally does justice" to its "breathtaking" Great South Bay vista with a "top-notch" menu and a "brighter", "updated dining room"; alfresco seating and "happy hour" "on the deck" are "what summer is all about", though some still view the service as unduly "slow."

Villa D'Aqua *Italian*   21 | 19 | 20 | $48

Bellmore | 2565 Bellmore Ave. (Public Hwy.) | 516-308-4900

Fans of this upscale, boat-accessible Bellmore newcomer "on the canal", from the folks behind Wantagh's Per Un Angelo, are fond of the "very good" Northern Italian fare focusing on "fresh" seafood; the owners work hard to "make sure guests are satisfied", and though the "cozy" interior looks a bit "dated", the outdoor deck attracts "many locals" in the summer.

Villa D'Este *Italian*   22 | 20 | 22 | $42

Floral Park | 186 Jericho Tpke. (bet. Flower & Tyson Aves.) | 516-354-1355 | www.villadesterestaurant.com

An "old favorite" in Floral Park, this "down-to-earth" Northern Italian is a "quiet" haven that's "always satisfying" for the "staples one would expect"; the "attentive staff" and "bargain" prix fixe menus for both lunch and dinner ensure the regulars "keep going back."

Village Lanterne *German*   ∇ 25 | 22 | 21 | $34

Lindenhurst | 143 N. Wellwood Ave. (bet. Auburn & Bristol Sts.) | 631-225-1690 | www.thevillagelanterne.com

The "party atmosphere" will "make you want to don your lederhosen" at this "cozy" Lindenhurst hideaway, which delivers the "authentic German" experience with "*wunderbar*" grub – from "sauerbraten to die for" to desserts from partner Black Forest Bakery – and wall-to-wall Bavarian decor; *ja*, the going can be "slow", but with servers in "costumes", a "large beer menu" and "live music" on weekends, it's like "Oktoberfest all year."

	FOOD	DECOR	SERVICE	COST

Vincent's Clam Bar *Italian* | 22 | 16 | 19 | $32 |

Carle Place | Carle Place Commons | 179 Old Country Rd.
(Glen Cove Rd.) | 516-742-4577 | www.vincentsclambar.com

Typically "jam-packed", this slice of "Mulberry Street" in Carle Place
is a local "institution" where marinara lovers "carbo-load" on "classic" Italian dishes big enough to "feed a small Sicilian village"; you
"can't beat the sauce" (though you can buy a bottle to go) or the
easy-to-digest prices, but the "frenetic" scene and "unbearable
noise level" drown out any intimate conversations, and live music on
Sundays only "adds to the din"; P.S. reservations accepted for five or
more (except Saturdays).

Vine Street Café *American* | 25 | 20 | 23 | $64 |

Shelter Island | 41 S. Ferry Rd. (Cartwright Rd.) | 631-749-3210 |
www.vinestreetcafe.com

An "out-of-the-way oasis of culinary delights", this "quaint" Shelter
Islander "consistently delivers" "on all counts" with a "market
menu" of "superbly prepared" American dishes, "timely" service
and a "sweet little" "cottage" setting with a "porch in the back";
since "it's such a hot ticket" there may be "noise and tumult", but it's
"definitely worth the ferry ride"; P.S. closed Tuesday and Wednesday
in the winter.

Vine Wine Bar and   ∇ | 22 | 23 | 18 | $43 |
First Street Restaurant Ⓜ *American*

Greenport | 100 South St. (1st St.) | 631-477-6238 | www.vinewinebar.com

"Hidden" "in sleepy little Greenport", this "über-cool wine bar" proffers a limited but "fantastic" selection of New American "small
plates" highlighting "local ingredients" (and "well matched" with
"outstanding" vinos) while the adjoining First Street Restaurant dining room features dinner entrees; the "warm" and "romantic" atmo
extends from the "handsome" interior to the vine-adorned patio.

Vintage Port ⓏⓂ *French*   ∇ | 19 | 19 | 19 | $31 |

Port Washington | 109D Main St. (bet. Central Dr. & Irma Ave.) |
516-883-1033

It's a "lovely place to stop after the movies or to catch up with
friends", say fans of this Port Washington wine bar that's "worth a
detour" for its "fine" vino, "excellent" cheeses and "limited menu" of
French small plates, including crêpes and sandwiches; the staff "ex-
plains the pairings well", while the "intimate" (some say "cramped")
space, with exposed-brick walls and mosaic table tops, hosts occasional "great live music."

Vintage Prime Steakhouse *Steak* | 25 | 21 | 23 | $67 |

St. James | 433 N. Country Rd. (Clinton Ave.) | 631-862-6440

Carnivores compliment the "phenomenal" steaks, "fabulous sides"
and "extensive wine list" at this "pricey" St. James steakhouse with
"quality" service; the Western "lodge atmosphere" isn't for
everyone – some feel the vibe could be "cozier" and are bothered by
"animals on the wall looking at" them – but the majority maintains
they've "never had a bad meal" here.

NEW Vitae *Continental*
| | - | - | - | E |

Huntington | 54 New St. (W. Carver St.) | 631-385-1919 | www.vitaeli.com

This classy newcomer in the former Abel Conklin's space in Huntington features dark wood and big, semi-circular red leather booths as a plush surround for upscale Continental fare such as the house veal chop and crab-crusted sole; a bluestone patio beckons in summer, hidden from the street by a high brick wall.

Vittorio's Restaurant & Wine Bar *American/Italian*
| | 25 | 22 | 25 | $48 |

Amityville | 184 Broadway (Greene Ave.) | 631-264-3333 | www.vittorios.biz

Amityville "locals" in the know confirm that this "charming" eatery-cum-enoteca is "always on the money" whether for "fabulous" American-Italian fare or "excellent" cuts of beef on Wednesday "steak nights"; a 150-label wine list and "gracious" servers who treat everyone like "the most important person in the room" have loyalists "going back" regardless of the "slightly high price."

Viva Juan *Mexican*
| | ▽ 21 | 16 | 19 | $28 |

Selden | 280 Middle Country Rd. (bet. New Ln. & Patchogue-Mt. Sinai Rd.) | 631-698-8172

The Mexican "comfort" chow is "decent", "filling and cheap" report fans of this casual Selden cantina; a few purists lament "Americanized" cooking that's "not even close to authentic", but the margarita-fueled "karaoke nights" are "so much fun."

Viva La Vida *Mexican/Spanish*
| | ▽ 20 | 16 | 22 | $36 |

Oakdale | 1611 Montauk Hwy. (bet. Idlehour & Vanderbilt Blvds.) | 631-589-2300 | www.viva-la-vida.com

"Not your typical" south-of-the-border spot, this Oakdale outpost caters to compadres "willing to try" real-deal Spanish-Mexican cuisine via "very satisfying" traditional dishes ("the paella is especially great") accompanied by "housemade" sangria; a "super staff" that "aims to please" further confirms "this is a special place."

Voila! 🛇 *French*
| | 24 | 22 | 26 | $48 |

St. James | 244 Lake Ave. (Woodlawn Ave.) | 631-584-5686 | www.voilathebistro.com

Habitués hope this St. James "sleeper" "stays a secret" so they can have the "superb" Provençal fare and "cute", homey setting all to themselves; with a chef-owner who "goes out of his way to please", "professional" service and a "bonus" no-corkage BYO policy (though there's a full bar as well), this "special place" "holds its own against the best of Long Island."

Walk Street *American*
| | 21 | 19 | 20 | $36 |

Garden City | 176 Seventh St. (Franklin Ave.) | 516-746-2592 | www.walkstreetgc.com

"Consistently good" New American "from burgers to fancy fish" puts a hop in the step of Garden City neighbors who rely on this "hangout" for "relaxed" weekday lunches and "solid" midpriced dinners; sidewalk seating and live music on Fridays make it more "en-joyable", though a few feel the menu "needs updating."

Wall's Wharf *American/Seafood*   17 | 19 | 16 | $42

Bayville | 18 Greenwich Ave. (off Bayville Ave.) | 516-628-9696 | www.wallswharf.com

"Sit outside" and "enjoy a beautiful sunset" from the "awesome" split-level deck at this "beachfront" Bayville "standby" with a "spectacular" "up-close view of the Sound"; if some think the "simple" New American and seafood options are "only so-so" and service is "unorganized", followers still "look forward to going" for the "unbeatable" "scenery."

Waterview Restaurant *Continental/Seafood*   18 | 19 | 19 | $41

Port Washington | Brewer Capri Marina E. | 45 Orchard Beach Blvd. (S. Norwood Rd.) | 516-944-5900 | www.thewaterview.net

As the name suggests, it's all about the "incredible" view of Long Island Sound, especially from the outdoor deck that "makes you feel like you're on vacation", at this Port Washington Continental sea-fooder; the dishes are "good but not spectacular" and the interior fairly "ordinary", but that's all "irrelevant" to most when they're "sit-ting outside in the summer, watching the boats."

☑ Waterzooi Belgian Bistro *Belgian*   24 | 19 | 21 | $42

Garden City | 850 Franklin Ave. (bet. 9th St. & Stewart Ave.) | 516-877-2177 | www.waterzooi.com

"Mussel mania" prevails at this "boisterous" Belgian bistro in Garden City that pots "plump, delicious" moules seemingly "by the ton", bathes them in "delectable" broths and matches them with an "unparalleled selection" of hard-to-find brews (more than 130 avail-able); the vibe is "cool" and "convivial" with a "popping bar scene", and though it does get "loud", that's just the sound of everyone "rav-ing" about the "fabulous frites" and clinking their Chimays.

Wave *American*   19 | 23 | 19 | $47

Port Jefferson | Danfords on the Sound | 25 E. Broadway (E. Main St.) | 631-928-5200 | www.danfords.com

It "made a huge comeback" after a complete makeover a few years back say Port Jeff guests about this New American in Danfords on the Sound with "fresh, beautiful" decor that complements the "un-believable" harbor views; the food is less impressive (ranging from "pretty good" to "decidedly average"), but that doesn't stop the "real bar scene" with "wonderful 'tenders" at "happy hour on Friday nights."

West East Bistro *Asian*   25 | 21 | 23 | $37

Hicksville | 758 S. Broadway (bet. Hazel St. & Oyster Bay Rd.) | 516-939-6618 | www.westeastbistro.com

Proponents praise the "extraordinary" Asian fusion fare at this "best-kept secret" hidden in a "practically deserted" Hicksville strip mall, saying the "varied", "city-caliber" menu "never disappoints"; a "hospitable" owner oversees "accommodating" service in the "sophisticated" dining room, and prices are "reasonable", so it's "worth seeking out."

	FOOD	DECOR	SERVICE	COST

⚡ West End Cafe *American* | 25 | 20 | 22 | $43 |

Carle Place | Clocktower Shopping Ctr. | 187 Glen Cove Rd. (bet. Old Country Rd. & Westbury Ave.) | 516-294-5608 | www.westendli.com

Despite its "oddball" location in the back of a strip mall, the "crowds" have "discovered" this "exceptional" Carle Place bistro whose "imaginative" New American creations deliver a "fantastic" "culinary experience"; a "mature, well-trained" staff and "NYC ambiance" complete the picture, but since the "tight" space is in demand, be sure to reserve "weeks in advance"; P.S. if you nab a seat for the early-bird, "you've scored a home run."

NEW Whale's Tale *Seafood* ▽ | 20 | 17 | 19 | $29 |

Northport | Brittania Yachting Ctr. | 81 Fort Salonga Rd. (Callahan's Beach Rd.) | East Northport | 631-651-8844 | www.brityacht.com

It's "quickly become a local favorite" say fans of this "publike" new-comer in Northport's Brittania Yachting Center (from a former partner of Zim Zari and Mercato), which serves up "surprisingly good" seafood in a "casual waterfront setting"; "don't expect a gourmet meal, just a fun night out" (plastic forks and all) on a spacious patio in summer, or inside, where the fare "tastes better than the place looks"; P.S. arrive early for the "great sunsets."

NEW When Pigs Fly ⊠Ⓜ *BBQ* ▽ | 18 | 14 | 17 | $24 |

Montauk | 10 S. Etna Ave. (S. Edison St.) | 631-668-8070 | www.whenpigsflymtk.com

After winging it to Montauk with their knack for BBQ in tow, "amazing" owners Michael and Lisa Antolini dish "darn good" ribs and chicken out of this little "shack" in the heart of the village; though a few smoke hounds are "not impressed", pork partisans are happy to grab their "take-out" babybacks and enjoy them "on the beach."

Wild Fig *Mediterranean/Turkish* | 19 | 15 | 18 | $28 |

Garden City | 829 Franklin Ave. (Stewart Ave.) | 516-739-1002
Glen Cove | 167 Glen St. (bet. Pearsall Ave. & Town Path) | 516-656-5645
Syosset | 631 Jericho Tpke. (Cedar St.) | 516-558-7744
www.wildfigonline.com

The "endless menu" means there's "something for everyone" at this "casual" Med-Turkish triumvirate, "consistently" "solid" sources of both "staples" and "more adventurous" choices (e.g. "pizzalike *pides*"); sticklers are less wild about the "sparsely decorated" digs and "sometimes slow" service, but "ample portions" at "economical prices" keep them "relatively busy."

Wildfish *Seafood* | 21 | 20 | 20 | $40 |

Freeport | 507 Guy Lombardo Ave. (Front St.) | 516-442-0565 | www.wildfishli.com

Since "redoing the interior" the owners have made this Freeport seafooder much "more inviting", and the "innovative", "price-conscious" menu is "excellent" too; guests "love" to "sit outside" and enjoy the "beautiful views", and the "helpful" service, "enter-

tainment on weekends" and boat slips for sailors are further draws;
P.S. hours vary by season.

Wild Ginger *Asian* | 21 | 20 | 19 | $36 |

Great Neck | The Gdns. | 48 Great Neck Rd. (bet. Brompton &
Middle Neck Rds.) | 516-487-8288
East Northport | 3018 Jericho Tpke. (bet. Daly & Larkfield Rds.) |
631-858-1888
www.wildgingerrestaurant.net

With their "full-flavored dishes", "zippy" decor and "rocking" atmospherics, this "popular" Pan-Asian pair in Great Neck and East
Northport rises "a cut above the usual neighborhood" options; but
since the tables are "close", the "noise level's insane" at "peak
times" and "service is so fast you can get whiplash", they're perhaps
not the places to go "for a relaxing meal."

Wild Honey Dining & Wine *American* | 25 | 20 | 23 | $46 |

Oyster Bay | 1 E. Main St. (South St.) | 516-922-4690

Wild Honey on Main Ⓜ *American*

NEW Port Washington | 172 Main St. (bet. Madison & Monroe Sts.) |
516-439-5324
www.wildhoneyrestaurant.com

"Eclectic, flavorful" New American dishes "deliver a wallop" at this
"delightful", upscale twosome: a "romantic little hideaway" with
sidewalk seating and "SoHo" flair in Oyster Bay, and its "teeny-tiny"
but "wonderful" Port Washington "sequel"; both benefit from
"pleasant" service, and though they can get "hectic" and quite
"noisy at times", they're still a top choice for "date night."

World Pie ❶ *Pizza* | 19 | 15 | 17 | $37 |

Bridgehampton | 2402 Montauk Hwy.
(bet. Bridgehampton-Sag Harbor Tpke. & Corwith Ave.) |
631-537-7999

"Choices abound" at this "gourmet" Bridgehampton pizza joint featuring a "gazillion" wood-fired pies with "unusual toppings" that
keep "families, couples and even seniors" lining up to dine before
the late-night "bar scene" gets cooking; it always works "in a pinch"
or for "people-watching" on the patio, but even though moderate
prices (for the Hamptons) leave some change in the pocket, crusty
critics don't buy the "hype."

NEW XO Wine & Chocolate Bar ❶Ⓜ *Eclectic* | – | – | – | E |

Huntington | 24 Clinton Ave. (bet. Gerard & Main Sts.) | 631-923-2224 |
www.xowinebar.com

Fire-engine red and black decor makes a striking setting at this tiny
new Huntington Eclectic where the granite bar and high-top tables
are filled with patrons nibbling on small plates (e.g. New Zealand
lamb chops with candied bacon and maple glaze) and large ones
(Kobe beef sliders with truffle Parmesan fries); for dessert – what
else? – chocolate in many forms; a selection of wines by the bottle
and glass completes the package.

 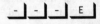

	FOOD	DECOR	SERVICE	COST

RESTAURANTS

Yamaguchi Ⓜ *Japanese* — 25 | 14 | 21 | $39

Port Washington | 63 Main St. (Herbert Ave.) | 516-883-3500

An "intimate" Port Washington "jewel" for "high-quality" sushi (rather than "contrived" rolls) and "top-notch" Japanese dishes, this "always crowded" "fixture" is a "home away from home" for many; the "generous" hosts "treasure" their customers ("regulars get delicious extras"), but nitpickers pout over decor that "needs an update" and caution "make reservations or plan to wait a long time."

Yama Q ⓈⓂ *Japanese/Vegetarian* — ▽ 23 | 15 | 19 | $44

Bridgehampton | 2393 Montauk Hwy. (bet. Ocean Rd. & School St.) | 631-537-0225

This "quiet" Bridgehampton "find" provides "fresh, healthy" Japanese dishes with an emphasis on sushi and vegetarian options and some "eclectic" global touches as well; the small, "quaint" space has an "almost private" feel, and while tabs are marked up with a slight Hamptons premium, the dishes are "worth it."

Yokohama *Japanese* — 23 | 17 | 23 | $37

East Northport | 3082 Jericho Tpke. (Verleye Ave.) | 631-462-2464

"Fresh, well-prepared sushi is the priority" at this East Northport "go-to", "one of the best" around that pleases with "amazing" specialty rolls and Japanese cooking with "inventive" twists; the decor's "a little tired", but the "welcoming" owner "treats the locals right" and everything comes at a "fair price."

Yuki's Palette Too Ⓜ *Japanese* — ▽ 24 | 17 | 22 | $31

Merrick | 151 Merrick Ave. (Loines Ave.) | 516-867-8738 | www.yukispalette.info

"Tender, delicious" sushi and "standout" rolls full of "exciting flavors" reel in regulars to this affordable Merrick Japanese with a "friendly" staff; the room itself is "not much to look at", but "it's the little touches", and often "stellar" quality, that "make it special" for fans.

Zim Zari *Californian/Mexican* — 22 | 19 | 20 | $20

Massapequa Park | Southgate Shopping Ctr. | 4964 Merrick Rd. (Whitewood Dr.) | 516-809-6960 | www.zimzari.com

The folks behind Mercato, in the same Massapequa Park shopping center, have brought this "West Coast surfer shack to Long Island" where the "refreshing", beach-bum environs and "tasty", "cheap" "Cali-cool" Mex eats "cater to a young crowd" (and work for "families" too); despite sometimes "long waits for a table", there's "decent service", and deals like $2 "Taco Tuesdays rock."

Zorba the Greek *Greek* — 19 | 13 | 19 | $25

Hicksville | 620 S. Oyster Bay Rd. (Old Country Rd.) | 516-932-9701
Port Jefferson Station | 572 Port Jefferson Plaza (Rte. 112) | 631-473-9220 | www.zorbathegreekpjs.com

"Consistent", "basic" Greek food for "super prices" satisfies customers at these separately owned "standbys" in Hicksville and Port Jefferson Station; maybe the decor "lacks" and the service varies, but they're "quick, easy" choices for dinner and "even better for lunch."

INDEXES

Cuisines

Includes names, locations and Food ratings.

AFGHAN

Afghan Grill	**New Hyde Pk**	20
Ariana	**Huntington**	20
Kabul Afghani	**Huntington**	23

AMERICAN

Amarelle	**Wading River**	25
Z American Hotel	**Sag Harbor**	25
Argyle Grill	**Babylon**	22
NEW Arthur Ave.	**Smithtown**	–
Z Atlantica	**Long Bch**	20
Z Barney's	**Locust Valley**	26
Bayview Inn	**S Jamesport**	22
Beacon	**Sag Harbor**	22
Bella Vita Grill	**St. James**	21
Bellport	**Bellport**	22
Birchwood	**Riverhead**	20
Bistro 44	**Northport**	23
Bistro M	**Glen Head**	25
NEW Bistro 72	**Riverhead**	–
B.K. Sweeney's	**multi.**	18
Blackwells	**Wading River**	23
Bliss	**E Setauket**	22
Blond	**Miller Pl**	21
Blue	**Blue Pt**	22
NEW Bluepoint B & G	**Blue Pt**	–
Bob's Place	**Floral Pk**	21
Brass Rail	**Locust Valley**	25
Brian Scotts	**Miller Pl**	19
Bridgehampton Candy	**Bridgehampton**	15
Broadway Beanery	**Lynbrook**	21
Buckram Stables	**Locust Valley**	19
Bulldog Grille	**Amityville**	–
Butterfields	**Hauppauge**	20
Cafe Joelle	**Sayville**	22
Cafe Max	**E Hampton**	23
Café Red/Rest.	**multi.**	25
Canterbury	**Oyster Bay**	19
Catfish Max	**Seaford**	21

NEW Cattlemen's	**Port Jefferson Station**	19
NEW Cedar Creek	**Glen Cove**	–
Z Chachama	**E Patchogue**	27
Chadwicks	**Rockville Ctr**	22
Chalet Rest.	**Roslyn**	18
Z Cheesecake	**multi.**	20
Chequit Inn	**Shelter Is Hts**	19
Chop Shop	**Smithtown**	24
Cirella's	**Huntington Station**	21
City Cellar	**Westbury**	21
Claudio's	**Greenport**	16
Coach Grill	**Oyster Bay**	22
Coast Grill	**Southampton**	22
Cooperage Inn	**Baiting Hollow**	22
Z Country House	**Stony Brook**	23
NEW Crave 11025	**Great Neck**	18
Crew Kitchen	**Huntington**	24
Crossroads Cafe	**E Northport**	22
NEW Dark Horse	**Riverhead**	–
Declan Quinn's	**Bay Shore**	19
NEW Deco 1600	**Plainview**	–
Z Della Femina	**E Hampton**	24
Desmond's	**Wading River**	20
Dish	**Water Mill**	27
Duke Falcon's	**Long Bch**	22
East by Northeast	**Montauk**	21
Z E. Hampton Pt.	**E Hampton**	19
E. B. Elliot's	**Freeport**	18
Estia's Kitchen	**Sag Harbor**	23
Farm Country Kit.	**Riverhead**	23
NEW Farmhouse	**Greenport**	26
F.H. Riley's	**Huntington**	23
Fifth Season	**Port Jefferson**	26
56th Fighter	**Farmingdale**	16
Fork & Vine	**Glen Head**	23
Four Food Studio	**Melville**	21
NEW 490 West	**Carle Pl**	–
Fresno	**E Hampton**	22
Garden Grill	**Smithtown**	21

George Martin | **Rockville Ctr**	22
George Martin's Grill | **multi.**	20
Georgica | **Wainscott**	18
Golden Pear | **multi.**	18
Gonzalo's | **Glen Cove**	21
Graffiti | **Woodbury**	20
Grasso's | **Cold Spring**	24
Grey Horse | **Bayport**	23
NEW Grill on Pantigo | **E Hampton**	21
Grill Room | **Hauppauge**	21
Gulf Coast | **Montauk**	21
Harbor Bistro/Grill | **E Hampton**	21
NEW Harbor Mist | **Cold Spring**	19
Hemingway's | **Wantagh**	19
Hildebrandt's | **Williston Pk**	19
Honu | **Huntington**	22
Horace/Sylvia's | **Babylon**	20
Houston's | **Garden City**	22
H.R. Singleton's | **Bethpage**	18
Hudson's Mill | **Massapequa**	22
Indian Cove | **Hampton Bays**	18
Indian Wells | **Amagansett**	17
International Delight | **multi.**	18
Island Mermaid | **Ocean Beach**	20
Ivy Cottage | **Williston Pk**	23
Izumi | **Bethpage**	23
NEW Jack Halyards | **Oyster Bay**	23
NEW Jackson Hall | **E Islip**	–
Jamesport Country | **Jamesport**	23
Z Jamesport Manor | **Jamesport**	23
NEW Janine's | **Hauppauge**	–
Jean Marie | **Great Neck**	22
Jonathan's | **Garden City Pk**	20
JT's Corner Cafe | **Nesconset**	23
La Cocina de Marcia | **Freeport**	–
Z Lake House | **Bay Shore**	28
NEW La Maison | **Sag Harbor**	18
Library Cafe | **Farmingdale**	18
Living Room | **E Hampton**	25
Lola's | **Long Bch**	20
Love Ln. Kitchen | **Mattituck**	23
Z Luce & Hawkins | **Jamesport**	25
Lucy's Café | **Babylon**	25
Ludlow Bistro | **Deer Park**	24
Maguire's | **Ocean Beach**	19
Maureen's Kitchen | **Smithtown**	25
Maxwell's | **Islip**	–
Meeting House | **Amagansett**	20
Mercato | **Massapequa Pk**	20
Meritage | **Bellport**	25
NEW Met. Bistro | **Sea Cliff**	22
Michaels'/Maidstone | **E Hampton**	18
Milk & Sugar Café | **Bay Shore**	21
Milleridge Inn | **Jericho**	16
Mim's | **multi.**	20
Mirabelle Tavern | **Stony Brook**	21
Modern Snack | **Aquebogue**	18
Z Mosaic | **St. James**	28
Mother Kelly's | **multi.**	21
Muse | **Water Mill**	23
NEW Navy Beach | **Montauk**	19
New Paradise | **Sag Harbor**	22
Nicholas James | **Merrick**	22
Nichol's | **E Hampton**	17
Z Noah's | **Greenport**	26
Z North Fork Table | **Southold**	29
Oakland's/Sunday | **Hampton Bays**	18
Oasis Waterfront | **Sag Harbor**	24
Ocean Grill | **Freeport**	23
NEW Old Fields | **Greenlawn**	–
Old Mill Inn | **Mattituck**	20
O'Mally's | **Southold**	18
Page One | **Glen Cove**	22
Z Palm Court | **E Meadow**	24
Panama Hatties | **Huntington Station**	25
NEW Park Place | **Floral Pk**	–
Patio/54 Main | **Westhampton Bch**	19
PeraBell | **Patchogue**	26
Z Piccolo | **Huntington**	27
Pine Island | **Bayville**	18
NEW Portly Grape | **Greenport**	–

Post Office | **Babylon**	19
Post Stop | **Westhampton Bch**	17
Z Prime | **Huntington**	23
Public House 49 | **Patchogue**	20
NEW Race Lane | **E Hampton**	19
Rachel's Waterside | **Freeport**	20
Ram's Head | **Shelter Is**	20
Rare 650 | **Syosset**	24
red bar | **Southampton**	22
Red Fish | **Plainview**	23
Red Rooster | **Cutchogue**	16
Rein | **Garden City**	23
Restaurant/The Inn | **Quogue**	21
Robinson's Tea | **Stony Brook**	23
Rockwell's | **Smithtown**	22
Roots | **Sea Cliff**	26
Rugosa | **Wainscott**	21
Runyon's | **Seaford**	18
NEW Sapsuckers | **Huntington**	–
Sarabeth's | **Garden City**	20
Savanna's | **Southampton**	20
Scrimshaw | **Greenport**	23
Sea Grille | **Montauk**	21
Sea Levels | **Brightwaters**	22
Second House | **Montauk**	19
Shagwong | **Montauk**	18
Z Snaps | **Wantagh**	26
Southampton Publick | **Southampton**	18
NEW South Edison | **Montauk**	22
Squiretown | **Hampton Bays**	20
Star Confectionery | **Riverhead**	22
Z Starr Boggs | **Westhampton Bch**	26
NEW Stone Turtle | **Island Pk**	21
Stonewalls | **Riverhead**	23
Strawberry's | **Huntington**	18
NEW Sugar | **Carle Pl**	–
Sullivan's Quay | **Port Washington**	18
Surf Lodge | **Montauk**	19
NEW Swallow | **Huntington**	–
Sweet Mama's | **Northport**	19
Table 9 | **E Hills**	22
Taste 99 | **Farmingdale**	18
NEW Tate's | **Nesconset**	26
Thyme | **Roslyn**	21
Tide Runners | **Hampton Bays**	16
Toast & Co. | **Huntington**	18
Top of the Bay | **Cherry Grove**	–
NEW Trattachino | **Wantagh**	–
Tricia's Café | **Babylon**	23
Trio | **Holbrook**	21
Z Trumpets | **Eastport**	22
Tweeds | **Riverhead**	21
Upper Crust | **Garden City**	–
Varney's | **Brookhaven**	23
View | **Oakdale**	22
Vine Street | **Shelter Is**	25
Vine Wine Bar | **Greenport**	22
Vittorio's | **Amityville**	25
Walk St. | **Garden City**	21
Wall's Wharf | **Bayville**	17
Wave | **Port Jefferson**	19
Z West End | **Carle Pl**	25
Wild Honey | **multi.**	25

ARGENTINEAN

Café Buenos Aires | **Huntington**	24

ASIAN

Asian Moon | **multi.**	23
Cho-Sen | **multi.**	19
Dao | **Huntington**	23
East by Northeast | **Montauk**	21
Elaine's | **Great Neck**	22
Haiku Bistro/Sushi | **Woodbury**	24
Izumi | **Bethpage**	23
NEW J&C 68 | **Farmingville**	–
Long River | **Kings Park**	21
NEW Marco Polo's | **Westbury**	–
Matsulin | **Hampton Bays**	22
Meritage | **Bellport**	25
MoCa Asian | **Hewlett**	18
NEW Sensasian | **Levittown**	–
NEW Sugar | **Carle Pl**	–
Sunset Beach | **Shelter Is Hts**	18
Taiko | **Rockville Ctr**	24

Thom Thom | **Wantagh**	20
🔁 Toku | **Manhasset**	25
Tony's | **multi.**	19
West East | **Hicksville**	25
Wild Ginger | **multi.**	21

BAKERIES

Main St. Bakery | **Port Washington**	–
Roe's Casa Dolce | **Rockville Ctr**	24

BARBECUE

Big Daddy's | **Massapequa**	24
BobbiQue | **Patchogue**	21
Dixie's | **Kings Park**	–
Famous Dave's | **multi.**	19
Foody's | **Water Mill**	21
Harbor-Q | **Port Washington**	21
🔁 Smokin' Al's | **multi.**	23
Spare Rib | **multi.**	18
Spicy's BBQ | **multi.**	20
Swingbelly's | **Long Bch**	23
Townline | **Sagaponack**	19
Turtle Crossing | **E Hampton**	22

BELGIAN

Moules et Frites | **Syosset**	19
🔁 Waterzooi | **Garden City**	24

BURGERS

American Burger | **Smithtown**	18
Bay Burger | **Sag Harbor**	21
Bobby's Burger | **Lake Grove**	21
Buckram Stables | **Locust Valley**	19
Bulldog Grille | **Amityville**	–
Chalet Rest. | **Roslyn**	18
NEW Downtown Burger | **Sayville**	–
🔁 Five Guys | **multi.**	21
Frank-N-Burger | **St. James**	19
George Martin's Grill | **multi.**	20
Gonzalo's | **Glen Cove**	21
NEW LT Burger | **Sag Harbor**	16
O'Mally's | **Southold**	18
Post Stop | **Westhampton Bch**	17
Rowdy Hall | **E Hampton**	20

CAJUN

Bayou | **N Bellmore**	23
Big Daddy's | **Massapequa**	24
Blackbirds' Grille | **Sayville**	20
B.Smith's | **Sag Harbor**	18

CALIFORNIAN

Salsa Salsa | **multi.**	23
Zim Zari | **Massapequa Pk**	22

CARIBBEAN

Tequila Jacks | **Port Jefferson**	18

CHINESE

(* dim sum specialist)

Albert's Mandarin | **Huntington**	20
Ancient Ginger | **St. James**	21
Best Buffet | **Huntington Station**	18
Chi | **Westbury**	25
Dynasty/Pt. Wash. | **Port Washington**	20
Fortune Wheel* | **Levittown**	22
Hunan Taste | **Greenvale**	22
Lotus East | **multi.**	21
Nanking | **New Hyde Pk**	19
Orchid | **Garden City**	23
🔁 Orient* | **Bethpage**	27
Pearl East | **Manhasset**	23
P.F. Chang's | **Westbury**	20
Philippe | **multi.**	24
Shang Hai Pavilion | **multi.**	21
Tony's | **Westhampton Bch**	19
Uncle Dai | **Glen Cove**	18

COFFEEHOUSES

Broadway Beanery | **Lynbrook**	21
Golden Pear | **multi.**	18
Hampton Coffee | **multi.**	19

COFFEE SHOPS/ DINERS

Bozena Polish | **Lindenhurst**	23
Bridgehampton Candy | **Bridgehampton**	15
International Delight | **multi.**	18
Star Confectionery | **Riverhead**	22
Sweet Mama's | **Northport**	19

Thomas's Eggery | **Carle Pl** 22

Tricia's Café | **Babylon** 23

COLOMBIAN

NEW Chicken Coop | _-_
Valley Stream

NEW Sabor a Colombia | _-_
Levittown

CONTINENTAL

Babylon Carriage | **Babylon** 21

Barolo | **Melville** 25

Bayview Inn | **S Jamesport** 22

Bellport | **Bellport** 22

Bulldog Grille | **Amityville** _-_

Cafe Testarossa | **Syosset** 22

Chadwicks | **Rockville Ctr** 22

Chez Kama | **Great Neck** 25

Cirella's | **Melville** 21

Claudio's | **Greenport** 16

Cooperage Inn | **Baiting Hollow** 22

Crabtree's | **Floral Pk** 21

Z Dave's Grill | **Montauk** 27

Frederick's | **Melville** 23

Irish Coffee | **E Islip** 23

Koenig's | **Floral Pk** 19

La Gioconda | **Great Neck** 21

Le Chef | **Southampton** 22

Meson Iberia | **Island Pk** 22

Oak Chalet | **Bellmore** 19

Z Palm Court | **E Meadow** 24

Palmer's | **Farmingdale** 21

Peppercorns | **Hicksville** 19

Ritz Cafe | **Northport** 19

Surfside Inn | **Montauk** 18

Z Trumpets | **Eastport** 22

View | **Oakdale** 22

NEW Vitae | **Huntington** _-_

Waterview | **Port Washington** 18

CREOLE

Bayou | **N Bellmore** 23

CRÊPES

Fresco Crêperie | **Williston Pk** 23

Tasty Crepes | **multi.** 18

CUBAN

Cafe Havana | **Smithtown** 18

DELIS

Z Ben's Deli | **multi.** 19

Deli King | **New Hyde Pk** 19

Pastrami King | **Merrick** 20

DESSERT

Bridgehampton Candy | 15
Bridgehampton

Broadway Beanery | **Lynbrook** 21

Z Cheesecake | **multi.** 20

Fresco Crêperie | **Long Bch** 23

Hildebrandt's | **Williston Pk** 19

Tasty Crepes | **multi.** 18

ECLECTIC

Babette's | **E Hampton** 20

Batata Café | **Northport** 21

Best Buffet | **Huntington Station** 18

NEW Bistro 25 | **Sayville** _-_

Café Joelle | **Sayville** 22

Cafe Max | **E Hampton** 23

Chalet Rest. | **Roslyn** 18

Chequit Inn | **Shelter Is Hts** 19

Chi | **Westbury** 25

Cirella's | **Huntington Station** 21

NEW Dark Horse | **Riverhead** _-_

Duke Falcon's | **Long Bch** 22

Frisky Oyster | **Greenport** 25

Grand Lux | **Garden City** 19

Hideaway | **Ocean Beach** 19

Inn Spot/Bay | **Hampton Bays** 19

Z La Plage | **Wading River** 27

Legends | **New Suffolk** 23

Lola | **Great Neck** 24

Z Maroni Cuisine | **Northport** 28

Michael Anthony's | **Wading River** 24

Z Mirko's | **Water Mill** 26

Muse | **Water Mill** 23

New Paradise | **Sag Harbor** 22

Page One | **Glen Cove** 22

Painters' | **Brookhaven Hamlet** 20

Pastrami King | **Merrick** 20

PeraBell | **Patchogue**	26
Planet Bliss | **Shelter Is**	20
Ram's Head | **Shelter Is**	20
Salamander's | **Greenport**	24
Silver's | **Southampton**	23
NEW Sip City | **Great Neck**	-
NEW Stone Turtle | **Island Pk**	21
34 New St. | **Huntington**	18
Toast | **Port Jefferson**	24
Tula Kitchen | **Bay Shore**	24
NEW XO | **Huntington**	-

EUROPEAN

Brasserie 214 | **New Hyde Pk**	20

FONDUE

Melting Pot | **Farmingdale**	18
Simply Fondue | **Great Neck**	17

FRENCH

Z American Hotel | **Sag Harbor**	25
Z Barney's | **Locust Valley**	26
Z Chez Noëlle | **Port Washington**	27
Fresco Crêperie | **multi.**	23
La Coquille | **Manhasset**	24
La Marmite | **Williston Pk**	24
Le Chef | **Southampton**	22
Z Le Soir | **Bayport**	27
Mirabelle, Rest. | **Stony Brook**	25
Moules et Frites | **Syosset**	19
O's Food | **St. James**	22
Pierre's | **Bridgehampton**	21
red bar | **Southampton**	22
Sage Bistro | **Woodbury**	24
Z Stone Creek | **E Quogue**	26
Stonewalls | **Riverhead**	23
Vintage Port | **Port Washington**	19

FRENCH (BISTRO)

NEW Aperitif | **Rockville Ctr**	25
NEW Bar Frites | **Greenvale**	18
Z Bistro Cassis | **Huntington**	24
Bistro Citron | **Roslyn**	21
Bistro Toulouse | **Port Washington**	22
Chat Noir | **Rockville Ctr**	21

NEW Comtesse Thérèse | **Aquebogue**	-
Cuvée | **Greenport**	22
Z Kitchen A Bistro | **St. James**	27
La P'tite Framboise | **Port Washington**	22
Sage Bistro | **Bellmore**	24
Sunset Beach | **Shelter Is Hts**	18
Voila! | **St. James**	24

FRENCH (BRASSERIE)

Brasserie Cassis | **Plainview**	23
Brasserie Persil | **Oceanside**	25
NEW Dark Horse | **Riverhead**	-

GERMAN

Koenig's | **Floral Pk**	19
Oak Chalet | **Bellmore**	19
Pumpernickels | **Northport**	21
Village Lanterne | **Lindenhurst**	25

GREEK

Alexandros | **Mount Sinai**	23
Chicken Kebab | **Roslyn Hts**	21
Ethos | **Great Neck**	21
Greek Village | **Commack**	19
Hellenic Snack | **E Marion**	20
Med. Snack | **Huntington**	22
Souvlaki Palace | **Commack**	24
Surf 'N Turf | **Merrick**	24
Trata | **multi.**	22
Zorba/Greek | **multi.**	19

HEALTH FOOD

(See also Vegetarian)

Babette's | **E Hampton**	20

HOT DOGS

Frank-N-Burger | **St. James**	19

INDIAN

Akbar | **Garden City**	22
Curry Club | **E Setauket**	20
Diwan | **multi.**	21
Dosa Diner | **Hicksville**	23
Hampton Chutney | **Amagansett**	22

House of Dosas	**Hicksville**	25
House of India	**Huntington**	21
Kiran Palace	**multi.**	24
Madras/India	**New Hyde Pk**	22
New Chilli/Curry	**Hicksville**	26
Rangmahal	**Hicksville**	23
Royal Bukhara Grill	**Hicksville**	22

IRISH

| Irish Coffee | **E Islip** | 23 |
| Sullivan's Quay | **Port Washington** | 18 |

ISRAELI

| Tel Aviv | **Great Neck** | 22 |

ITALIAN

(N=Northern; S=Southern)

Absolutely Mario	**Farmingdale**	20
Allison's Amalfi	**Sea Cliff**	21
Almarco	**Huntington**	20
A Mano	**Mattituck**	24
Angelina's	**multi.**	23
Arturo's	**Floral Pk**	22
Baby Moon	S	**Westhampton Bch**	18
Barolo	**Melville**	25
Basil Leaf	**Locust Valley**	21
Bella Vita Grill	**St. James**	21
Bellissimo Rist.	**Deer Park**	23
NEW Bel Posto	**Huntington**	-
Benny's	N	**Westbury**	25
Bertucci's	**multi.**	17
Bevanda	N	**Great Neck**	22
Blue Moon	**Rockville Ctr**	20
Boccaccio	N	**Hicksville**	21
☑ Branzino	N	**Lynbrook**	26
Bravo Nader!/Fish	S	**Huntington**	24
Brio	N	**Port Washington**	21
☑ Butera's	**multi.**	21
☑ Cafe Baci	**Westbury**	22
Café Formaggio	**Carle Pl**	20
Cafe La Strada	**Hauppauge**	23
Cafe Rustica	**Great Neck**	22
Cafe Symposio	**Bellmore**	18
Cafe Toscano	**Massapequa**	21
La Bottega	**multi.**	21

Caffe Laguna	**Long Bch**	19
Capriccio	N	**Hicksville**	24
Caracalla	**Syosset**	23
Carnival	S	**Port Jefferson Station**	22
Carrabba's	**multi.**	19
Caruso's	**Rocky Pt**	23
Casa Rustica	**Smithtown**	25
Chefs of NY	**E Northport**	19
Ciao Baby	**multi.**	20
Cielo Rist.	N	**Rockville Ctr**	20
Cinelli's	**multi.**	18
Cipollini	**Manhasset**	21
Circa	**Mineola**	22
Cirella's	N	**Melville**	21
Ciro's	**Kings Park**	22
cittanuova	N	**E Hampton**	20
☑ Dario's	N	**Rockville Ctr**	26
Da Ugo	N	**Rockville Ctr**	25
NEW Deco 1600	**Plainview**	-
Dee Angelo's	**Westhampton Bch**	19
DiMaggio's	**Port Washington**	19
Dodici	**Rockville Ctr**	24
Edgewater	**Hampton Bays**	22
El Parral	**Syosset**	21
Emilio's	**Commack**	23
Epiphany	**Glen Cove**	21
Ernesto's East	**Glen Head**	22
Fanatico	**Jericho**	20
Franina	**Syosset**	26
Galleria Dominick	N	**Westbury**	26
Giulio Cesare	N	**Westbury**	25
☑ Harvest	N	**Montauk**	26
Iavarone Cafe	**New Hyde Pk**	21
Il Capuccino	**Sag Harbor**	19
Il Classico	N	**Massapequa Pk**	23
☑ Il Mulino NY	N	**Roslyn Estates**	27
Il Villagio	**Malverne**	24
Intermezzo	**Ft Salonga**	23
Jonathan's Rist.	**Huntington**	24
King Umberto	**Elmont**	23
☑ Kitchen A Tratt.	**St. James**	28
La Bussola	**Glen Cove**	23

La Famiglia | **multi.**	22
La Ginestra | S | **Glen Cove**	25
La Gioconda | S | **Great Neck**	21
La Marmite | N | **Williston Pk**	24
La Nonna Bella | **Garden City**	21
La Novella | N | **E Meadow**	19
La Pace/Chef Michael | N | **Glen Cove**	25
⚡ La Parma | S | **multi.**	23
La Parmigiana | **Southampton**	22
La Piazza | **multi.**	21
⚡ La Piccola | N | **Port Washington**	27
La Pizzetta | **E Norwich**	21
La Rotonda | **Great Neck**	19
La Spada | S | **Huntington Station**	21
La Strada | **Merrick**	20
La Tavola | **Sayville**	22
La Terrazza | **Cedarhurst**	22
La Viola | **Cedarhurst**	20
La Volpe | **Center Moriches**	23
Livorno | S | **Port Washington**	21
Lombardi's/Sound | **Port Jefferson**	21
Lucé | **E Norwich**	22
Luigi Q | **Hicksville**	23
Mama's | **multi.**	21
Mamma Lombardi's | S | **Holbrook**	23
Manucci's | **Montauk**	19
NEW Marco Polo's | **Westbury**	-
Mario | N | **Hauppauge**	25
⚡ Maroni Cuisine | **Northport**	28
⚡ Matteo's | S | **multi.**	23
Mercato | **Massapequa Pk**	20
Montebello | N | **Port Washington**	21
Mother Kelly's | **multi.**	21
Nello Summertimes | N | **Southampton**	16
⚡ Nick & Toni's | **E Hampton**	24
Nick's | **Rockville Ctr**	23
Nick's Tuscan | N | **Long Bch**	21
Nonnina | **W Islip**	25
Novitá | **Garden City**	23
Oevo | **Great Neck**	21
Olive Oils | **Point Lookout**	20
Osteria da Nino | N | **Huntington**	24
Osteria Toscana | **Huntington**	23
Panini Café | **Roslyn**	23
Papa Razzi | N | **Westbury**	18
Pasta-eria | **Hicksville**	23
Pasta Pasta | **Port Jefferson**	25
Pasta Vino | **Mineola**	22
Pentimento | **Stony Brook**	22
NEW Pepe Rosso | **Port Washington**	-
Per Un Angelo | N | **Wantagh**	22
Piccola Bussola | **multi.**	23
⚡ Piccolo | **Huntington**	27
Piccolo's | N | **Mineola**	24
Pomodorino | **multi.**	19
Porto Bello | **Greenport**	22
Porto Vivo | **Huntington**	22
NEW Puglia's/Garden City | **Garden City**	-
Rachel's Cafe | **Syosset**	22
Rialto | N | **Carle Pl**	26
Rist. Gemelli | **Babylon**	24
Rist. Italiano | **Port Washington**	24
Riviera Grill | **Glen Cove**	26
Robert's | **Water Mill**	25
Roe's Casa Dolce | **Rockville Ctr**	24
Ruvo | S | **multi.**	22
Sam's | **E Hampton**	18
⚡ San Marco | N | **Hauppauge**	26
Sant Ambroeus | N | **Southampton**	24
Scotto's | **Westbury**	20
Sea Basin | **Rocky Pt**	19
Sea Grille | **Montauk**	21
⚡ Sempre Vivolo | **Hauppauge**	27
NEW Serafina | **E Hampton**	18
Seventh St. Cafe | N | **Garden City**	20
75 Main | **Southampton**	18
Solé | **Oceanside**	26
Stella Ristorante | **Floral Pk**	24
Steve's Piccola | **multi.**	24
Strawberry's | **Huntington**	18
Stresa | **Manhasset**	25
Sundried Tomato | **Nesconset**	21

Surf's Out | **Kismet**	17
Table 9 | **E Hills**	22
NEW Tate's | **Nesconset**	26
Tesoro | **Westbury**	23
Torcellos | **E Northport**	21
Tratt. Diane | N | **Roslyn**	25
Tratt. Di Meo | **Roslyn Hts**	21
Tratt. Lucia | **E Meadow**	22
Tuscan House | **Southampton**	22
Tutto Il Giorno | **Sag Harbor**	25
Tutto Pazzo | **Huntington**	20
Umberto's | S | **multi.**	22
Uncle Bacala's | S | **Garden City Pk**	21
Venere | **Westbury**	20
Z Verace | **Islip**	26
NEW Vero | **Amityville**	–
Vespa | N | **Great Neck**	22
Villa D'Aqua | N | **Bellmore**	21
Villa D'Este | N | **Floral Pk**	22
Vincent's | **Carle Pl**	22
Vittorio's | **Amityville**	25
World Pie | **Bridgehampton**	19

JAPANESE

(* sushi specialist)

Z Aji 53 | **Bay Shore**	27
Azuma | **Greenlawn**	23
Benihana | **multi.**	19
Benkei Japanese* | **Northport**	23
Blue* | **Blue Pt**	22
NEW Blue Fish | **Hicksville**	–
Bonbori Tiki* | **Huntington**	20
Bonsai* | **Port Washington**	22
Carousel* | **Great Neck**	21
Chez Kama | **Great Neck**	25
Daruma of Tokyo* | **Great Neck**	23
NEW Domo Sushi | **E Setauket**	21
Fatty Fish | **Glen Cove**	22
Galangal* | **Syosset**	23
Gasho of Japan | **Hauppauge**	20
Haiku* | **Riverhead**	–
Hinata | **Great Neck**	23
Homura Sushi* | **Williston Pk**	23
Hotoke | **Smithtown**	21

NEW Imperial Seoul | **New Hyde Pk**	–
Kawasaki Steak | **Long Bch**	19
NEW Kinha* | **Garden City**	–
Kiraku | **Glen Head**	26
Kiss'o* | **New Hyde Pk**	21
Z Kotobuki* | **multi.**	27
Kumo Sushi* | **Plainview**	25
Kurabarn* | **Huntington**	24
Kurofune* | **Commack**	23
Matsuya* | **Great Neck**	21
Minado* | **Carle Pl**	21
Minami* | **Massapequa**	26
Mitsui* | **Bay Shore**	24
Mumon | **Garden City**	22
Z Nagahama* | **Long Bch**	28
Nagashima* | **Jericho**	24
Nisen* | **multi.**	25
NEW Onsen Sushi* | **Oakdale**	–
Osaka* | **Huntington**	24
Ozumo* | **Bethpage**	23
Robata* | **Plainview**	20
Rock 'n Sake* | **Port Washington**	22
NEW Sakaya | **Albertson**	–
Samurai | **Huntington**	24
Sapporo* | **Wantagh**	23
Sen* | **Sag Harbor**	21
Shiki* | **Babylon**	24
Shiki* | **E Hampton**	–
Shiro of Japan* | **Carle Pl**	22
Shogi* | **Westbury**	25
Show Win* | **multi.**	20
Suki Zuki* | **Water Mill**	24
Sushi Palace* | **Great Neck**	24
Sushi Ya* | **multi.**	21
Tai-Show* | **multi.**	23
Takara* | **Islandia**	28
Tokyo* | **E Northport**	24
Tomo Hibachi* | **Huntington**	20
Tony's | **Westhampton Bch**	19
Tsubo* | **Syosset**	23
Z Two Steak/Sushi | **New Hyde Pk**	24

Yamaguchi* | **Port Washington** 25

Yama Q | **Bridgehampton** 23

Yokohama | **E Northport** 23

Yuki's Palette* | **Merrick** 24

KOREAN

NEW Imperial Seoul | _

New Hyde Pk

Tokyo | **E Northport** 24

KOSHER/ KOSHER-STYLE

Z Ben's Deli | **multi.** 19

Cho-Sen | **multi.** 19

Colbeh | **multi.** 21

Deli King | **New Hyde Pk** 19

Madras/India | **New Hyde Pk** 22

MEDITERRANEAN

Alexandros | **Mount Sinai** 23

Allison's Amalfi | **Sea Cliff** 21

Ayhan's Shish | **multi.** 18

Ayhan's Trodos | **Westbury** 21

Azerbaijan | **Westbury** 22

Backyard | **Montauk** 23

Z Barrique Kitchen | **Babylon** 24

Cafe Rustica | **Great Neck** 22

Crabtree's | **Floral Pk** 21

fatfish | **Bay Shore** 21

Z Harvest | **Montauk** 26

Z Limani | **Roslyn** 26

Med. Grill | **Hewlett** 21

Med. Snack | **Huntington** 22

Meeting House | **Amagansett** 20

NEW Miraj | **Williston Pk** _

Z Nick & Toni's | **E Hampton** 24

Pier 95 | **Freeport** 24

Pita House | **multi.** 22

Z Stone Creek | **E Quogue** 26

Tulip Bar & Grill | **Great Neck** 19

Wild Fig | **multi.** 19

MEXICAN

Baja Fresh | **New Hyde Pk** 18

Baja Grill | **multi.** 18

Besito | **multi.** 24

Chipotle | **Farmingdale** 20

Cozymel's Mex. | **Westbury** 17

Goldmine Mex. | **Greenlawn** 21

Green Cactus | **multi.** 20

La Panchita | **Smithtown** 22

Los Compadres | 23

Huntington Station

Oaxaca Mexican | **Huntington** 23

Poco Loco | **Roslyn** 17

Quetzalcoatl | **Huntington** 20

Salsa Salsa | **multi.** 23

Viva Juan | **Selden** 21

Viva La Vida | **Oakdale** 20

Zim Zari | **Massapequa Pk** 22

NEW ENGLAND

Bigelow's | **Rockville Ctr** 24

NEW WORLD

Planet Bliss | **Shelter Is** 20

NUEVO LATINO

Laguna Grille | **Woodbury** 20

PAKISTANI

Spice Village | **Huntington** 20

PAN-LATIN

NEW Perfecto Mundo | 24

Commack

Pollo Rico | **multi.** 20

PERSIAN

Azerbaijan | **Westbury** 22

Colbeh | **multi.** 21

NEW Miraj | **Williston Pk** _

Ravagh | **multi.** 22

Spice Village | **Huntington** 20

PIZZA

Baby Moon | **Westhampton Bch** 18

Bertucci's | **multi.** 17

Blue Moon | **Rockville Ctr** 20

Chefs of NY | **E Northport** 19

Cirella's | **multi.** 21

California Pizza Kitchen | **multi.** 17

Eddie's Pizza | **New Hyde Pk** 21

Emilio's | **Commack** 23

Foody's | **Water Mill** 21

Giaccone's Pizza | **Mineola** -

Grimaldi's | **Garden City** 23

King Umberto | **Elmont** 23

La Piazza | **multi.** 21

La Pizzetta | **E Norwich** 21

La Rotonda | **Great Neck** 19

Manucci's | **Montauk** 19

Massa's | **Huntington Station** 23

Nick's | **Rockville Ctr** 23

Pasta-eria | **Hicksville** 23

Pie | **Port Jefferson** 21

Salvatore's | **multi.** 25

Pizza Place | **Bridgehampton** 24

Sam's | **E Hampton** 18

Scotto's | **Westbury** 20

Sundried Tomato | **Nesconset** 21

Torcellos | **E Northport** 21

Umberto's | **multi.** 22

World Pie | **Bridgehampton** 19

POLISH

Birchwood | **Riverhead** 20

Bozena Polish | **Lindenhurst** 23

PORTUGUESE

A Taberna | **Island Pk** 23

Churrasq. Bairrada | **Mineola** 25

NEW Fado | **Huntington** 21

Heart of Portugal | **Mineola** 20

Lareira | **Mineola** 20

Luso | **Smithtown** 22

PUB FOOD

John Harvard's | **Lake Grove** 16

O'Mally's | **Southold** 18

Peppercorns | **Hicksville** 19

Post Office | **Babylon** 19

Rockwell's | **Smithtown** 22

Rowdy Hall | **E Hampton** 20

Runyon's | **Seaford** 18

Southampton Publick | **Southampton** 18

Sullivan's Quay | **Port Washington** 18

SANDWICHES

Batata Café | **Northport** 21

Greenport Tea | **Greenport** 21

Hampton Coffee | **multi.** 19

Lucy's Café | **Babylon** 25

Main St. Bakery | **Port Washington** -

Panini Café | **Roslyn** 23

Pastrami King | **Merrick** 20

NEW Press 195 | **Rockville Ctr** -

SEAFOOD

Z Atlantica | **Long Bch** 20

Ayhan's Fish | **Port Washington** 19

Bigelow's | **Rockville Ctr** 24

Black & Blue | **Huntington** 22

Z Blackstone Steak | **Melville** 24

NEW Boathouse | **E Hampton** 19

Bostwick's | **E Hampton** 20

Bravo Nader!/Fish | **Huntington** 24

B.Smith's | **Sag Harbor** 18

Buccaneer Crab | **Freeport** 23

Buoy One | **multi.** 23

Cafe Max | **E Hampton** 23

Canterbury | **Oyster Bay** 19

Catfish Max | **Seaford** 21

Chop Shop | **Smithtown** 24

Clam Bar | **Amagansett** 21

Claudio's | **Greenport** 16

Coast Grill | **Southampton** 22

Z Coolfish | **Syosset** 24

Cull House | **Sayville** 20

Cyril's Fish | **Amagansett** 18

Z Dave's Grill | **Montauk** 27

Dock B&G | **Montauk** -

Dockers Waterside | **E Quogue** 20

Dockside B&G | **Sag Harbor** 21

Duryea's Lobster | **Montauk** 22

fatfish | **Bay Shore** 21

Fishbar | **Montauk** 18

Fisherman's Catch | **Point Lookout** 20

Fishery | **E Rockaway** 19

NEW Fish Store | **Bayport** -

Fulton Prime | **Syosset** 23

Gosman's Dock | **Montauk** 19

Harbor Crab | **Patchogue** 18

H2O Seafood | **Smithtown** 23

Hudson/McCoy | **Freeport** 18

Indian Cove | **Hampton Bays** 18

Inlet Seafood | **Montauk** 21

Inn Spot/Bay | **Hampton Bays** 19

Island Mermaid | **Ocean Beach** 20

NEW Jack Halyards | **Oyster Bay** 23

Jeff's Seafood | **E Northport** 20

Jolly Fisherman | **Roslyn** 21

Z Kitchen A Bistro | **St. James** 27

Legal Sea Foods | **multi.** 20

Z Limani | **Roslyn** 26

Lobster Inn | **Southampton** 19

Lobster Roll | **Amagansett** 19

Lobster Roll N. | **Baiting Hollow** 20

Lombardi's/Bay | **Patchogue** 23

Louie's Oyster | **Port Washington** 17

Matthew's | **Ocean Beach** 22

Mill Creek | **Bayville** 21

Mill Pond House | **Centerport** 25

Nautilus Cafe | **Freeport** 24

Oakland's/Sunday | **Hampton Bays** 18

Oar Steak | **Patchogue** 21

Ocean Grill | **Freeport** 23

Old Mill Inn | **Mattituck** 20

Paddy McGees | **Island Pk** 18

Z Palm | **E Hampton** 26

NEW Park Place | **Floral Pk** -

Pier 95 | **Freeport** 24

Z Plaza Cafe | **Southampton** 26

Porters | **Bellport** 20

NEW Prime Catch | **Rockville Ctr** -

Rachel's Waterside | **Freeport** 20

Rare 650 | **Syosset** 24

Red Fish | **Plainview** 23

Z Riverbay | **Williston Pk** 23

Schooner | **Freeport** 17

Sea Basin | **Rocky Pt** 19

Sea Grille | **Montauk** 21

Sea Levels | **Brightwaters** 22

Shagwong | **Montauk** 18

Snapper Inn | **Oakdale** 18

NEW Southfork | **Bridgehampton** -

Southside Fish | **Lindenhurst** 20

Z Starr Boggs | **Westhampton Bch** 26

Surfside Inn | **Montauk** 18

Surf's Out | **Kismet** 17

Tequila Jacks | **Port Jefferson** 18

Thom Thom | **Wantagh** 20

Trata | **multi.** 22

Turquoise | **Great Neck** 21

Uncle Bacala's | **Garden City Pk** 21

Varney's | **Brookhaven** 23

Wall's Wharf | **Bayville** 17

Waterview | **Port Washington** 18

NEW Whale's Tale | **Northport** 20

Wildfish | **Freeport** 21

SMALL PLATES

(See also Spanish tapas specialist)

Z Barrique Kitchen | Med. | **Babylon** 24

Brass Rail | Amer. | **Locust Valley** 25

Café Buenos Aires | Argent. | **Huntington** 24

Carousel | Japanese | **Great Neck** 21

Fork & Vine | Amer. | **Glen Head** 23

Lola | Eclectic | **Great Neck** 24

Meeting House | Amer./Med. | **Amagansett** 20

Z Noah's | Amer. | **Greenport** 26

O's Food | Eclectic | **St. James** 22

NEW Sugar | Amer./Asian | **Carle Pl** -

NEW Swallow | Amer. | **Huntington** -

Toast | Eclectic | **Port Jefferson** 24

Z Verace | Italian | **Islip** 26

NEW Vero | Italian | **Amityville**	─
Vintage Port | French | **Port Washington**	19

SOUTHERN

Blackbirds' Grille | **Sayville**	20
B.Smith's | **Sag Harbor**	18
LL Dent | **Carle Pl**	23

SOUTHWESTERN

RS Jones | **Merrick**	22

SPANISH

(* tapas specialist)

Bin 56* | **Huntington**	24
Casa Luis | **Smithtown**	22
Copa Wine* | **Bridgehampton**	20
El Parral | **Syosset**	21
La Cocina de Marcia | **Freeport**	─
La Panchita | **Smithtown**	22
Meson Iberia | **Island Pk**	22
Viva La Vida | **Oakdale**	20

STEAKHOUSES

Benihana | **multi.**	19
Black & Blue | **Huntington**	22
Z Blackstone Steak | **Melville**	24
Blackwells | **Wading River**	23
Bobby Van's | **Bridgehampton**	22
Boulder Creek | **multi.**	─
Brooks & Porter | **Merrick**	22
Z Bryant & Cooper | **Roslyn**	26
Burton & Doyle | **Great Neck**	24
NEW Cattlemen's | **multi.**	19
Chop Shop | **Smithtown**	24
Cliff's | **multi.**	22
Clubhouse | **Huntington**	21
Dockers Waterside | **E Quogue**	20
Elbow East | **Southold**	19
Frank's Steaks | **multi.**	21
Fulton Prime | **Syosset**	23
Gasho of Japan | **Hauppauge**	20
NEW George Martin's Steak | **Great River**	─
Hotoke | **Smithtown**	21
NEW JD Steakhouse | **Southold**	19

Jimmy Hays | **Island Pk**	25
Jolly Fisherman | **Roslyn**	21
Lombardi's/Bay | **Patchogue**	23
Mac's Steak | **Huntington**	23
Majors Steak | **multi.**	19
Mill Creek | **Bayville**	21
Mill Pond House | **Centerport**	25
Z Morton's | **Great Neck**	25
Nautilus Cafe | **Freeport**	24
Oar Steak | **Patchogue**	21
NEW Old Fields | **Greenlawn**	─
1 North Steak | **Hampton Bays**	22
Pace's Steak | **multi.**	22
Z Palm | **E Hampton**	26
Peppercorns | **Hicksville**	19
Z Peter Luger | **Great Neck**	27
PG Steak | **Huntington**	22
Porters | **Bellport**	20
Rare 650 | **Syosset**	24
Z Rothmann's | **E Norwich**	25
Z Ruth's Chris | **Garden City**	25
Schooner | **Freeport**	17
Z Tellers | **Islip**	26
Thom Thom | **Wantagh**	20
Tomo Hibachi | **Huntington**	20
21 Main | **W Sayville**	23
Z Two Steak/Sushi | **New Hyde Pk**	24
Vintage Prime | **St. James**	25

TEAROOMS

Chat Noir | **Rockville Ctr**	21
Greenport Tea | **Greenport**	21
Robinson's Tea | **Stony Brook**	23

TEX-MEX

Blue Parrot | **E Hampton**	15
Pancho's | **multi.**	19

THAI

Bonbori Tiki | **Huntington**	20
Galangal | **Syosset**	23
Jaiya | **Hicksville**	19
Lemonleaf Grill | **multi.**	22

Vote at ZAGAT.com

Lemonleaf Thai | **multi.**	20
Nanking | **New Hyde Pk**	19
Onzon Thai | **Bellmore**	24
Phao Thai | **Sag Harbor**	21
Sabai Thai | **Miller Pl**	22
Sarin Thai | **multi.**	24
Seeda Thai | **Valley Stream**	23
☒ Siam Lotus | **Bay Shore**	28
Simply Thai | **Rockville Ctr**	21
Sripraphai | **Williston Pk**	25
Sri Thai | **Huntington**	22
Thai Gourmet | **Port Jefferson Station**	26
Thai Green Leaf | **multi.**	21
Thai House | **Smithtown**	24
Thai Table | **Rockville Ctr**	23
Thai USA | **Huntington**	23
Tony's | **Westhampton Bch**	19

TURKISH

Ayhan's Fish | **Port Washington**	19
Ayhan's Shish | **multi.**	18
Azerbaijan | **Westbury**	22
Chicken Kebab | **Roslyn Hts**	21
Pita House | **multi.**	22
Surf 'N Turf | **Merrick**	24
Tava | **Port Washington**	18
Tulip Bar & Grill | **Great Neck**	19
Wild Fig | **multi.**	19

VEGETARIAN

Ariana | **Huntington**	20
NEW Crave 11025 | **Great Neck**	18
Dosa Diner | **Hicksville**	23
House of Dosas | **Hicksville**	25
Madras/India | **New Hyde Pk**	22
Yama Q | **Bridgehampton**	23

CUISINES

Locations

Includes names, cuisines and Food ratings.

Nassau

ALBERTSON

NEW Sakaya | *Japanese* —

BALDWIN

Ayhan's Shish | *Med./Turkish* 18

BAYVILLE

Mill Creek | *Seafood/Steak* 21

Pine Island | *Amer.* 18

Wall's Wharf | *Amer./Seafood* 17

BELLMORE

Cafe Symposio | *Italian* 18

International Delight | *Amer./Diner* 18

Z Matteo's | *Italian* 23

Oak Chalet | *Continental/German* 19

Onzon Thai | *Thai* 24

Sage Bistro | *French* 24

Shang Hai Pavilion | *Chinese* 21

Villa D'Aqua | *Italian* 21

BETHPAGE

B.K. Sweeney's | *Amer.* 18

H.R. Singleton's | *Amer.* 18

Izumi | *Asian* 23

Z Orient | *Chinese* 27

Ozumo | *Japanese* 23

CARLE PLACE

Z Ben's Deli | *Deli* 19

Café Formaggio | *Italian* 20

NEW 490 West | *Amer.* —

Lemonleaf Thai | *Thai* 20

LL Dent | *Southern* 23

Minado | *Japanese* 21

Rialto | *Italian* 26

Shiro of Japan | *Japanese* 22

NEW Sugar | *Amer./Asian* —

Tasty Crepes | *Crêpes* 18

Thomas's Eggery | *Diner* 22

Vincent's | *Italian* 22

Z West End | *Amer.* 25

CEDARHURST

La Terrazza | *Italian* 22

La Viola | *Italian* 20

Mother Kelly's | *Amer./Italian* 21

EAST HILLS

Table 9 | *Amer./Italian* 22

EAST MEADOW

La Novella | *Italian* 19

Majors Steak | *Steak* 19

Z Palm Court | *Amer./Continental* 24

Tratt. Lucia | *Italian* 22

EAST NORWICH

Angelina's | *Italian* 23

La Pizzetta | *Italian* 21

Lucé | *Italian* 22

Z Rothmann's | *Steak* 25

EAST ROCKAWAY

Fishery | *Seafood* 19

ELMONT

King Umberto | *Italian* 23

FARMINGDALE

Absolutely Mario | *Italian* 20

Chipotle | *Mex.* 20

56th Fighter | *Amer.* 16

Library Cafe | *Amer.* 18

Melting Pot | *Fondue* 18

Palmer's | *Continental* 21

Taste 99 | *Amer.* 18

FLORAL PARK

Arturo's | *Italian* 22

Bob's Place | *Amer.* 21

Crabtree's | *Continental/Med.* 21

Koenig's | *Continental/German* 19

La Bottega | *Italian* 21

NEW Park Place	Amer./Seafood	–
Stella Ristorante	Italian	24
Umberto's	Italian/Pizza	22
Villa D'Este	Italian	22

FRANKLIN SQUARE

| Boulder Creek | Steak | – |
| Cinelli's | Italian | 18 |

FREEPORT

Buccaneer Crab	Seafood	23
E. B. Elliot's	Amer.	18
Hudson/McCoy	Seafood	18
La Cocina de Marcia	Amer./Spanish	–
Nautilus Cafe	Seafood/Steak	24
Ocean Grill	Amer./Seafood	23
Pier 95	Med.	24
Rachel's Waterside	Amer./Seafood	20
Schooner	Seafood/Steak	17
Wildfish	Seafood	21

GARDEN CITY

Akbar	Indian	22
Asian Moon	Asian	23
B.K. Sweeney's	Amer.	18
La Bottega	Italian	21
Grand Lux	Eclectic	19
Grimaldi's	Pizza	23
Houston's	Amer.	22
NEW Kinha	Japanese	–
La Nonna Bella	Italian	21
Legal Sea Foods	Seafood	20
Mumon	Japanese	22
Novitá	Italian	23
Orchid	Chinese	23
NEW Puglia's/Garden City	Italian	–
Rein	Amer.	23
Z Ruth's Chris	Steak	25
Sarabeth's	Amer.	20
Seventh St. Cafe	Italian	20
Sushi Ya	Japanese	21
Umberto's	Italian/Pizza	22

Upper Crust	Amer.	–
Walk St.	Amer.	21
Z Waterzooi	Belgian	24
Wild Fig	Med./Turkish	19

GARDEN CITY PARK

Green Cactus	Mex.	20
Jonathan's	Amer.	20
Uncle Bacala's	Italian/Seafood	21

GLEN COVE

NEW Cedar Creek	Amer.	–
Epiphany	Italian	21
Fatty Fish	Japanese	22
Gonzalo's	Amer.	21
La Bussola	Italian	23
La Ginestra	Italian	25
La Pace/Chef Michael	Italian	25
Page One	Amer./Eclectic	22
Riviera Grill	Italian	26
Uncle Dai	Chinese	18
Wild Fig	Med./Turkish	19

GLEN HEAD

Bistro M	Amer.	25
Ernesto's East	Italian	22
Fork & Vine	Amer.	23
Kiraku	Japanese	26

GREAT NECK

Bevanda	Italian	22
Burton & Doyle	Steak	24
Cafe Rustica	Italian/Med.	22
Carousel	Japanese	21
Chez Kama	Continental/Japanese	25
Cho-Sen	Asian/Kosher	19
Colbeh	Persian	21
NEW Crave 11025	Amer./Veg.	18
Daruma of Tokyo	Japanese	23
Elaine's	Asian	22
Ethos	Greek	21
Hinata	Japanese	23
Jean Marie	American	22
La Gioconda	Continental/Italian	21
La Rotonda	Pizza	19

Lola | *Eclectic* 24
Matsuya | *Asian* 21
🅉 Morton's | *Steak* 25
Oevo | *Italian* 21
Pancho's | *Tex-Mex* 19
🅉 Peter Luger | *Steak* 27
Simply Fondue | *Fondue* 17
NEW Sip City | *Eclectic* -
Sushi Palace | *Japanese* 24
Tel Aviv | *Israeli* 22
Tulip Bar & Grill | *Med./Turkish* 19
Turquoise | *Seafood* 21
Vespa | *Italian* 22
Wild Ginger | *Asian* 21

GREENVALE

NEW Bar Frites | *French* 18
🅉 Ben's Deli | *Deli* 19
Hunan Taste | *Chinese* 22
Sarin Thai | *Thai* 24

HEWLETT

Med. Grill | *Med.* 21
MoCa Asian | *Asian* 18

HICKSVILLE

NEW Blue Fish | *Japanese* -
Boccaccio | *Italian* 21
Boulder Creek | *Steak* -
Capriccio | *Italian* 24
Diwan | *Indian* 21
Dosa Diner | *Indian/Veg.* 23
🅉 Five Guys | *Burgers* 21
House of Dosas | *Indian/Veg.* 25
Jaiya | *Thai* 19
Kiran Palace | *Indian* 24
Lemonleaf Grill | *Thai* 22
Luigi Q | *Italian* 23
New Chilli/Curry | *Indian* 26
Pasta-eria | *Italian* 23
Peppercorns | *Continental* 19
Rangmahal | *Indian* 23
Royal Bukhara Grill | *Indian* 22
Spare Rib | *BBQ* 18

West East | *Asian* 25
Zorba/Greek | *Greek* 19

ISLAND PARK

A Taberna | *Portug.* 23
Jimmy Hays | *Steak* 25
Meson Iberia | *Continental/Spanish* 22
Paddy McGees | *Seafood* 18
Pancho's | *Tex-Mex* 19
NEW Stone Turtle | *Amer./Eclectic* 21

JERICHO

Fanatico | *Italian* 20
Frank's Steaks | *Steak* 21
Milleridge Inn | *Amer.* 16
Nagashima | *Japanese* 24
Philippe | *Chinese* 24

LAWRENCE

Cho-Sen | *Asian/Kosher* 19

LEVITTOWN

🅉 Five Guys | *Burgers* 21
Fortune Wheel | *Chinese* 22
Kiran Palace | *Indian* 24
NEW Sabor a Colombia | *Colombian* -
NEW Sensasian | *Asian* -
Tai-Show | *Japanese* 23

LOCUST VALLEY

🅉 Barney's | *Amer./French* 26
Basil Leaf | *Italian* 21
Brass Rail | *Amer.* 25
Buckram Stables | *Amer.* 19

LONG BEACH

🅉 Atlantica | *Amer./Seafood* 20
Caffe Laguna | *Italian* 19
Duke Falcon's | *Amer./Eclectic* 22
🅉 Five Guys | *Burgers* 21
Fresco Crêperie | *French* 23
George Martin's Grill | *Burgers* 20
Kawasaki Steak | *Japanese* 19
Lola's | *Amer.* 20
🅉 Matteo's | *Italian* 23
🅉 Nagahama | *Japanese* 28

Nick's Tuscan | *Italian* 21

Sugo | *Amer.* 23

Swingbelly's | *BBQ* 23

LYNBROOK

Ⓩ Branzino | *Italian* 26

Broadway Beanery | *Amer.* 21

MALVERNE

Il Villagio | *Italian* 24

MANHASSET

Benihana | *Japanese/Steak* 19

Cipollini | *Italian* 21

La Coquille | *French* 24

Pearl East | *Chinese* 23

Stresa | *Italian* 25

Ⓩ Toku | *Asian* 25

MASSAPEQUA/
MASSAPEQUA PARK

Asian Moon | *Asian* 23

Big Daddy's | *BBQ/Cajun* 24

Cafe Toscano | *Italian* 21

Ciao Baby | *Italian* 20

Hudson's Mill | *Amer.* 22

Il Classico | *Italian* 23

La Bottega | *Italian* 21

Mercato | *Amer./Italian* 20

Minami | *Japanese* 26

Ⓩ Smokin' Al's | *BBQ* 23

Tai-Show | *Japanese* 23

Zim Zari | *Cal./Mex.* 22

MERRICK

Brooks & Porter | *Steak* 22

Ⓩ Five Guys | *Burgers* 21

George Martin's Grill | *Burgers* 20

La Piazza | *Pizza* 21

La Strada | *Italian* 20

Nicholas James | *Amer.* 22

Pastrami King | *Deli/Sandwiches* 20

RS Jones | *SW* 22

Surf 'N Turf | *Greek/Turkish* 24

Yuki's Palette | *Japanese* 24

MINEOLA

Churrasq. Bairrada | *Portug.* 25

Circa | *Italian* 22

Giaccone's Pizza | *Pizza* -

Heart of Portugal | *Portug.* 20

Lareira | *Portug.* 20

Lemonleaf Thai | *Thai* 20

Pasta Vino | *Italian* 22

Piccola Bussola | *Italian* 23

Piccolo's | *Italian* 24

NEW HYDE PARK

Afghan Grill | *Afghan* 20

Baja Fresh | *Mex.* 18

Brasserie 214 | *European* 20

Deli King | *Deli* 19

Eddie's Pizza | *Pizza* 21

Iavarone Cafe | *Italian* 21

NEW Imperial Seoul | -
   Japanese/Korean

Kiss'o | *Japanese* 21

Madras/India | *Indian/Veg.* 22

Nanking | *Chinese/Thai* 19

Sushi Ya | *Japanese* 21

Ⓩ Two Steak/Sushi | 24
   Japanese/Steak

Umberto's | *Italian/Pizza* 22

NORTH BELLMORE

Bayou | *Cajun/Creole* 23

OCEANSIDE

Brasserie Persil | *French* 25

Cinelli's | *Italian* 18

La Bottega | *Italian* 21

Ⓩ La Parma | *Italian* 23

Solé | *Italian* 26

OYSTER BAY

Canterbury | *Amer./Seafood* 19

Coach Grill | *Amer.* 22

NEW Jack Halyards | 23
   Amer./Seafood

Wild Honey | *Amer.* 25

LOCATIONS

PLAINVIEW

Ayhan's Shish | Med./Turkish — 18
Brasserie Cassis | French — 23
NEW Deco 1600 | Amer./Italian — -
Green Cactus | Mex. — 20
Kumo Sushi | Japanese — 25
La Bottega | Italian — 21
La Famiglia | Italian — 22
La Piazza | Pizza — 21
Red Fish | Amer./Seafood — 23
Robata | Japanese — 20

POINT LOOKOUT

Fisherman's Catch | Seafood — 20
Olive Oils | Italian — 20

PORT WASHINGTON

Ayhan's Fish | Seafood/Turkish — 19
Ayhan's Shish | Med./Turkish — 18
Bistro Toulouse | French — 22
Bonsai | Japanese — 22
Brio | Italian — 21
Z Chez Noëlle | French — 27
DiMaggio's | Italian — 19
Diwan | Indian — 21
Dynasty/Pt. Wash. | Chinese — 20
Harbor-Q | BBQ — 21
La Bottega | Italian — 21
Z La Parma | Italian — 23
Z La Piccola | Italian — 27
La P'tite Framboise | French — 22
Livorno | Italian — 21
Louie's Oyster | Seafood — 17
Main St. Bakery | Bakery/Sandwiches — -
Montebello | Italian — 21
NEW Pepe Rosso | Italian — -
Rist. Italiano | Italian — 24
Rock 'n Sake | Japanese — 22
Salvatore's | Pizza — 25
Shang Hai Pavilion | Chinese — 21
Sullivan's Quay | Pub — 18
Tava | Turkish — 18
Vintage Port | French — 19

Waterview | Continental/Seafood — 18
Wild Honey | Amer. — 25
Yamaguchi | Japanese — 25

ROCKVILLE CENTRE

NEW Aperitif | French — 25
Ayhan's Shish | Med./Turkish — 18
Bigelow's | New Eng./Seafood — 24
Blue Moon | Italian/Pizza — 20
Chadwicks | Amer./Continental — 22
Chat Noir | French/Tea — 21
Cielo Rist. | Italian — 20
Z Dario's | Italian — 26
Da Ugo | Italian — 25
Dodici | Italian — 24
Frank's Steaks | Steak — 21
George Martin | Amer. — 22
George Martin's Grill | Burgers — 20
Green Cactus | Mex. — 20
International Delight | Diner — 18
La Bottega | Italian — 21
Nick's | Pizza — 23
NEW Press 195 | Sandwiches — -
NEW Prime Catch | Seafood — -
Roe's Casa Dolce | Bakery/Italian — 24
Simply Thai | Thai — 21
Taiko | Asian — 24
Tasty Crepes | Crêpes — 18
Thai Table | Thai — 23

ROSLYN/ ROSLYN HTS./ ROSLYN ESTATES

Z Besito | Mex. — 24
Bistro Citron | French — 21
Z Bryant & Cooper | Steak — 26
Chalet Rest. | Amer./Eclectic — 18
Chicken Kebab | Greek/Turkish — 21
Colbeh | Persian — 21
Green Cactus | Mex. — 20
Z Il Mulino NY | Italian — 27
Jolly Fisherman | Seafood/Steak — 21
Z Kotobuki | Japanese — 27
La Bottega | Italian — 21

Z Limani | *Med./Seafood* 26

Z Matteo's | *Italian* 23

Mim's | *Amer.* 20

Panini Café | *Sandwiches* 23

Poco Loco | *Mex.* 17

Ravagh | *Persian* 22

NEW 388 Rest. | *Amer./Italian* 20

Thyme | *Amer.* 21

Trata | *Greek/Seafood* 22

Tratt. Diane | *Italian* 25

Tratt. Di Meo | *Italian* 21

SEA CLIFF

Allison's Amalfi | *Italian/Med.* 21

NEW Met. Bistro | *Amer.* 22

Roots | *Amer.* 26

SEAFORD

Z Butera's | *Italian* 21

Catfish Max | *Amer./Seafood* 21

Pomodorino | *Italian* 19

Runyon's | *Amer.* 18

SYOSSET

Angelina's | *Italian* 23

Cafe Testarossa | *Continental* 22

Caracalla | *Italian* 23

Z Coolfish | *Seafood* 24

El Parral | *Italian/Spanish* 21

Franina | *Italian* 26

Fulton Prime | *Seafood/Steak* 23

Galangal | *Japanese/Thai* 23

Mim's | *Amer.* 20

Mother Kelly's | *Amer./Italian* 21

Moules et Frites | *Belgian/French* 19

Rachel's Cafe | *Italian* 22

Rare 650 | *Amer./Steak* 24

Steve's Piccola | *Italian* 24

Tsubo | *Japanese* 23

Wild Fig | *Med./Turkish* 19

VALLEY STREAM

NEW Chicken Coop | *Colombian* –

Seeda Thai | *Thai* 23

WANTAGH

Green Cactus | *Mex.* 20

Hemingway's | *Amer.* 19

Per Un Angelo | *Italian* 22

Sapporo | *Japanese* 23

Z Snaps | *Amer.* 26

Thom Thom | *Seafood/Steak* 20

NEW Trattachino | *Amer.* –

Umberto's | *Italian/Pizza* 22

WESTBURY

Ayhan's Trodos | *Med.* 21

Azerbaijan | *Mideast.* 22

Benihana | *Japanese/Steak* 19

Benny's | *Italian* 25

Bertucci's | *Italian* 17

Z Cafe Baci | *Italian* 22

Z Cheesecake | *Amer.* 20

Chi | *Chinese/Eclectic* 25

City Cellar | *Amer.* 21

Cozymel's Mex. | *Mex.* 17

California Pizza Kitchen | *Pizza* 17

Famous Dave's | *BBQ* 19

Galleria Dominick | *Italian* 26

Giulio Cesare | *Italian* 25

NEW Marco Polo's | *Asian/Italian* –

Papa Razzi | *Italian* 18

P.F. Chang's | *Chinese* 20

Scotto's | *Italian/Pizza* 20

Shogi | *Japanese* 25

Steve's Piccola | *Italian* 24

Tesoro | *Italian* 23

Venere | *Italian* 20

WILLISTON PARK

Fresco Crêperie | *French* 23

Hildebrandt's | *Amer.* 19

Homura Sushi | *Japanese* 23

Ivy Cottage | *Amer.* 23

La Marmite | *French/Italian* 24

Z La Parma | *Italian* 23

NEW Miraj | *Med./Persian* –

Z Riverbay | *Seafood* 23

Sripraphai | *Thai* 25

LOCATIONS

WOODBURY

☑ Ben's Deli | *Deli*	19
☑ Butera's | *Italian*	21
Graffiti | *Amer.*	20
Haiku Bistro/Sushi | *Asian*	24
Laguna Grille | *Nuevo Latino*	20
Majors Steak | *Steak*	19
Nisen | *Japanese*	25
Sage Bistro | *French*	24

Suffolk

AMAGANSETT

Clam Bar | *Seafood*	21
Cyril's Fish | *Seafood*	18
Hampton Chutney | *Indian*	22
Indian Wells | *Amer.*	17
Lobster Roll | *Seafood*	19
Meeting House | *Amer./Med.*	20
Show Win | *Japanese*	20

AMITYVILLE

Bulldog Grille | *Amer./Continental*	-
☑ Five Guys | *Burgers*	21
NEW Vero | *Italian*	-
Vittorio's | *Amer./Italian*	25

AQUEBOGUE

NEW Comtesse Thérèse | *French*	-
Modern Snack | *Amer.*	18

BABYLON/ NORTH BABYLON

Argyle Grill | *Amer.*	22
Babylon Carriage | *Continental*	21
☑ Barrique Kitchen | *Med.*	24
Green Cactus | *Mex.*	20
Horace/Sylvia's | *Amer.*	20
☑ Kotobuki | *Japanese*	27
Lucy's Café | *Amer.*	25
Pomodorino | *Italian*	19
Post Office | *Amer.*	19
Rist. Gemelli | *Italian*	24
Shiki | *Japanese*	24
Tricia's Café | *Amer.*	23

BAITING HOLLOW

Cooperage Inn | *Amer./Continental*	22
Lobster Roll N. | *Seafood*	20

BAYPORT

NEW Fish Store | *Seafood*	-
Grey Horse | *Amer.*	23
☑ Le Soir | *French*	27
Salsa Salsa | *Cal./Mex.*	23

BAY SHORE

☑ Aji 53 | *Japanese*	27
Boulder Creek | *Steak*	-
Declan Quinn's | *Amer.*	19
fatfish | *Med./Seafood*	21
☑ Lake House | *Amer.*	28
Milk & Sugar Café | *Amer.*	21
Mitsui | *Japanese*	24
Salvatore's | *Pizza*	25
☑ Siam Lotus | *Thai*	28
☑ Smokin' Al's | *BBQ*	23
Tula Kitchen | *Eclectic*	24

BELLPORT

Bellport | *Amer./Continental*	22
Meritage | *Amer./Asian*	25
Porters | *Seafood/Steak*	20
Spicy's BBQ | *BBQ*	20

BLUE POINT

Blue | *Amer.*	22
NEW Bluepoint B & G | *Amer.*	-

BRIDGEHAMPTON

Bobby Van's | *Steak*	22
Bridgehampton Candy | *Diner*	15
Copa Wine | *Spanish*	20
Golden Pear | *Amer./Coffee*	18
Pierre's | *French*	21
Pizza Place | *Pizza*	24
NEW Southfork | *Seafood*	-
World Pie | *Pizza*	19
Yama Q | *Japanese/Veg.*	23

BRIGHTWATERS

Sea Levels | *Amer./Seafood*	22

BROOKHAVEN HAMLET

Painters' | *Eclectic* — 20

BROOKHAVEN/ ROCKY POINT

Caruso's | *Italian* — 23
Sea Basin | *Italian/Seafood* — 19
Varney's | *Amer./Seafood* — 23

CENTEREACH

Mama's | *Italian* — 21
Pollo Rico | *Pan-Latin* — 20

CENTER MORICHES

La Volpe | *Italian* — 23

CENTERPORT

Mill Pond House | *Seafood/Steak* — 25

COLD SPRING HARBOR

Grasso's | *Amer.* — 24
NEW Harbor Mist | *Amer.* — 19

COMMACK

Ciao Baby | *Italian* — 20
Emilio's | *Pizza* — 23
Greek Village | *Greek* — 19
Kiran Palace | *Indian* — 24
Kurofune | *Japanese* — 23
Nisen | *Japanese* — 25
NEW Perfecto Mundo | *Pan-Latin* — 24
Souvlaki Palace | *Greek* — 24
Spare Rib | *BBQ* — 18

COPIAGUE

Thai Green Leaf | *Thai* — 21

CUTCHOGUE

Red Rooster | *Amer.* — 16

DEER PARK

Bellissimo Rist. | *Italian* — 23
Z Five Guys | *Burgers* — 21
Ludlow Bistro | *Amer.* — 24

EAST HAMPTON

Babette's | *Eclectic* — 20
Blue Parrot | *Tex-Mex* — 15

NEW Boathouse | *Seafood* — 19
Bostwick's | *Seafood* — 20
Cafe Max | *Amer./Eclectic* — 23
cittanuova | *Italian* — 20
Z Della Femina | *Amer.* — 24
Z E. Hampton Pt. | *Amer.* — 19
Fresno | *Amer.* — 22
Golden Pear | *Amer./Coffee* — 18
NEW Grill on Pantigo | *Amer.* — 21
Harbor Bistro/Grill | *Amer.* — 21
Living Room | *Amer.* — 25
Michaels'/Maidstone | *Amer.* — 18
Nichol's | *Amer.* — 17
Z Nick & Toni's | *Italian/Med.* — 24
Z Palm | *Seafood/Steak* — 26
Philippe | *Chinese* — 24
NEW Race Lane | *Amer.* — 19
Rowdy Hall | *Pub* — 20
Sam's | *Italian/Pizza* — 18
NEW Serafina | *Italian* — 18
Z 1770 House | *Amer.* — 25
Shiki | *Japanese* — –
Turtle Crossing | *Amer./BBQ* — 22

EAST MARION

Hellenic Snack | *Greek* — 20

EAST MORICHES

Tony's | *Asian* — 19

EAST NORTHPORT

Baja Grill | *Mex.* — 18
Chefs of NY | *Italian/Pizza* — 19
Crossroads Cafe | *Amer.* — 22
Jeff's Seafood | *Seafood* — 20
Thai Green Leaf | *Thai* — 21
Tokyo | *Japanese/Korean* — 24
Torcellos | *Italian* — 21
Wild Ginger | *Asian* — 21
Yokohama | *Japanese* — 23

EAST PATCHOGUE

Z Chachama | *Amer.* — 27

EASTPORT

Z Trumpets | *Amer./Continental* — 22

EAST SETAUKET

Bliss	*Amer.*	22
Curry Club	*Indian*	20
NEW Domo Sushi	*Japanese*	21
Pita House	*Med./Turkish*	22
Tai-Show	*Japanese*	23

FARMINGVILLE

NEW J&C 68	*Asian*	-

FIRE ISLAND

Hideaway	*Eclectic*	19
Island Mermaid	*Amer./Seafood*	20
Maguire's	*Amer.*	19
Matthew's	*Seafood*	22
Surf's Out	*Italian/Seafood*	17
Top of the Bay	*Amer.*	-

FORT SALONGA

Intermezzo	*Italian*	23

GREAT RIVER

NEW George Martin's Steak	*Steak*	-

GREENLAWN

Azuma	*Asian/Japanese*	23
Goldmine Mex.	*Mex.*	21
NEW Old Fields	*Amer./Steak*	-
Ruvo	*Italian*	22

GREENPORT

Claudio's	*Amer./Continental*	16
Cuvée	*French*	22
NEW Farmhouse	*Amer.*	26
Frisky Oyster	*Eclectic*	25
Greenport Tea	*Tea*	21
Z Noah's	*Amer.*	26
NEW Portly Grape	*Amer.*	-
Porto Bello	*Italian*	22
Salamander's	*Eclectic*	24
Scrimshaw	*Amer.*	23
Vine Wine Bar	*Amer.*	22

HAMPTON BAYS

Edgewater	*Italian*	22
Indian Cove	*Amer./Seafood*	18
Inn Spot/Bay	*Eclectic/Seafood*	19
Matsulin	*Asian*	22
Oakland's/Sunday	*Amer./Seafood*	18
1 North Steak	*Steak*	22
Squiretown	*Amer.*	20
Tide Runners	*Amer.*	16
Tony's	*Asian*	19

HAUPPAUGE

Bertucci's	*Italian*	17
Butterfields	*Amer.*	20
Cafe La Strada	*Italian*	23
Z Five Guys	*Burgers*	21
Gasho of Japan	*Japanese/Steak*	20
Grill Room	*Amer.*	21
NEW Janine's	*Amer.*	-
Z Kotobuki	*Japanese*	27
Mario	*Italian*	25
Pace's Steak	*Steak*	22
Pomodorino	*Italian*	19
Z San Marco	*Italian*	26
Z Sempre Vivolo	*Italian*	27

HOLBROOK

Mama's	*Italian*	21
Mamma Lombardi's	*Italian*	23
Trio	*Amer.*	21

HUNTINGTON/HUNTINGTON STATION

Albert's Mandarin	*Chinese*	20
Almarco	*Italian*	20
Ariana	*Afghan/Veg.*	20
NEW Bel Posto	*Italian*	-
Z Besito	*Mex.*	24
Best Buffet	*Chinese/Eclectic*	18
Bin 56	*Spanish*	24
Z Bistro Cassis	*French*	24
Black & Blue	*Seafood/Steak*	22
Bonbori Tiki	*Japanese/Thai*	20
Bravo Nader!/Fish	*Italian/Seafood*	24
Café Buenos Aires	*Argent.*	24
Z Cheesecake	*Amer.*	20

Cirella's | *Amer./Eclectic* 21
Clubhouse | *Steak* 21
California Pizza Kitchen | *Pizza* 17
Crew Kitchen | *Amer.* 24
Dao | *Asian* 23
NEW Fado | *Portug.* 21
F.H. Riley's | *Amer.* 23
Z Five Guys | *Burgers* 21
Green Cactus | *Mex.* 20
Honu | *Amer.* 22
House of India | *Indian* 21
Jonathan's Rist. | *Italian* 24
Kabul Afghani | *Afghan* 23
Kurabarn | *Japanese* 24
La Bottega | *Italian* 21
Z La Parma | *Italian* 23
La Spada | *Italian* 21
Legal Sea Foods | *Seafood* 20
Los Compadres | *Mex.* 23
Mac's Steak | *Steak* 23
Massa's | *Pizza* 23
Z Matteo's | *Italian* 23
Med. Snack | *Greek/Med.* 22
Oaxaca Mexican | *Mex.* 23
Osaka | *Japanese* 24
Osteria da Nino | *Italian* 24
Osteria Toscana | *Italian* 23
Panama Hatties | *Amer.* 25
PG Steak | *Steak* 22
Piccola Bussola | *Italian* 23
Z Piccolo | *Amer./Italian* 27
Pomodorino | *Italian* 19
Porto Vivo | *Italian* 22
Z Prime | *Amer.* 23
Quetzalcoatl | *Mex.* 20
Ravagh | *Persian* 22
Café Red/Rest. | *Amer.* 25
Samurai | *Japanese* 24
NEW Sapsuckers | *Amer.* -
Spice Village | *Pakistani/Persian* 20
Sri Thai | *Thai* 22
Strawberry's | *Amer./Italian* 18

NEW Swallow | *Amer.* -
Thai USA | *Thai* 23
34 New St. | *Eclectic* 18
Toast & Co. | *Amer.* 18
Tomo Hibachi | *Japanese* 20
Tutto Pazzo | *Italian* 20
Umberto's | *Italian/Pizza* 22
NEW Vitae | *Continental* -
NEW XO | *Eclectic* -

ISLANDIA
Takara | *Japanese* 28

ISLIP
(Including Central, East, West)
Carrabba's | *Italian* 19
Irish Coffee | *Continental/Irish* 23
NEW Jackson Hall | *Amer.* -
Maxwell's | *Amer.* -
Nonnina | *Italian* 25
Z Tellers | *Steak* 26
Z Verace | *Italian* 26

JAMESPORT/ SOUTH JAMESPORT
Bayview Inn | *Amer./Continental* 22
Cliff's | *Steak* 22
Jamesport Country | *Amer.* 23
Z Jamesport Manor | *Amer.* 23
Z Luce & Hawkins | *Amer.* 25

KINGS PARK
Café Red/Rest. | *Amer.* 25
Ciro's | *Italian* 22
Dixie's | *BBQ* -
Long River | *Asian* 21
Sarin Thai | *Thai* 24

LAKE GROVE
Bobby's Burger | *Burgers* 21
Z Cheesecake | *Amer.* 20
California Pizza Kitchen | *Pizza* 17
John Harvard's | *Pub* 16

LAUREL
Cliff's | *Steak* 22

LINDENHURST

Bozena Polish | *Polish*	23
NEW Cattlemen's | *Steak*	19
Southside Fish | *Seafood*	20
Village Lanterne | *German*	25

MATTITUCK

A Mano | *Italian*	24
Love Ln. Kitchen | *Amer.*	23
Old Mill Inn | *Amer./Seafood*	20

MELVILLE

Barolo | *Continental/Italian*	25
Bertucci's | *Italian*	17
Z Blackstone Steak | *Steak*	24
Cirella's | *Continental/Italian*	21
Four Food Studio | *Amer.*	21
Frederick's | *Continental*	23
La Piazza | *Pizza*	21

MILLER PLACE

Blond | *Amer.*	21
Brian Scotts | *Amer.*	19
Sabai Thai | *Thai*	22

MONTAUK

Backyard | *Med.*	23
Crow's Nest | *Seafood*	19
Z Dave's Grill | *Continental/Seafood*	27
Dock B&G | *Seafood*	-
Duryea's Lobster | *Seafood*	22
East by Northeast | *Amer./Asian*	21
Fishbar | *Seafood*	18
Gosman's Dock | *Seafood*	19
Gulf Coast | *Amer.*	21
Z Harvest | *Italian/Med.*	26
Inlet Seafood | *Seafood*	21
Manucci's | *Italian/Pizza*	19
NEW Navy Beach | *Amer.*	19
Sea Grille | *Amer./Italian*	21
Second House | *Amer.*	19
Shagwong | *Amer./Seafood*	18
NEW South Edison | *Amer.*	22

Surf Lodge | *Amer.*	19
Surfside Inn | *Continental/Seafood*	18
NEW When Pigs Fly | *BBQ*	18

MOUNT SINAI

Alexandros | *Greek/Med.*	23
Lotus East | *Chinese*	21

NESCONSET

JT's Corner Cafe | *Amer.*	23
Sundried Tomato | *Italian/Pizza*	21
NEW Tate's | *Amer./Italian*	26

NEW SUFFOLK

Legends | *Eclectic*	23

NORTHPORT

Batata Café | *Eclectic*	21
Benkei Japanese | *Japanese*	23
Bistro 44 | *Amer.*	23
Z Maroni Cuisine | *Eclectic/Italian*	28
Pumpernickels | *German*	21
Ritz Cafe | *Continental*	19
Show Win | *Japanese*	20
Sweet Mama's | *Diner*	19
NEW Whale's Tale | *Seafood*	20

OAKDALE

Green Cactus | *Mex.*	20
Mama's | *Italian*	21
NEW Onsen Sushi | *Japanese*	-
Snapper Inn | *Seafood*	18
Tai-Show | *Japanese*	23
View | *Amer./Continental*	22
Viva La Vida | *Mex./Spanish*	20

PATCHOGUE

BobbiQue | *BBQ*	21
Harbor Crab | *Seafood*	18
Lombardi's/Bay | *Seafood/Steak*	23
Oar Steak | *Seafood/Steak*	21
PeraBell | *Amer./Eclectic*	26
Pita House | *Med./Turkish*	22
Pollo Rico | *Pan-Latin*	20
Public House 49 | *Amer.*	20

PORT JEFFERSON/ PORT JEFFERSON STATION

Carnival	*Italian*	22
NEW Cattlemen's	*Steak*	19
Fifth Season	*Amer.*	26
Lemonleaf Grill	*Thai*	22
Lombardi's/Sound	*Italian*	21
Pace's Steak	*Steak*	22
Pasta Pasta	*Italian*	25
Pie	*Pizza*	21
Ruvo	*Italian*	22
Salsa Salsa	*Cal./Mex.*	23
Tequila Jacks	*Carib./Seafood*	18
Thai Gourmet	*Thai*	26
Toast	*Eclectic*	24
Wave	*Amer.*	19
Zorba/Greek	*Greek*	19

QUOGUE/ EAST QUOGUE

Dockers Waterside	*Seafood/Steak*	20
Restaurant/The Inn	*Amer.*	21
Z Stone Creek	*French/Med.*	26
Tony's	*Asian*	19

RIVERHEAD

Birchwood	*Amer./Polish*	20
NEW Bistro 72	*Amer.*	-
Boulder Creek	*Steak*	-
Buoy One	*Seafood*	23
Cliff's	*Steak*	22
NEW Dark Horse	*Amer./Eclectic*	-
Farm Country Kit.	*Amer.*	23
Haiku	*Japanese*	-
Spicy's BBQ	*BBQ*	20
Star Confectionery	*Amer./Diner*	22
Stonewalls	*Amer./French*	23
Tweeds	*Amer.*	21

SAGAPONACK

Townline	*BBQ*	19

SAG HARBOR

Z American Hotel	*Amer./French*	25
Bay Burger	*Burgers*	21

Beacon	*Amer.*	22
B.Smith's	*Cajun/Southern*	18
Dockside B&G	*Seafood*	21
Estia's Kitchen	*Amer.*	23
Golden Pear	*Amer./Coffee*	18
Il Capuccino	*Italian*	19
NEW La Maison	*Amer.*	18
NEW LT Burger	*Burgers*	16
New Paradise	*Amer./Eclectic*	22
Oasis Waterfront	*Amer.*	24
Phao Thai	*Thai*	21
Sen	*Japanese*	21
Tutto Il Giorno	*Italian*	25

SAYVILLE

NEW Bistro 25	*Eclectic*	-
Blackbirds' Grille	*Cajun/Southern*	20
Z Butera's	*Italian*	21
Cafe Joelle	*Amer./Eclectic*	22
Cull House	*Seafood*	20
NEW Downtown Burger	*Amer./Burgers*	-
La Tavola	*Italian*	22

SELDEN

Viva Juan	*Mex.*	21

SHELTER ISLAND/ SHELTER ISLAND HEIGHTS

Chequit Inn	*Amer./Eclectic*	19
Planet Bliss	*Eclectic/New World*	20
Ram's Head	*Amer./Eclectic*	20
Sunset Beach	*Asian/French*	18
Vine Street	*Amer.*	25

SMITHTOWN

American Burger	*Burgers*	18
NEW Arthur Ave.	*Amer.*	-
Baja Grill	*Mex.*	18
Z Butera's	*Italian*	21
Cafe Havana	*Cuban*	18
Carrabba's	*Italian*	19
Casa Luis	*Spanish*	22
Casa Rustica	*Italian*	25
Chop Shop	*Amer.*	24

Famous Dave's | *BBQ* 19

Garden Grill | *Amer.* 21

Hotoke | *Japanese/Steak* 21

H2O Seafood | *Seafood* 23

La Famiglia | *Italian* 22

La Panchita | *Mex./Spanish* 22

Luso | *Portug.* 22

Maureen's Kitchen | *Amer.* 25

Rockwell's | *Amer.* 22

Salsa Salsa | *Cal./Mex.* 23

Thai House | *Thai* 24

SOUTHAMPTON

Coast Grill | *Amer./Seafood* 22

Golden Pear | *Amer./Coffee* 18

La Parmigiana | *Italian* 22

Le Chef | *Continental/French* 22

Lobster Inn | *Seafood* 19

Nello Summertimes | *Italian* 16

🗹 Plaza Cafe | *Seafood* 26

red bar | *Amer./French* 22

Sant Ambroeus | *Italian* 24

Savanna's | *Amer.* 20

75 Main | *Italian* 18

Silver's | *Eclectic* 23

Southampton Publick | *Pub* 18

Tuscan House | *Italian* 22

SOUTHOLD

Elbow East | *Steak* 19

🆕 JD Steakhouse | *Steak* 19

🗹 North Fork Table | *Amer.* 29

O'Mally's | *Pub* 18

ST. JAMES

Ancient Ginger | *Chinese* 21

Bella Vita Grill | *Amer./Italian* 21

Frank-N-Burger | 19
Burgers/Hot Dogs

🗹 Kitchen A Bistro | *French* 27

🗹 Kitchen A Tratt. | *Italian* 28

Lotus East | *Chinese* 21

🗹 Mosaic | *Amer.* 28

O's Food | *French* 22

Vintage Prime | *Steak* 25

Voila! | *French* 24

STONY BROOK

🗹 Country House | *Amer.* 23

Green Cactus | *Mex.* 20

Mirabelle, Rest. | *French* 25

Mirabelle Tavern | *Amer.* 21

Pentimento | *Italian* 22

Robinson's Tea | *Tea* 23

WADING RIVER

Amarelle | *Amer.* 25

Blackwells | *Steak* 23

Desmond's | *Amer.* 20

🗹 La Plage | *Eclectic* 27

Michael Anthony's | *Eclectic* 24

WAINSCOTT

Georgica | *Amer.* 18

Rugosa | *Amer.* 21

WATER MILL

Dish | *Amer.* 27

Foody's | *BBQ/Pizza* 21

Hampton Coffee | *Coffee* 19

🗹 Mirko's | *Eclectic* 26

Muse | *Amer./Eclectic* 23

Robert's | *Italian* 25

Suki Zuki | *Japanese* 24

Trata | *Greek/Seafood* 22

WESTHAMPTON/ WESTHAMPTON BEACH

Baby Moon | *Italian* 18

Buoy One | *Seafood* 23

Dee Angelo's | *Italian* 19

Hampton Coffee | *Coffee* 19

Patio/54 Main | *Amer.* 19

Post Stop | *Amer.* 17

🗹 Starr Boggs | *Amer./Seafood* 26

Tony's | *Asian* 19

WEST SAYVILLE

21 Main | *Steak* 23

Special Features

Listings cover the best in each category and include names, locations and Food ratings. Multi-location restaurants' features may vary by branch.

BOAT DOCKING

NEW Boathouse	E Hampton	19
B.Smith's	Sag Harbor	18
Catfish Max	Seaford	21
Claudio's	Greenport	16
Coast Grill	Southampton	22
Dockers Waterside	E Quogue	20
Z E. Hampton Pt.	E Hampton	19
fatfish	Bay Shore	21
Fishbar	Montauk	18
Fisherman's Catch	Point Lookout	20
Gosman's Dock	Montauk	19
Harbor Crab	Patchogue	18
Indian Cove	Hampton Bays	18
Lobster Inn	Southampton	19
Louie's Oyster	Port Washington	17
Maguire's	Ocean Beach	19
Oakland's/Sunday	Hampton Bays	18
Oar Steak	Patchogue	21
Oasis Waterfront	Sag Harbor	24
Old Mill Inn	Mattituck	20
Paddy McGees	Island Pk	18
Pier 95	Freeport	24
Z Prime	Huntington	23
Rachel's Waterside	Freeport	20
Ram's Head	Shelter Is	20
Schooner	Freeport	17
Scrimshaw	Greenport	23
Snapper Inn	Oakdale	18
Surf's Out	Kismet	17
Tide Runners	Hampton Bays	16
View	Oakdale	22
Villa D'Aqua	Bellmore	21
Waterview	Port Washington	18
Wildfish	Freeport	21

BREAKFAST

(See also Hotel Dining)

Ayhan's Shish	Port Washington	18
Babette's	E Hampton	20
Batata Café	Northport	21
Bridgehampton Candy	Bridgehampton	15
Buckram Stables	Locust Valley	19
Cuvée	Greenport	22
Estia's Kitchen	Sag Harbor	23
Golden Pear	multi.	18
Hampton Coffee	Water Mill	19
Hellenic Snack	E Marion	20
International Delight	multi.	18
JT's Corner Cafe	Nesconset	23
Lombardi's/Sound	Port Jefferson	21
Love Ln. Kitchen	Mattituck	23
Maureen's Kitchen	Smithtown	25
Post Stop	Westhampton Bch	17
Robinson's Tea	Stony Brook	23
Star Confectionery	Riverhead	22
Sweet Mama's	Northport	19
Thomas's Eggery	Carle Pl	22
Toast	Port Jefferson	24

BRUNCH

Ayhan's Shish	multi.	18
Z Bistro Cassis	Huntington	24
Bistro Citron	Roslyn	21
NEW Bistro 25	Sayville	-
Blackbirds' Grille	Sayville	20
Bobby Van's	Bridgehampton	22
B.Smith's	Sag Harbor	18
Cafe Joelle	Sayville	22
Cafe Max	E Hampton	23
Canterbury	Oyster Bay	19
Z Cheesecake	Westbury	20
Cooperage Inn	Baiting Hollow	22
Desmond's	Wading River	20
Z E. Hampton Pt.	E Hampton	19

56th Fighter | **Farmingdale**	16
Garden Grill | **Smithtown**	21
Gonzalo's | **Glen Cove**	21
Hemingway's | **Wantagh**	19
H.R. Singleton's | **Bethpage**	18
☒ Jamesport Manor | **Jamesport**	23
Jonathan's | **Garden City Pk**	20
Library Cafe | **Farmingdale**	18
☒ Limani | **Roslyn**	26
Lombardi's/Sound | **Port Jefferson**	21
Louie's Oyster | **Port Washington**	17
Milleridge Inn | **Jericho**	16
Paddy McGees | **Island Pk**	18
Painters' | **Brookhaven Hamlet**	20
☒ Palm Court | **E Meadow**	24
Pierre's | **Bridgehampton**	21
Pine Island | **Bayville**	18
☒ Prime | **Huntington**	23
Rachel's Waterside | **Freeport**	20
Ram's Head | **Shelter Is**	20
Rein | **Garden City**	23
Ritz Cafe | **Northport**	19
☒ Rothmann's | **E Norwich**	25
Snapper Inn | **Oakdale**	18
Southampton Publick | **Southampton**	18
Stonewalls | **Riverhead**	23
☒ Trumpets | **Eastport**	22
☒ Waterzooi | **Garden City**	24
Wild Ginger | **Great Neck**	21
World Pie | **Bridgehampton**	19

BUSINESS DINING

Amarelle | **Wading River**	25
☒ Atlantica | **Long Bch**	20
Benihana | **Manhasset**	19
Benny's | **Westbury**	25
☒ Blackstone Steak | **Melville**	24
Bobby Van's | **Bridgehampton**	22
☒ Bryant & Cooper | **Roslyn**	26
Burton & Doyle | **Great Neck**	24
Butterfields | **Hauppauge**	20

Caracalla | **Syosset**	23
Clubhouse | **Huntington**	21
☒ E. Hampton Pt. | **E Hampton**	19
Fork & Vine | **Glen Head**	23
Franina | **Syosset**	26
Frederick's | **Melville**	23
Fulton Prime | **Syosset**	23
Giulio Cesare | **Westbury**	25
☒ Il Mulino NY | **Roslyn Estates**	27
☒ Jamesport Manor | **Jamesport**	23
Jolly Fisherman | **Roslyn**	21
Jonathan's Rist. | **Huntington**	24
La Coquille | **Manhasset**	24
La Pace/Chef Michael | **Glen Cove**	25
☒ La Piccola | **Port Washington**	27
☒ Limani | **Roslyn**	26
Lola | **Great Neck**	24
Lombardi's/Sound | **Port Jefferson**	21
☒ Luce & Hawkins | **Jamesport**	25
Mac's Steak | **Huntington**	23
Manucci's | **Montauk**	19
Mirabelle, Rest. | **Stony Brook**	25
☒ Morton's | **Great Neck**	25
Nick's Tuscan | **Long Bch**	21
Nonnina | **W Islip**	25
Oevo | **Great Neck**	21
☒ Palm | **E Hampton**	26
Palmer's | **Farmingdale**	21
Panama Hatties | **Huntington Station**	25
Patio/54 Main | **Westhampton Bch**	19
☒ Peter Luger | **Great Neck**	27
☒ Piccolo | **Huntington**	27
☒ Plaza Cafe | **Southampton**	26
☒ Prime | **Huntington**	23
Rare 650 | **Syosset**	24
☒ Riverbay | **Williston Pk**	23
Robert's | **Water Mill**	25
☒ Rothmann's | **E Norwich**	25
☒ Ruth's Chris | **Garden City**	25
Sea Grille | **Montauk**	21

❷ Sempre Vivolo | **Hauppauge**	27	❷ Coolfish | **Syosset**	24
Show Win | **Northport**	20	**NEW** Crave 11025 | **Great Neck**	18
❷ Stone Creek | **E Quogue**	26	Crossroads Cafe | **E Northport**	22
Stresa | **Manhasset**	25	Deli King | **New Hyde Pk**	19
Table 9 | **E Hills**	22	❷ Della Femina | **E Hampton**	24
Taste 99 | **Farmingdale**	18	Dish | **Water Mill**	27
❷ Tellers | **Islip**	26	Dockers Waterside | **E Quogue**	20
Trata | **Roslyn**	22	Dockside B&G | **Sag Harbor**	21
Trio | **Holbrook**	21	Dosa Diner | **Hicksville**	23
❷ Trumpets | **Eastport**	22	Duryea's Lobster | **Montauk**	22
Vespa | **Great Neck**	22	East by Northeast | **Montauk**	21
		❷ E. Hampton Pt. | **E Hampton**	19

BYO

Afghan Grill | **New Hyde Pk**	20	Elbow East | **Southold**	19
Almarco | **Huntington**	20	Ernesto's East | **Glen Head**	22
Angelina's | **Syosset**	23	Farm Country Kit. | **Riverhead**	23
Asian Moon | **Massapequa Pk**	23	Fork & Vine | **Glen Head**	23
❷ Barney's | **Locust Valley**	26	Fresco Crêperie | **Williston Pk**	23
Barolo | **Melville**	25	Frisky Oyster | **Greenport**	25
❷ Barrique Kitchen | **Babylon**	24	Fulton Prime | **Syosset**	23
Bay Burger | **Sag Harbor**	21	Galleria Dominick | **Westbury**	26
Bayview Inn | **S Jamesport**	22	**NEW** George Martin's Steak | **Great River**	–
NEW Bel Posto | **Huntington**	–	Gosman's Dock | **Montauk**	19
Bigelow's | **Rockville Ctr**	24	**NEW** Grill on Pantigo | **E Hampton**	21
❷ Bistro Cassis | **Huntington**	24	Haiku | **Riverhead**	–
Bistro Citron | **Roslyn**	21	Harbor Bistro/Grill | **E Hampton**	21
Bistro M | **Glen Head**	25	❷ Harvest | **Montauk**	26
Bistro Toulouse | **Port Washington**	22	Heart of Portugal | **Mineola**	20
❷ Blackstone Steak | **Melville**	24	Hellenic Snack | **E Marion**	20
Bob's Place | **Floral Pk**	21	Il Capuccino | **Sag Harbor**	19
Brasserie Persil | **Oceanside**	25	Indian Wells | **Amagansett**	17
Broadway Beanery | **Lynbrook**	21	Inn Spot/Bay | **Hampton Bays**	19
❷ Bryant & Cooper | **Roslyn**	26	International Delight | **multi.**	18
Burton & Doyle | **Great Neck**	24	Jeff's Seafood | **E Northport**	20
Cafe Testarossa | **Syosset**	22	Jimmy Hays | **Island Pk**	25
Caffe Laguna | **Long Bch**	19	Kiran Palace | **Levittown**	24
❷ Chez Noëlle | **Port Washington**	27	❷ Kitchen A Bistro | **St. James**	27
Ciao Baby | **Massapequa Pk**	20	❷ Kitchen A Tratt. | **St. James**	28
Cipollini | **Manhasset**	21	La Pace/Chef Michael | **Glen Cove**	25
Ciro's | **Kings Park**	22	❷ La Plage | **Wading River**	27
Clubhouse | **Huntington**	21	La P'tite Framboise | **Port Washington**	22
Coach Grill | **Oyster Bay**	22		
Colbeh | **Roslyn Estates**	21		

SPECIAL FEATURES

Le Chef | **Southampton**	22
Living Room | **E Hampton**	25
Main St. Bakery | **Port Washington**	-
NEW Marco Polo's | **Westbury**	-
⛿ Maroni Cuisine | **Northport**	28
Massa's | **Huntington Station**	23
Matsulin | **Hampton Bays**	22
Meeting House | **Amagansett**	20
Meritage | **Bellport**	25
Michael Anthony's | **Wading River**	24
Michaels'/Maidstone | **E Hampton**	18
Muse | **Water Mill**	23
Nautilus Cafe | **Freeport**	24
New Chilli/Curry | **Hicksville**	26
Nichol's | **E Hampton**	17
⛿ Nick & Toni's | **E Hampton**	24
Nick's Tuscan | **Long Bch**	21
Nonnina | **W Islip**	25
Novitá | **Garden City**	23
Oasis Waterfront | **Sag Harbor**	24
Onzon Thai | **Bellmore**	24
O's Food | **St. James**	22
Osteria da Nino | **Huntington**	24
Osteria Toscana | **Huntington**	23
Pace's Steak | **multi.**	22
⛿ Palm | **E Hampton**	26
⛿ Palm Court | **E Meadow**	24
Panama Hatties | **Huntington Station**	25
Pasta Vino | **Mineola**	22
Patio/54 Main | **Westhampton Bch**	19
PeraBell | **Patchogue**	26
PG Steak | **Huntington**	22
Piccola Bussola | **multi.**	23
⛿ Piccolo | **Huntington**	27
Piccolo's | **Mineola**	24
Pie | **Port Jefferson**	21
Salvatore's | **Bay Shore**	25
Pierre's | **Bridgehampton**	21
Planet Bliss | **Shelter Is**	20

Poco Loco | **Roslyn**	17
Porto Bello | **Greenport**	22
Porto Vivo | **Huntington**	22
Ram's Head | **Shelter Is**	20
Rare 650 | **Syosset**	24
Red Fish | **Plainview**	23
Café Red/Rest. | **Huntington**	25
Rein | **Garden City**	23
Rist. Gemelli | **Babylon**	24
Rock 'n Sake | **Port Washington**	22
Roe's Casa Dolce | **Rockville Ctr**	24
Roots | **Sea Cliff**	26
Sabai Thai | **Miller Pl**	22
NEW Sakaya | **Albertson**	-
Salsa Salsa | **Smithtown**	23
⛿ 1770 House | **E Hampton**	25
Spice Village | **Huntington**	20
Sushi Palace | **Great Neck**	24
Taiko | **Rockville Ctr**	24
Tasty Crepes | **Rockville Ctr**	18
NEW Tate's | **Nesconset**	26
Thai Gourmet | **Port Jefferson Station**	26
Tratt. Diane | **Roslyn**	25
Trio | **Holbrook**	21
Turquoise | **Great Neck**	21
NEW Vero | **Amityville**	-
Vespa | **Great Neck**	22
Vine Street | **Shelter Is**	25
Voila! | **St. James**	24
Walk St. | **Garden City**	21
West East | **Hicksville**	25
Wild Honey | **multi.**	25
World Pie | **Bridgehampton**	19

CATERING

Akbar | **Garden City**	22
Barolo | **Melville**	25
Bayou | **N Bellmore**	23
Bella Vita Grill | **St. James**	21
Bellport | **Bellport**	22
Big Daddy's | **Massapequa**	24
Bistro M | **Glen Head**	25

Blond | **Miller Pl**	21	**Z** Maroni Cuisine | **Northport**	28
Brio | **Port Washington**	21	Meritage | **Bellport**	25
Butterfields | **Hauppauge**	20	Mirabelle, Rest. | **Stony Brook**	25
Z Cafe Baci | **Westbury**	22	Mother Kelly's | **Cedarhurst**	21
Cafe Joelle | **Sayville**	22	Nagashima | **Jericho**	24
Cafe La Strada | **Hauppauge**	23	Nicholas James | **Merrick**	22
Cafe Toscano | **Massapequa**	21	Nick's | **Rockville Ctr**	23
Caffe Laguna | **Long Bch**	19	Nisen | **Commack**	25
Capriccio | **Hicksville**	24	Orchid | **Garden City**	23
Casa Rustica | **Smithtown**	25	O's Food | **St. James**	22
Ciao Baby | **multi.**	20	Pace's Steak | **multi.**	22
Colbeh | **Great Neck**	21	Page One | **Glen Cove**	22
Z Coolfish | **Syosset**	24	**Z** Palm Court | **E Meadow**	24
Curry Club | **E Setauket**	20	Pasta-eria | **Hicksville**	23
Cuvée | **Greenport**	22	Pasta Pasta | **Port Jefferson**	25
Z Dario's | **Rockville Ctr**	26	Pastrami King | **Merrick**	20
Z Della Femina | **E Hampton**	24	Piccola Bussola | **multi.**	23
E. B. Elliot's | **Freeport**	18	Pita House | **Patchogue**	22
Fresno | **E Hampton**	22	Planet Bliss | **Shelter Is**	20
Galleria Dominick | **Westbury**	26	**Z** Plaza Cafe | **Southampton**	26
George Martin | **Rockville Ctr**	22	Rachel's Waterside | **Freeport**	20
Golden Pear | **multi.**	18	Rangmahal | **Hicksville**	23
Heart of Portugal | **Mineola**	20	Restaurant/The Inn | **Quogue**	21
House of Dosas | **Hicksville**	25	RS Jones | **Merrick**	22
H.R. Singleton's | **Bethpage**	18	Salamander's | **Greenport**	24
Iavarone Cafe | **New Hyde Pk**	21	Salsa Salsa | **multi.**	23
Il Classico | **Massapequa Pk**	23	**Z** San Marco | **Hauppauge**	26
Ivy Cottage | **Williston Pk**	23	Sapporo | **Wantagh**	23
NEW Jack Halyards | **Oyster Bay**	23	Shiki | **Babylon**	24
Jamesport Country | **Jamesport**	23	**Z** Siam Lotus | **Bay Shore**	28
Kiran Palace | **Hicksville**	24	**Z** Smokin' Al's | **Bay Shore**	23
La Famiglia | **Smithtown**	22	**Z** Snaps | **Wantagh**	26
La Gioconda | **Great Neck**	21	Solé | **Oceanside**	26
Laguna Grille | **Woodbury**	20	Southside Fish | **Lindenhurst**	20
La Piazza | **multi.**	21	Spare Rib | **multi.**	18
Z La Plage | **Wading River**	27	**Z** Stone Creek | **E Quogue**	26
La Terrazza | **Cedarhurst**	22	Stresa | **Manhasset**	25
Lemonleaf Grill | **Hicksville**	22	Sundried Tomato | **Nesconset**	21
Lemonleaf Thai | **Carle Pl**	20	Taiko | **Rockville Ctr**	24
Lombardi's/Sound | **Port Jefferson**	21	Tai-Show | **multi.**	23
Lotus East | **multi.**	21	Tesoro | **Westbury**	23
Mamma Lombardi's | **Holbrook**	23	Thai Gourmet | **Port Jefferson Station**	26

Thai Table	**Rockville Ctr**	23
Thyme	**Roslyn**	21
Umberto's	**New Hyde Pk**	22
Uncle Dai	**Glen Cove**	18
Venere	**Westbury**	20
Viva La Vida	**Oakdale**	20
Voila!	**St. James**	24
Walk St.	**Garden City**	21
Z West End	**Carle Pl**	25
World Pie	**Bridgehampton**	19

CELEBRITY CHEFS

Starr Boggs

| Z Starr Boggs | **Westhampton Bch** | 26 |

Philippe Chow

| Philippe | **multi.** | 24 |

Claudia Fleming/Gerry Hayden

| Z North Fork Table | **Southold** | 29 |

Philippe Corbet

| O's Food | **St. James** | 22 |

Massimo Fedozzi

| NEW Vero | **Amityville** | - |

Bobby Flay

| Bobby's Burger | **Lake Grove** | 21 |

Nader Gebrin

| Bravo Nader!/Fish | **Huntington** | 24 |

Chris Gerdes

| Blackwells | **Wading River** | 23 |

Michael Ginor

| Lola | **Great Neck** | 24 |
| Tel Aviv | **Great Neck** | 22 |

Doug Gulija

| Z Plaza Cafe | **Southampton** | 26 |

Joe Isidori

| NEW Southfork | **Bridgehampton** | - |

Todd Jacobs

| Z Atlantica | **Long Bch** | 20 |

Paul LaBue

| NEW Navy Beach | **Montauk** | 19 |

Richard Lanza

| NEW Farmhouse | **Greenport** | 26 |

Eric Lomando

| Z Kitchen A Bistro | **St. James** | 27 |
| Z Kitchen A Tratt. | **St. James** | 28 |

Keith Luce

| Z Luce & Hawkins | **Jamesport** | 25 |

Michael Maroni

| Z Maroni Cuisine | **Northport** | 28 |

Michael Meehan

| H2O Seafood | **Smithtown** | 23 |

Todd Mitgang

| NEW South Edison | **Montauk** | 22 |

Kent Monkan

| Brass Rail | **Locust Valley** | 25 |

Guy Reuge

| Mirabelle, Rest. | **Stony Brook** | 25 |
| Mirabelle Tavern | **Stony Brook** | 21 |

Rosa Ross

| Scrimshaw | **Greenport** | 23 |

Tom Schaudel

| A Mano | **Mattituck** | 24 |
| Z Coolfish | **Syosset** | 24 |

Sam Talbot

| Surf Lodge | **Montauk** | 19 |

Laurent Tourondel

| NEW LT Burger | **Sag Harbor** | 16 |

CHILD-FRIENDLY

(Alternatives to the usual fast-food places; * children's menu available)

Albert's Mandarin	**Huntington**	20
Angelina's	**E Norwich**	23
Argyle Grill*	**Babylon**	22
Ayhan's Fish*	**Port Washington**	19
Ayhan's Shish*	**multi.**	18
Babylon Carriage*	**Babylon**	21
Baby Moon	**Westhampton Bch**	18
Baja Fresh*	**New Hyde Pk**	18
Baja Grill*	**multi.**	18
Bella Vita Grill*	**St. James**	21
Bellport	**Bellport**	22
Benihana*	**multi.**	19
Big Daddy's*	**Massapequa**	24
Bigelow's*	**Rockville Ctr**	24
Bliss*	**E Setauket**	22

Boccaccio | **Hicksville**	21	Green Cactus | **multi.**	20
Bonsai | **Port Washington**	22	Grimaldi's | **Garden City**	23
Bostwick's | **E Hampton**	20	Hampton Chutney* |	22
Boulder Creek* | **multi.**	-	**Amagansett**	
Bozena Polish* | **Lindenhurst**	23	Hellenic Snack | **E Marion**	20
Bridgehampton Candy |	15	House of Dosas | **Hicksville**	25
Bridgehampton		Il Capuccino* | **Sag Harbor**	19
⚡ Butera's* | **Woodbury**	21	Indian Cove* | **Hampton Bays**	18
Butterfields* | **Hauppauge**	20	Jamesport Country* | **Jamesport**	23
⚡ Cafe Baci* | **Westbury**	22	Jolly Fisherman* | **Roslyn**	21
Cafe La Strada | **Hauppauge**	23	Kiran Palace | **Hicksville**	24
Cafe Rustica | **Great Neck**	22	Kiss'o | **New Hyde Pk**	21
Cafe Toscano | **Massapequa**	21	Kurofune | **Commack**	23
Caffe Laguna | **Long Bch**	19	La Bussola | **Glen Cove**	23
Canterbury* | **Oyster Bay**	19	La Famiglia | **Smithtown**	22
Capriccio | **Hicksville**	24	Laguna Grille* | **Woodbury**	20
Carousel* | **Great Neck**	21	⚡ La Parma | **multi.**	23
Carrabba's* | **Smithtown**	19	La Parmigiana | **Southampton**	22
Casa Luis | **Smithtown**	22	La Pizzetta | **E Norwich**	21
⚡ Cheesecake | **Westbury**	20	Legal Sea Foods* | **multi.**	20
Chefs of NY | **E Northport**	19	Lobster Roll* | **Amagansett**	19
Churrasq. Bairrada | **Mineola**	25	Lobster Roll N.* | **Baiting Hollow**	20
Cirella's* | **Huntington Station**	21	Lombardi's/Sound* |	21
Cooperage Inn* | **Baiting Hollow**	22	**Port Jefferson**	
⚡ Country House | **Stony Brook**	23	Los Compadres |	23
Crossroads Cafe* | **E Northport**	22	**Huntington Station**	
Curry Club* | **E Setauket**	20	Louie's Oyster* | **Port Washington**	17
DiMaggio's* | **Port Washington**	19	Lucy's Café | **Babylon**	25
Dodici* | **Rockville Ctr**	24	Mamma Lombardi's* | **Holbrook**	23
Duke Falcon's | **Long Bch**	22	⚡ Matteo's | **multi.**	23
Eddie's Pizza | **New Hyde Pk**	21	Maureen's Kitchen | **Smithtown**	25
Emilio's* | **Commack**	23	Med. Snack | **Huntington**	22
Estia's Kitchen | **Sag Harbor**	23	Meritage | **Bellport**	25
Frank's Steaks | **multi.**	21	Mim's* | **multi.**	20
Frederick's | **Melville**	23	Minado | **Carle Pl**	21
Galleria Dominick* | **Westbury**	26	Mirabelle, Rest.* | **Stony Brook**	25
George Martin's Grill* |	20	Modern Snack* | **Aquebogue**	18
Rockville Ctr		⚡ Nagahama | **Long Bch**	28
Golden Pear* | **multi.**	18	Nagashima | **Jericho**	24
Goldmine Mex. | **Greenlawn**	21	Nautilus Cafe* | **Freeport**	24
Gonzalo's* | **Glen Cove**	21	Nicholas James* | **Merrick**	22
Gosman's Dock* | **Montauk**	19	Nick's | **Rockville Ctr**	23
Graffiti* | **Woodbury**	20	Oaxaca Mexican | **Huntington**	23

O'Mally's*	Southold	18
Orchid	Garden City	23
O's Food*	St. James	22
Ozumo*	Bethpage	23
Pace's Steak*	multi.	22
Page One*	Glen Cove	22
Painters'*	Brookhaven Hamlet	20
Pancho's*	multi.	19
Pasta-eria	Hicksville	23
Pentimento	Stony Brook	22
Per Un Angelo	Wantagh	22
Pier 95	Freeport	24
Pita House	Patchogue	22
Poco Loco*	Roslyn	17
Pomodorino*	multi.	19
Post Stop*	Westhampton Bch	17
Pumpernickels*	Northport	21
Rangmahal	Hicksville	23
Red Fish*	Plainview	23
Rein*	Garden City	23
Rist. Gemelli*	Babylon	24
☑ Riverbay	Williston Pk	23
RS Jones	Merrick	22
Salamander's	Greenport	24
Salsa Salsa*	multi.	23
Sam's*	E Hampton	18
Sapporo*	Wantagh	23
Seeda Thai	Valley Stream	23
Shiki*	Babylon	24
Shogi	Westbury	25
☑ Siam Lotus	Bay Shore	28
☑ Smokin' Al's*	Bay Shore	23
☑ Snaps*	Wantagh	26
Solé*	Oceanside	26
Spare Rib*	Commack	18
Spicy's BBQ*	multi.	20
Star Confectionery	Riverhead	22
Steve's Piccola	Westbury	24
Sundried Tomato*	Nesconset	21
Sushi Ya*	Garden City	21
Taiko	Rockville Ctr	24
Tai-Show*	Massapequa	23

Tesoro	Westbury	23
Thai Gourmet	Port Jefferson Station	26
Thai Table	Rockville Ctr	23
34 New St.*	Huntington	18
Thomas's Eggery*	Carle Pl	22
Thom Thom*	Wantagh	20
Thyme*	Roslyn	21
Turtle Crossing*	E Hampton	22
Tutto Pazzo*	Huntington	20
Umberto's	New Hyde Pk	22
Uncle Dai	Glen Cove	18
Venere*	Westbury	20
Villa D'Este	Floral Pk	22
Voila!	St. James	24
World Pie	Bridgehampton	19

DANCING

NEW Arthur Ave.	Smithtown	–
Bellport	Bellport	22
Black & Blue	Huntington	22
Blue	Blue Pt	22
Brian Scotts	Miller Pl	19
Butterfields	Hauppauge	20
E. B. Elliot's	Freeport	18
56th Fighter	Farmingdale	16
Hudson/McCoy	Freeport	18
Island Mermaid	Ocean Beach	20
Oakland's/Sunday	Hampton Bays	18
Oar Steak	Patchogue	21
Phao Thai	Sag Harbor	21
NEW Prime Catch	Rockville Ctr	–
NEW Puglia's/Garden City	Garden City	–
Sea Grille	Montauk	21
75 Main	Southampton	18
Snapper Inn	Oakdale	18
NEW Stone Turtle	Island Pk	21
NEW Sugar	Carle Pl	–
Trata	Roslyn	22
Tulip Bar & Grill	Great Neck	19
View	Oakdale	22

DELIVERY/TAKEOUT

(D=delivery, T=takeout)

Albert's Mandarin | T | **Huntington**	20
Angelina's | T | **multi.**	23
Ayhan's Shish | D, T | **Port Washington**	18
Baby Moon | T | **Westhampton Bch**	18
Baja Grill | T | **multi.**	18
Bella Vita Grill | T | **St. James**	21
Big Daddy's | T | **Massapequa**	24
Bigelow's | T | **Rockville Ctr**	24
Bliss | T | **E Setauket**	22
Blond | T | **Miller Pl**	21
Bonbori Tiki | T | **Huntington**	20
Bonsai | D, T | **Port Washington**	22
Bridgehampton Candy | T | **Bridgehampton**	15
Brio | D | **Port Washington**	21
Buckram Stables | T | **Locust Valley**	19
☑ Butera's | T | **Woodbury**	21
Cafe La Strada | T | **Hauppauge**	23
Cafe Toscano | T | **Massapequa**	21
Caffe Laguna | D | **Long Bch**	19
Chicken Kebab | T | **Roslyn Hts**	21
Churrasq. Bairrada | D, T | **Mineola**	25
Cirella's | T | **multi.**	21
Clam Bar | T | **Amagansett**	21
Curry Club | T | **E Setauket**	20
Cyril's Fish | T | **Amagansett**	18
DiMaggio's | T | **Port Washington**	19
Duryea's Lobster | T | **Montauk**	22
Dynasty/Pt. Wash. | D | **Port Washington**	20
Eddie's Pizza | T | **New Hyde Pk**	21
Emilio's | T | **Commack**	23
Fortune Wheel | T | **Levittown**	22
Frederick's | T | **Melville**	23
Fresco Crêperie | T | **Long Bch**	23
Galangal | T | **Syosset**	23
Golden Pear | D, T | **multi.**	18
Goldmine Mex. | T | **Greenlawn**	21
Gonzalo's | D, T | **Glen Cove**	21
Green Cactus | T | **multi.**	20
Grimaldi's | T | **Garden City**	23
Hampton Chutney | T | **Amagansett**	22
Hampton Coffee | T | **Water Mill**	19
Hellenic Snack | T | **E Marion**	20
Hinata | D | **Great Neck**	23
Iavarone Cafe | D | **New Hyde Pk**	21
Intermezzo | D | **Ft Salonga**	23
Kawasaki Steak | D | **Long Bch**	19
Kiran Palace | D, T | **Hicksville**	24
Kiss'o | T | **New Hyde Pk**	21
Kurabarn | T | **Huntington**	24
Kurofune | T | **Commack**	23
Laguna Grille | T | **Woodbury**	20
☑ La Parma | T | **multi.**	23
La Parmigiana | T | **Southampton**	22
La Pizzetta | T | **E Norwich**	21
La Viola | D | **Cedarhurst**	20
Lemonleaf Grill | D | **Hicksville**	22
Lemonleaf Thai | D | **Carle Pl**	20
Lobster Inn | T | **Southampton**	19
Lobster Roll | T | **Amagansett**	19
Lobster Roll N. | T | **Baiting Hollow**	20
Lombardi's/Sound | T | **Port Jefferson**	21
Long River | T | **Kings Park**	21
Los Compadres | T | **Huntington Station**	23
Lucy's Café | T | **Babylon**	25
☑ Maroni Cuisine | T | **Northport**	28
Matsuya | D | **Great Neck**	21
☑ Matteo's | T | **multi.**	23
Maureen's Kitchen | T | **Smithtown**	25
Med. Snack | T | **Huntington**	22
Mim's | T | **multi.**	20
Minami | T | **Massapequa**	26
Modern Snack | T | **Aquebogue**	18
Mother Kelly's | D | **Cedarhurst**	21
☑ Nagahama | D, T | **Long Bch**	28
Nagashima | T | **Jericho**	24

Nautilus Cafe	T	**Freeport**	24
Nicholas James	T	**Merrick**	22
Nick's	T	**Rockville Ctr**	23
O'Mally's	T	**Southold**	18
Onzon Thai	T	**Bellmore**	24
Orchid	T	**Garden City**	23
O's Food	T	**St. James**	22
Ozumo	T	**Bethpage**	23
Pace's Steak	T	**multi.**	22
Pancho's	T	**multi.**	19
Pasta-eria	T	**Hicksville**	23
Pasta Pasta	T	**Port Jefferson**	25
Pearl East	D, T	**Manhasset**	23
Pita House	T	**Patchogue**	22
Pomodorino	T	**multi.**	19
Post Stop	T	**Westhampton Bch**	17
Pumpernickels	T	**Northport**	21
Rangmahal	D, T	**Hicksville**	23
Ravagh	D, T	**Roslyn Hts**	22
Red Fish	T	**Plainview**	23
Rowdy Hall	T	**E Hampton**	20
RS Jones	T	**Merrick**	22
Salamander's	T	**Greenport**	24
Salsa Salsa	T	**multi.**	23
Sam's	T	**E Hampton**	18
🔣 San Marco	T	**Hauppauge**	26
Sant Ambroeus	T	**Southampton**	24
Sapporo	T	**Wantagh**	23
Sarin Thai	T	**Greenvale**	24
Seeda Thai	T	**Valley Stream**	23
Shagwong	T	**Montauk**	18
Shogi	T	**Westbury**	25
Show Win	D, T	**Northport**	20
🔣 Siam Lotus	T	**Bay Shore**	28
Silver's	T	**Southampton**	23
🔣 Smokin' Al's	T	**Bay Shore**	23
🔣 Snaps	T	**Wantagh**	26
Southampton Publick	T	**Southampton**	18
Southside Fish	T	**Lindenhurst**	20
Spicy's BBQ	D, T	**multi.**	20
Star Confectionary	T	**Riverhead**	22
Suki Zuki	T	**Water Mill**	24

Sushi Ya	T	**Garden City**	21
Taiko	T	**Rockville Ctr**	24
Tai-Show	T	**multi.**	23
Tesoro	T	**Westbury**	23
Thai Gourmet	T	**Port Jefferson Station**	26
Thai Green Leaf	D, T	**E Northport**	21
Thai Table	T	**Rockville Ctr**	23
Thai USA	T	**Huntington**	23
34 New St.	D, T	**Huntington**	18
Thomas's Eggery	T	**Carle Pl**	22
Thom Thom	T	**Wantagh**	20
Thyme	T	**Roslyn**	21
Tokyo	T	**E Northport**	24
Tony's	D	**E Quogue**	19
Tratt. Di Meo	T	**Roslyn Hts**	21
Turtle Crossing	T	**E Hampton**	22
Tutto Pazzo	T	**Huntington**	20
Umberto's	T	**New Hyde Pk**	22
Uncle Dai	D, T	**Glen Cove**	18
Venere	T	**Westbury**	20
Wild Ginger	D, T	**Great Neck**	21
World Pie	T	**Bridgehampton**	19
Yamaguchi	T	**Port Washington**	25

DINING ALONE

(Other than hotels and places with counter service)

Babette's	**E Hampton**	20
🔣 Ben's Deli	**multi.**	19
Bliss	**E Setauket**	22
Bridgehampton Candy	**Bridgehampton**	15
🔣 Coolfish	**Syosset**	24
Estia's Kitchen	**Sag Harbor**	23
Frisky Oyster	**Greenport**	25
Golden Pear	**multi.**	18
Graffiti	**Woodbury**	20
Hampton Chutney	**Amagansett**	22
Lobster Roll N.	**Baiting Hollow**	20
Panini Café	**Roslyn**	23
Salamander's	**Greenport**	24
Sen	**Sag Harbor**	21

Show Win	**Northport** 20	Toku	**Manhasset** 25
Star Confectionery	**Riverhead** 22	Trata	**Roslyn** 22
Sushi Ya	**Garden City** 21	Tula Kitchen	**Bay Shore** 24
Tava	**Port Washington** 18	Tweeds	**Riverhead** 21
Townline	**Sagaponack** 19	Two Steak/Sushi	24
Vine Wine Bar	**Greenport** 22	**New Hyde Pk**
	View	**Oakdale** 22
	Wave	**Port Jefferson** 19

DRAMATIC INTERIORS

American Hotel | **Sag Harbor** 25

Atlantica | **Long Bch** 20

Chi | **Westbury** 25

City Cellar | **Westbury** 21

Claudio's | **Greenport** 16

Country House | **Stony Brook** 23

Dao | **Huntington** 23

E. B. Elliot's | **Freeport** 18

56th Fighter | **Farmingdale** 16

Fisherman's Catch | **Point Lookout** 20

Four Food Studio | **Melville** 21

Garden Grill | **Smithtown** 21

Honu | **Huntington** 22

Jamesport Manor | **Jamesport** 23

Library Cafe | **Farmingdale** 18

Limani | **Roslyn** 26

Luce & Hawkins | **Jamesport** 25

Ludlow Bistro | **Deer Park** 24

Milleridge Inn | **Jericho** 16

Mumon | **Garden City** 22

Nanking | **New Hyde Pk** 19

Nisen | **multi.** 25

Nonnina | **W Islip** 25

Novitá | **Garden City** 23

Palm Court | **E Meadow** 24

Porto Vivo | **Huntington** 22

Ram's Head | **Shelter Is** 20

Café Red/Rest. | **Huntington** 25

Rist. Gemelli | **Babylon** 24

Robert's | **Water Mill** 25

1770 House | **E Hampton** 25

Taste 99 | **Farmingdale** 18

Tellers | **Islip** 26

Thom Thom | **Wantagh** 20

ENTERTAINMENT

(Call for days and times of performances)

Babette's | jazz | **E Hampton** 20

Backyard | DJ | **Montauk** 23

Bayou | bands | **N Bellmore** 23

Big Daddy's | live music | 24
Massapequa

NEW Bistro 25 | acoustic ─
guitar | **Sayville**

Blackbirds' Grille | live music | 20
Sayville

Blond | jazz | **Miller Pl** 21

Blue | DJ/live music | **Blue Pt** 22

Bulldog Grille | rock bands | ─
Amityville

Cafe Symposio | piano | **Bellmore** 18

Capriccio | piano | **Hicksville** 24

Chequit Inn | rock | 19
Shelter Is Hts

Ciao Baby | vocals | **multi.** 20

Coolfish | varies | **Syosset** 24

Curry Club | varies | **E Setauket** 20

Dockers Waterside | varies | 20
E Quogue

E. Hampton Pt. | reggae | 19
E Hampton

E. B. Elliot's | karaoke | **Freeport** 18

fatfish | acoustic rock | 21
Bay Shore

Fishery | varies | **E Rockaway** 19

Galleria Dominick | piano | 26
Westbury

Gosman's Dock | jazz | 19
Montauk

Grasso's | jazz | **Cold Spring** 24

Grey Horse	live music	**Bayport**	23
Grill Room	live music	**Hauppauge**	21
H2O Seafood	live music	**Smithtown**	23
Hudson/McCoy	live music	**Freeport**	18
Indian Cove	live music	**Hampton Bays**	18
Irish Coffee	Irish folk/piano	**E Islip**	23
NEW Jack Halyards	live music	**Oyster Bay**	23
Kabul Afghani	belly dancing	**Huntington**	23
La Coquille	harpist	**Manhasset**	24
Library Cafe	varies	**Farmingdale**	18
Lobster Roll N.	guitar	**Baiting Hollow**	20
Lombardi's/Sound	varies	**Port Jefferson**	21
Milleridge Inn	piano	**Jericho**	16
Mill Pond House	piano	**Centerport**	25
Nisen	DJ; varies	**Woodbury**	25
Oakland's/Sunday	varies	**Hampton Bays**	18
Oar Steak	varies	**Patchogue**	21
Pace's Steak	live music	**Port Jefferson**	22
Paddy McGees	DJ	**Island Pk**	18
Painters'	bands	**Brookhaven Hamlet**	20
☑ Palm Court	varies	**E Meadow**	24
Patio/54 Main	varies	**Westhampton Bch**	19
Per Un Angelo	varies	**Wantagh**	22
☑ Piccolo	piano	**Huntington**	27
Pierre's	jazz	**Bridgehampton**	21
Pollo Rico	guitar/harp	**Centereach**	20
Post Office	live music	**Babylon**	19
Ram's Head	jazz	**Shelter Is**	20

RS Jones	varies	**Merrick**	22
Sea Grille	DJ/karaoke	**Montauk**	21
Snapper Inn	piano	**Oakdale**	18
Southampton Publick	DJ	**Southampton**	18
Swingbelly's	acoustic	**Long Bch**	23
Taste 99	varies	**Farmingdale**	18
Tava	guitar/piano	**Port Washington**	18
Tide Runners	bands	**Hampton Bays**	16
Tulip Bar & Grill	belly dancing/live music	**Great Neck**	19
Turtle Crossing	jazz	**E Hampton**	22
Tweeds	piano	**Riverhead**	21
21 Main	varies	**W Sayville**	23
View	bands	**Oakdale**	22
Village Lanterne	folk	**Lindenhurst**	25
Walk St.	live band	**Garden City**	21

FAMILY-STYLE

Albert's Mandarin	**Huntington**	20
Benny's	**Westbury**	25
Buckram Stables	**Locust Valley**	19
☑ Butera's	**Sayville**	21
Cafe Toscano	**Massapequa**	21
Capriccio	**Hicksville**	24
Ciao Baby	**multi.**	20
Dynasty/Pt. Wash.	**Port Washington**	20
Fanatico	**Jericho**	20
NEW George Martin's Steak	**Great River**	-
☑ Harvest	**Montauk**	26
NEW Imperial Seoul	**New Hyde Pk**	-
La Famiglia	**multi.**	22
☑ La Parma	**multi.**	23
La Parmigiana	**Southampton**	22
La Viola	**Cedarhurst**	20
Mamma Lombardi's	**Holbrook**	23

NEW Marco Polo's | **Westbury** ⌐⌐

☑ Matteo's | **multi.** 23

Montebello | **Port Washington** 21

Nick's | **Rockville Ctr** 23

P.F. Chang's | **Westbury** 20

Piccola Bussola | **multi.** 23

Porto Vivo | **Huntington** 22

Steve's Piccola | **multi.** 24

NEW 388 Rest. | **Roslyn Hts** 20

FIREPLACES

Absolutely Mario | **Farmingdale** 20

Amarelle | **Wading River** 25

☑ American Hotel | **Sag Harbor** 25

Angelina's | **Syosset** 23

Babylon Carriage | **Babylon** 21

Baby Moon | **Westhampton Bch** 18

☑ Barney's | **Locust Valley** 26

Basil Leaf | **Locust Valley** 21

Bayview Inn | **S Jamesport** 22

Bellport | **Bellport** 22

Bertucci's | **Hauppauge** 17

Birchwood | **Riverhead** 20

NEW Bistro 72 | **Riverhead** ⌐

Blackbirds' Grille | **Sayville** 20

☑ Blackstone Steak | **Melville** 24

Blackwells | **Wading River** 23

Blue | **Blue Pt** 22

NEW Boathouse | **E Hampton** 19

Bob's Place | **Floral Pk** 21

Brasserie 214 | **New Hyde Pk** 20

Brooks & Porter | **Merrick** 22

☑ Bryant & Cooper | **Roslyn** 26

Buccaneer Crab | **Freeport** 23

Burton & Doyle | **Great Neck** 24

Cafe Havana | **Smithtown** 18

Casa Rustica | **Smithtown** 25

Chalet Rest. | **Roslyn** 18

Chequit Inn | **Shelter Is Hts** 19

Cielo Rist. | **Rockville Ctr** 20

Circa | **Mineola** 22

Cooperage Inn | **Baiting Hollow** 22

☑ Country House | **Stony Brook** 23

Cozymel's Mex. | **Westbury** 17

Crossroads Cafe | **E Northport** 22

Cuvée | **Greenport** 22

NEW Dark Horse | **Riverhead** ⌐

NEW Deco 1600 | **Plainview** ⌐

☑ Della Femina | **E Hampton** 24

E. B. Elliot's | **Freeport** 18

Famous Dave's | **multi.** 19

56th Fighter | **Farmingdale** 16

Fisherman's Catch | **Point Lookout** 20

Franina | **Syosset** 26

Galleria Dominick | **Westbury** 26

Garden Grill | **Smithtown** 21

NEW George Martin's Steak |
   Great River ⌐

NEW Harbor Mist | **Cold Spring** 19

Heart of Portugal | **Mineola** 20

Hemingway's | **Wantagh** 19

Honu | **Huntington** 22

Horace/Sylvia's | **Babylon** 20

H.R. Singleton's | **Bethpage** 18

Hudson/McCoy | **Freeport** 18

Il Classico | **Massapequa Pk** 23

Irish Coffee | **E Islip** 23

☑ Jamesport Manor | **Jamesport** 23

Jimmy Hays | **Island Pk** 25

Jolly Fisherman | **Roslyn** 21

Jonathan's | **Garden City Pk** 20

☑ Lake House | **Bay Shore** 28

La Pace/Chef Michael |
   Glen Cove 25

Legends | **New Suffolk** 23

Living Room | **E Hampton** 25

Lobster Roll N. | **Baiting Hollow** 20

☑ Luce & Hawkins | **Jamesport** 25

Maguire's | **Ocean Beach** 19

Majors Steak | **multi.** 19

Mamma Lombardi's | **Holbrook** 23

Mario | **Hauppauge** 25

Milk & Sugar Café | **Bay Shore** 21

Mill Creek | **Bayville** 21

Milleridge Inn | **Jericho** 16

Mirabelle, Rest. | **Stony Brook** 25

Mirabelle Tavern | **Stony Brook**	21
Z Mirko's | **Water Mill**	26
Nello Summertimes | **Southampton**	16
Nichol's | **E Hampton**	17
Nonnina | **W Islip**	25
Z North Fork Table | **Southold**	29
Oak Chalet | **Bellmore**	19
Old Mill Inn | **Mattituck**	20
1 North Steak | **Hampton Bays**	22
O's Food | **St. James**	22
Osteria Toscana | **Huntington**	23
Z Palm | **E Hampton**	26
Z Palm Court | **E Meadow**	24
Panama Hatties | **Huntington Station**	25
Papa Razzi | **Westbury**	18
Per Un Angelo | **Wantagh**	22
Piccolo's | **Mineola**	24
Pierre's | **Bridgehampton**	21
Z Plaza Cafe | **Southampton**	26
Porto Bello | **Greenport**	22
Post Office | **Babylon**	19
Z Prime | **Huntington**	23
NEW Puglia's/Garden City | **Garden City**	–
NEW Race Lane | **E Hampton**	19
Ram's Head | **Shelter Is**	20
Rein | **Garden City**	23
Restaurant/The Inn | **Quogue**	21
Rist. Gemelli | **Babylon**	24
Robert's | **Water Mill**	25
Z Rothmann's | **E Norwich**	25
Rowdy Hall | **E Hampton**	20
Runyon's | **Seaford**	18
Z 1770 House | **E Hampton**	25
Seventh St. Cafe | **Garden City**	20
Snapper Inn | **Oakdale**	18
Spare Rib | **Hicksville**	18
Z Starr Boggs | **Westhampton Bch**	26
Z Stone Creek | **E Quogue**	26
NEW Stone Turtle | **Island Pk**	21

Sullivan's Quay | **Port Washington**	18
Surfside Inn | **Montauk**	18
Taste 99 | **Farmingdale**	18
Tesoro | **Westbury**	23
NEW 388 Rest. | **Roslyn Hts**	20
Thyme | **Roslyn**	21
Tratt. Di Meo | **Roslyn Hts**	21
Z Trumpets | **Eastport**	22
Tutto Il Giorno | **Sag Harbor**	25
Tutto Pazzo | **Huntington**	20
Tweeds | **Riverhead**	21
21 Main | **W Sayville**	23
Umberto's | **New Hyde Pk**	22
Venere | **Westbury**	20
View | **Oakdale**	22
Vintage Prime | **St. James**	25
Wall's Wharf | **Bayville**	17

GREEN/LOCAL/ORGANIC

A Mano | **Mattituck**	24
Amarelle | **Wading River**	25
Z Atlantica | **Long Bch**	20
Babette's | **E Hampton**	20
Backyard | **Montauk**	23
NEW Bistro 72 | **Riverhead**	–
NEW Bistro 25 | **Sayville**	–
Coast Grill | **Southampton**	22
NEW Comtesse Thérèse | **Aquebogue**	–
Cuvée | **Greenport**	22
Z Dave's Grill | **Montauk**	27
Dish | **Water Mill**	27
Farm Country Kit. | **Riverhead**	23
NEW Farmhouse | **Greenport**	26
Fifth Season | **Port Jefferson**	26
Gosman's Dock | **Montauk**	19
Grey Horse | **Bayport**	23
Inlet Seafood | **Montauk**	21
Jamesport Country | **Jamesport**	23
Z Jamesport Manor | **Jamesport**	23
Living Room | **E Hampton**	25
Love Ln. Kitchen | **Mattituck**	23

Z Luce & Hawkins | **Jamesport** 25

Michael Anthony's | 24
  Wading River

Z Mirko's | **Water Mill** 26

Z Nick & Toni's | **E Hampton** 24

Z Noah's | **Greenport** 26

Z North Fork Table | **Southold** 29

Old Mill Inn | **Mattituck** 20

1 North Steak | **Hampton Bays** 22

Planet Bliss | **Shelter Is** 20

Scrimshaw | **Greenport** 23

NEW South Edison | **Montauk** 22

NEW Southfork | **Bridgehampton** -

Z Starr Boggs | 26
  Westhampton Bch

Vine Street | **Shelter Is** 25

Vine Wine Bar | **Greenport** 22

HISTORIC PLACES

(Year opened; * building)

1647 | Nello Summertimes* | 16
  Southampton

1663 | 1770 House* | 25
  E Hampton

1672 | Milleridge Inn* | **Jericho** 16

1699 | Palm* | **E Hampton** 26

1700 | Living Room* | **E Hampton** 25

1710 | Country House* | 23
  Stony Brook

1751 | Mirabelle, Rest.* | 25
  Stony Brook

1785 | Restaurant/The Inn* | 21
  Quogue

1821 | Old Mill Inn* | **Mattituck** 20

1824 | Brian Scotts* | **Miller Pl** 19

1826 | Garden Grill* | **Smithtown** 21

1842 | Chalet Rest.* | **Roslyn** 18

1846 | American Hotel* | 25
  Sag Harbor

1850 | Bistro 44* | **Northport** 23

1850 | Farm Country Kit.* | 23
  Riverhead

1857 | Inn Spot/Bay* | 19
  Hampton Bays

1863 | Luce & Hawkins* | 25
  Jamesport

1865 | Babylon Carriage* | 21
  Babylon

1870 | Claudio's | **Greenport** 16

1872 | Chequit Inn* | 19
  Shelter Is Hts

1888 | View* | **Oakdale** 22

1891 | 21 Main* | **W Sayville** 23

1896 | Tweeds* | **Riverhead** 21

1898 | Ayhan's Fish* | 19
  Port Washington

1900 | Brasserie 214* | 20
  New Hyde Pk

1900 | O's Food* | **St. James** 22

1900 | Porters* | **Bellport** 20

1902 | Silver's* | **Southampton** 23

1902 | Wild Honey* | 25
  Oyster Bay

1903 | Spicy's BBQ* | **Riverhead** 20

1904 | La Marmite* | 24
  Williston Pk

1905 | Louie's Oyster | 17
  Port Washington

1906 | Mill Pond House* | 25
  Centerport

1907 | Main St. Bakery* | -
  Port Washington

1907 | Rothmann's* | **E Norwich** 25

1910 | Ariana* | **Huntington** 20

1911 | Star Confectionery* | 22
  Riverhead

1914 | Post Stop* | 17
  Westhampton Bch

1915 | Duryea's Lobster* | 22
  Montauk

1920 | Alexandros* | 23
  Mount Sinai

1920 | Ayhan's Shish* | 18
  Port Washington

1920 | Second House* | **Montauk** 19

1926 | Bridgehampton Candy | 15
  Bridgehampton

1926 | Tellers* | **Islip** 26

1927 | Hildebrandt's | **Williston Pk** _19_

1927 | Shagwong* | **Montauk** _18_

1928 | Post Office* | **Babylon** _19_

1929 | Backyard* | **Montauk** _23_

1929 | Birchwood* | **Riverhead** _20_

1929 | Gulf Coast* | **Montauk** _21_

1929 | Jimmy Hays | **Island Pk** _25_

1929 | Ram's Head* | **Shelter Is** _20_

1929 | Snapper Inn | **Oakdale** _18_

1930 | Meritage* | **Bellport** _25_

1934 | Southside Fish | **Lindenhurst** _20_

1935 | red bar* | **Southampton** _22_

1936 | Maguire's | **Ocean Beach** _19_

1937 | Blue Moon* | **Rockville Ctr** _20_

1938 | Declan Quinn's* | **Bay Shore** _19_

1939 | Bigelow's | **Rockville Ctr** _24_

1941 | Eddie's Pizza | **New Hyde Pk** _21_

1943 | Gosman's Dock | **Montauk** _19_

1944 | Koenig's | **Floral Pk** _19_

1945 | Fulton Prime | **Syosset** _23_

1945 | Wall's Wharf | **Bayville** _17_

1946 | Thomas's Eggery | **Carle Pl** _22_

1947 | Sam's | **E Hampton** _18_

1950 | Harbor Bistro/Grill* | **E Hampton** _21_

1950 | Modern Snack | **Aquebogue** _18_

1950 | 1 North Steak* | **Hampton Bays** _22_

1950 | Pier 95* | **Freeport** _24_

1955 | Carnival | **Port Jefferson Station** _22_

1956 | Dockers Waterside* | **E Quogue** _20_

1956 | Dockside B&G* | **Sag Harbor** _21_

1957 | Jolly Fisherman | **Roslyn** _21_

1958 | Cliff's | **Jamesport** _22_

1960 | Peter Luger | **Great Neck** _27_

1960 | Stella Ristorante | **Floral Pk** _24_

1961 | Arturo's | **Floral Pk** _22_

HOLIDAY MEALS

(Special prix fixe meals offered at major holidays)

Benihana | **Manhasset** _19_

Z Country House | **Stony Brook** _23_

Milleridge Inn | **Jericho** _16_

Ram's Head | **Shelter Is** _20_

HOTEL DINING

Allegria Hotel

Z Atlantica | **Long Bch** _20_

American Hotel, The

Z American Hotel | **Sag Harbor** _25_

Andrew Hotel

Colbeh | **Great Neck** _21_

Bayview Inn

Bayview Inn | **S Jamesport** _22_

Chequit Inn

Chequit Inn | **Shelter Is Hts** _19_

c/o The Maidstone

Living Room | **E Hampton** _25_

Days Inn

NEW Blue Fish | **Hicksville** _–_

Garden City Hotel

Rein | **Garden City** _23_

Gurney's Inn

Sea Grille | **Montauk** _21_

Hotel Indigo

NEW Bistro 72 | **Riverhead** _–_

Housers Hotel, Fire Island

Hideaway | **Ocean Beach** _19_

Huntting Inn

Z Palm | **E Hampton** _26_

Inn at East Wind

Desmond's | **Wading River** _20_

Inn at New Hyde Park

Brasserie 214 | **New Hyde Pk** _20_

Inn at Quogue, The

Restaurant/The Inn | **Quogue** _21_

Jedediah Hawkins Inn		
ⓩ Luce & Hawkins | **Jamesport**		25
Jones Beach Hotel		
Per Un Angelo | **Wantagh**		22
Kenny's Tipperary Inn		
Manucci's | **Montauk**		19
Montauk Yacht Club Resort		
Gulf Coast | **Montauk**		21
Nello Summertimes		
Nello Summertimes | **Southampton**		16
North Fork Table & Inn		
ⓩ North Fork Table | **Southold**		29
Portly Grape Inn		
NEW Portly Grape | **Greenport**		-
Ram's Head Inn		
Ram's Head | **Shelter Is**		20
1770 House		
ⓩ 1770 House | **E Hampton**		25
Solé East		
Backyard | **Montauk**		23
Stone Lion Inn		
East by Northeast | **Montauk**		21
Sunset Beach Hotel		
Sunset Beach | **Shelter Is Hts**		18
Surf Lodge		
Surf Lodge | **Montauk**		19
Surfside Inn		
Surfside Inn | **Montauk**		18
Three Village Inn		
Mirabelle, Rest. | **Stony Brook**		25
Mirabelle Tavern | **Stony Brook**		21
Viana Hotel & Spa		
NEW Marco Polo's | **Westbury**		-

LATE DINING

(Weekday closing hour)

NEW Arthur Ave. | varies | **Smithtown**		-
Bin 56 | 12 AM | **Huntington**		24
Bulldog Grille | 12 AM | **Amityville**		-
Carnival | 12 AM | **Port Jefferson Station**		22
Chalet Rest. | 12 AM | **Roslyn**		18
Copa Wine | 11:30 PM | **Bridgehampton**		20
E. B. Elliot's | 4 AM | **Freeport**		18
Eddie's Pizza | varies | **New Hyde Pk**		21
Inn Spot/Bay | 12 AM | **Hampton Bays**		19
Library Cafe | 1 AM | **Farmingdale**		18
Maxwell's | varies | **Islip**		-
O'Mally's | 12 AM | **Southold**		18
O's Food | 12 AM | **St. James**		22
Philippe | 12 AM | **E Hampton**		24
Porto Vivo | 12 AM | **Huntington**		22
Post Office | varies | **Babylon**		19
NEW Serafina | 12 AM | **E Hampton**		18
75 Main | 12 AM | **Southampton**		18
Strawberry's | varies | **Huntington**		18
Swingbelly's | 12:30 AM | **Long Bch**		23
Trata | 12 AM | **Water Mill**		22
World Pie | 12 AM | **Bridgehampton**		19
NEW XO | varies | **Huntington**		-

LOCAL FAVORITES

Angelina's | **multi.**		23
Arturo's | **Floral Pk**		22
Azuma | **Greenlawn**		23
Bellport | **Bellport**		22
Benny's | **Westbury**		25
Bigelow's | **Rockville Ctr**		24
ⓩ Bistro Cassis | **Huntington**		24
B.K. Sweeney's | **Garden City**		18
Blackbirds' Grille | **Sayville**		20
Blue Moon | **Rockville Ctr**		20
Brass Rail | **Locust Valley**		25
Bravo Nader!/Fish | **Huntington**		24
Bridgehampton Candy | **Bridgehampton**		15

Broadway Beanery | **Lynbrook**	21
Buckram Stables | **Locust Valley**	19
Bulldog Grille | **Amityville**	-
Cafe Toscano | **Massapequa**	21
Canterbury | **Oyster Bay**	19
Ciao Baby | **Commack**	20
Cliff's | **multi.**	22
Coast Grill | **Southampton**	22
Cooperage Inn | **Baiting Hollow**	22
Crossroads Cafe | **E Northport**	22
Curry Club | **E Setauket**	20
☑ Dario's | **Rockville Ctr**	26
Da Ugo | **Rockville Ctr**	25
☑ Dave's Grill | **Montauk**	27
Duke Falcon's | **Long Bch**	22
Duryea's Lobster | **Montauk**	22
East by Northeast | **Montauk**	21
Eddie's Pizza | **New Hyde Pk**	21
Emilio's | **Commack**	23
Fork & Vine | **Glen Head**	23
Graffiti | **Woodbury**	20
Greenport Tea | **Greenport**	21
Hellenic Snack | **E Marion**	20
Hemingway's | **Wantagh**	19
Hildebrandt's | **Williston Pk**	19
Il Capuccino | **Sag Harbor**	19
Ivy Cottage | **Williston Pk**	23
Jamesport Country | **Jamesport**	23
Jimmy Hays | **Island Pk**	25
JT's Corner Cafe | **Nesconset**	23
☑ Kotobuki | **multi.**	27
La Parmigiana | **Southampton**	22
La Piazza | **multi.**	21
Legends | **New Suffolk**	23
Lobster Roll | **Amagansett**	19
Lobster Roll N. | **Baiting Hollow**	20
Love Ln. Kitchen | **Mattituck**	23
Ludlow Bistro | **Deer Park**	24
Maureen's Kitchen | **Smithtown**	25
Michaels'/Maidstone | **E Hampton**	18
Mill Creek | **Bayville**	21
Mim's | **multi.**	20

Modern Snack | **Aquebogue**	18
☑ Nagahama | **Long Bch**	28
Nichol's | **E Hampton**	17
Orchid | **Garden City**	23
Page One | **Glen Cove**	22
Panini Café | **Roslyn**	23
Pierre's | **Bridgehampton**	21
Rachel's Cafe | **Syosset**	22
red bar | **Southampton**	22
Rowdy Hall | **E Hampton**	20
Ruvo | **Port Jefferson**	22
Sage Bistro | **Bellmore**	24
Salsa Salsa | **Smithtown**	23
Salvatore's | **Port Washington**	25
Sam's | **E Hampton**	18
Sen | **Sag Harbor**	21
Shagwong | **Montauk**	18
☑ Siam Lotus | **Bay Shore**	28
Silver's | **Southampton**	23
☑ Smokin' Al's | **Bay Shore**	23
Southampton Publick | **Southampton**	18
Star Confectionery | **Riverhead**	22
Surfside Inn | **Montauk**	18
Taiko | **Rockville Ctr**	24
Tesoro | **Westbury**	23
Thai Gourmet | **Port Jefferson Station**	26
Thomas's Eggery | **Carle Pl**	22
Umberto's | **New Hyde Pk**	22
Varney's | **Brookhaven**	23
Wall's Wharf | **Bayville**	17
☑ West End | **Carle Pl**	25
Wild Honey | **Oyster Bay**	25

MEET FOR A DRINK

Amarelle | **Wading River**	25
☑ Atlantica | **Long Bch**	20
Babylon Carriage | **Babylon**	21
Backyard | **Montauk**	23
NEW Bar Frites | **Greenvale**	18
Bayou | **N Bellmore**	23
Bayview Inn | **S Jamesport**	22

Vote at ZAGAT.com

☑ Besito	**Huntington**	24	
Bin 56	**Huntington**	24	
Birchwood	**Riverhead**	20	
NEW Bistro 25	**Sayville**	-	
B.K. Sweeney's	**Garden City**	18	
☑ Blackstone Steak	**Melville**	24	
Blackwells	**Wading River**	23	
NEW Boathouse	**E Hampton**	19	
Bobby Van's	**Bridgehampton**	22	
Brass Rail	**Locust Valley**	25	
B.Smith's	**Sag Harbor**	18	
Bulldog Grille	**Amityville**	-	
Burton & Doyle	**Great Neck**	24	
Café Buenos Aires	**Huntington**	24	
Canterbury	**Oyster Bay**	19	
NEW Cedar Creek	**Glen Cove**	-	
Chalet Rest.	**Roslyn**	18	
Chi	**Westbury**	25	
Cipollini	**Manhasset**	21	
cittanuova	**E Hampton**	20	
City Cellar	**Westbury**	21	
Claudio's	**Greenport**	16	
Clubhouse	**Huntington**	21	
Coach Grill	**Oyster Bay**	22	
Coast Grill	**Southampton**	22	
☑ Coolfish	**Syosset**	24	
Copa Wine	**Bridgehampton**	20	
Cuvée	**Greenport**	22	
Cyril's Fish	**Amagansett**	18	
Dao	**Huntington**	23	
☑ E. Hampton Pt.	**E Hampton**	19	
E. B. Elliot's	**Freeport**	18	
fatfish	**Bay Shore**	21	
F.H. Riley's	**Huntington**	23	
Fishery	**E Rockaway**	19	
Fork & Vine	**Glen Head**	23	
George Martin's Grill	**Rockville Ctr**	20	
Grand Lux	**Garden City**	19	
Grey Horse	**Bayport**	23	
Hemingway's	**Wantagh**	19	
Hideaway	**Ocean Beach**	19	

Honu	**Huntington**	22	
Horace/Sylvia's	**Babylon**	20	
Houston's	**Garden City**	22	
Hudson/McCoy	**Freeport**	18	
Hunan Taste	**Greenvale**	22	
Indian Wells	**Amagansett**	17	
☑ La Piccola	**Port Washington**	27	
Legends	**New Suffolk**	23	
☑ Limani	**Roslyn**	26	
Lobster Inn	**Southampton**	19	
Mac's Steak	**Huntington**	23	
Maguire's	**Ocean Beach**	19	
Matthew's	**Ocean Beach**	22	
Maxwell's	**Islip**	-	
Mirabelle Tavern	**Stony Brook**	21	
☑ Morton's	**Great Neck**	25	
Muse	**Water Mill**	23	
NEW Navy Beach	**Montauk**	19	
Nello Summertimes	**Southampton**	16	
☑ Nick & Toni's	**E Hampton**	24	
Nick's Tuscan	**Long Bch**	21	
Nonnina	**W Islip**	25	
Novitá	**Garden City**	23	
Oasis Waterfront	**Sag Harbor**	24	
Old Mill Inn	**Mattituck**	20	
Painters'	**Brookhaven Hamlet**	20	
Philippe	**E Hampton**	24	
Pine Island	**Bayville**	18	
Porto Vivo	**Huntington**	22	
Post Office	**Babylon**	19	
☑ Prime	**Huntington**	23	
Public House 49	**Patchogue**	20	
NEW Race Lane	**E Hampton**	19	
Café Red/Rest.	**Huntington**	25	
Rein	**Garden City**	23	
Restaurant/The Inn	**Quogue**	21	
Rockwell's	**Smithtown**	22	
☑ Rothmann's	**E Norwich**	25	
Rowdy Hall	**E Hampton**	20	
NEW Sakaya	**Albertson**	-	
NEW Serafina	**E Hampton**	18	
NEW Sip City	**Great Neck**	-	

SPECIAL FEATURES

Southampton Publick | **Southampton**	18
NEW Southfork | **Bridgehampton**	-
Strawberry's | **Huntington**	18
NEW Sugar | **Carle Pl**	-
Sunset Beach | **Shelter Is Hts**	18
Surf Lodge | **Montauk**	19
Surfside Inn | **Montauk**	18
Taste 99 | **Farmingdale**	18
Tide Runners | **Hampton Bays**	16
Z Toku | **Manhasset**	25
Townline | **Sagaponack**	19
Trata | **multi.**	22
Z Two Steak/Sushi | **New Hyde Pk**	24
Z Verace | **Islip**	26
NEW Vero | **Amityville**	-
Vintage Port | **Port Washington**	19
Wall's Wharf | **Bayville**	17
Waterview | **Port Washington**	18
Z Waterzooi | **Garden City**	24

NEWCOMERS

Aperitif | **Rockville Ctr**	25
Arthur Ave. | **Smithtown**	-
Bar Frites | **Greenvale**	18
Bel Posto | **Huntington**	-
Bistro 72 | **Riverhead**	-
Bistro 25 | **Sayville**	-
Blue Fish | **Hicksville**	-
Bluepoint B & G | **Blue Pt**	-
Boathouse | **E Hampton**	19
Cattlemen's | **multi.**	19
Cedar Creek | **Glen Cove**	-
Chicken Coop | **Valley Stream**	-
Comtesse Thérèse | **Aquebogue**	-
Crave 11025 | **Great Neck**	18
Dark Horse | **Riverhead**	-
Deco 1600 | **Plainview**	-
Domo Sushi | **E Setauket**	21
Downtown Burger | **Sayville**	-
Fado | **Huntington**	21
Farmhouse | **Greenport**	26

Fish Store | **Bayport**	-
490 West | **Carle Pl**	-
George Martin's Steak | **Great River**	-
Grill on Pantigo | **E Hampton**	21
Harbor Mist | **Cold Spring**	19
Imperial Seoul | **New Hyde Pk**	-
Jack Halyards | **Oyster Bay**	23
Jackson Hall | **E Islip**	-
J&C 68 | **Farmingville**	-
Janine's | **Hauppauge**	-
JD Steakhouse | **Southold**	19
Kinha | **Garden City**	-
La Maison | **Sag Harbor**	18
LT Burger | **Sag Harbor**	16
Marco Polo's | **Westbury**	-
Met. Bistro | **Sea Cliff**	22
Miraj | **Williston Pk**	-
Navy Beach | **Montauk**	19
Old Fields | **Greenlawn**	-
Onsen Sushi | **Oakdale**	-
Park Place | **Floral Pk**	-
Pepe Rosso | **Port Washington**	-
Perfecto Mundo | **Commack**	24
Philippe | **Jericho**	24
Portly Grape | **Greenport**	-
Press 195 | **Rockville Ctr**	-
Prime Catch | **Rockville Ctr**	-
Puglia's/Garden City | **Garden City**	-
Race Lane | **E Hampton**	19
Sabor a Colombia | **Levittown**	-
Sakaya | **Albertson**	-
Sapsuckers | **Huntington**	-
Sensasian | **Levittown**	-
Serafina | **E Hampton**	18
Sip City | **Great Neck**	-
South Edison | **Montauk**	22
Southfork | **Bridgehampton**	-
Stone Turtle | **Island Pk**	21
Sugar | **Carle Pl**	-
Swallow | **Huntington**	-
Tate's | **Nesconset**	26

388 Rest. | **Roslyn Hts**	20
Trattachino | **Wantagh**	-_
Vero | **Amityville**	-_
Vitae | **Huntington**	-_
Whale's Tale | **Northport**	20
When Pigs Fly | **Montauk**	18
XO | **Huntington**	-_

OFFBEAT

Ariana | **Huntington**	20
Baby Moon | **Westhampton Bch**	18
Backyard | **Montauk**	23
Benihana | **multi.**	19
Big Daddy's | **Massapequa**	24
Bliss | **E Setauket**	22
Chalet Rest. | **Roslyn**	18
Cuvée | **Greenport**	22
Cyril's Fish | **Amagansett**	18
Farm Country Kit. | **Riverhead**	23
Hampton Chutney | **Amagansett**	22
House of Dosas | **Hicksville**	25
LL Dent | **Carle Pl**	23
Los Compadres | **Huntington Station**	23
Melting Pot | **Farmingdale**	18
New Paradise | **Sag Harbor**	22
Nichol's | **E Hampton**	17
Painters' | **Brookhaven Hamlet**	20
Planet Bliss | **Shelter Is**	20
Poco Loco | **Roslyn**	17
Roots | **Sea Cliff**	26
RS Jones | **Merrick**	22
Samurai | **Huntington**	24
☑ Smokin' Al's | **Bay Shore**	23
Spicy's BBQ | **multi.**	20
Sunset Beach | **Shelter Is Hts**	18
Surfside Inn | **Montauk**	18
Swingbelly's | **Long Bch**	23
Toast | **Port Jefferson**	24
Tomo Hibachi | **Huntington**	20
Townline | **Sagaponack**	19
Tula Kitchen | **Bay Shore**	24

Tweeds | **Riverhead**	21
Vine Wine Bar | **Greenport**	22

OUTDOOR DINING

(G=garden; P=patio; S=sidewalk; T=terrace)

A Mano | P | **Mattituck**	24
Amarelle | P | **Wading River**	25
Babette's | S | **E Hampton**	20
Backyard | T | **Montauk**	23
Bay Burger | P | **Sag Harbor**	21
Beacon | T | **Sag Harbor**	22
Bistro Citron | T | **Roslyn**	21
Blue | P | **Blue Pt**	22
Blue Parrot | P | **E Hampton**	15
B.Smith's | P | **Sag Harbor**	18
Chequit Inn | P | **Shelter Is Hts**	19
Cipollini | P | **Manhasset**	21
cittanuova | P, S | **E Hampton**	20
Clam Bar | P | **Amagansett**	21
Crew Kitchen | T | **Huntington**	24
Cyril's Fish | P | **Amagansett**	18
Dee Angelo's | P | **Westhampton Bch**	19
☑ Della Femina | T | **E Hampton**	24
Dockers Waterside | T | **E Quogue**	20
Duryea's Lobster | T | **Montauk**	22
☑ E. Hampton Pt. | P, T | **E Hampton**	19
Fishbar | P | **Montauk**	18
Fishery | T | **E Rockaway**	19
Fork & Vine | G | **Glen Head**	23
Fresno | P | **E Hampton**	22
Gosman's Dock | P | **Montauk**	19
Graffiti | P | **Woodbury**	20
☑ Harvest | G, P | **Montauk**	26
Hellenic Snack | P | **E Marion**	20
Hideaway | T | **Ocean Beach**	19
Indian Cove | P | **Hampton Bays**	18
Inlet Seafood | T | **Montauk**	21
Inn Spot/Bay | T | **Hampton Bays**	19
Island Mermaid | T | **Ocean Beach**	20
Livorno | P | **Port Washington**	21

Lobster Inn | P | **Southampton** 19

Lombardi's/Sound | T | **Port Jefferson** 21

Louie's Oyster | T | **Port Washington** 17

☑ Maroni Cuisine | P | **Northport** 28

Mill Pond House | P | **Centerport** 25

☑ Mirko's | P | **Water Mill** 26

Mumon | T | **Garden City** 22

Nello Summertimes | P, T | **Southampton** 16

New Paradise | T | **Sag Harbor** 22

Nichol's | P | **E Hampton** 17

☑ Nick & Toni's | G | **E Hampton** 24

☑ Noah's | S | **Greenport** 26

Oakland's/Sunday | T | **Hampton Bays** 18

Old Mill Inn | T | **Mattituck** 20

☑ Palm Court | P | **E Meadow** 24

Pine Island | T | **Bayville** 18

Planet Bliss | T | **Shelter Is** 20

Poco Loco | P | **Roslyn** 17

Post Stop | T | **Westhampton Bch** 17

Ram's Head | T | **Shelter Is** 20

Sant Ambroeus | S | **Southampton** 24

Savanna's | G | **Southampton** 20

Scrimshaw | P | **Greenport** 23

Sea Grille | P | **Montauk** 21

☑ Starr Boggs | P | **Westhampton Bch** 26

Stonewalls | P | **Riverhead** 23

Sunset Beach | T | **Shelter Is Hts** 18

Surf Lodge | P | **Montauk** 19

Surfside Inn | P | **Montauk** 18

Surf's Out | P, T | **Kismet** 17

Taste 99 | P | **Farmingdale** 18

Tasty Crepes | P | **Carle Pl** 18

Tide Runners | T | **Hampton Bays** 16

Trio | P | **Holbrook** 21

☑ Trumpets | T | **Eastport** 22

☑ Verace | P, S | **Islip** 26

Villa D'Aqua | P | **Bellmore** 21

Vine Street | T | **Shelter Is** 25

Waterview | P | **Port Washington** 18

☑ Waterzooi | P | **Garden City** 24

World Pie | G, P | **Bridgehampton** 19

PEOPLE-WATCHING

☑ American Hotel | **Sag Harbor** 25

☑ Atlantica | **Long Bch** 20

Babette's | **E Hampton** 20

Babylon Carriage | **Babylon** 21

Backyard | **Montauk** 23

🆕 Bar Frites | **Greenvale** 18

☑ Barney's | **Locust Valley** 26

🆕 Boathouse | **E Hampton** 19

Bobby Van's | **Bridgehampton** 22

B.Smith's | **Sag Harbor** 18

Burton & Doyle | **Great Neck** 24

Cipollini | **Manhasset** 21

cittanuova | **E Hampton** 20

Clam Bar | **Amagansett** 21

☑ Coolfish | **Syosset** 24

Copa Wine | **Bridgehampton** 20

Dao | **Huntington** 23

☑ Della Femina | **E Hampton** 24

☑ E. Hampton Pt. | **E Hampton** 19

Grill Room | **Hauppauge** 21

Hudson/McCoy | **Freeport** 18

☑ Il Mulino NY | **Roslyn Estates** 27

🆕 La Maison | **Sag Harbor** 18

☑ Limani | **Roslyn** 26

Lobster Inn | **Southampton** 19

Lobster Roll | **Amagansett** 19

☑ Luce & Hawkins | **Jamesport** 25

Mill Pond House | **Centerport** 25

Mirabelle Tavern | **Stony Brook** 21

☑ Morton's | **Great Neck** 25

Muse | **Water Mill** 23

🆕 Navy Beach | **Montauk** 19

Nello Summertimes | **Southampton** 16

☑ Nick & Toni's | **E Hampton** 24

Nisen | **Woodbury** 25

Oasis Waterfront | **Sag Harbor** 24

☑ Palm | **E Hampton** 26

Panama Hatties | **Huntington Station**	25
🛂 Peter Luger | **Great Neck**	27
Philippe | **multi.**	24
Porto Vivo | **Huntington**	22
red bar | **Southampton**	22
Rein | **Garden City**	23
Robert's | **Water Mill**	25
Sant Ambroeus | **Southampton**	24
Savanna's | **Southampton**	20
Second House | **Montauk**	19
🛂 1770 House | **E Hampton**	25
75 Main | **Southampton**	18
NEW Southfork | **Bridgehampton**	–
🛂 Starr Boggs | **Westhampton Bch**	26
🛂 Stone Creek | **E Quogue**	26
Stresa | **Manhasset**	25
Sunset Beach | **Shelter Is Hts**	18
Surf Lodge | **Montauk**	19
Table 9 | **E Hills**	22
🛂 Toku | **Manhasset**	25
Trata | **Water Mill**	22
Tratt. Diane | **Roslyn**	25
Tutto Il Giorno | **Sag Harbor**	25
🛂 Verace | **Islip**	26
NEW Vero | **Amityville**	–
🛂 Waterzooi | **Garden City**	24
World Pie | **Bridgehampton**	19

POWER SCENES

🛂 American Hotel | **Sag Harbor**	25
🛂 Barney's | **Locust Valley**	26
Barolo | **Melville**	25
🛂 Blackstone Steak | **Melville**	24
Bobby Van's | **Bridgehampton**	22
🛂 Bryant & Cooper | **Roslyn**	26
Burton & Doyle | **Great Neck**	24
Crew Kitchen | **Huntington**	24
🛂 Della Femina | **E Hampton**	24
🛂 E. Hampton Pt. | **E Hampton**	19
Franina | **Syosset**	26
🛂 Il Mulino NY | **Roslyn Estates**	27

La Coquicio | **Manhasset**	24
🛂 Limani | **Roslyn**	26
Mac's Steak | **Huntington**	23
Mirabelle, Rest. | **Stony Brook**	25
🛂 Morton's | **Great Neck**	25
🛂 Nick & Toni's | **E Hampton**	24
🛂 Palm | **E Hampton**	26
🛂 Palm Court | **E Meadow**	24
Panama Hatties | **Huntington Station**	25
🛂 Peter Luger | **Great Neck**	27
Philippe | **E Hampton**	24
🛂 Plaza Cafe | **Southampton**	26
Porto Vivo | **Huntington**	22
🛂 Prime | **Huntington**	23
🛂 Ruth's Chris | **Garden City**	25
🛂 1770 House | **E Hampton**	25
🛂 Stone Creek | **E Quogue**	26
Stresa | **Manhasset**	25
Table 9 | **E Hills**	22
🛂 Tellers | **Islip**	26
🛂 Toku | **Manhasset**	25

PRIVATE ROOMS

(Restaurants charge less at off
times; call for capacity)

🛂 American Hotel | **Sag Harbor**	25
Babylon Carriage | **Babylon**	21
Barolo | **Melville**	25
Basil Leaf | **Locust Valley**	21
Bella Vita Grill | **St. James**	21
Birchwood | **Riverhead**	20
Blackwells | **Wading River**	23
Blue Moon | **Rockville Ctr**	20
Boccaccio | **Hicksville**	21
B.Smith's | **Sag Harbor**	18
Burton & Doyle | **Great Neck**	24
Cafe La Strada | **Hauppauge**	23
Capriccio | **Hicksville**	24
Carnival | **Port Jefferson Station**	22
Casa Rustica | **Smithtown**	25
Chi | **Westbury**	25
Coast Grill | **Southampton**	22
Cooperage Inn | **Baiting Hollow**	22

Restaurant	Location	Rating
🔲 Country House	Stony Brook	23
Crabtree's	Floral Pk	21
Curry Club	E Setauket	20
Dodici	Rockville Ctr	24
Dynasty/Pt. Wash.	Port Washington	20
🔲 E. Hampton Pt.	E Hampton	19
E. B. Elliot's	Freeport	18
Emilio's	Commack	23
Fisherman's Catch	Point Lookout	20
Frank's Steaks	Rockville Ctr	21
Frederick's	Melville	23
Galleria Dominick	Westbury	26
George Martin	Rockville Ctr	22
Giulio Cesare	Westbury	25
Gosman's Dock	Montauk	19
Grasso's	Cold Spring	24
Heart of Portugal	Mineola	20
H2O Seafood	Smithtown	23
Iavarone Cafe	New Hyde Pk	21
Il Capuccino	Sag Harbor	19
Il Classico	Massapequa Pk	23
Inn Spot/Bay	Hampton Bays	19
Irish Coffee	E Islip	23
Jaiya	Hicksville	19
Jimmy Hays	Island Pk	25
Jolly Fisherman	Roslyn	21
Kiss'o	New Hyde Pk	21
La Marmite	Williston Pk	24
🔲 La Plage	Wading River	27
Lareira	Mineola	20
Legal Sea Foods	Garden City	20
🔲 Limani	Roslyn	26
Lobster Inn	Southampton	19
Lombardi's/Sound	Port Jefferson	21
Louie's Oyster	Port Washington	17
Lucé	E Norwich	22
Mamma Lombardi's	Holbrook	23
Mario	Hauppauge	25
🔲 Maroni Cuisine	Northport	28
Mill Pond House	Centerport	25
Mim's	Roslyn Hts	20
Minado	Carle Pl	21
🔲 Morton's	Great Neck	25
Mother Kelly's	Cedarhurst	21
Nagashima	Jericho	24
Nicholas James	Merrick	22
Nonnina	W Islip	25
Oasis Waterfront	Sag Harbor	24
Orchid	Garden City	23
🔲 Orient	Bethpage	27
O's Food	St. James	22
Pace's Steak	multi.	22
Panama Hatties	Huntington Station	25
Pasta Pasta	Port Jefferson	25
Peppercorns	Hicksville	19
Per Un Angelo	Wantagh	22
Piccola Bussola	Mineola	23
🔲 Piccolo	Huntington	27
Piccolo's	Mineola	24
Pierre's	Bridgehampton	21
Pine Island	Bayville	18
Porto Vivo	Huntington	22
Ram's Head	Shelter Is	20
Rare 650	Syosset	24
Restaurant/The Inn	Quogue	21
Rialto	Carle Pl	26
🔲 Riverbay	Williston Pk	23
Robert's	Water Mill	25
🔲 Rothmann's	E Norwich	25
🔲 Ruth's Chris	Garden City	25
🔲 San Marco	Hauppauge	26
Sea Grille	Montauk	21
🔲 1770 House	E Hampton	25
Seventh St. Cafe	Garden City	20
Shiki	Babylon	24
Solé	Oceanside	26
Southampton Publick	Southampton	18
Southside Fish	Lindenhurst	20
🔲 Stone Creek	E Quogue	26
Sundried Tomato	Nesconset	21

Sunset Beach | **Shelter Is Hts**	18
Table 9 | **E Hills**	22
☑ Tellers | **Islip**	26
Tesoro | **Westbury**	23
Thom Thom | **Wantagh**	20
Thyme | **Roslyn**	21
Tratt. Diane | **Roslyn**	25
Trio | **Holbrook**	21
☑ Two Steak/Sushi | **New Hyde Pk**	24
Umberto's | **New Hyde Pk**	22
Vespa | **Great Neck**	22
Villa D'Este | **Floral Pk**	22
Vintage Prime | **St. James**	25
World Pie | **Bridgehampton**	19

PRIX FIXE MENUS

(Call for prices and times)

Albert's Mandarin | **Huntington**	20
Angelina's | **Syosset**	23
Argyle Grill | **Babylon**	22
Arturo's | **Floral Pk**	22
Azerbaijan | **Westbury**	22
Babylon Carriage | **Babylon**	21
☑ Barney's | **Locust Valley**	26
Bayou | **N Bellmore**	23
Bellport | **Bellport**	22
Benny's | **Westbury**	25
Big Daddy's | **Massapequa**	24
Bistro Citron | **Roslyn**	21
Bistro 44 | **Northport**	23
Bistro M | **Glen Head**	25
Bistro Toulouse | **Port Washington**	22
Bobby Van's | **Bridgehampton**	22
Bob's Place | **Floral Pk**	21
Brasserie 214 | **New Hyde Pk**	20
Brio | **Port Washington**	21
Broadway Beanery | **Lynbrook**	21
Butterfields | **Hauppauge**	20
Cafe Max | **E Hampton**	23
Cafe Rustica | **Great Neck**	22
Capriccio | **Hicksville**	24
Caracalla | **Syosset**	23
Casa Rustica | **Smithtown**	25

☑ Chachama | **E Patchogue**	27
☑ Chez Noëlle | **Port Washington**	27
Cho-Sen | **multi.**	19
☑ Coolfish | **Syosset**	24
☑ Country House | **Stony Brook**	23
Crossroads Cafe | **E Northport**	22
Declan Quinn's | **Bay Shore**	19
☑ Della Femina | **E Hampton**	24
Desmond's | **Wading River**	20
Dish | **Water Mill**	27
Duke Falcon's | **Long Bch**	22
Elaine's | **Great Neck**	22
Fifth Season | **Port Jefferson**	26
Fisherman's Catch | **Point Lookout**	20
Fork & Vine | **Glen Head**	23
Fortune Wheel | **Levittown**	22
Fresno | **E Hampton**	22
Garden Grill | **Smithtown**	21
George Martin's Grill | **multi.**	20
Hemingway's | **Wantagh**	19
Hudson's Mill | **Massapequa**	22
Indian Cove | **Hampton Bays**	18
☑ Jamesport Manor | **Jamesport**	23
Jolly Fisherman | **Roslyn**	21
Jonathan's Rist. | **Huntington**	24
La Coquille | **Manhasset**	24
La Tavola | **Sayville**	22
Le Chef | **Southampton**	22
☑ Limani | **Roslyn**	26
Living Room | **E Hampton**	25
Lola's | **Long Bch**	20
Mama's | **Centereach**	21
☑ Maroni Cuisine | **Northport**	28
Matsulin | **Hampton Bays**	22
Michaels'/Maidstone | **E Hampton**	18
Milleridge Inn | **Jericho**	16
Mill Pond House | **Centerport**	25
Mirabelle, Rest. | **Stony Brook**	25
Nicholas James | **Merrick**	22

Page One | **Glen Cove**	22
🆉 Palm Court | **E Meadow**	24
Panama Hatties | **Huntington Station**	25
Pearl East | **Manhasset**	23
Peppercorns | **Hicksville**	19
Pierre's | **Bridgehampton**	21
🆉 Plaza Cafe | **Southampton**	26
red bar | **Southampton**	22
Café Red/Rest. | **Huntington**	25
Restaurant/The Inn | **Quogue**	21
Rist. Gemelli | **Babylon**	24
RS Jones | **Merrick**	22
Runyon's | **Seaford**	18
Ruvo | **multi.**	22
Schooner | **Freeport**	17
Sea Levels | **Brightwaters**	22
🆉 1770 House | **E Hampton**	25
Shagwong | **Montauk**	18
🆉 Snaps | **Wantagh**	26
Southampton Publick | **Southampton**	18
🆉 Stone Creek | **E Quogue**	26
Stresa | **Manhasset**	25
Table 9 | **E Hills**	22
Tava | **Port Washington**	18
🆉 Tellers | **Islip**	26
34 New St. | **Huntington**	18
Thyme | **Roslyn**	21
Tratt. Diane | **Roslyn**	25
Uncle Bacala's | **Garden City Pk**	21
Villa D'Este | **Floral Pk**	22
Voila! | **St. James**	24
Wild Honey | **Oyster Bay**	25

QUIET CONVERSATION

Allison's Amalfi | **Sea Cliff**	21
Ariana | **Huntington**	20
Basil Leaf | **Locust Valley**	21
Bayview Inn | **S Jamesport**	22
Bevanda | **Great Neck**	22
Cafe Max | **E Hampton**	23
Cafe Symposio | **Bellmore**	18

Caracalla | **Syosset**	23
Chat Noir | **Rockville Ctr**	21
🆉 Chez Noëlle | **Port Washington**	27
E. B. Elliot's | **Freeport**	18
Ernesto's East | **Glen Head**	22
Estia's Kitchen | **Sag Harbor**	23
Franina | **Syosset**	26
Garden Grill | **Smithtown**	21
Greenport Tea | **Greenport**	21
Haiku | **Riverhead**	-
Hampton Chutney | **Amagansett**	22
Inn Spot/Bay | **Hampton Bays**	19
Jonathan's Rist. | **Huntington**	24
Kurabarn | **Huntington**	24
La Coquille | **Manhasset**	24
La Pace/Chef Michael | **Glen Cove**	25
🆉 La Plage | **Wading River**	27
La Spada | **Huntington Station**	21
Living Room | **E Hampton**	25
🆉 Luce & Hawkins | **Jamesport**	25
Mac's Steak | **Huntington**	23
Michaels'/Maidstone | **E Hampton**	18
Mill Pond House | **Centerport**	25
Mirabelle, Rest. | **Stony Brook**	25
🆉 Mirko's | **Water Mill**	26
🆉 Mosaic | **St. James**	28
Osteria da Nino | **Huntington**	24
Page One | **Glen Cove**	22
Patio/54 Main | **Westhampton Bch**	19
NEW Portly Grape | **Greenport**	-
Ram's Head | **Shelter Is**	20
Robert's | **Water Mill**	25
Robinson's Tea | **Stony Brook**	23
Sant Ambroeus | **Southampton**	24
Sarin Thai | **Greenvale**	24
🆉 1770 House | **E Hampton**	25
Stonewalls | **Riverhead**	23
Stresa | **Manhasset**	25
Thai Green Leaf | **E Northport**	21

Tratt. Diane | **Roslyn**	25
🉑 Trumpets | **Eastport**	22
Vespa | **Great Neck**	22

RAW BARS

🉑 Aji 53 | **Bay Shore**	27
🉑 Atlantica | **Long Bch**	20
NEW Bistro 25 | **Sayville**	-
🉑 Blackstone Steak | **Melville**	24
Blue | **Blue Pt**	22
NEW Boathouse | **E Hampton**	19
Bonbori Tiki | **Huntington**	20
Brasserie Persil | **Oceanside**	25
Brass Rail | **Locust Valley**	25
Brian Scotts | **Miller Pl**	19
Buoy One | **multi.**	23
Café Formaggio | **Carle Pl**	20
Caffe Laguna | **Long Bch**	19
Canterbury | **Oyster Bay**	19
Claudio's | **Greenport**	16
🉑 E. Hampton Pt. | **E Hampton**	19
Hudson/McCoy | **Freeport**	18
NEW Kinha | **Garden City**	-
NEW La Maison | **Sag Harbor**	18
Legal Sea Foods | **multi.**	20
Louie's Oyster | **Port Washington**	17
Mill Pond House | **Centerport**	25
🉑 Noah's | **Greenport**	26
Oar Steak | **Patchogue**	21
Paddy McGees | **Island Pk**	18
Porters | **Bellport**	20
NEW Prime Catch | **Rockville Ctr**	-
🉑 Riverbay | **Williston Pk**	23
Sage Bistro | **Bellmore**	24
Second House | **Montauk**	19
NEW Sensasian | **Levittown**	-
Snapper Inn | **Oakdale**	18
NEW South Edison | **Montauk**	22
Southside Fish | **Lindenhurst**	20
Squiretown | **Hampton Bays**	20
Tai-Show | **Massapequa**	23
🉑 Tellers | **Islip**	26
🉑 Toku | **Manhasset**	25

Tony's | **Westhampton Bch**	19
Trata | **Roslyn**	22
🉑 Two Steak/Sushi | **New Hyde Pk**	24
View | **Oakdale**	22
Vincent's | **Carle Pl**	22
Waterview | **Port Washington**	18
Wildfish | **Freeport**	21

ROMANTIC PLACES

Amarelle | **Wading River**	25
🉑 American Hotel | **Sag Harbor**	25
🉑 Atlantica | **Long Bch**	20
🉑 Barney's | **Locust Valley**	26
Benny's | **Westbury**	25
Bistro M | **Glen Head**	25
Blackwells | **Wading River**	23
Bliss | **E Setauket**	22
Cafe Joelle | **Sayville**	22
Caffe Laguna | **Long Bch**	19
Caracalla | **Syosset**	23
Casa Rustica | **Smithtown**	25
Chadwicks | **Rockville Ctr**	22
🉑 Chez Noëlle | **Port Washington**	27
NEW Comtesse Thérèse | **Aquebogue**	-
Cooperage Inn | **Baiting Hollow**	22
🉑 Country House | **Stony Brook**	23
E. B. Elliot's | **Freeport**	18
Elaine's | **Great Neck**	22
Grasso's | **Cold Spring**	24
🉑 Jamesport Manor | **Jamesport**	23
Kurabarn | **Huntington**	24
La Coquille | **Manhasset**	24
🉑 Lake House | **Bay Shore**	28
La Pace/Chef Michael | **Glen Cove**	25
🉑 La Plage | **Wading River**	27
La Spada | **Huntington Station**	21
🉑 Le Soir | **Bayport**	27
Lola | **Great Neck**	24

Lombardi's/Sound | **Port Jefferson**	21
Lucé | **E Norwich**	22
Z Luce & Hawkins | **Jamesport**	25
Mac's Steak | **Huntington**	23
Mill Pond House | **Centerport**	25
Mirabelle, Rest. | **Stony Brook**	25
Z Mirko's | **Water Mill**	26
NEW Navy Beach | **Montauk**	19
Z North Fork Table | **Southold**	29
Osteria Toscana | **Huntington**	23
Z Palm Court | **E Meadow**	24
Per Un Angelo | **Wantagh**	22
Z Piccolo | **Huntington**	27
Pine Island | **Bayville**	18
Z Plaza Cafe | **Southampton**	26
Ram's Head | **Shelter Is**	20
Restaurant/The Inn | **Quogue**	21
Rist. Gemelli | **Babylon**	24
Robert's | **Water Mill**	25
Sant Ambroeus | **Southampton**	24
Z Sempre Vivolo | **Hauppauge**	27
Z 1770 House | **E Hampton**	25
Z Stone Creek | **E Quogue**	26
Stresa | **Manhasset**	25
Taste 99 | **Farmingdale**	18
Tratt. Diane | **Roslyn**	25
Trio | **Holbrook**	21
Z Trumpets | **Eastport**	22
21 Main | **W Sayville**	23
Vespa | **Great Neck**	22
Villa D'Aqua | **Bellmore**	21

SENIOR APPEAL

Afghan Grill | **New Hyde Pk**	20
Basil Leaf | **Locust Valley**	21
Cafe Max | **E Hampton**	23
Cafe Rustica | **Great Neck**	22
Capriccio | **Hicksville**	24
Greenport Tea | **Greenport**	21
Jolly Fisherman | **Roslyn**	21
Le Chef | **Southampton**	22
Lombardi's/Sound | **Port Jefferson**	21

Med. Snack | **Huntington**	22
Michaels'/Maidstone | **E Hampton**	18
Milleridge Inn | **Jericho**	16
Modern Snack | **Aquebogue**	18
Nicholas James | **Merrick**	22
Page One | **Glen Cove**	22
Pastrami King | **Merrick**	20
Schooner | **Freeport**	17
Sea Grille | **Montauk**	21
Sweet Mama's | **Northport**	19
Villa D'Este | **Floral Pk**	22
Zorba/Greek | **Hicksville**	19

SINGLES SCENES

Argyle Grill | **Babylon**	22
Babylon Carriage | **Babylon**	21
Backyard | **Montauk**	23
B.K. Sweeney's | **Garden City**	18
Blue Parrot | **E Hampton**	15
NEW Boathouse | **E Hampton**	19
Z Bryant & Cooper | **Roslyn**	26
Bulldog Grille | **Amityville**	–
Burton & Doyle | **Great Neck**	24
Cafe Testarossa | **Syosset**	22
Cipollini | **Manhasset**	21
Copa Wine | **Bridgehampton**	20
Cyril's Fish | **Amagansett**	18
Dao | **Huntington**	23
Z E. Hampton Pt. | **E Hampton**	19
Four Food Studio | **Melville**	21
George Martin's Grill | **Rockville Ctr**	20
Hudson/McCoy | **Freeport**	18
Legal Sea Foods | **Huntington Station**	20
Legends | **New Suffolk**	23
Library Cafe | **Farmingdale**	18
Z Limani | **Roslyn**	26
Melting Pot | **Farmingdale**	18
Muse | **Water Mill**	23
Nisen | **Woodbury**	25
Oakland's/Sunday | **Hampton Bays**	18

Oasis Waterfront | **Sag Harbor**	24
Porto Vivo | **Huntington**	22
Post Office | **Babylon**	19
Public House 49 | **Patchogue**	20
Rockwell's | **Smithtown**	22
Z Rothmann's | **E Norwich**	25
Rugosa | **Wainscott**	21
NEW Sip City | **Great Neck**	-
Southampton Publick | **Southampton**	18
Strawberry's | **Huntington**	18
NEW Sugar | **Carle Pl**	-
Sunset Beach | **Shelter Is Hts**	18
Surf Lodge | **Montauk**	19
Z Tellers | **Islip**	26
Tide Runners | **Hampton Bays**	16
Z Toku | **Manhasset**	25
Trata | **Water Mill**	22
Z Two Steak/Sushi | **New Hyde Pk**	24
Z Verace | **Islip**	26
Wall's Wharf | **Bayville**	17
Z Waterzooi | **Garden City**	24
Wild Ginger | **Great Neck**	21

SLEEPERS

(Good food, but little known)

Backyard | **Montauk**	23
Bellissimo Rist. | **Deer Park**	23
Benkei Japanese | **Northport**	23
Bin 56 | **Huntington**	24
Bozena Polish | **Lindenhurst**	23
Chi | **Westbury**	25
Cuvée | **Greenport**	22
Dish | **Water Mill**	27
Il Villagio | **Malverne**	24
Izumi | **Bethpage**	23
La Terrazza | **Cedarhurst**	22
Los Compadres | **Huntington Station**	23
Madras/India | **New Hyde Pk**	22
Matthew's | **Ocean Beach**	22
Mumon | **Garden City**	22
Ocean Grill | **Freeport**	23

Osaka | **Huntington**	24
Panini Café | **Roslyn**	23
Pizza Place | **Bridgehampton**	24
Ravagh | **multi.**	22
Rist. Italiano | **Port Washington**	24
Rockwell's | **Smithtown**	22
Roe's Casa Dolce | **Rockville Ctr**	24
Roots | **Sea Cliff**	26
Royal Bukhara Grill | **Hicksville**	22
Sabai Thai | **Miller Pl**	22
Salamander's | **Greenport**	24
Samurai | **Huntington**	24
Shiki | **Babylon**	24
Shogi | **Westbury**	25
Star Confectionery | **Riverhead**	22
Surf 'N Turf | **Merrick**	24
Sushi Palace | **Great Neck**	24
Takara | **Islandia**	28
Tokyo | **E Northport**	24
Tratt. Lucia | **E Meadow**	22
Tsubo | **Syosset**	23

TASTING MENUS

Z Barney's | **Locust Valley**	26
Bin 56 | **Huntington**	24
NEW Bistro 72 | **Riverhead**	-
Bob's Place | **Floral Pk**	21
Cafe Rustica | **Great Neck**	22
Chadwicks | **Rockville Ctr**	22
Z Coolfish | **Syosset**	24
Crew Kitchen | **Huntington**	24
Crossroads Cafe | **E Northport**	22
Daruma of Tokyo | **Great Neck**	23
Z Della Femina | **E Hampton**	24
Fork & Vine | **Glen Head**	23
Z Kitchen A Tratt. | **St. James**	28
Lola | **Great Neck**	24
Z Maroni Cuisine | **Northport**	28
Mirabelle, Rest. | **Stony Brook**	25
Z Mosaic | **St. James**	28
1 North Steak | **Hampton Bays**	22
O's Food | **St. James**	22
Panama Hatties | **Huntington Station**	25

Philippe | **E Hampton** — 24

ℤ **Plaza Cafe** | **Southampton** — 26

Café Red/Rest. | **Huntington** — 25

ℤ **Snaps** | **Wantagh** — 26

Tel Aviv | **Great Neck** — 22

Voila! | **St. James** — 24

TEEN APPEAL

Baby Moon | **Westhampton Bch** — 18

Bigelow's | **Rockville Ctr** — 24

Blackbirds' Grille | **Sayville** — 20

Green Cactus | **multi.** — 20

Grimaldi's | **Garden City** — 23

La Pizzetta | **E Norwich** — 21

Melting Pot | **Farmingdale** — 18

Salsa Salsa | **Port Jefferson** — 23

ℤ **Smokin' Al's** | **Bay Shore** — 23

Southside Fish | **Lindenhurst** — 20

Turtle Crossing | **E Hampton** — 22

TRENDY

ℤ **Aji 53** | **Bay Shore** — 27

Babette's | **E Hampton** — 20

Babylon Carriage | **Babylon** — 21

Backyard | **Montauk** — 23

NEW **Bar Frites** | **Greenvale** — 18

ℤ **Barney's** | **Locust Valley** — 26

ℤ **Besito** | **Huntington** — 24

Bistro M | **Glen Head** — 25

Blue Parrot | **E Hampton** — 15

NEW **Boathouse** | **E Hampton** — 19

ℤ **Bryant & Cooper** | **Roslyn** — 26

B.Smith's | **Sag Harbor** — 18

Burton & Doyle | **Great Neck** — 24

Chi | **Westbury** — 25

Cipollini | **Manhasset** — 21

cittanuova | **E Hampton** — 20

ℤ **Coolfish** | **Syosset** — 24

Copa Wine | **Bridgehampton** — 20

Dao | **Huntington** — 23

ℤ **Della Femina** | **E Hampton** — 24

East by Northeast | **Montauk** — 21

Fork & Vine | **Glen Head** — 23

Four Food Studio | **Melville** — 21

Frisky Oyster | **Greenport** — 25

Georgica | **Wainscott** — 18

Honu | **Huntington** — 22

Hudson/McCoy | **Freeport** — 18

ℤ **Il Mulino NY** | **Roslyn Estates** — 27

ℤ **Limani** | **Roslyn** — 26

Ludlow Bistro | **Deer Park** — 24

Minado | **Carle Pl** — 21

ℤ **Morton's** | **Great Neck** — 25

Muse | **Water Mill** — 23

NEW **Navy Beach** | **Montauk** — 19

Nello Summertimes | **Southampton** — 16

ℤ **Nick & Toni's** | **E Hampton** — 24

Nisen | **Woodbury** — 25

Novitá | **Garden City** — 23

Panama Hatties | **Huntington Station** — 25

ℤ **Peter Luger** | **Great Neck** — 27

Philippe | **multi.** — 24

ℤ **Piccolo** | **Huntington** — 27

Porto Vivo | **Huntington** — 22

red bar | **Southampton** — 22

Rein | **Garden City** — 23

Savanna's | **Southampton** — 20

Sen | **Sag Harbor** — 21

NEW **Serafina** | **E Hampton** — 18

NEW **South Edison** | **Montauk** — 22

ℤ **Starr Boggs** | **Westhampton Bch** — 26

ℤ **Stone Creek** | **E Quogue** — 26

NEW **Sugar** | **Carle Pl** — –

Sunset Beach | **Shelter Is Hts** — 18

Surf Lodge | **Montauk** — 19

ℤ **Toku** | **Manhasset** — 25

Trata | **multi.** — 22

Tratt. Diane | **Roslyn** — 25

ℤ **Two Steak/Sushi** | **New Hyde Pk** — 24

NEW **Vero** | **Amityville** — –

NEW **Vitae** | **Huntington** — –

ℤ **Waterzooi** | **Garden City** — 24

Wild Ginger | **multi.** — 21

VALET PARKING

Akbar | **Garden City**	22
NEW Arthur Ave. | **Smithtown**	–
Arturo's | **Floral Pk**	22
Z Atlantica | **Long Bch**	20
Bistro Citron | **Roslyn**	21
Bistro M | **Glen Head**	25
Z Blackstone Steak | **Melville**	24
Blue | **Blue Pt**	22
Bob's Place | **Floral Pk**	21
Z Branzino | **Lynbrook**	26
Brasserie 214 | **New Hyde Pk**	20
Brio | **Port Washington**	21
Brooks & Porter | **Merrick**	22
Z Bryant & Cooper | **Roslyn**	26
Burton & Doyle | **Great Neck**	24
Café Formaggio | **Carle Pl**	20
Cafe La Strada | **Hauppauge**	23
Cafe Testarossa | **Syosset**	22
Capriccio | **Hicksville**	24
Casa Rustica | **Smithtown**	25
NEW Cedar Creek | **Glen Cove**	–
Chi | **Westbury**	25
Cielo Rist. | **Rockville Ctr**	20
Circa | **Mineola**	22
Cirella's | **Melville**	21
Clubhouse | **Huntington**	21
Coach Grill | **Oyster Bay**	22
Crabtree's | **Floral Pk**	21
Crew Kitchen | **Huntington**	24
Z Dario's | **Rockville Ctr**	26
Desmond's | **Wading River**	20
fatfish | **Bay Shore**	21
Fisherman's Catch | **Point Lookout**	20
Four Food Studio | **Melville**	21
Franina | **Syosset**	26
Frank's Steaks | **Rockville Ctr**	21
Frederick's | **Melville**	23
Hudson/McCoy | **Freeport**	18
Z Il Mulino NY | **Roslyn Estates**	27
Jimmy Hays | **Island Pk**	25
Jolly Fisherman | **Roslyn**	21
La Bottega | **Port Washington**	21
La Bussola | **Glen Cove**	23
La Famiglia | **multi.**	22
La Marmite | **Williston Pk**	24
La Pace/Chef Michael | **Glen Cove**	25
Z La Parma | **multi.**	23
Legal Sea Foods | **Garden City**	20
Z Limani | **Roslyn**	26
Living Room | **E Hampton**	25
Lombardi's/Bay | **Patchogue**	23
Lombardi's/Sound | **Port Jefferson**	21
Luigi Q | **Hicksville**	23
Mac's Steak | **Huntington**	23
NEW Marco Polo's | **Westbury**	–
Mario | **Hauppauge**	25
Z Matteo's | **multi.**	23
Mill Pond House | **Centerport**	25
Mim's | **multi.**	20
Z Morton's | **Great Neck**	25
Moules et Frites | **Syosset**	19
Nautilus Cafe | **Freeport**	24
Nello Summertimes | **Southampton**	16
Nonnina | **W Islip**	25
Oasis Waterfront | **Sag Harbor**	24
Pace's Steak | **Hauppauge**	22
Paddy McGees | **Island Pk**	18
Z Palm | **E Hampton**	26
Z Palm Court | **E Meadow**	24
Pearl East | **Manhasset**	23
Per Un Angelo | **Wantagh**	22
Z Peter Luger | **Great Neck**	27
Piccola Bussola | **multi.**	23
Pine Island | **Bayville**	18
Porto Bello | **Greenport**	22
Porto Vivo | **Huntington**	22
Z Prime | **Huntington**	23
NEW Puglia's/Garden City | **Garden City**	–
Rare 650 | **Syosset**	24
Rein | **Garden City**	23

Restaurant/The Inn	Quogue	21
Rist. Gemelli	Babylon	24
☑ Riverbay	Williston Pk	23
Robert's	Water Mill	25
☑ Ruth's Chris	Garden City	25
☑ San Marco	Hauppauge	26
Savanna's	Southampton	20
Schooner	Freeport	17
Sea Grille	Montauk	21
Solé	Oceanside	26
Steve's Piccola	Westbury	24
☑ Stone Creek	E Quogue	26
NEW Sugar	Carle Pl	-
Surfside Inn	Montauk	18
Table 9	E Hills	22
☑ Tellers	Islip	26
NEW 388 Rest.	Roslyn Hts	20
Thyme	Roslyn	21
NEW Trattachino	Wantagh	-
Tratt. Diane	Roslyn	25
Tratt. Di Meo	Roslyn Hts	21
Tutto Pazzo	Huntington	20
21 Main	W Sayville	23
☑ Two Steak/Sushi	New Hyde Pk	24
Uncle Bacala's	Garden City Pk	21
Vespa	Great Neck	22
View	Oakdale	22
Wall's Wharf	Bayville	17

VIEWS

Amarelle	Wading River	25
☑ Atlantica	Long Bch	20
Beacon	Sag Harbor	22
Blackwells	Wading River	23
NEW Boathouse	E Hampton	19
Brian Scotts	Miller Pl	19
B.Smith's	Sag Harbor	18
Catfish Max	Seaford	21
Chequit Inn	Shelter Is Hts	19
Claudio's	Greenport	16
Coast Grill	Southampton	22
Dockers Waterside	E Quogue	20

Duryea's Lobster	Montauk	22
East by Northeast	Montauk	21
☑ E. Hampton Pt.	E Hampton	19
E. B. Elliot's	Freeport	18
Edgewater	Hampton Bays	22
fatfish	Bay Shore	21
Fishbar	Montauk	18
Fisherman's Catch	Point Lookout	20
Fishery	E Rockaway	19
Georgica	Wainscott	18
Gosman's Dock	Montauk	19
Harbor Bistro/Grill	E Hampton	21
☑ Harvest	Montauk	26
Hideaway	Ocean Beach	19
Hudson/McCoy	Freeport	18
Indian Cove	Hampton Bays	18
Inlet Seafood	Montauk	21
Inn Spot/Bay	Hampton Bays	19
Island Mermaid	Ocean Beach	20
Jolly Fisherman	Roslyn	21
☑ Lake House	Bay Shore	28
Lobster Inn	Southampton	19
Lombardi's/Bay	Patchogue	23
Lombardi's/Sound	Port Jefferson	21
Louie's Oyster	Port Washington	17
Maguire's	Ocean Beach	19
Matthew's	Ocean Beach	22
Meeting House	Amagansett	20
Mill Pond House	Centerport	25
Nautilus Cafe	Freeport	24
Oakland's/Sunday	Hampton Bays	18
Oar Steak	Patchogue	21
Oasis Waterfront	Sag Harbor	24
Ocean Grill	Freeport	23
Old Mill Inn	Mattituck	20
Pine Island	Bayville	18
Porto Bello	Greenport	22
☑ Prime	Huntington	23
Ram's Head	Shelter Is	20

Schooner | **Freeport**	17	Fishery | **E Rockaway**	19
Scrimshaw | **Greenport**	23	Georgica | **Wainscott**	18
Sea Grille | **Montauk**	21	Gosman's Dock | **Montauk**	19
Second House | **Montauk**	19	Gulf Coast | **Montauk**	21
Snapper Inn | **Oakdale**	18	Harbor Bistro/Grill | **E Hampton**	21
Stonewalls | **Riverhead**	23	Harbor Crab | **Patchogue**	18
Sunset Beach | **Shelter Is Hts**	18	☑ Harvest | **Montauk**	26
Surf Lodge | **Montauk**	19	Hideaway | **Ocean Beach**	19
Surfside Inn | **Montauk**	18	Indian Cove | **Hampton Bays**	18
Surf's Out | **Kismet**	17	Inlet Seafood | **Montauk**	21
Thyme | **Roslyn**	21	Inn Spot/Bay | **Hampton Bays**	19
Tide Runners | **Hampton Bays**	16	Island Mermaid | **Ocean Beach**	20
Top of the Bay | **Cherry Grove**	-	☑ Lake House | **Bay Shore**	28
Trio | **Holbrook**	21	Lobster Inn | **Southampton**	19
☑ Trumpets | **Eastport**	22	Lombardi's/Sound | **Port Jefferson**	21
View | **Oakdale**	22	Louie's Oyster | **Port Washington**	17
Villa D'Aqua | **Bellmore**	21	Maguire's | **Ocean Beach**	19
Wall's Wharf | **Bayville**	17	Matthew's | **Ocean Beach**	22
Waterview | **Port Washington**	18	Mill Pond House | **Centerport**	25
NEW Whale's Tale | **Northport**	20	Nautilus Cafe | **Freeport**	24

WATERSIDE

☑ Atlantica | **Long Bch**	20	Oakland's/Sunday | **Hampton Bays**	18
Beacon | **Sag Harbor**	22	Oar Steak | **Patchogue**	21
Bistro Citron | **Roslyn**	21	Old Mill Inn | **Mattituck**	20
NEW Boathouse | **E Hampton**	19	Paddy McGees | **Island Pk**	18
B.Smith's | **Sag Harbor**	18	Pier 95 | **Freeport**	24
Catfish Max | **Seaford**	21	Pine Island | **Bayville**	18
NEW Cattlemen's | **Lindenhurst**	19	Porto Bello | **Greenport**	22
Claudio's | **Greenport**	16	☑ Prime | **Huntington**	23
Coast Grill | **Southampton**	22	Rachel's Waterside | **Freeport**	20
☑ Dave's Grill | **Montauk**	27	Schooner | **Freeport**	17
Dockers Waterside | **E Quogue**	20	Scrimshaw | **Greenport**	23
Duryea's Lobster | **Montauk**	22	Sea Grille | **Montauk**	21
East by Northeast | **Montauk**	21	Snapper Inn | **Oakdale**	18
☑ E. Hampton Pt. | **E Hampton**	19	Surf Lodge | **Montauk**	19
E. B. Elliot's | **Freeport**	18	Surf's Out | **Kismet**	17
Farm Country Kit. | **Riverhead**	23	Tide Runners | **Hampton Bays**	16
fatfish | **Bay Shore**	21	Top of the Bay | **Cherry Grove**	-
Fishbar | **Montauk**	18	☑ Trumpets | **Eastport**	22
Fisherman's Catch | **Point Lookout**	20	View | **Oakdale**	22
		Wall's Wharf | **Bayville**	17

SPECIAL FEATURES

Restaurant	Score
Waterview | **Port Washington**	18
Wildfish | **Freeport**	21

WINNING WINE LISTS

Restaurant	Score
Allison's Amalfi | **Sea Cliff**	21
Z American Hotel | **Sag Harbor**	25
Arturo's | **Floral Pk**	22
Z Barney's | **Locust Valley**	26
Barolo | **Melville**	25
Z Blackstone Steak | **Melville**	24
Blackwells | **Wading River**	23
Z Branzino | **Lynbrook**	26
Z Bryant & Cooper | **Roslyn**	26
Burton & Doyle | **Great Neck**	24
Butterfields | **Hauppauge**	20
Cafe La Strada | **Hauppauge**	23
Cafe Max | **E Hampton**	23
Caracalla | **Syosset**	23
Z Chez Noëlle | **Port Washington**	27
City Cellar | **Westbury**	21
Z Coolfish | **Syosset**	24
Crew Kitchen | **Huntington**	24
Cuvée | **Greenport**	22
Z Della Femina | **E Hampton**	24
Dodici | **Rockville Ctr**	24
East by Northeast | **Montauk**	21
Z E. Hampton Pt. | **E Hampton**	19
Epiphany | **Glen Cove**	21
Fork & Vine | **Glen Head**	23
Franina | **Syosset**	26
Fresno | **E Hampton**	22
Galleria Dominick | **Westbury**	26
Z Harvest | **Montauk**	26
Z Il Mulino NY | **Roslyn Estates**	27
NEW Jack Halyards | **Oyster Bay**	23
Jamesport Country | **Jamesport**	23
Jonathan's Rist. | **Huntington**	24
La Coquille | **Manhasset**	24
La Marmite | **Williston Pk**	24
La Pace/Chef Michael | **Glen Cove**	25

Restaurant	Score
Z La Piccola | **Port Washington**	27
Z La Plage | **Wading River**	27
Legal Sea Foods | **Huntington Station**	20
Z Le Soir | **Bayport**	27
Z Limani | **Roslyn**	26
Lucé | **E Norwich**	22
Z Luce & Hawkins | **Jamesport**	25
Mac's Steak | **Huntington**	23
Melting Pot | **Farmingdale**	18
Mill Pond House | **Centerport**	25
Mirabelle, Rest. | **Stony Brook**	25
Z Mirko's | **Water Mill**	26
Z Morton's | **Great Neck**	25
Z Nick & Toni's | **E Hampton**	24
Novitá | **Garden City**	23
Pace's Steak | **multi.**	22
Z Palm Court | **E Meadow**	24
Panama Hatties | **Huntington Station**	25
Pentimento | **Stony Brook**	22
Z Piccolo | **Huntington**	27
Z Plaza Cafe | **Southampton**	26
Z Prime | **Huntington**	23
Ram's Head | **Shelter Is**	20
Rare 650 | **Syosset**	24
red bar | **Southampton**	22
Café Red/Rest. | **Huntington**	25
Restaurant/The Inn | **Quogue**	21
Z Riverbay | **Williston Pk**	23
Robert's | **Water Mill**	25
Z Rothmann's | **E Norwich**	25
Rugosa | **Wainscott**	21
Z Ruth's Chris | **Garden City**	25
Z San Marco | **Hauppauge**	26
Z Sempre Vivolo | **Hauppauge**	27
Z 1770 House | **E Hampton**	25
Z Starr Boggs | **Westhampton Bch**	26
Z Stone Creek | **E Quogue**	26
Stresa | **Manhasset**	25
Z Tellers | **Islip**	26
Tratt. Diane | **Roslyn**	25

SPECIAL FEATURES

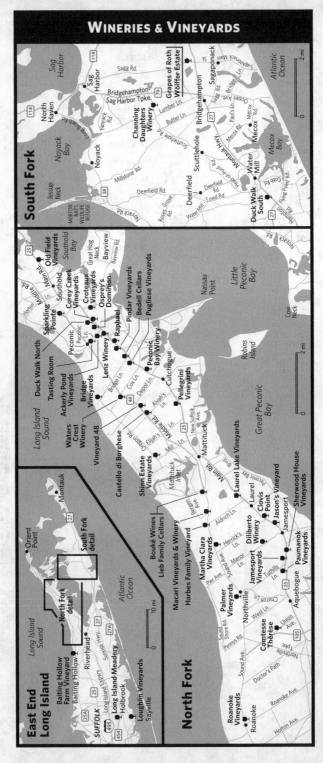

WINERIES & VINEYARDS

South Fork

Sag Harbor
Sagaponack
Atlantic Ocean
Sagg Rd.
Sag Harbor
North Haven
Grapes of Roth
Wölffer Estate
Bridgehampton-Sag Harbor Tpke.
Channing Daughters Winery
Bridgehampton
Noyack
Scuttlehole
Water Mill
Mecox
Mecox Bay
Deerfield
Duck Walk South
Montauk Hwy.
MORTON NAT'L WILDLIFE REFUGE

North Fork

Old Field Vineyards
Southold
Corey Creek Vineyards
Croteaux Vineyards
Osprey's Dominion
Bayview
Sparkling Pointe
Raphael
Pindar Vineyards
Bedell Cellars
Pugliese Vineyards
Duck Walk North
Tasting Room
Lenz Winery
Peconic Bay Winery
Ackerly Pond Vineyards
Bridge Vineyards
Cutchogue
Pellegrini Vineyards
Waters Crest Winery
Vineyard 48
Little Peconic Bay
Robins Island
Nassau Point
Cow Neck
Castello di Borghese
Shinn Estate Vineyards
Mattituck
Great Peconic Bay
Laurel Lake Vineyards
Bo_ké Wines
Lieb Family Cellars
Sherwood House Vineyards
Macari Vineyards & Winery
Harbes Family Vineyard
Martha Clara Vineyards
Clovis Point
Jason's Vineyard
Diliberto Winery
Jamesport Vineyards
Laurel
Jamesport
Paumanok Vineyards
Palmer Vineyards
Northville
Aquebogue
Comtesse Thérèse

East End Long Island

Orient Point
Montauk
South Fork detail
North Fork detail
Long Island Sound
Atlantic Ocean
Baiting Hollow Farm Vineyard
Baiting Hollow
Riverhead
Long Island Meadery
Holbrook
Loughlin Vineyards
Sayville
SUFFOLK
Roanoke Vineyards
Roanoke

Wineries & Vineyards

Ackerly Pond Vineyards
1375 Peconic Ln. | Peconic | 631-765-6861 |
www.ackerlypondvineyards.com

Baiting Hollow Farm Vineyard
2114 Sound Ave. | Baiting Hollow | 631-369-0100 |
www.baitinghollowfarmvineyard.com

Bedell Cellars
36225 Main Rd./Rte. 25 | Cutchogue | 631-734-7537 |
www.bedellcellars.com

Bouké Wines
35 Cox Neck Rd. | Mattituck | 877-877-0527 | www.boukewines.com

Bridge Vineyards
8850 Bridge Ln. | Cutchogue | 917-439-6592 | www.bridgevineyards.com

Castello di Borghese
17150 County Rd. | Cutchogue | 631-734-5111 |
www.castellodiborghese.com

Channing Daughters Winery
1927 Scuttlehole Rd. | Bridgehampton | 631-537-7224 |
www.channingdaughters.com

Clovis Point
1935 Main Rd. | Jamesport | 631-722-4222 |
www.clovispointwines.com

Comtesse Thérèse
Union Ave./Rte. 105 | Aquebogue | 631-765-6404 |
www.comtessetherese.com

Corey Creek Vineyards
45470 Main Rd./Rte. 25 | Southold | 631-765-4168 |
www.bedellcellars.com

Croteaux Vineyards
1450 S. Harbor Rd. | Southold | 631-765-6099 | www.croteaux.com

Diliberto Winery
250 Manor Ln. | Jamesport | 631-722-3416 | www.dilibertowinery.com

Duck Walk North
44535 Main Rd./Rte. 25 | Southold | 631-765-3500 | www.duckwalk.com

Duck Walk South
231 Montauk Hwy. | Water Mill | 631-726-7555 |
www.duckwalk.com

Grapes of Roth
P.O. Box 114 | Sag Harbor | 631-725-7999 | www.thegrapesofroth.com

Harbes Family Vineyard
715 Sound Ave. | Mattituck | 631-298-0700 |
www.harbesfamilyfarm.com

rt Vineyards
ain Rd./Rte. 25 | Jamesport | 631-722-5256 |
..jamesport-vineyards.com

ason's Vineyard
1785 Main Rd./Rte. 25 | Jamesport | 631-238-5801 |
www.jasonsvineyard.com

Laurel Lake Vineyards
3165 Main Rd./Rte. 25 | Laurel | 631-298-1420 | www.llwines.com

Lenz Winery, The
Main Rd./Rte. 25 | Peconic | 631-734-6010 | www.lenzwine.com

Lieb Family Cellars
35 Cox Neck Rd. | Mattituck | 631-734-1100 | www.liebcellars.com

Long Island Meadery
1347 Lincoln Ave. | Holbrook | 631-285-7469 | www.limeadery.com

Loughlin Vineyards
S. Main St. | Sayville | 631-589-0027 | www.loughlinvineyard.com

Macari Vineyards & Winery
150 Bergen Ave. | Mattituck | 631-298-0100 | www.macariwines.com

Martha Clara Vineyards
6025 Sound Ave. | Riverhead | 631-298-0075 |
www.marthaclaravineyards.com

Old Field Vineyards, The
59600 Main Rd./Rte. 25 | Southold | 631-765-0004 |
www.theoldfield.com

Osprey's Dominion
44075 Main Rd./Rte. 25 | Peconic | 631-765-6188 |
www.ospreysdominion.com

Palmer Vineyards
108 Sound Ave./Rte. 48 | Aquebogue | 631-722-9463 |
www.palmervineyards.com

Paumanok Vineyards
1074 Main Rd./Rte. 25 | Aquebogue | 631-722-8800 |
www.paumanok.com

Peconic Bay Winery
31320 Main Rd./Rte. 25 | Cutchogue | 631-734-7361 |
www.peconicbaywinery.com

Pellegrini Vineyards
23005 Main Rd./Rte. 25 | Cutchogue | 631-734-4111 |
www.pellegrinivineyards.com

Pindar Vineyards
37645 Main Rd./Rte. 25 | Peconic | 631-734-6200 | www.pindar.net

Pugliese Vineyards
34515 Main Rd./Rte. 25 | Cutchogue | 631-734-4057 |
www.pugliesevineyards.com

WINERIES & VINEYARDS

Raphael
39390 Main Rd./Rte. 25 | Peconic | 631-765-1100 | www.raphaelwine.com

Roanoke Vineyards
3543 Sound Ave. | Riverhead | 631-727-4161 | www.roanokevineyards.com

Sherwood House Vineyards
1291 Main Rd./Rte. 25 | Jamesport | 631-779-2817 |
www.sherwoodhousevineyards.com

Shinn Estate Vineyards
2000 Oregon Rd. | Mattituck | 631-804-0367 |
www.shinnestatevineyards.com

Sparkling Pointe
39750 Rte. 48 | Southold | 631-765-0200 | www.sparklingpointe.com

Tasting Room, The
2885 Peconic Ln. | Peconic | 631-765-6404 | www.tastingroomli.com

Vineyard 48
18910 Rte. 48 | Cutchogue | 631-734-5200 | www.vineyard48.net

Waters Crest Winery
22355 Rte. 48 | Cutchogue | 631-734-5065 | www.waterscrestwinery.com

Wölffer Estate
139 Sagg Rd. | Sagaponack | 631-537-5106 | www.wolffer.com

Wine Vintage Chart

This chart is based on our 0 to 30 scale. The ratings (by U. of South Carolina law professor **Howard Stravitz**) reflect vintage quality and the wine's readiness to drink. A dash means the wine is past its peak or too young to rate. Loire ratings are for dry whites.

Whites	95	96	97	98	99	00	01	02	03	04	05	06	07	08	09
France:															
Alsace	24	23	23	25	23	25	26	23	21	24	25	24	26	25	25
Burgundy	27	26	22	21	24	24	24	27	23	26	27	25	26	25	25
Loire Valley	-	-	-	-	-	-	-	26	21	23	27	23	24	24	26
Champagne	26	27	24	23	25	24	21	26	21	-	-	-	-	-	-
Sauternes	21	23	25	23	24	24	29	24	26	21	26	24	27	25	27
California:															
Chardonnay	-	-	-	-	22	21	25	26	22	26	29	24	27	25	-
Sauvignon Blanc	-	-	-	-	-	-	-	-	26	25	27	25	24	25	-
Austria:															
Grüner V./Riesl.	22	-	25	22	25	21	22	25	26	25	24	26	25	23	27
Germany:	21	26	21	22	24	20	29	25	26	27	28	25	27	25	25

Reds	95	96	97	98	99	00	01	02	03	04	05	06	07	08	09
France:															
Bordeaux	26	25	23	25	24	29	26	24	26	25	28	24	23	25	27
Burgundy	26	27	25	24	27	22	24	27	25	23	28	25	25	24	26
Rhône	26	22	23	27	26	27	26	-	26	25	27	25	26	23	26
Beaujolais	-	-	-	-	-	-	-	-	-	-	27	24	25	23	27
California:															
Cab./Merlot	27	25	28	23	25	-	27	26	25	24	26	23	26	23	25
Pinot Noir	-	-	-	-	-	-	25	26	25	26	24	23	27	25	24
Zinfandel	-	-	-	-	-	-	25	23	27	22	24	21	21	25	23
Oregon:															
Pinot Noir	-	-	-	-	-	-	-	26	24	26	25	24	23	27	25
Italy:															
Tuscany	25	24	29	24	27	24	27	-	25	27	26	26	25	24	-
Piedmont	21	27	26	25	26	28	27	-	24	27	26	25	26	26	-
Spain:															
Rioja	26	24	25	-	25	24	28	-	23	27	26	24	24	-	26
Ribera del Duero/Priorat	26	27	25	24	25	24	27	-	24	27	26	24	26	-	-
Australia:															
Shiraz/Cab.	24	26	25	28	24	24	27	27	25	26	27	25	23	-	-
Chile:	-	-	-	-	25	23	26	24	25	24	27	25	24	26	-
Argentina:															
Malbec	-	-	-	-	-	-	-	-	-	25	26	27	25	24	-

Vote at ZAGAT.com